THE
AMERICAN
ACADEMIC
PROFESSION

THE AMERICAN ACADEMIC PROFESSION

Stephen R. Graubard, editor

Transaction Publishers
New Brunswick (U.S.A.) and London (U.K.)

Library of Congress Catalog Number: 2001027379
ISBN: 0-7658-0646-0
Printed in the United States of America

Library of Congress Cataloging-in-Publication Data

The American academic profession / edited by Stephen R. Graubard.
     p. cm.
  Includes bibliographical references and index.
  ISBN 0-7658-0646-0 (pbk.: alk. paper)
    1. College teachers—United States. 2. College teaching—United States. 3. Education, Higher—Aims and objectives—United States. I. Graubard, Stephen Richards.

LB1778.2 A52 2001
378.1'2'0973—dc21   2001027379

Contents

Preface

THE HISTORY OF AMERICAN HIGHER EDUCATION in the twentieth century, exploring the character of its universities and colleges, remains to be written. A *Dædalus* issue that deals with the American academic profession—that large company of men and women, unprecedented in its size and diversity, who have done so much to make academic institutions what they are today—can only recount a minuscule part of the tale that needs to be written of how political, economic, social, and intellectual forces have conspired to change a system that was already a mass enterprise even before World War I. No European society aspired to educate men and women in the number attending American universities and colleges in 1914. In no other country was there room in the curriculum for so many subjects—for so much that traditional Europe believed had no place in higher educational study. In most conventional histories, a great deal of attention is given to how much the German and British examples provided the incentives for the major post–Civil War reforms that made American higher education so different from what it had once been. Without wishing to deny the importance of such influences, the uniqueness of the American system needs to be emphasized, and not only because of the Morrill Act and the innovations introduced by the land-grant principle, with its emphasis on research in agriculture and in many other fields as well. The concept of "service" took on a wholly new meaning in state universities that pledged to assist their citizens in ways that had never previously been considered. If the introduction of a degree called the Ph.D. and the creation of something called a "seminar" did not a Heidelberg make, so the pedagogic innovations through individual and group tutorials or preceptorials and the building of undergraduate residences called houses or colleges did not an Oxford make. Before 1914, as after, Americans showed their originality in the diversity of their higher educational institutions but even more in the breadth of the offerings and in their accessibility to adolescents and adults who would never have thought to seek admission to Europe's universities; this was as evident in those colleges that could lay claim to colonial origins as those created by new wealth in the decades after the Civil War.

It is impossible to study the American academic profession independently of the universities and colleges that today provide employ for so many hundreds of thousands of men and women. Again, there is no comparable mass academic profession anywhere else in the world. How this profession has come to grow so large, and indeed how it has been able to provide so many services to so many, young and old, who seek instruction, again imagining that term to embrace such vastly different disciplines and competences, are distinctive features of an American higher educational system that defines scholarship and learning in quite new ways. While a fairly large historical literature exists dealing with America's universities and colleges, much of it, until very recently, was unashamedly hagiographic. If this did not preclude distinguished historians like Samuel Eliot Morison and Merle Curti from occasionally setting themselves the task of writing more measured and thoughtful studies of the institutions they valued, these were always exceptional works. Just as biography was once thought to be the study of great lives, university and college histories were once deemed to be the study of valued institutions, led by superbly endowed individuals, committed to high and worthy purposes. Books seeking to propound such ideas today would almost certainly be ridiculed. If biography has become largely the study of human imperfection, revealing the dark, deep secrets of an individual's life that were once deliberately concealed, institutional history, insofar as it exists at all, has taken on something of the same character. Heroes are conspicuous by their absence; failure, chicanery, intrigue, and pettiness are constantly explored themes. Since it is indeed conceivable that these are some of the defining characteristics of American higher educational institutions today—as many best-selling books proclaim—that possibility cannot be dismissed out of hand. Some of the more critical works, without ever deigning to make historical comparisons, see American universities as having become sclerotic and even decadent, if not in the way that the two great English universities had become in the eighteenth century, then certainly in no less dire need of massive reform.

Whatever truth there may be in such a charge, it is not one sustained by those who have written for this issue of *Dædalus*. This is not to say that all goes well in academe, that the authors are at all sanguine about what is currently happening in higher education or what they imagine the future portends. There are numerous complaints and grievances, and these are aired in ways that make it evident that this is not simply an elegy for a lost world and even less a call for maintaining the status quo. There is much to be concerned about, and no amount of enthusiasm for the number of students enrolled, or for the size of private benefactions to both private and public universities and colleges, can conceal the anxiety that many feel with a public less enthusiastic about higher education, with a Congress and state legislatures increasingly wary of making the ever-larger appropriations that had once been common. If there are silences in the issue—and there are many— they have to do with such matters as the exceptional costs of American higher education that leave so many students very heavily in debt, obliged to pay tuition and other fees that would be inconceivable in other countries. Other even more delicate issues are also skirted: whether many in the society, including prospective employers, on the whole are satisfied with what students appear to be learning, with what individual members of faculties are choosing to teach, with what the high schools of the country are doing to prepare students for colleges and universities—a great number of which are in a constant, surreptitious but desperate search for students who are able to pay. Does not the whole issue of graduate education for the professoriate in many disciplines need to be reconsidered, yet once again? How content are both younger and older members of faculties with present methods of appointment to faculty positions? Has the "old boy" network given way to other "networks," frequently unnamed but generally known, and no less insidious? Does the existing departmental structure, which owes so much to innovations in the late nineteenth century, still have great utility? If the injustices of another age in respect to social class, race, ethnicity, and religion have been largely superseded, are new exclusions being created, and what dangers do they pose and to whom? Are the values of a liberal-arts education being implicitly or explicitly denied, and is too much attention being given to employment as the principal rationale for all educational innovation? Is the level of discourse about higher educational issues not at all what it should be? Is there in fact the "dumbing down" of students—and some would say of faculty—that so many writers and commentators complain of? Can such criticisms be dismissed as the largely unsubstantiated charges of men and women who cannot accept change? What needs to be said about the federal presence in higher education, so beneficial in so many ways, so injurious in others? Is too much emphasis being given to what technology is likely to do to alter higher educational institutions and to the academic profession more generally, or are we not even beginning to understand the "revolution" that is at hand?

In asking these questions, but also the very large number of others posed in this issue, a more fundamental one is raised: Can a society know its universities and colleges when it has relied on hagiography for so many decades and when recently only the arguments of those who find fault with the system have come to the fore? Have we moved too quickly from an uncritical admiration to an uninformed and ungenerous complaint? In the process, have we concluded that objective truth in these matters is no longer possible? If this is so, we have departed very dramatically from the opinions that once informed those who helped create the higher learning in the United States in this century—a system perhaps more admired in great parts of the world today, and not only for its scholarship in many realms, including the scientific, than in any previous period. So long as Americans are unwilling to examine their beliefs and prejudices in regard to their own educational institutions, at every level, and not only as these have existed in some remote or recent past but as they survive today, a code of silence that passes for discretion will govern, and there will be no new innovations comparable to those that once expressed the pride of individuals and groups determined to create institutions different from those that had once existed.

Because it is relatively easy to retail horror stories about the inanities of any institution or profession—higher education cannot be uniquely vulnerable in that respect, certainly no more so than journalism, business, law, or medicine—one must ask why in recent years it has so often been the object of such unflattering attention. Why, in short, have universities and colleges been so frequently attacked, and why has it been so difficult to create effective defenses against such assaults? The short answer would be that it is difficult to counter confessional works or jeremiads that tell stories of fresh academic disasters with narratives of educational triumphs. The longer answer would be that too many of the influential books that have circulated recently, purporting to deal with higher education, have been largely self-referential; few, if any, have explored the social, economic, and political circumstances that have made America's colleges and universities what they are today; and even fewer have compared American institutions with others abroad, showing where they differ and why, which of their many intended purposes are in fact being realized. Scholarly detachment about the professoriate has not been at all common in recent years. The kinds of intellectual and cultural changes in American society and in the world beyond that, which figured so largely in the Winter 1997 issue of *Dædalus,* "American Academic Culture in Transformation," are too rarely thought of.

These national and international conditions, which have necessarily impinged on academic life, are fully considered in the book edited by Carl Schorske and Thomas Bender and published by the Princeton University Press in 1998, which developed themes that had their origin in the *Dædalus* issue. To indicate why specific academic disciplines have developed as they have, what new kinds of research topics and agendas have been proposed and adopted, and why much of what can only be seen as genuine curricular innovation has in fact proved divisive, both within the academy and outside, is part of a larger tale that relates to why the colleges and universities of the country have so often been savaged by the mass media in recent years. While it is incontestably true that passionate and sometimes unscrupulous individuals have sought to exploit the genuine and legitimate grievances and differences that exist in the professoriate, the cultural and intellectual divides that rend the late twentieth-century academy are increasingly spoken of. There is no virtue in denying them. Still, hyperbole can never be an adequate substitute for sober analysis. Certain conditions, if they exist, must be acknowledged, which is not to say that they must be accepted or that they will necessarily endure for very long.

In considering the American academic profession in the late twentieth century, attention must be given to how the growth of profit-making educational institutions threaten certain existing ones, particularly those with small endowments or purely local reputations. It is not modern technology alone that provides the opportunity for long-distance learning. If the credential—the degree—is the invaluable passport to career and employ, it can almost certainly be provided at a discounted price by institutions very different from those that now dot the higher educational landscape. If academic culture is today fragmented, and not only as between the sciences and the humanities, but also within the individual disciplines, if older and more traditional concerns with the "life of the mind" must often take second place to what are perceived to be other more pressing national demands, certified "expertness," as defined by prospective employers, becomes all-important. Where competence is often defined narrowly, the interest in a broader intellectual accomplishment may well atrophy. While it is reasonable that those who now seek academic appointments complain of how difficult entry into the profession has become, and what the decisions of institutions to economize, to opt for part-time or nontenure track positions, are doing to change the profession, this is but a single aspect of a much larger problem. It has to do with whether the academic profession, as presently constituted, will in fact attract the most able men and women, whether the prizes it offers are comparable to those offered by other no less desirable professions.

Thanks are due to two foundations, the Spencer Foundation and the Alfred P. Sloan Foundation, for their generous grants that made the conferences and meetings that preceded this publication possible. Without these sessions—so conspicuous for their candor—this issue would have been a very different one. To the Center for Advanced Study in the Behavioral Sciences and to its

Arthur Levine

How the Academic Profession is Changing

I N THE YEARS AHEAD, the academic profession can be expected to change dramatically. Five forces are propelling the change: 1) the changing attitudes and demands of higher education's patrons; 2) the changing characteristics of college students; 3) the changing conditions of employment in higher education; 4) the rise of new technologies; and 5) the growth of private-sector competitors. Most of the impetus for change is coming from sources outside the academy, over which higher education has little control.

THE CHANGING ATTITUDES AND DEMANDS OF HIGHER EDUCATION'S PATRONS

During the late 1980s and 1990s, government support for higher education decreased, both financially and politically. Two rationales have generally been offered to explain the reductions. The first is that these are hard times for the government, so it has less money to give away. The assumption is that when the government is flusher, higher education will receive additional support. The second explanation is that government priorities have changed. Higher education has given way in importance to prisons, health care, and highways. Even in the area of education, preference is now given to schools over colleges and children over adults. The assumption is that the change is temporary, and higher education's priority will rise again in the future—what goes around comes around.

Arthur Levine is President of Teachers College, Columbia University.

1

I would suggest a third reason, one that is likely to be far more permanent. American higher education has become a mature industry. More than 60 percent of all high-school graduates are now going on to some form of postsecondary education. Increasingly, this is viewed in state capitols as a sufficient number or even as an overexpansion of higher education. There is no government enthusiasm for increasing the college attendance rate to 70 or 80 percent.

This represents a dramatic change in the condition of American higher education. Throughout this century, colleges and universities have been a growth industry. Except during the world wars and for two years of the depression, enrollment has risen every year. In the decades following World War II, the first and most persistent demand that government made of higher education was to increase its capacity to provide a college education for more and more people. Rising government support was the norm; obstacles to increasing enrollments were swept away. Government's principal role was to expand higher education and increase opportunities for access. More and more faculty were hired, public institutions of higher education multiplied, and government aid was targeted at private schools to promote expansion. Few questions were asked. This is generally the lot of growth industries in America.

The government, however, treats mature industries very differently. It seeks to regularize or control them. It asks hard questions about their cost, efficiency, productivity, and effectiveness. It attempts to limit their size and funding. It diminishes their autonomy and demands greater accountability. This is precisely what is happening to higher education today. The government, in scrutinizing the cost of the enterprise, is asking questions of colleges and universities that have never been asked before. The price of higher education is being attacked loudly and continually, funding formulas are being reexamined, and financial aid is shifting from grants to loans.

Questions of productivity and efficiency are being raised, particularly in regard to the professoriate. How much should faculty teach? What is the appropriate balance between teaching and research? How much should it cost to educate a student? Can campuses and faculties be replaced by new technologies? Should there continue to be lifetime employment or tenure for faculty?

What programs should colleges offer? How much course and program redundancy is necessary? What should the balance be between graduate and undergraduate education? Should faculties continue to make these decisions, as they have historically?

Questions of effectiveness are being asked, too. Why are graduation rates not higher? Why should it take students more than four years to graduate from college? Why do colleges offer remedial education?

The government is shifting the terms of the relationship between higher education and the public. The focus is moving from teaching (what faculty do in their classrooms) to learning (what students get out of their classes). The emphasis is moving from courses and credits (process) to what students achieve as a result of a college education (outcomes). In short, the state is demanding greater accountability from higher education, and that burden is resting increasingly on the shoulders of the faculty. Several states, Florida for one, have already imposed tests on higher education to measure student achievement.

The effects of these changes on higher education are profound. As a growth industry, colleges and universities could generally rely on additional resources annually. Growth and progress were treated as synonyms. New activities were a matter of addition: the new was simply added to the old.

Today, with resources either stable or declining, this is no longer possible. Change is expected to occur by substitution. If something new is added, something old must be eliminated. If growth is to occur, it can occur only in selective areas. Colleges and universities are being forced to choose limited targets for investment. If colleges are unwilling to do this themselves, the government is increasingly willing to help them make the choices. The government is becoming more involved and is quite prepared to make decisions that were once regarded as the prerogative of the faculty.

The net result is likely to be a "boutique-ing" of higher education. That is, most colleges and universities in the country are fundamentally alike in terms of the curriculum and academic programs they offer. For the most part, institutions vary largely in terms of the number of professional programs they provide and the relative size of their upper division and graduate programs; in this sense, most institutions are comprehensive. This is increasingly the case even among colleges that were once exclusively devoted to liberal arts. Today, institutions of higher education are being forced to make selections, eliminate overlapping or redundant offerings, and make themselves more specialized. They are moving away from being something akin to full-service department stores toward being more sharply focused boutiques. The common wisdom today is that higher education must do more with less; the reality is that institutions will have to do less with less, putting existing programs and faculty positions in jeopardy, as is the case with downsizing in business today.

These changes are likely to be permanent. They will not go away when the government has more money or higher education's relative priority in the public agenda rises. And higher education's response to these new conditions has only served to further anger and frustrate the government. Instead of making cuts, as the government intended when resources were reduced, higher education's first response was to raise more money. Tuition prices were increased well above inflation. More admissions officers were hired to attract more students. More development staff was hired to raise more money. More student-affairs professionals were hired to reduce attrition. And more finance staff was hired to control spending. Higher education soon found that these steps only increased costs and did not produce more revenue—though they did set off a firestorm of criticism, especially regarding the price of tuition.

The second response was to cut costs around the edges, making across-the-board budget cuts, imposing hiring freezes, and deferring maintenance. The stated goal was to preserve institutional quality, staff morale, and student access. The reality was that preserving quality turned out to be a synonym for maintaining every program and every faculty member on campus, making it also a synonym for preserving morale. Only the commitment to access was allowed to wither. It has been preserved rhetorically and abandoned financially on many campuses. At bottom, this strategy sacrificed quality to avoid rocking the boat. Strong and weak programs were cut equally, and staff reductions followed. Random attrition patterns, rather than institutional priorities, determined the changes to be made. All in all, it was akin to a ship hitting an iceberg, and the captain announcing as the boat sinks that his highest priority is to save the crew. The next priority is to avoid any inconvenience as the ship goes down by continuing all activities—the midnight buffet, the bingo game, and the shuffleboard tournament. The third priority is to repair the ship. And the fourth and final priority, should time permit, is to save the passengers. Besides penalizing students and sacrificing academic quality, this approach does not save enough money, making campus decision-making and decisionmakers look very bad publicly, particularly the faculty, who are viewed as being self-concerned and intransigent.

This caused institutions of higher education to attempt a third response, that is, choosing priorities—distinguishing between the areas central to an institutional mission and more marginal activities that could be reduced or eliminated. To accomplish this, the usual mechanism has been to create a strategic planning committee comprised of at least eighty-seven members, which, after two years of weekly meetings, manages to select one program for cuts that has not had a student in three years. This gross intrusion into the fabric of the institution leads to a faculty vote of no confidence in the president, who then resigns. A new president is selected, who says the problem can be overcome by raising more money, and the cycle begins again.

This is, of course, a parody of decision-making in higher education. However, it is true that the government believes more and more that colleges and universities are dragging their feet and are selfish and unconcerned about the public good. The government is more critical of higher education today than it ever was of the schools.

This is likely to affect the professoriate in a variety of ways. In the years ahead, the faculty role in governance is likely to diminish. Boards of trustees will become more active in the management of educational institutions. Government regulation of higher education will increase and encompass such matters as faculty work loads and tenure. Higher education is entirely unready for this change. Not long ago, I visited a research university in a state in which the legislature was considering a bill that would tie faculty salaries entirely to the amount of time spent in the classroom. When I asked the faculty at this university what they thought about this, their answer was "intellectual McCarthyism." This represents a major communication failure. The faculty completely misread the message of disapproval and censure that the legislature was sending them. This kind of response is likely to lead to further criticism of the academy in general and of professors in particular. More sensational books like *ProfScam* can be anticipated, along with legislative inquiries. Demands for accountability from institutions and their faculties are also likely to increase and, if not heeded, to become mandates.

THE CHANGING CHARACTERISTICS OF STUDENTS

Perhaps the greatest change in higher education in recent years has to do with who the students are. During the 1980s and early 1990s, the lion's share of growth in college enrollment came from students often described as nontraditional. Half of new students were twenty-five years of age or older, 74 percent of the increase was female, and 56 percent were part-time students. By 1993, 38 percent of all college students were over twenty-five years of age; 61 percent were working; 56 percent were female, and 42 percent were attending part-time. Less than a fifth of all undergraduates fit the traditional stereotype of the American college student—eighteen to twenty-two years of age, attending full-time, and living on campus.[1]

What this means is that higher education is not as central to the lives of many of today's undergraduates as it was to previous generations. It is becoming just one of many activities in which they engage every day. For many, college is not even the most important of these activities—work and family often overshadow it.

As a consequence, older, part-time, and working students, especially those with children, said in a national study I conducted of undergraduate attitudes and experiences between 1992 and 1997 that they wanted a different type of relationship with their colleges than undergraduates have historically had. They preferred relationships like those they already enjoyed with their bank, their gas company, and their supermarket.

Think about what we want from our bank. We want an ATM on every corner. We want to know that when we get to the ATM, there will be no line. We want a parking spot right in front of the ATM. We want money available the moment our checks arrive at the bank—or perhaps the day before. And we want no mistakes unless they are in our favor. There are also things we do not want our bank to provide—softball leagues, psychological counseling, or religious services. We can arrange those things without their assistance or additional cost.

Students are asking for roughly the same kind of service from their colleges. They want their colleges nearby and open during the hours most useful to them—preferably, around the clock. They want easy, accessible parking (in the classroom would not be at all bad), no lines, and a polite, helpful, and efficient staff. They want high-quality education at a low cost. For the most part, they are willing to comparison shop, placing a premium on time and money. They do not want to pay for activities and programs they do not use or can get elsewhere. Increasingly, students are bringing to higher education exactly the same consumer expectations they have for every other commercial enterprise with which they deal. Their focus is on convenience, quality, service, and cost. They believe that since they are paying for their education, faculty should give them the education they want, and they make larger demands on faculty than students in the past ever have. They are also the target audience for alternatives to traditional higher education. They are likely to find distance education appealing, offering the convenience of instruction at home or in the office. They are prime candidates for stripped-down versions of college, located in the suburbs and business districts of our cities, that offer low-cost instruction made possible by heavy faculty teaching loads, with primarily a part-time faculty, limited numbers of majors, and few electives. Proprietary institutions of this type are springing up around the country.

Traditional undergraduates are also changing in ways that will affect the faculty who teach them. They are not as well prepared to enter college as their predecessors. As a result, there is a growing need for remediation. According to a national survey of student-affairs officers that I conducted in 1997, within the last decade nearly three-fourths (73 percent) of all colleges and universities experienced an increase in the proportion of students requiring remedial or developmental education at two-year (81 percent) and four-year (64 percent) colleges. Today, nearly one-third (32 percent) of all undergraduates report having taken a basic skills or remedial course in reading, writing, or math. In 1995, more than three-fourths of all colleges and universities offered remedial reading, writing, or math courses. Between 1990 and 1995, 39 percent of institutions reported that enrollments in these areas had increased while only 14 percent reported a decrease.[2]

According to a survey by the Higher Education Research Institute, only one-quarter (25 percent) of faculty believe their students are "well-prepared academically," while less than four in ten (39 percent) gave them even a "satisfactory" or "very satisfactory" rating in terms of their quality.[3] The result is that faculty are being forced to teach more and more basic-skills courses, dumb down the level of their classes, and reduce the number of advanced courses they offer, therefore enjoying their teaching and their students less than in the past. The 1997 student-affairs survey showed that 45 percent of faculty feel less comfortable with students today than in the past. This feeling is more pronounced at four-year schools (53 percent) than at two-year colleges (37 percent).

There is another hurdle even more daunting than remediation—the widening gap between the ways in which students prefer to learn and the ways in which faculty prefer to teach. According to research by Charles Schroeder of the University of Missouri–Columbia, more than half of today's students perform best in a learning situation characterized by "direct, concrete experience, moderate-to-high degrees of structure, and a linear approach to learning. They value the practical and the immediate, and the focus of their perception is primarily on the physical world." On the other hand, more than three-quarters (75 percent) of faculty "prefer the global to the particular, are stimulated by the realm of concepts, ideas, and abstractions, and assume that students, like themselves, need a high degree of autonomy in their work." In short, students are more likely to prefer concrete or practical subjects and active methods of learning while faculty are predisposed to abstract and theoretical subject matter and passive methods of learning. The result, says Schroeder, is frustration on both sides and a tendency for faculty to interpret as deficiencies what may simply be natural differences in learning patterns.[4] This mismatch may cause faculty to think every year that students are less and less well-prepared and for students to think their classes are incomprehensible. This is certainly the case with faculty. The 1997 student-affairs survey revealed that at 74 percent of colleges and universities, faculty complaints about students were on the rise; there is little difference between two-year (72 percent) and four-year (77 percent) colleges. In the years ahead, there will be enormous pressure on faculty to change the way they teach to match the ways in which students learn. In the final analysis, student tuition dollars are likely to be more powerful than faculty preferences.

There are other reasons that the classroom experience is becoming less appealing to faculty. Forty-four percent of institutions report rises in student disruptions of class over the past five years. Plagiarism or cheating has increased on more than a fifth of college campuses (21 percent) and three-quarters of deans of students say undergraduates are less likely to believe plagiarism is wrong. A majority also would describe their campuses as politically correct (57 percent) and report that students feel uncomfortable expressing unpopular opinions (54 percent). And on top of this, 40 percent of all colleges and universities are experiencing increased threats of litigation by students.[5] The campus is becoming less and less of a community for faculty and their students. Because a majority of undergraduates are now working and increasing proportions are attending college part-time, faculty are spending less time with their students and thus do not know their students as well. The degree to which this is occurring varies considerably across different types of colleges, as Burton Clark's essay in this issue of *Dædalus* indicates.

Finally, current undergraduates are costing their institutions more than their predecessors did. Student aid is growing dramatically on many campuses, as the fastest-growing populations in the country have the lowest incomes and can least afford to attend college. The cost of student services is also rising substantially. For instance, students are coming to college more damaged psychologically than in the past, owing to family, sexual, drug, eating, and other disorders. More than three out of five colleges and universities (61 percent) report expanded use of psychological counseling services.[6] The resources to support these activities are coming out of revenues that in the past would have been used to fund academic programs and faculty positions. For the past decade, administrative budget lines have been growing much more quickly than faculty lines.

THE CHANGING CONDITIONS OF FACULTY EMPLOYMENT[7]

College and university professors are being criticized today for low productivity—not working enough, with too little consequence. This criticism is coming in part from the states.

> Many state legislators and policy makers believe that faculty members at public colleges and universities care little about undergraduate education, especially education at the freshman and sophomore levels. Faculty members are viewed as being more concerned with graduate education and their research, publication, and other professional activities.[8]

The criticism is also coming from blue-ribbon commissions within higher education.

> Our best guess is that professors in 1990 spend less time in the classroom than their counterparts before the second world war. There is a general feeling that faculty spend less time advising, teach fewer courses outside their specialties, and are less committed to a commonly defined curriculum.[9]

And several distinguished academics have also joined the fray.

> When I began to teach, a "full load" was six courses a year; it is commonly five now and there is movement underway to reduce it to four. Seven courses a year would seem to me to be a reasonable number, a number that...would allow all the research activity a professor felt compelled to do.[10]

A raft of sensational books have been published, seemingly on a daily basis, on the shortcomings of higher education. One of the earliest described college professors this way: 1) They are overpaid, grotesquely underworked, and the architects of academe's vast empire of waste; 2) they have abandoned their teaching responsibilities and their students. To the average undergraduate, the professoriate is unapproachable, uncommunicative, and unavailable; 3) in pursuit of their own interest and research, academic politicking, and cushier grants, they have left the nation's students in the care of an ill-trained, ill-paid, and bitter academic underclass; 4) they have distorted university curriculums to accommodate their own narrow and selfish interests rather than the interests of their own students; 5) they have created a culture in which bad teaching goes unnoticed and unsanctioned and good teaching is penalized; and 6) they insist that their obligations to research justify their flight from the college classroom, despite the fact that fewer than one in ten makes any significant contribution to their field.[11]

What is ironic is that the mounting criticism of faculty and their work loads does not comport with the facts. The realities are these: Faculty members are working longer, not shorter hours. The first study of faculty work load, conducted in 1919, found that professors worked 46.8 hours a week.[12] Research in the 1970s showed roughly the same length for a faculty week (44 hours). However, by 1992 that number had risen to 53 hours. Faculty at research universities worked the longest week (56 hours) and those at two-year colleges worked the shortest (47 hours).[13]

Moreover, faculty hours in the classroom have not systematically declined in recent years. What has occurred is far more complex. In 1975, 1984, and 1989, the Carnegie Foundation studied the median number of hours faculty spent in the classroom each week. [14] They examined five different types of institutions—research universities, doctoral-granting universities, comprehensive colleges and universities, liberal-arts colleges, and two-year colleges. Over the decade and a half of the study, median classroom hours, which the foundation reported in ranges, changed in a variety of ways, as shown in Table 1. The minimum number of hours in the classroom declined across all institutional types. However, the maximum number of hours remained constant at research universities and actually increased at doctoral universities and community colleges. In contrast, declines in maximum hours occurred at liberal-arts and community colleges. In short, faculty are teaching undergraduates both less and more, depending upon where they teach and how they fit into the median range. Plummeting faculty work loads are merely a figment in the minds of higher education's most productive critics. The reality—particularly if one includes graduate teaching hours, which have risen since the 1970s—is very different.

Table 1. Estimated Median Undergraduate Classroom Hours per Week for Full-Time Faculty

Institutional Type	1975	1984	1989
Research universities	3.4 - 3.8	3.4 - 3.6	2.6 - 3.8
Doctoral universities	5.6 - 6.0	5.5 - 5.7	4.6 - 6.4
Comprehensive universities	9.6 - 9.8	9.2 - 9.3	8.4 - 8.8
Liberal-arts colleges	9.7 - 9.9	9.5 - 9.6	9.2 - 9.6
Two-year colleges	13.8 - 13.9	14.2 - 14.6	13.7 - 14.6
Total	8.9 - 9.3	7.7 - 9.0	8.4 - 9.2

Source: Carnegie Foundation Faculty Studies, 1975, 1984, 1989.

It is also true that faculty are spending a smaller proportion of their time teaching, but they are nonetheless spending more hours teaching. In the original 1919 study, faculty spent 63 percent of their time on teaching, 8 percent on research, and 29 percent on other activities.[15] A 1988 study found that faculty now spend 56 percent of their time teaching, 16 percent on research, 13 percent on administration, 4 percent on community service, 5 percent on professional development, and 7 percent on other activities. However, faculty at two-year colleges were spending an even higher percentage of their time teaching (71 percent), while those at four-year colleges spent less time (52 percent).[16] Yet even for faculty at four-year institutions, this translates into a greater number of teaching hours than the 1919 faculty.

On top of this, teaching still remains the key interest of most faculty. In surveys in 1969, 1975, and 1989, the Carnegie Foundation asked faculty whether their interests were primarily in teaching or research. Roughly the same question was asked by the Higher Education Research Institute in 1996. Over nearly thirty years, the proportion of faculty responding affirmatively to teaching remained an astounding seven out of ten, as shown in Table 2.[17]

Table 2. Do Your Interests Lie Primarily in Teaching or Research?

Year	Percent answering teaching
1969	76
1975	73
1984	69
1989	71

Source: Carnegie Foundation, 1989; Higher Education Research Institute, 1996.[18]

The picture that emerges of the professoriate is very different from the popular image. Despite claims to the contrary, academic life has changed relatively little in recent years. However, disenchantment with higher education on the part of the government and the public over issues such as cost and lack of responsiveness seems sufficient to render the facts irrelevant. Accordingly, substantial changes can be expected in the years ahead. There are currently approximately 584,000 college and university faculty. "Seven in ten hold an earned doctorate, half are age 40 to 54 years, and more than six in ten have the security of a tenured position."[19]

Relatively new laws ending mandatory retirement are likely to have a major effect on faculty. They raise large questions about the future of tenure. In the past, colleges and universities could offer faculty permanent appointments, with an understood termination date. Permanent now means lifetime, and people are living longer than in the past. There is no longer any recognition in law that a faculty member's abilities may decline with age or that institutional needs are changing quickly while the length of tenure is increasing. Tenure now means, for all intents and purposes, a thirty-year appointment. In the future, it could mean fifty years. This will present a major issue for college and university boards of trustees. At a minimum, higher education will be forced to create a variety of appointment alternatives to allow older faculty to move from full-time to part-time status, rather than directly into retirement. This will increase the proportion of part-time faculty on the nation's campuses. And add to this the fact that the majority of the current faculty are under the age of fifty-four, and more than three out of five have tenure. This means that it will be more difficult for institutions to remain vital by continually bringing new blood into the academy, because they will already have on board a relatively young, highly tenured faculty, who will probably remain on staff for extended periods of time.

Compounding this situation are changes in the traditional disciplines and departments that employ faculty. Some staple fields, such as sociology, are deeply troubled, and several major institutions have chosen to close their departments. Other subject areas, particularly new area studies, ethnic studies, and technology and cognitive studies, are on the rise, and new departments and programs are being created. This too will raise questions about the utility of tenure at a time when a majority of faculty are in the arts and sciences while a majority of students are choosing majors in professional areas. This mismatch is exacerbated by the lengthening condition of tenure.

The issue of affirmative action will be another pressure on tenure for those campuses and higher education systems that continue to embrace it. The proportion of faculty of color still remains woefully low in American higher education and is even lower among tenured faculty. Increases in the length of tenure will only make this inequity worse.[20]

Finally, 73 percent of the contemporary faculty are full-time,[21] and the proportion of part-time faculty has been growing in recent years, a result largely of economics. Four part-time faculty are considerably cheaper than one full-time staffer. They are also more flexible. Part-timers have been a useful vehicle for plugging holes in faculty coverage of subject areas, for teaching in specialty areas requiring less than a full-time faculty member, and for teaching introductory courses full-time faculty have not wanted to teach. The labor pool for part-time faculty is growing and will expand even more quickly in the future. With the aging of the baby boomers, the supply of retirement-aged academics can be expected to balloon. This will provide a huge pool of very able potential part-time staffers. Higher education has mounting reasons for turning to these staff members. Beginning in 1997, the number of eighteen-year-olds in the US population started to expand. This influx of new students is coming to higher education at a time when collegiate financial resources are either declining or steady. As a result, for both programmatic and economic reasons, the temptation to hire part-time faculty may be irresistible.

THE RISE OF NEW TECHNOLOGIES

The wild card that has the greatest capacity to change faculty life in this situation is new technologies. Several years ago, I had a conversation with the editor of one of the nation's major metropolitan daily newspapers. He said his newspaper would be out of the newspaper business within the next two decades. Instead, he said, the news would be delivered electronically. Subscribers would be able to design the newspaper they receive. For instance, they might want to begin the day with sports. The headlines and front-page news on their daily paper would accordingly focus on athletics. They might have young children and therefore ask that political news be excised, and so forth. This has enormous import for curriculum design; it means the age of textbooks is coming to an end. Faculty will be expected to custom design their own course readings, and these readings will be geared to the demographics of the class being taught. They can and should be updated with each subsequent class. The days of teaching from old yellow lecture notes is approaching an abrupt conclusion.

In the same vein, I recently read an article in an airline magazine that described the travel agency of the future. Through virtual reality, a traveler considering different vacation venues would be able to experience various possibilities. The traveler would be able to smell, hear, feel, and see different locales. She could walk the beaches, climb the mountains, enter the historic landmarks, and inspect the restaurants, hotels, and shops. The same could be done with historic locales. One could visit fifth-century Rome, eighteenth-century America, or fifteenth-century Paris. Imagine smelling the smells of fifteenth-century Paris—they must have been putrid. Imagine walking the cobblestones, entering the great and not-so-great buildings, and seeing the people on the street. This would have revolutionary consequences for pedagogy. How will a standard lecture on fifteenth-century Paris compare with the experience of actually being there? As technology advances, we can anticipate profound changes in the nature of instruction. The only real question is the degree to which this will be something that replaces the faculty or whether it will supplement the faculty. In either case, it will mean a very different role for the professoriate.

Already, technology is available with the capacity to fundamentally change the nature of college instruction. Today, it is possible for Stephen Graubard to give a lecture at the House of the Academy in Cambridge, for me to attend that lecture in New York, and for a third person to watch and listen to it in Tokyo, for example. All of us would, for all intents and purposes, be in the same classroom. I could, for instance, electronically nudge the student in Tokyo and say I missed Professor Graubard's last comment. My question would be translated into Japanese, and the update would be translated back into English. Professor Graubard could ask my Japanese colleague and me to prepare a joint project for the following class session. The point is this: if we can do all of these things electronically, why does higher education any longer need the physical plant called a campus? In the years since World War II, the goal for American higher education has been to overcome geographic barriers to attending college by putting a campus within reach of most Americans. Geography is a barrier that electronic education minimizes and perhaps has the capacity to eliminate. If that is the case, why would a state like California need nine research universities? Why does New York need sixty-four state colleges? Why should any university be forced to employ a lesser scholar or teacher? Faculty will work across campus and state boundaries, as they already have begun to do. Reducing the barrier of geography will profoundly change the nature of the college and university faculty, perhaps in number, but certainly in expectations, roles, and activities.

THE GROWTH OF PRIVATE-SECTOR COMPETITORS

Higher education is a business with revenues in the hundreds of billions of dollars and a reputation for low productivity. This is causing the private sector to look increasingly at postsecondary education with a gleam in its keen eyes. As the chair of a major university's board of trustees confided recently, if higher education were a publicly traded stock, it would be overripe for a hostile takeover.

In this regard, two recent activities are worth noting. The first is the development of a new breed of higher education institution, characterized by the University of Phoenix, now the largest private college in America, enrolling fifty thousand students. Traded on the NASDAQ exchange, this profit-making college is regionally accredited, offering degrees from associate through masters and soon the doctorate. The faculty, which boast traditional academic credentials, are all part-timers, having other forms of primary employment in the fields in which they teach. The equivalent of a full-time faculty member would teach a dozen courses a year. Class syllabi are uniform, prepared every three years by professionals and practitioners in the subject area. In other words, faculty teach the courses; they do not prepare or design them. Students attend classes at convenient hours as a cohort, taking precisely the same courses in sequence. There are no electives. In recent years, the University of Phoenix has added an on-line version of their courses, used by three thousand students. They offer programs from coast to coast, put an emphasis on assessment of student learning and faculty teaching, and have plans to expand enrollment to two hundred thousand students over the next decade.

The University of Phoenix is the largest example of proprietary higher education, but it is not unique, and its example is being watched not only by other entrepreneurs but also by Wall Street and venture capital firms. We will see more institutions like it in the future. What they will mean for faculty is a vastly different role, one that does not include participation in governance, and minimal activity in curriculum planning. The emphasis will be on increasing teaching productivity and eliminating scholarly expectations. Total salary costs will be lower, and all or most faculty will be part-time.

Other, more traditional corporations are also eyeing the higher education market. There is an underlying belief that colleges and universities are making precisely the same mistake that the railroads made. The railroads believed they were in the railroad business; they focused on making bigger and better railroads. The problem is that they were actually in the transportation industry and, as a result, were derailed by the airlines. Similarly, it can be said that higher education is making the mistake of thinking it is in the campus business, when in reality it is in the very lucrative education business. High-technology and entertainment companies are viewing noncampus-based education as an opportunity. The head of one of the major state university systems in the United States recently said his biggest fear is that, before long, the private sector will go to the state capitol demanding the opportunity to bid on the state university contract. At the moment several major companies, such as Disney, IBM, and Bell Atlantic, are exploring technology and learning as an investment opportunity, with greater capital and speed than higher education. Partnerships between the private sector and campuses in this area are mushrooming. Industry is the driving force and senior partner in most of these relationships. With the right company offering education and degrees—

that is, a company with an admired name, a record of cutting-edge accomplishments, and a consumer orientation—the public may well find the alternative very attractive. The implications for faculty of this new education alternative are difficult to contemplate, but one can be assured that the change will be profound.

CONCLUSION

In 1819 Washington Irving wrote "Rip Van Winkle," a story about a man who fell asleep for twenty years. He awakened unaware of the length of his slumber and proceeded to walk around the village in which he lived. He found that "the very village was altered; it was larger and more populous. There were rows of houses which he had never seen before, and those which had been his familiar haunts had disappeared. Strange names were over the doors—strange faces at the windows—everything was strange." The same was true of the village populace: "The very character of the people seemed changed. There was a busy, bustling, disputatious tone to it, instead of the accustomed phlegm and drowsy tranquillity." Rip Van Winkle concluded: "Everything changed and I'm changed and I can't tell what's my name, or who I am."

Washington Irving's story was an allegory. It was more than a tale of a man who overslept; it was an account of the relentlessness of change in America, of an era of overwhelming demographic, economic, global, and technological changes called the Industrial Revolution. Rip Van Winkle was intended to be Everyman trying to orient himself to an unfamiliar world, which seemed to be changing radically overnight.

Today's faculty may be living through a comparable period. As one *Newsweek* observer put it, "It wasn't until recently that I began to get some inkling of what poor Rip must have been feeling the day he finally opened his eyes and rejoined that world." This just might be an equally eye-opening period for all of us who live and work in the world of academe.

ENDNOTES

[1] *The Digest of Educational Statistics* (Washington, D.C.: Department of Education, 1995), 167, 179, 189; *Digest of Educational Statistics* (Washington, D.C.: Department of Education, 1996), 179, 189, 324; *Condition of Education* (Washington, D.C.: Department of Education, 1995), 142, 379; Youth Indicators, *Indicator* 67 (1996).

[2] National Center for Educational Statistics, "Remedial Education at Higher Education Institutions, Fall 1995–October 1996," NCES-97-584.

[3] Eric L. Dey, Alexander W. Astin, and William S. Korn, "The American Freshman: Twenty-Five Year Trends, 1966–1990," Higher Education Research Institute, Graduate School of Education, University of California, Los Angeles, September 1991, 37–38.

[4] Charles C. Schroeder, "New Students—New Learning Styles," *Change* 25 (4) (September/October 1993): 21–26.

[5] Arthur Levine, student affairs survey, 1997.

[6] Ibid.

[7] The material on criticism of the professoriate and the research on a changing work load come from an unpublished manuscript by Arthur Levine and Jana Nidiffer, "Faculty Productivity: A Background Paper," 1994.

[8] Daniel T. Layzell (Legislative Budget Office, State of Arizona), "Tight Budgets Demand Studies of Faculty Productivity," *Chronicle of Higher Education,* 19 February 1992, B2-B3.

[9] Pew Foundation Higher Education Roundtable, "The Lattice and the Ratchet," *Policy Perspectives* 2 (4) (1990).

[10] Page Smith, *Killing the Spirit: Higher Education in America* (New York: Viking, 1990), 192–193.

[11] Charles Sykes, *ProfScam: Professors and the Demise of Higher Education* (New York: St. Martin's Press, 1990), 5.

[12] Leonard Koos, *The Adjustment of Teaching Load in a University* (Washington, D.C.: US Government Printing Office, 1919).

[13] *Digest of Educational Statistics,* 1996, Table 223.

[14] Unfortunately, this data is now eight years old. More recent studies have used categories of institutional types or other divisions of faculty activities, so they are not comparable to the earlier Carnegie studies. The most recent Carnegie Foundation study conducted in 1992–1993 is not yet available either.

[15] Koos, *The Adjustment of Teaching Load in a University.*

[16] S. M. Russell, F. S. Fairweather, and R. N. Hendrickson, *Profiles of Faculty in Higher Education Institutions, 1988* (Washington, D.C.: National Center for Educational Statistics, August 1992), 51–52.

[17]Carnegie Foundation for the Advancement of Teaching, *The Condition of the Professoriate: Attitudes and Trends* (Princeton, N.J.: Carnegie Foundation for the Advancement of Teaching, 1989), 63.

[18]Higher Education Research Institute, "The American College Teacher: National Norms for the 1995–96 HERI Faculty Survey," University of California, Los Angeles, 1997.

[19]Eugene J. Haas, "The American Academic Profession," in Philip G. Altbach, ed., *The International Academic Profession: Portraits of Fourteen Countries* (Princeton, N.J.: Carnegie Foundation, 1996), 342.

[20]*Digest of Educational Statistics*, 1996, Table 221.

[21]Ibid., 342.

Burton R. Clark

Small Worlds, Different Worlds: The Uniquenesses and Troubles of American Academic Professions

T HE ACADEMIC PROFESSION is a multitude of academic tribes and territories.[1] As in days of old, it is law, medicine, and theology. It is now also high-energy physics, molecular biology, Renaissance literature, childhood learning, and computer science. Built upon a widening array of disciplines and specialties, it hosts subcultures that speak in the strange tongues of econometrics, biochemistry, ethnomethodology, and deconstructionism. Driven by a research imperative that rewards specialization, its fragmentation is slowed, though not fully arrested, by limited resources to fund all the new and old lines of effort in which academics would like to engage. Already very great, knowledge growth builds in a self-amplifying fashion. Subject differentiation follows in train, not least in a national system of universities and colleges, such as the American, that is both hugely based on research and generously inclusive in adding subjects to the now-endless list of what legitimately can be taught. As subjects fragment, so does the academic profession, turning it evermore into a profession of professions.

No less important in the differentiation of the academic profession in America is the dispersion of faculty among institutions in a system that, when viewed internationally, must be seen as inordinately large, radically decentralized, extremely diversified, uniquely

Burton R. Clark is Allan M. Cartter Professor of Higher Education Emeritus in the Graduate School of Education and Information Studies at the University of California, Los Angeles.

21

competitive, and uncommonly entrepreneurial. A high degree of institutional dispersion positions American faculty in many varied sectors of a national "system" that totaled 3,600 institutions in the mid-1990s: a hundred-plus "research universities" of high research intensity; another hundred "doctoral-granting" universities that grant only a few doctorates and operate off of a small research base; five hundred and more "master's colleges and universities," a catch-all category of private and public institutions that have graduate as well as undergraduate programs, offering master's degrees but not doctorates; still another six hundred "baccalaureate colleges," heavily private and varying greatly in quality and in degree of concentration on the liberal arts; a huge array of over 1,400 two-year colleges, 95 percent public in enrollment, whose individual comprehensiveness includes college-transfer programs, short-term vocational offerings, and adult education; and finally a leftover miscellany of some seven hundred "specialized institutions" that do not fit into the above basic categories.[2]

These major categories in turn contain much institutional diversity. Buried within them are historically black colleges, Catholic universities, women's colleges, fundamentalist religious universities and colleges, and such distinctive institutions as the Julliard School (of Music), the Bank Street College of Education, and Rockefeller University. The American faculty is distributed institutionally all over the map, located in the educational equivalents of the farm and the big city, the ghetto and the suburbs, the darkened ravine located next to a coal mine and the sunny hill overlooking a lovely valley.

Disciplinary and institutional locations together compose the primary matrix of induced and enforced differences among American academics. These two internal features of the system itself are more important than such background characteristics of academics as class, race, religion, and gender in determining work-centered thought and behavior. These primary dimensions convert simple statements about "the professor" in "the college" or "the university" into stereotypes. We deceive ourselves every time we speak of *the* college professor, a common habit among popular critics of the professoriate who fail to talk to academics in their varied locations and to listen to what they say. Simple summary figures and averages extracted from surveys, e.g., "68 percent of

American professors like their mothers" or "On the average, American professors teach eight and a half hours a week," also should be avoided. Understanding begins with a willingness to pursue diversity.

DIFFERENT WORLDS, SMALL WORLDS

The disciplinary creation of different academic worlds becomes more striking with each passing year. In the leading universities, the clinical professor of medicine is as much a part of the basic work force as the professor of English. The medical academic might be found in a cancer ward, interacting intensively with other doctors, nurses, orderlies, laboratory assistants, a few students perhaps, and many patients in a round of tightly scheduled activities that can begin at six in the morning and extend into the evenings and weekends. Such academics are often under considerable pressure to generate income from patient-care revenues; their faculty groups negotiate with third-party medical plans and need a sizeable administrative staff to handle patient billing. Salaries may well depend on group income, which fluctuates from year to year and is directly affected by changes in the health-care industry and the competitive position of a particular medical school–hospital complex. Even in a tenured post, salary may not be guaranteed. Sizeable research grants must be actively and repetitively pursued; those who do not raise funds from research grants will find themselves encumbered with more clinical duties.

The humanities professor in the leading universities operates in a totally different environment. To begin with, teaching "loads" are in the range of four to six hours a week, office hours are at one's discretion, and administrative assignments vary considerably with one's willingness to cooperate. The humanities academic typically interacts with large numbers of beginning students in introductory classes in lecture halls; with small numbers of juniors and seniors in specialized upper-division courses; and with a few graduate students in seminars and dissertation supervision around such highly specialized topics as Elizabethan lyric and Icelandic legend. Much valuable work time can be spent at home, away from the "distractions" of the university office.

About what is the humanities academic thinking and writing? Attention may center on a biography of Eugene O'Neill, an interpretation of what Jane Austen really meant, an effort to trace Lillian Hellman's political passions, or a critique of Derrida and deconstructionism. Professors seek to master a highly specialized segment of literature and maximize individual interpretation. The interests of humanities professors are reflected not only in the many sections and byways of such omnibus associations as the Modern Language Association but also in the specificities of the Shakespeare Association of America, the Dickens Society, the D. H. Lawrence Society of North America, the Speech Association of America, the Thomas Hardy Society of America, and the Vladimir Nabokov Society. Tocqueville's famous comment on the propensity of Americans to form voluntary associations is nowhere more true than in the academic world.

Disciplinary differences are of course not limited to the sharp contrast between life in a medical school and in a department of English. The work of Tony Becher and others on the cultures of individual disciplines has shown that bodies of knowledge variously determine the behavior of individuals and departments.[3] Disciplines exhibit discernible differences in individual behavior and group action, notably between "hard" and "soft" subjects and "pure" and "applied" fields: in a simple fourfold classification, between hard-pure (physics), hard-applied (engineering), soft-pure (history), and soft-applied (social work). Across the many fields of the physical sciences, the biological sciences, the social sciences, the humanities, and the arts, face-to-face research reveals varied work assignments, symbols of identity, modes of authority, career lines, and associational linkages. Great differences in the academic life often appear between letters and science departments and the many professional-school domains in which a concern for the ways and needs of an outside profession must necessarily be combined with the pursuit of science and truth for its own sake. The popular images of Mr. Chips chatting up undergraduates and Einsteinian, white-haired, remote scholars dreaming up esoteric mathematical equations are a far cry from the realities of academic work that helps prepare schoolteachers, librarians, social workers, engineers, computer experts, architects, nurses, pharmacists, business managers, lawyers, and doctors—and, in some academic locales, also morticians, military personnel, auto mechanics, airport technicians, secretaries, lathe operators, and cosmetologists. For over a century, American higher education has been generous to a fault in admitting former outside fields, and new occupations, into the academy—a point made by historians of higher education and of the professions.[4]

Because research is the first priority of leading universities, the disciplinary differentiation of every modern system of higher education is self-amplifying. The American system is currently the extreme case of this phenomenon. Historic decentralization and competitiveness prompted Charles William Eliot at Harvard and others at the old colleges of the last half of the nineteenth century to speed up the nascent evolution from the age of the college to the age of the university. This evolution turned professors loose to pursue specialized research and to teach specialized subjects at the newly created graduate level, even as students were turned loose to pick and choose from an array of undergraduate courses that was to become ever more bewildering. Throughout the twentieth century and especially in the last fifty years, the reward system of promoting academics on the grounds of research and published scholarship has become more deeply rooted in the universities (and would-be universities and leading four-year colleges) with almost every passing decade. The many proliferating specialties of the knowledge-producing disciplines are like tributaries flowing into a mammoth river of the research imperative.

The most serious operational obstacles to this research-driven amplification are the limitations of funding and the institutional need to teach undergraduates and beginning graduate students the codified introductory knowledge of the various fields. There also remains in American higher education the long-standing belief in the importance of liberal or general education—a task, we may note, that Europeans largely assign to secondary schools. The saving remnant of academics who uphold the banner of liberal and general education are able to sally forth in full cry periodically— the 1920s, the late 1940s, the 1990s—to group some specialties into more general courses, narrow the options in distribution requirements from, say, four hundred to one hundred courses, insist that teaching take priority over research, and in general raise a ruckus about the dangers of the specialized mind. Meanwhile, promotion committees on campus continue their steady scrutiny of individual records of research-based scholarship. Central administrators work to build an institutional culture of first-rateness, as it is defined competitively across the nation and the world according to the reputations of noted scholars and departments. Sophisticated general educators and liberal-arts proponents in the universities recognize the primacy of the substantive impulse and learn how to work incrementally within its limits.

Institutional Differentiation

As powerful as self-amplifying disciplinary differences have become in dividing the American professoriate, institutional diversity now plays an even more important role. This axis of differentiation places approximately two-thirds of American academics in settings other than that of doctoral-granting universities. We find about a fourth of the total faculty in the colleges and universities that offer degree work as far as the master's; a small share, about 7 percent, in the liberal-arts colleges; and a major bloc of a third or so (over 250,000) in the nearly 1,500 community colleges.[5] In student numbers in 1994, the universities had just 26 percent of the total enrollment; the master's level institutions, 21 percent; the baccalaureate colleges, 7 percent; the specialized institutions, 4 percent; and the community colleges, 43 percent—by far the largest share.[6] The two-year colleges admit over 50 percent of entering students. There is no secret that academics in this latter section do an enormous amount of the work of the system at large.

These major locales exhibit vast differences in the very basis of academic life, namely, the balance of effort between undergraduate teaching and advanced research and research training. Teaching loads in the leading universities come in at around four to six hours a week, occasionally tapering down to two to three hours— a class a week, a seminar a week—while sometimes, especially in the humanities, rising above six. The flip side is that faculty commonly expect to spend at least half their time in research, alone or in the company of graduate students, other faculty, and research staff. We need not stray very far among the institutional types, however, before we encounter teaching loads that are 50, 100, and 200 percent higher. The "doctoral-granting universities" that are not well supported to do research often exact teaching loads of nine to twelve hours, as do the liberal-arts colleges, especially those outside the top fifty. In master's colleges, loads of twelve hours a week in the classroom are common. In the community colleges, the standard climbs to fifteen hours and loads of eighteen and twenty-one hours are not unknown. Notably, as we move from the research universities through the middle types to the two-year institutions, faculty involvement shifts from advanced students to beginning students; from highly selected students to an open-door clientele; from young students in the traditional college age-group to a mix of students of all ages in short-term vocational programs as well as in course work leading toward a bachelor's degree. In the community colleges, students in the college-transfer track are numerically overshadowed by students in terminal vocational programs, and both are frequently outnumbered by nonmatriculated adults who turn the "college" into a "community center."

The burdens of remedial education are also much heavier as we move from the most to the least prestigious institutions. The open-door approach, standard in two-year colleges and also operational in tuition-dependent four-year colleges that take virtually all comers, means that college teachers are confronted with many underprepared students. Those who work in the less-selective settings also more frequently work part-time. During the last two decades, the ranks of the part-timers have swollen to over 40 percent of the total academic work force,[7] with heavy concentrations in the less prestigious colleges and especially in the community colleges, where over half the faculty operate on a part-time schedule. At the extreme opposite end of the institutional prestige hierarchy from those who serve primarily in graduate schools and graduate-level professional schools in the major universities we find the full-time and, especially, part-time teachers of English and mathematics in downtown community colleges, who teach introductory and subintroductory courses over and over again—the rudiments of English composition, the basic courses in mathematics—to high-school graduates who need remediation and to adults struggling with basic literacy.

With the nature of work varying enormously across the many types of institutions that make up American postsecondary education, other aspects of the academic life run on a parallel course. If we examine the cultures of institutions by discussing with faculty members their basic academic beliefs, we find different worlds. Among the leading research universities, the discipline is front and center, the institution is prized for its reputation of scholarship and research, and peers are the primary reference group. A professor of physics says, "What I value the most is the presence of the large number and diverse collection of scientists who are constantly doing things that I find stimulating." A professor of biology tells us that his university "has a lot of extremely good departments...there are a lot of fascinating, interesting people here." A political scientist adds that what he values most "is the intellectual level of the faculty and the graduate students.... Good graduate students are very important to me personally and always have been, and having colleagues that are smart is important." And a professor of English states that his institution "is a first-rate university...we have a fine library, and we have excellent teachers here, and we have first-rate scholars." Academics in this favored site have much with which to identify. They are proud of the quality they believe surrounds them, experiencing it directly in their own and neighboring departments and inferring it indirectly from institutional reputation. The strong symbolic thrust of the institution incorporates the combined strengths of the departments that in turn represent the disciplines. Thus, for faculty, disciplinary and institutional cultures converge, creating a happy state indeed.

The leading private liberal-arts colleges provide a second favored site. Here, professors often waxed lyrical in interviews about the small-college environment tailored to undergraduate teaching: "It is a very enjoyable setting. The students—the students we get in physics—are a delight to work with," "I can't put it in a word, but I think that it is one of the least constraining environments I know of," "It is a better form of life," or "My colleagues are fantastic. The people in this department are sane, which in an English department is not always the case." These institutions retain the capacity to appear as academic communities, not bureaucracies, in their overall integration and symbolic unity.

But soon we encounter sites where faculty members are troubled by inchoate institutional character and worried about the quality of their environment. In the lesser universities, and especially in the comprehensive colleges that have evolved out of a teachers-college background, at the second, third, and fourth levels of the institutional prestige hierarchy, the setting may be summed up in the words of one professor:

> I think the most difficult thing about being at an institution like [this one] is that it has a difficult time coming to terms with itself. I think the more established institutions with strong academic backgrounds don't have the problem that an institution that pretty much is in the middle range of higher educational institutions around the country does. I'm not saying that [this place] is a bad institution, but it certainly doesn't have the quality students, the quality faculty, the quality programs of the University of Chicago, Harvard, Yale.... When it talks about standards, what sort of standards? When it talks about practicality, how practical does it have to be?...It doesn't have a strong sense of tradition.

Compared to the research universities, the overall institutional culture is weaker and less satisfying for many faculty members at the same time that disciplinary identifications are weakened as heavy teaching loads suppress research and its rewards.

In these middle-level institutions, professors often spoke of their relationship with students as the thing they value most. Students begin to replace peers as the audience of first resort. That shift is completed in the community colleges, with the identifications of faculty reaching a high point of student-centeredness. In a setting that is distinctly opposed to disciplinary definitions of quality and excellence, pleasures and rewards have to lie in the task of working with poorly prepared students who pour in through the open door. For example: "We are a practical teaching college. We serve our community and we serve...the students in our community and give them a good, basic, strong education....We are not sitting here on our high horses looking to publish" and "I really do like to teach, and this place allows me to teach. It doesn't bog me down with having to turn out papers." In the community colleges, the equity values of open door and open access have some payoff as anchoring points in the faculty culture. But in the overall institutional hierarchy, where the dominant values emphasize quality, selection, and advanced work, the community-college ideology can play only a subsidiary role. The limitations cannot be missed: "It would be nice to be able to teach upper-division classes."

As go work and culture, so go authority, careers, and associational life. To sum up the story on authority: in the leading universities faculty influence is relatively strong. Many individuals have personal bargaining power; departments and professional schools are semiautonomous units; and all-campus faculty bodies such as senates have primacy in personnel and curricular decisions. University presidents speak lovingly of the faculty as the core of the institution and walk gently around entrenched faculty prerogatives. But as we move to other types of institutions, faculty authority weakens and managerialism increases. Top-down command is noticeably stronger in public master's colleges, especially when they have evolved out of a teachers-college background. The two-year colleges, operating under local trustees much like K-12 schools, are quite managerial. Faculty in these places often feel powerless, even severely put upon. Their answer (where possible under state law) has been to band together by means of unionization. The further down the general hierarchy of institutional prestige, the more widespread the unions become, especially among public-sector institutions.

To sum up the associational life of faculty: in the leading universities, faculty interact with one another across institutional boundaries in an extensive network of disciplinary linkages— formal and informal; large and small; visible and invisible; local, regional, national, and international. When university specialists find national "monster meetings" not to their liking, they go anyway to participate in a smaller division or section that best represents their specific interests, or they find kindred souls in small, autonomous meetings of several dozen people. In the other sectors, however, involvement in the mainline disciplinary associations declines; there is less to learn that is relevant to one's everyday life, and travel money is scarce in the institutional budget. Academics then go to national meetings when they are held in their part of the country. They look for special sessions on teaching; they break away to form associations (and journals) appropriate to their sector. Community-college teachers have developed associations in such broad areas as the social sciences and the humanities, e.g., the Community College Humanities Association, and in such special fields as mathematics and biology, e.g., the American Mathematics Association for Two-Year Colleges.[8]

Different worlds, small worlds. Institutional differentiation interacts with disciplinary differentiation in a bewildering fashion that steadily widens and deepens the matrix of differences that separate American academics from each other.

SYSTEMIC PROBLEMS

When we pursue the different worlds of American professors by emphasizing disciplinary and institutional conditions, deep-rooted problems that are otherwise relegated to the background or only dimly perceived come to the fore. Five systemic concerns may be briefly stated as problems of secondarization, excessive teaching, attenuated professional control, fragmented academic culture, and diminished intrinsic reward and motivation.

Secondarization and Remediation

The long evolution from elite to mass to universal access in American postsecondary education has not been without its costs. One major undesirable effect is a change in the conditions of the academic life that occurs when academics confront poorly educated students who come out of a defective secondary-school system and flow into higher education by means of open access. Academic work then revolves considerably around remedial education. Faced with entering students whose academic achievement is, for example, at the level of ninth-grade English, faculty first have to help the student progress to the twelfth-grade or traditional college-entry level, thereby engaging in the work of the high school. Mathematics instructors may find themselves facing students whose achievements measure at the sixth-grade level and hence need to complete some elementary schoolwork as well as their secondary education. Well known by those who teach in nonselective four-year colleges and especially in community colleges, this situation may seem surprising, even shocking, to others. But like the night and the day, it follows from the structure and orientation of American secondary and postsecondary education. If secondary schools graduate students whose achievement is below the twelfth-grade level, as they commonly do, and if some colleges admit all or virtually all who approach their doors, then college faculties will engage in K-12 work. Remedial education is spread throughout American higher education, from leading universities to community colleges, but it is relatively light when selectivity is high and quite heavy when selection is low or even nonexistent.

The problem of teaching poorly prepared students is compounded in the two-year college by its concentration on the first two years of the four-year undergraduate curriculum and on short-term vocational and semiprofessional programs. This curricular context calls for repetitive teaching of introductory courses. Since community colleges experience much student attrition during and after the first year of study, due to a variety of personal, occupational, and academic reasons, teaching is concentrated in first-year courses. In each department it is usually the general introductory course or two that must be taught over and over again, with little or no surcease. Upper-division courses, let alone graduate courses, are rarely available. While some course diversity can be found at the second-year level, the departmental task is to cover the introductory materials semester by semester, year in and year out. The teaching task is then closer to secondary-school teaching than what is found in selective universities. The task of remedial education adds to the downward thrust, requiring subcollege work on a plane below the regular first-year instruction.

Inherent and widespread in current American education, this teaching context receives relatively little attention in academic and public discussions. It is virtually an institutional secret that academic life is so often reduced to the teaching of secondary-school subjects. With due respect to the difficulties of the work, and the often deep devotion of involved staff to the welfare of underprepared students and immigrant populations, this widely found situation amounts to a dumbing down of the intellectual life of academic staff. Subject content is limited to codified introductory material. Educational euphemisms allow us to blink at this undesired effect of American-style comprehensive secondary schooling and universal higher education, but they do not allow us to escape it. The situation marginalizes faculty. Eroding "the essential intellectual core of faculty work," it deprofessionalizes them.[9]

Excessive Teaching

The complaint that professors do too much research and too little teaching has been prevalent for almost a hundred years. When William James wrote about "the Ph.D. octopus" shortly after the turn of the century, he pointed to the increasing preoccupation of professors in the emerging universities with specialized research, graduate students, and doctoral programs. Since then the protest of too much research has been a perennial battle cry of the American reformer seeking more emphasis on undergraduate programs and on their general or liberal education components in particular. The 1980s and early 1990s have seen a strong resurgence of this point of view inside and outside the academy. Careful critics beamed their messages at research universities, would-be universities, and even four-year private and public colleges that have opened their faculty reward systems to the research imperative. They understand that professors teach when they supervise students in the preparation of master's and doctoral theses. They are sometimes aware that in the best private liberal-arts colleges professors involve their undergraduate students in research as an effective way to teach and to learn.[10] But the critical comment overall has turned into a generalized charge that "professors" should do less research and more teaching, meaning undergraduate teaching. In the popular press, and even in the academic press, careful targeting is forgone. In the extreme, a minimization of teaching by professors is portrayed as part of a "scam."

But across the dispersed American professoriate, the reality is the reverse: more academics teach too much than teach too little. Fifteen hours of classroom teaching each week is far too much for the maintenance of a scholarly life; even twelve hours is excessive. But as noted earlier, most institutional sectors present such loads, specifying assignments that are two to three times greater than that of professors in research-based institutions. Twelve and fifteen hours a week in the classroom at the college level tend to push professors out of their disciplines. A sense of being a scholar is reduced as the "physicist" becomes entirely a "teacher of physics," the "political scientist" a "teacher of political science"—and then mainly as teachers of introductory courses only. Interest flags in what is going on in the revision of advanced topics; command of the literature weakens. Excessive teaching loads apparently are now becoming a source of academic burnout, importing into higher education the teacher burnout long noted as a problem in the K–12 system. A 1989 Carnegie Foundation faculty survey found that the share of the full-time faculty "intending to retire early" was 25 percent in research universities, 26 percent in liberal-arts colleges, and a huge 49 percent in two-year colleges.[11] A setting characterized by heavy introductory teaching propels academics toward early retirement twice as much—one-half of the total staff!—as settings where professors have light teaching loads, involvement in research, and a more scholarly life as traditionally defined.

Weakened Professional Control

As indicated earlier, command structures are not unheard of in American colleges and universities. Professors in research universities and leading private four-year colleges certainly encounter trustee and administrator influence. Their professional position is also increasingly challenged by the professionalization of administrative occupations clustered around central management; in the words of Gary Rhoades, "faculty are increasingly 'managed' professionals in organizations increasingly run by 'managerial professionals.'"[12] But academics in these favored sites generally have strong countervailing power of a professional kind that is rooted in their personal and collective expertise. Department by department, professional school by professional school, they exercise much internal control. They expect to dominate in choosing who to add to the faculty and what courses should be taught. They expect to be consulted in many matters rather than to receive orders from those in nominally superior positions. But in public and private comprehensive colleges and especially in community colleges, the foundations of authority change. Subject expertise becomes more diffuse, occasionally amounting only to sufficient knowledge in the discipline to teach the introductory course to poorly prepared students, while at the same time the role of trustees and administrators is strengthened, sometimes approaching the top-down supervision found in local school districts. Such managerialism is particularly evident in public-sector institutions, especially when they are exposed to state assertions of accountability.

Adding greatly to the vulnerability of academic professionals to political and administrative dictate is the marginal position of part-time faculty. In all institutional sectors, part-timers have long been with us: witness the traditional use and abuse of faculty spouses in part-time work in foreign language departments of research universities. But the use of part-timers grew greatly during the last two decades as a form of mobile and inexpensive labor. It unfortunately turns out that floating student "clienteles" require dispensable academic staff, hence the deteriorating situation for staff in community colleges where a majority of faculty now serve part-time. The part-timers themselves have only marginal influence, and their large numbers weaken the influence of full-time faculty vis-à-vis trustees and administrative staff. A relatively powerless proletariat exists in American academic life, centered in employment that is part-time and poorly paid.

Experiments are underway in the two-year colleges, we should note, to create new forms of academic professionalism that are centered on "the disciplines of instruction" rather than on disciplinary affiliation.[13] This approach emphasizes the importance of translating knowledge into more understandable forms by such means as course revision and media preparation. Certain attitudes about teaching, as well as forms of teaching, become the possible basis for professional identity. But while community-college instruction has become a career in its own right, it remains highly unlikely that a strong sense of professionalism can be constructed when disciplinary foundations are weak, part-time work is the main form of employment, and top-down bureaucratic control remains widespread.

Fragmented Academic Culture

All-encompassing academic values are increasingly hard to find in American academic life. The claims frequently made by reformers that academics must somehow find their way back to agreement on core values and assume an overarching common framework become less realistic with each passing year. Different contexts, especially institutional ones, promote different values. Even common terms assume different meanings. "Academic freedom" in one context means mainly the right to do as one pleases in pursuing new ideas; in another, not to have an administrator dictate the teaching syllabus one uses; in another, the right to teach evolution in a college where the local board of trustees is dominated by creationists; in yet another, the right to join an extremist political group. Promotion criteria vary from an all-out emphasis on research productivity to weight put solely on undergraduate instruction, from complicated mixtures of teaching and research and several forms of "service" to heavy weighting of years on the job and seniority rights. As mentioned earlier, professional schools must value their connection to outside professions as well as to other parts of their universities, thereby balancing themselves between two sets of values in a way not required in the letters and science departments. The grounds for advancement then become particularly contentious. All such differences in outlook among academics widen as differentiation of academic work continues.

Diminished Intrinsic Reward and Motivation

Under all the strengths and weaknesses of American academic life, we find the persistent problem of the professional calling. When academic work becomes just a job and a routine career, then such material rewards as salary are placed front and center. Academics stay at their work or leave for other pursuits according to how much they are paid. They come to work "on time" because they must (it is nailed down in the union contract); they leave on time because satisfaction is found after work is concluded. But when academic work is still a calling, it "constitutes a practical ideal of activity and character that makes a person's work morally inseparable from his or her life. It subsumes the self into a community of disciplined practice and sound judgment whose activity has meaning and value in itself, not just in the output or profit that results from it."[14] A calling transmutes narrow self-interest into other-regarding and ideal-regarding interests: one is linked to peers and to a version of a larger common good. The calling has moral content; it contributes to civic virtue.

Professionalization projects seek to provide vehicles by which multitudes of workers are transported to a calling, where they find intrinsic motivation as well as the glories of high status and the trappings of power. The academic profession is lucky in that it has abundant sources of intrinsic motivation in the fascinations of research and the enchantments of teaching. Many academic contexts offer a workaday existence rich in content and consequence. As a confederate gathering, the academic profession's continuing promise lies considerably in the provision of a variety of contexts that generate "absorbing errands."[15] In that promise lies the best hope in the long term for the recruitment and retention of talent.

But when such contexts fade away or become severely weakened, the errands run down and talented people search for other fascinations and enchantments. The systemic problems I have identified—secondarization, excessive teaching, weakened professional control, fragmented academic culture—point to structural and cultural conditions that run down the academic calling.

WHAT, IF ANYTHING, CAN BE DONE?

In a large, decentralized, and competitive system of higher education, apace with great differentiation of institutions and disciplines, student growth and knowledge growth have badly fractured the American academic profession. From a cross-national perspective, the resulting system has had major advantages. More than elsewhere, the system at large has been able to combine academic excellence and scientific preeminence with universal access and weak standards. It has been flexible, even to a fault, with various sectors adjusting to different demands and numerous colleges and universities fashioning individual niches. But a heavy price has been paid, not least in the systemic problems I have identified that seriously weaken the American academic work force. The ever-extending differentiation that is integral to the success of the system produces a host of academic subworlds that downgrade the academic profession overall. They establish conditions hostile to the best features of professionalism.

Can these conditions be reduced, reversing the drift toward secondarization, the weight of excessive teaching, the weakening of professional control, the fragmentation of academic culture, and the diminishing of intrinsic motivation and reward? These weaknesses do not just hurt the professoriate; they also injure universities and colleges. They undermine the hopes of the nation that a well-trained and highly motivated professoriate will continue to staff an academic system second to none.

Four broad ideas can frame future directions of reform. First, *the intellectual core of academic work throughout the system should be protected and strengthened.* It may be helpful to students in the short run to offer them remedial instruction; it may be helpful to high-turnover clienteles and tight institutional budgets to invest heavily in part-time academics. But such major developments are injurious to the state of the academic profession and hence in the long term to the institutions that depend upon its capability. Higher education has enough to do without including the work of the secondary school. Success in secondary-school reform that instilled serious standards for the high-school diploma would be a major step for those who teach in postsecondary education. Part-timeness needs to be taken seriously, since nothing runs down a profession faster than to shift its work from full-time labor requiring credentialed experts to an operation that can be staffed by casual laborers who must live by their wits as they flit among jobs. Limits on the use of part-timers can be set in institutions: 20 or 25 percent of the total staff is enough; 50 percent is highly excessive and should be seen as institutionally injurious.

Second, *constant attention must be paid to the integration of academic personnel with managerial personnel.* As the gap grows between "faculty" and "administration" inside universities and colleges, faculty seek to promote their special interests more and administrators increasingly see themselves as the only ones who uphold overall institutional concerns. "Shared governance" only works when it is shared to the point where some academics sit in central councils and the rest of the academic staff feel they are appropriately represented, or where decision-making is extensively decentralized to deans and department heads and faculty sit close to these newly strengthened "line managers," or in various other complicated combinations of centralized and decentralized decision-making.

Personal leadership has its place in academe, but the window of opportunity for arbitrary top-down policy generally does not last very long. Anything worth doing in a university or college requires a number of people who want it to happen and will work at it for a number of years. Academic values, as defined by the academic staff, need to be constantly mixed throughout the organizational structure with the influence of the new managerial values that will be even more necessary in academic institutions in the future than they are now. The linking of academics with overall, long-term institutional interests is central in academic management; with it comes extended professional authority.

Third, *indirect forms of linkage among divergent academic cultures need to be better understood and promoted.* The search for clarified common goals comes up empty-handed. Rhetoric that embraces complex universities and colleges falls back on eternal clichés about research, teaching, and service. Meanwhile, the separate departments and professional schools go on generating their separate cultures. How do these cultures then connect, if at all? Both as modes of reasoning and as knowledge domains, they often have some overlap with neighboring fields. With interdisciplinary fields also helping to bridge the gaps, the many specialties of academics may be seen (in the words of three acute observers) as connected in "chains of overlapping neighborhoods." The connections produce "a continuous texture of narrow specialties," a "collective communication," and "a collective competence and breadth." Academics are partially integrated through "interlocking cultural communities."[16] Then, too, the socialization of graduate students into academic ways still counts for something—an integrating force among university graduates spread out among different types of institutions. Models of behavior also radiate from one type of institution to another. For example, the image of liberal education most strongly embodied in small private liberal-arts colleges clearly serves as a model of what undergraduate education in large public four-year colleges could be if appropriately funded and properly carried out. The many different types of institutions comprising the American system do not operate as value-tight compartments.

Fourth, *the intrinsic rewards of the academic life need to be highlighted and respected.* As earlier reported, academics in diverse settings point to the special joys of teaching, or of doing research, or of combining the two. They speak of the pleasure of shaping the minds of the young, of making discoveries, of carrying forward the intellectual heritage of the nation and the world. They sense that at the end of the day they may have done something worthwhile. They point to such psychic rewards as reasons to be in academic work and as reasons to resist the lure of greater material rewards elsewhere. There is still some devotion to a calling.

Academic fanatics who are fully caught up in this now oddly shaped calling can even feel, as Max Weber put it in a famous essay, that they are in the grip of "a demon who holds the fibers of their very lives."[17] We find the academic demon everywhere: in the professor so intensely interested in her writing that she never checks the clock; in the college teacher who acts way beyond the call of duty as personal mentor and substitute parent for marginal students; in the academic scientist who is in the laboratory instead of at home at two o'clock in the morning; in the lecturer who will not stop talking long after the bell has rung and has to be forced out of the lecture hall or classroom; in the dying academic who works up to the last week, even the last day. George Steiner wrote of the world of "the absolute scholar" as "a haunting and haunted business," a place where "sleep is a puzzle of wasted time, and flesh a piece of torn luggage that the spirit must drag after it. . . ."[18]

Even in modest dosages, academic professionalism centered on intrinsic features of the work at hand leads to committed productivity that political and bureaucratic controls cannot generate— nor can "market forces" guarantee. Those who seek to replace professional commitment with the nuts and bolts of bureaucratic regulation run down the calling; they take intellectual absorption out of the absorbing errand. Wise academic leaders and sophisticated critics sense that only professional norms and practices are ingrained, person by person, in everyday activity to constructively shape motivation and steer behavior. They then attend to the conditions of professional inspiration and self-regulation. Positioned between state and market, academic professionalism, however fragmented, remains a necessary foundation for performance and progress in higher education.

ENDNOTES

[1]This essay is based largely on two books and two prior articles that report the results of research on academic life in Europe and America: Burton R. Clark, ed., *The Academic Profession: National, Disciplinary and Institutional Settings* (Berkeley and Los Angeles, Calif.: University of California Press, 1987); Burton R. Clark, *The Academic Life: Small Worlds, Different Worlds* (Princeton, N.J.: Carnegie Foundation for the Advancement of Teaching and Princeton University Press, 1987); Burton R. Clark, "The Academic Life: Small Worlds, Different Worlds," *Educational Researcher* 18 (5) (1989): 4–8; and Burton R. Clark, "Faculty: Differentiation and Dispersion," in Arthur Levine, ed., *Higher Learning in America: 1980–2000* (Baltimore, Md.: Johns Hopkins University Press, 1993), 163–178. For other research-based studies of American academics reported in the 1980s and 1990s, see Martin J. Finkelstein, *The American Academic Profession: A Synthesis of Social Scientific Inquiry Since World War II* (Columbus, Ohio: Ohio State University Press, 1984); Howard R. Bowen

and Jack H. Schuster, *American Professors: A National Resource Imperiled* (New York: Oxford University Press, 1986); and Robert T. Blackburn and Janet H. Lawrence, *Faculty at Work: Motivation, Expectation, Satisfaction* (Baltimore, Md.: Johns Hopkins University Press, 1995).

[2]Carnegie Foundation for the Advancement of Teaching, *A Classification of Institutions of Higher Education,* 1994 ed. (Princeton, N.J.: Carnegie Foundation for the Advancement of Teaching, 1994), xiv.

[3]Tony Becher, *Academic Tribes and Territories: Intellectual Enquiry and the Cultures of Disciplines* (Milton Keynes, England: The Open University Press, 1989).

[4]See Walter Metzger, "The Academic Profession in the United States," in Clark, ed., *The Academic Profession: National, Disciplinary, and Institutional Settings,* 123–208; and R. H. Wiebe, *The Search for Order, 1877–1920* (New York: Hill and Wang, 1967).

[5]Arthur M. Cohen and Florence B. Brawer, *The American Community College,* 3d ed. (San Francisco, Calif.: Jossey-Bass, 1996), 86.

[6]Carnegie Foundation for the Advancement of Teaching, *A Classification of Institutions of Higher Education,* xiv.

[7]For tracking the growth of part-time faculty, see David W. Leslie, Samuel E. Kellams, and G. M. Gunne, *Part-Time Faculty in American Higher Education* (New York: Praeger, 1982); Judith M. Gappa, *Part-Time Faculty: Higher Education at a Crossroads,* ASHE-ERIC Higher Education Research Report No. 3 (Washington, D.C.: Association for the Study of Higher Education, 1984); and Judith M. Gappa and David W. Leslie, *The Invisible Faculty: Improving the Status of Part-Timers in Higher Education* (San Francisco, Calif.: Jossey-Bass, 1993).

[8]Cohen and Brawer, *The American Community College,* 98.

[9]Earl Seidman, *In the Words of the Faculty: Perspectives on Improving Teaching and Educational Quality in Community Colleges* (San Francisco, Calif.: Jossey-Bass, 1985), 275.

[10]See Robert A. McCaughey, *Scholars and Teachers: The Faculties of Select Liberal Arts Colleges and Their Place in American Higher Learning* (New York: Barnard College, Columbia University, 1994).

[11]Carnegie Foundation for the Advancement of Teaching, "Early Faculty Retirees: Who, Why, and with What Impact?," *Change* (July/August 1990): 31–34. On burnout in community colleges, see Cohen and Brawer, *The American Community College,* 90–93.

[12]Gary Rhoades, "Reorganizing the Faculty Work Force for Flexibility," *Journal of Higher Education* 67 (6) (November/December 1996): 656.

[13]Cohen and Brawer, *The American Community College,* 96–100.

[14]Robert N. Bellah, Richard Madsen, William M. Sullivan, Ann Swidler, and Steven M. Tipton, *Habits of the Heart: Individualism and Commitment in American Life* (Berkeley and Los Angeles, Calif.: University of California Press, 1985), 66.

[15]A metaphor attributed to Henry James. Exact reference unknown.

[16]For a fuller account of these metaphors and perspectives offered respectively by Michael Polanyi, Donald T. Campbell, and Diana Crane, see Clark, *The Academic Life,* 140–142.

[17]Max Weber, "Science as a Vocation," in H. H. Gerth and C. Wright Mills, eds., *From Max Weber: Essays in Sociology* (New York: Oxford University Press, 1946), 156.

[18]George Steiner, "The Cleric of Treason," in *George Steiner: A Reader* (New York: Penguin Books, 1984), 197–198.

Francis Oakley

The Elusive Academic Profession: Complexity and Change

THE REASSURINGLY FAMILIAR AND UNPROBLEMATIC RING of the phrase "academic profession" invites an ease of generalization that is, in fact, belied by the elusive and shifting nature of the phenomenon to which it refers. Those who have concerned themselves as scholars with one or another aspect of that phenomenon often tend to be somewhat skeptical about the propriety of even speaking about any single such profession.[1] That skepticism becomes understandably prominent among those seeking to understand the academic world in some sort of comparative or cross-national terms.[2] Professionalism itself may not necessarily be an "Anglo-American disease,"[3] but it is hard not to be struck by the degree to which academics in continental Western Europe fail, unlike their British and American counterparts, to perceive themselves as members of a profession analogous to the professions of medicine and law. Instead, they tend to view themselves as being part of the *grand corps d'État,* of an academic estate "closely related to, or intimately a part of, the state."[4] And even if one restricts oneself to the American scene, it is only after signaling the need for caution that one should permit oneself to deploy what Laurence Vesey has called "the somewhat loose and imprecise concept of higher education as a profession." One reason for this is the sheer complexity of the vast and sprawling American system of higher education taken as a whole. Another is the further complexity of the university itself, which, Vesey argues, "may well be the most internally diverse institution there is," sheltering an

Francis Oakley is Edward Dorr Griffin Professor of the History of Ideas at Williams College and President Emeritus of the College.

43

enormously numerous, various, and "indeed incongruous" range of specialties as well as "a multitude of what are called professions."[5] Both of these reasons call for some preliminary commentary before we proceed with the task at hand.

That so many of the recent commentators on the ills of American higher education appear to have drawn their negative conclusions from what is purported to have been going on at little more than a dozen of the nation's leading research universities and liberal-arts colleges should not encourage us to proceed in similar fashion. A focus on such prominent institutions necessarily affords only the most partial of insights into the extremely varied realities of the 3,595 institutions that the Carnegie Foundation for the Advancement of Teaching recognized in 1994 as institutions of higher education.[6] The conditions of work, range of subjects taught, target group of students served, institutional mission pursued—all of these differ widely among those institutions. Two-year junior and community colleges alone, which stand closer in mission to the world of secondary education than to the research university sector, make up no less than 41 percent of the total, while the group of specialized institutions that award most of their degrees in a single subject (whether Bible studies, engineering, management, law, music, or design) make up a further 20 percent. Even in the university sector (whether research, doctoral-granting, or comprehensive in category), something of a gulf divides the intellectual and teaching preoccupations characteristic of arts and sciences people from those characteristic of the professional schools.[7] And at the liberal-arts colleges as well as at the universities, the professional interests of arts and sciences faculty are themselves diffused among a constantly proliferating array of disciplines, subdisciplines, and cross-disciplinary areas of interest, each with its own distinctive array of professional organizations, specialized journals, and fluctuating affinity groups, as well as its own persistent purchase on loyalties, attention, and time.

Such factors should loom large in one's mind in attempting to address the issue of change in the profession as a whole. The changes experienced over the past thirty years by those teaching in the comprehensive sector, for example, have been far more dramatic than those experienced by people working in the liberal-arts college sector and in many ways different in kind from those evident in the research university sector.[8] Moreover, given the propensity of in-house commentators on the academic scene to filter their perceptions of change through an autobiographical lens and to frame their reportage in loosely anecdotal fashion, one has to keep a discerning eye out for the gap that has so often in the past turned out to exist between individual and localized perceptions of academic reality and the aggregate situation in the academic world at large to which carefully collected statistical data testify. Faculty commentators at the start of the century, for example, not infrequently portrayed themselves as belonging to an underpaid and poorly rewarded profession, and historians have sometimes taken such self-portrayals at face value. But during the period stretching from the 1890s to World War I (as public opinion polls suggest and salary figures testify) the profession in fact stood at something of a high point in terms of both economic status and public esteem. Indeed, one contemporary academic leader subsequently looked back at those years as "the richest in our lives," and, more recently, they have been described as constituting "a golden age for the academic profession."[9]

Furthermore, even if, chastened by such examples, one sets out accordingly to discipline an impressionistic sense of the way things stand by factoring in evidence drawn from the available statistical data, one must be aware of the drawbacks often attendant upon the use of survey data—the way in which questions were framed may well have had the effect of introducing ambiguities into the results obtained. More specifically, one has to be conscious, too, of the degree to which the chronological point of departure settled on for purposes of statistical comparison can determine the nature, direction, and amount of change one perceives in the ensuing period. The harrowing slide in both public esteem and economic status that the profession experienced in the 1970s and 1980s should not tempt one to view the conditions of the years immediately preceding that time as representing some sort of norm. Instead, the mid-1950s to 1971 was an unusual period of partial recovery that turns out, in retrospect, merely to have punctuated the more persistent process of decline in the fortunes of the profession that had set in after World War I.[10] Similarly, once one recovers and tracks the statistics back beyond the commonly chosen point of analytic departure in the late 1960s, it becomes clear that the startling decline in liberal-arts enrollments evident in the 1970s and early 1980s represents no unprecedented declension from any long-term higher norm. Instead, it reflects a falling back from the all-time peak in such enrollments produced by an unprecedented surge lasting from the late 1950s to around 1970. It becomes clear, too, that the effect of that falling back has been merely to return us to something like the long-term "trajectory [of gradual decline] established over the past century."[11]

Such putative pitfalls, craven caveats, and squeamish qualifications duly recorded, it is in fact possible to frame a few observations about the nature, dimension, speed, and focus of the changes that the profession has experienced since the quickening in the pace of growth that set in somewhere around forty years ago. These observations are essentially of three types: First, there are those in which it seems safe to repose a high degree of confidence, grounded as they are in the basic descriptive statistical data concerning the world of higher education, which from the late 1960s onward have grown considerably in both volume and precision. Second, there are those observations that are attitudinal in focus and that lean for support (somewhat uneasily, it must be confessed) upon aggregated statistical data both national and international in scope. With these, it is true, the vagueness of some of the questions asked and the marked disparities evident in the conditions of work in the various institutional sectors of higher education both tend to obscure the clarity of their message and to diminish the confidence with which one can assess their import. Used, however, with a due measure of caution and supplemented, whenever possible, by the findings of studies that (like those of Howard Bowen and Jack Schuster, David Breneman, or Robert McCaughey)[12] rely not simply on survey data but on some measure of direct fieldwork, such data are not to be ignored. If nothing else, they can serve as a chastening corrective to the species of disheveled anecdotalism that, in the recent surge of critical commentary on American higher education, has so often and so regrettably been substituted for any more responsible or systematic effort to penetrate to an understanding of the complex realities being addressed.[13] Third, and in an attempt to counteract the flattening effect of generalizations based on data drawn from the full and disparate array of institutional sectors, I will offer a few observations grounded in the intimations of change evident in one particular sector—namely, that of the baccalaureate/liberal-arts colleges, the sector I myself know most intimately and with which I have had the longest acquaintance. These three types of observations I propose to advance in sequence.

Under the first heading, the initial observation to be made is so obvious that it would be all too easy (though no less unwise) simply to take it for granted. Namely, there are far more universities and colleges than there were forty years ago and, accordingly, far more of us in the profession than was formerly the case. Here, change has been unquestionably dramatic and in some measure unprecedented. On the eve of the Civil War the United States boasted some 250 institutions of higher education. A century later (1960) the comparable figure stood at 2,026, and a further increase of similar dimensions (up to 3,595) has been crammed into the years since then.[14] In 1960 the academic profession included approximately 280,000 members; by 1970 there were over 530,000, the biggest jump (of about 150,000) having occurred between 1965 and 1970, "with the number of *new* positions created and filled exceeding the *entire number* of faculty slots that [had] existed in 1940."[15] After the early 1970s, of course, as student enrollment levels stabilized, the demand for new faculty dried up, and the growth rate accordingly slowed down. Even so, by 1988, when the National Center for Education Statistics initiated—for the first time since 1963—a National Survey of Postsecondary Faculty, and even excluding those with "acting, affiliate, adjunct, or visiting faculty status," it came up with a total of approximately 670,000 faculty members. And initial data released from the Center's 1993 National Study of Postsecondary Faculty, which was somewhat more inclusive in its definition of faculty, indicate a global figure of approximately 886,000.[16]

Of the faculty total of 670,000 established in 1988, approximately 494,000 were full-time and 176,000 part-time. Of the full-time faculty, approximately 28 percent taught at research universities, 26 percent at comprehensive institutions, 19 percent at public two-year colleges, and 8 percent at liberal-arts colleges of one sort or another. The distribution of part-time faculty was markedly different. No less than 46 percent of them were concentrated in the two-year colleges, with the next largest group (approximately 18 percent) at the comprehensive institutions, and only 11 and 8 percent, respectively, at the research universities and liberal-arts colleges. A similarly sharp contrast is evident in the overall percentages of full-time (around 35 percent) and part-time (around 19 percent) faculty teaching in the arts and sciences as opposed to programs of professional education.[17]

As far as seniority is concerned, some 60 percent of the full-time faculty at both four-year and two-year institutions were tenured, ranging from a high of 69 percent at the public research universities to a low of 48 percent at the private doctoral institutions; the liberal-arts colleges came in towards the low end, at 51 percent, with above-average tenured cohorts in the arts and sciences. The mean age of the full-time group was forty-seven; at forty-four, their part-time colleagues were slightly younger. Of the full-time faculty, only 2 percent were under thirty, 40 percent were between thirty and forty-five, and 55 percent between forty-five and sixty-four. With this dimension, no statistically significant differences were evident across either subject area or institutional sector. And the same is by and large true among both part-time and full-time faculty for representation of the several racial and ethnic groupings across the several institutional sectors. Eighty-nine percent of the full-time and 90 percent of the part-time faculty were white; Asians constituted some 4 percent approximately of the total; blacks, Hispanics, and Native Americans, 3, 2, and 1 percent respectively.[18] So far as gender is concerned, however, there was a fairly marked difference between full-time and part-time faculty. Whereas men constituted 73 percent of the full-time contingent, they totaled no more than 56 percent of the part-timers. Not surprisingly, then, in relation to their average of 27 percent of the full-time contingent, women were comparatively overrepresented at the public two-year institutions (38 percent) and underrepresented at the research universities (approximately 20 percent). At 29 percent, they possessed a comparatively strong presence in the liberal-arts colleges.[19]

From the responses of faculty members in the 1988 survey, we learn that in the fall semester of 1987 they reported themselves as working, on average, some 53 hours per week at all their professional activities, whether institutional or non-institutional, paid or unpaid. Eighty-seven percent of that average work load involved work at their academic institutions, while mean hours of unremunerated professional service constituted 6 percent and mean hours of remunerated outside work, such as consulting, were 7 percent of the total. Faculty at the public and private research universities and at the public doctoral universities put in on average the longest hours (at 57, 56, and 54 hours per week); those at the two-year colleges (at 47 hours) the shortest.[20] If academic rank seemed to make no appreciable difference in the number of working hours devoted either to the institution itself or to outside professional activities, whether remunerated or not,[21] field of study or program area clearly did. Faculty in the fine arts, for example, while putting in the same number of hours as the overall mean and as the mean for unpaid professional service "outside," committed less time to the institution (44 hours) and more to paid outside activities (6 hours). In contrast, faculty in the humanities, who also aligned with the mean in relation both to overall work load and to amount of time devoted to outside unpaid professional services, devoted more time to the institution (48 hours) and less to outside remunerated activities (2 hours).[22]

Differences in the way in which faculty members allocated their working hours showed up also by institutional sector. At all types of institutions, teaching activities accounted for the bulk of that time, with the overall mean being 56 percent for teaching, student advising, grading, course preparation, and so on; 16 percent for scholarly research (and, presumably, writing); 13 percent for administrative and governance activities of one sort or another; and 15 percent for such other activities as working with student organizations, community or public service, and outside counseling or free-lance work. But in regard to the balance between teaching and research, whereas faculty at the two-year colleges devoted 71 percent of their time to teaching and only 3 percent to research, those at the private research universities (not surprisingly) devoted an average of only 40 percent to teaching and 30 percent to research. The comparable distribution of time for faculty at liberal-arts colleges was 65 percent to teaching, 8 percent to research. At all types of institutions, moreover, academic rank made some difference in the differential amounts of time allocated to teaching, research, and administration, with the full professors spending 5 percent less time on teaching and 6 percent more time on administrative activity than their assistant professor colleagues. Similarly, disparities also show up when one controls for academic field or program area, with the extremes being set by faculty in agriculture and home economics (46 percent teaching; 28 percent research), and by those in the humanities (61 percent teaching; 17 percent research).[23]

For their efforts, full-time faculty respondents in the 1988 survey reported themselves to be receiving on average a basic institutional salary of approximately $39,500 and a total annual income from all sources in the neighborhood of $49,000. Apart from an obvious differentiation in earnings by academic rank, institutional sector, program area or field, and gender also accounted for substantial differences in mean annual incomes. The highest annual income (about $75,000) was reported by faculty members teaching at private research universities; the lowest (about $33,000) by faculty at liberal-arts colleges. When broken down by academic field or program area—whatever the institutional sector involved—those in the health sciences emerged as the best remunerated ($75,000) and most likely to be in receipt of outside consulting income; those in the humanities, the worst ($33,000) and the least likely to make any money from consulting.[24] Cutting across these discrepancies, moreover, are gender-related differences in compensation, with the female members of the full-time regular faculty cohort receiving 32 percent less in total income from all sources and with compensation discrepancies evident at every academic rank.[25]

The 1988 survey report provides us with a fuller picture than any subsequent report and affords us a useful profile of the profession as it was slightly less than a decade ago. And while a glance at the data thus far released from the 1993 National Study of Postsecondary Faculty does, of course, reveal a measure of continuing change, it does not, I would judge, suggest any dramatic reshaping of that overall profile.[26]

That was far from being the case with the three decades previous, which had witnessed some very significant changes—for example, in the composition of the profession by race, ethnicity, and, above all, gender. At the same time, it is harder to use those decades to make reliable comparisons or chart the process of change in the profession. The reason is the simple lack of data, or—where pertinent sets were indeed collected but assuming shifting definitions and using varying methodologies—the lack of easily comparable data. In particular, given the insouciance with which commentators presume to generalize on the subject, it would have been helpful to have for the preceding decades survey data directly comparable to what was collected in 1988, which would enable us to ascertain with some precision the degree to which there has been a change in the way that faculty members characteristically divide their time between teaching and research. Such precisely comparable data we do not have. What we do have, however, are studies by scholars like Ernest Boyer, Howard Bowen, Oliver Fulton, Seymour Lipset, Everett Ladd, Jack Schuster, and Martin Trow—some of which are based on their own independent survey and interview data while others are based on the faculty surveys conducted at intervals from 1969 to 1989 by the Carnegie Commission on Higher Education and the American Council on Education and distinguished by their consistency of questioning.[27] These studies do help fill the gap.

Thus, in common with the 1988 data (and consistent with independent findings reported earlier by others in the 1960s),[28] they strongly suggest that the typical faculty member in the United States places a much higher priority on teaching and a lower priority on research than is usually alleged and nearly always assumed to be the case. The data from the 1989 survey reveal that 70 percent of the professoriate reported their interests as lying primarily with teaching rather than research, and 62 percent believe that teaching effectiveness should be the primary criterion for promotion of faculty. It should be noted, moreover, that on this matter (if not necessarily on all) their actual behavior appears to have been consonant with their affirmations. Thus, it turns out, 56 percent had never published or edited a book, whether alone or in collaboration (although 6 percent, presumably composed of compulsive recidivists, had published six or more); 59 percent had published *in toto* no more than five articles in an academic or professional journal, and 26 percent none at all.[29]

These data from 1989 do appear to attest to some degree of movement in a research-oriented direction across the two decades since 1969, when 76 percent of the professoriate had represented themselves as being primarily committed to teaching and 69 percent had never published or edited a book. But this shift would appear (at least in part) to be an artifact produced by the difference in composition of the group of respondents involved. Whereas the 1989 data "represent full-time campus faculty members," the 1969 figures "refer to all respondents" including, presumably, part-timers and adjuncts.[30] Whatever the case, the rather modest shift involved is dwarfed by the sheer growth in the overall size of the professoriate as already noted, and it is not particularly significant in scope when compared with several other changes occurring during this period.

First, although for the earlier years information about the age distribution of the faculty is not readily available, it is clear that the enormous influx of new people led to a significant drop in the average age of the professoriate, with the steady-state conditions of the 1970s and 1980s leading to a subsequent reversal of that change. In 1988 some 2 percent of the full-time faculty was thirty years old, 40 percent between thirty and forty-four, and 55 percent between forty-five and sixty-four. Also, the survey revealed no significant differences across subject area. That being so, the calculations that William Bowen and Julie Sosa have made concerning the change in the age distribution of arts and sciences faculty should be reasonably representative of the age distribution of the faculty as a whole. Those calculations reveal that in 1977, with 42 percent under forty years old, "the age distribution of arts and sciences faculty...was skewed dramatically to the younger age group (principally 30–34 and 35–39)." But by 1988 the percentage of those under forty had fallen precipitously from 42 to 22 percent, while the percentage over forty-nine had gone up by more than one third, from 27 to 39 percent. By the year 2000, indeed, if the projection made by the Carnegie Council in 1980 proves to be correct, there will be "far more faculty members 66 and over than there are faculty members 35 and younger." The "basic demographic message," Bowen and Sosa rightly conclude, "is striking in its clarity."[31]

Second, and not much less obvious, is the dramatic shift across time in the institutional location of the bulk of faculty members. In 1963, for example, as many as one faculty member in six taught at a liberal-arts college; by 1980, only one in twelve did so; and by 1988 the number had dropped to something closer to one in thirteen. On the other hand, whereas in 1963 only one faculty member in ten taught at a two-year college, by 1988 the figure was closer to one in five, and their numbers since then have grown still further.[32]

Third, and similarly apparent, is the fact that the roller-coaster conditions prevailing in the academic employment market in the years between 1960 and the present also had a marked impact on the economic status of the profession. Embedded, therefore, in the figures reported in the 1988 survey for annual income is the effect of some demoralizing swings as the excess demand for faculty generated by the surging enrollments of the 1960s (and prevailing until 1969) was replaced in subsequent years by a surplus in the number of candidates available for the rapidly dwindling number of openings. As a result, while "the rapid expansion of higher education in the 1960s was accompanied by the only significant, sustained improvement in the real income of faculty members since World War II," the subsequent slowdown led to a 19 percent decline in faculty salaries between 1970–1971 and 1983–1984 (in terms of real, non-inflated dollars), while in contrast "most other occupational groups experienced increases in real [non-inflated] earnings, of at least 20 percent." In fact "average real faculty salaries in 1983–84 were no higher than they had been in 1960–61," and, while the late 1980s and early 1990s saw something of a recovery, average real faculty salaries for 1994–1995 still lagged somewhat behind the 1970–1971 averages.[33]

Discussing these trends in compensation in 1986, W. Lee Hansen appears simply to have assumed a direct linkage between the loss in economic status that they reflected and the decline in faculty morale that was certainly much talked about at that time. But turning now, and in the second place, to what can safely be said about changing attitudes and perceptions on the part of members of the academic profession across the past few decades, it must be confessed that there are some puzzling fluctuations in the findings elicited by several attempts to survey the matter and that the outlines of the picture that emerges are somewhat blurred.

After riding high in public esteem during the early years of the century, the profession later lost ground, and it has been said that in the years immediately following World War II members of the professoriate had come to consider themselves as being part "of a beleaguered minority."[34] The boom years between the late 1950s and 1970 witnessed a clear measure of recovery both in the prosperity of the profession and the public esteem accorded to it. But on both accounts the hard-won ground was subsequently lost again. In 1983 a Harris poll revealed that while 61 percent of the populace had indicated in 1966 that they reposed a "great deal of confidence" in those involved in the enterprise of higher education, by 1983 that category had fallen precipitously to 36 percent.[35] Hardly surprising, then, that data collected by the Carnegie Foundation for the Advancement of Teaching in 1984 (at the very moment when compensation levels were approaching their nadir since the early 1960s) should reveal college and university faculty in America to be "deeply troubled." Sixty percent reported themselves to be unhappy with their salaries (i.e., they viewed them as "poor" or no more than "fair"), 40 percent claimed that within the next five years, they might well choose to leave the profession altogether, around 30 percent confessed to feeling "trapped" in the profession, and 20 percent regretted having chosen an academic career in the first place.[36]

Such aggregate data do not align fully with the findings produced by the more nuanced and in-depth probings undertaken by Bowen and Schuster in the same year, involving on-site visits and in-depth interviews with a total of 532 faculty members and administrators at some thirty-eight representatively chosen campuses. While they found the commitment to their institutions by the growing numbers of part-timers understandably to be minimal, and the attitudes of the numerous nomadic or "gypsy" faculty to reflect "despair and dogged determination rather than optimism," their findings concerning full-time faculty were far from being unambiguously negative. In the areas upon which they focused in order to help "evoke faculty attitudes" (morale, collegiality, autonomy, views of the administration) they found "neither a uniformly bleak outlook nor any sense of dramatic change from the past." Although the campus mood was marked by volatility, glumness, and uneasiness about the future—ranging all the way "from buoyance to deep depression"—the academic life was still found to be "on balance attractive to its practitioners." More than 90 percent indicated that, had they been starting over, they would have chosen the profession again. And the overall conclusion of the investigators was that "the condition of American faculty" was "neither bleak nor bountiful," that "the satisfactions and frustrations of faculty life. . .[appeared] to hang in uneasy balance," and that, in that most elusive dimension of the professional condition, "middling" morale appeared to represent the norm.[37]

Surveys of faculty attitudes conducted in the late 1980s and mid-1990s both appear to support the somewhat less negative appraisal that emerged from this particular piece of fieldwork. Asked in the 1989 Carnegie national survey of faculty to indicate their agreement or disagreement with the twin assertions "I feel trapped in a profession with limited opportunity for advancement" and "If I had it to do over again, I would not become a College teacher," only 6 percent in each case indicated strong agreement.[38] With the latter assertion, it is true, a further 8 percent indicated agreement "with reservations," for a total of 14 percent—a modestly higher proportion than the Bowen and Schuster study would suggest and higher, too, than the 11 percent of Americans who indicated their agreement with the same assertion in the survey of academics in fourteen countries that the Carnegie Foundation conducted in 1991–1992.[39]

This last survey also (and interestingly) revealed that, of the fourteen countries in North America, Europe, and Asia surveyed, only three (Sweden, Israel, and Korea) reported *lower* levels of discontent among academics with their choice of profession than did the United States. American academics also indicated the lowest degree of dissatisfaction with the courses they were teaching and, at least in comparison with their foreign counterparts, lower degrees of dissatisfaction with their level of compensation, the quality of administrative leadership on their campuses, and the protection afforded in their country to academic freedom. Those comparatively upbeat findings, moreover, have to be read in the context of a survey that is itself "at variance with much contemporary commentary," and that shows in general and with "considerable unanimity of views internationally" that even in troubled times the professoriate, far from being "acutely depressed" or "deeply demoralized or disaffected," is "remarkably sanguine about the future."[40]

That said, the authors of the survey confess that "the overall picture of faculty morale" conveyed "is neither good nor bad—but often quite blurred."[41] It would have taken, it seems, supplemental, targeted fieldwork and some disaggregation of the data, not only by nation but also by institutional sector within a given nation, to bring any greater clarity to the picture. Certainly, focusing on the American scene alone, it is clear that the aggregated data do mask some important disparities. The 1984 Carnegie data had themselves revealed a measure of difference by institutional sector, and the Bowen and Schuster study, conducted at more or less the same time, uncovered a good deal more—with the liberal-arts colleges manifesting a somewhat better perceived institutional climate and, accordingly, better faculty morale than the research universities, and significantly better than the two-year colleges and the institutions of the comprehensive sector.

That being so, let me turn in the third place, and by way of conclusion, to an exclusive (and tighter) focus on that particular sector—in current Carnegie terminology, the sector comprised of institutions in the two Baccalaureate (Liberal Arts) College categories. I do so not only because it constitutes the oldest stratum in American higher education, and happens to be the one I myself know best, but also because personal observation, in-depth field studies, and some of the survey data together suggest that it may have ridden out the demographic, fiscal, and cultural turbulence of the past several decades in somewhat better shape than the others. Certainly, the 1989 Carnegie data reveal it to be the institutional sector with the highest degree of agreement on the standards for good scholarship and the highest degree of commitment to the importance of institutional service, student advising, and the delivery, evaluation, and rewarding of effective teaching. Not surprisingly, faculty who teach in this sector are prominent among those who are at the highest end of the institutional loyalty and commitment scale, who feel least "trapped in a profession with limited opportunity for advancement," and who accordingly evince the greatest enthusiasm about their work.[42]

All this is doubtless true, but the first thing that a tighter focus on the sector reveals is that the overall impression of comparative well-being calls for a measure of qualification or, at least, complexification. Certainly, when placed in the context of the whole vast enterprise of higher education in America, institutions in this sector (once, after all, the norm) have decreased in comparative importance. They have dwindled in number, and they now teach a smaller percentage of the overall undergraduate popula-tion. As recently as 1970 there were 721 liberal-arts colleges, constituting approximately 25 percent of the higher educational institutions in the country and enrolling 8.1 percent of the student population. By 1987 they had dropped in number (partly by disappearance but mainly by reclassification, usually into the Com-prehensive Universities and Colleges category) to 572, constituting slightly less than 17 percent of the institutional total and educating 4.7 percent of the student population.[43] Some skepticism, more-over, has been expressed about the very viability of the Liberal Arts II category, which includes primarily undergraduate colleges that are less selective in their admissions than those falling into the Liberal Arts I category and award less than 40 percent of their baccalaureate degrees in liberal-arts fields. Thus, applying both educational and economic criteria and building upon site visits as well as analysis of statistical data, David Breneman has argued for excluding eleven of the 140 private colleges listed by Carnegie in 1987 as falling into the Liberal Arts I category on the grounds that they offer professional and graduate programs and are really "small universities." And applying to the private Liberal Arts II colleges the admittedly "weak criterion" constituted by the awarding of at least 40 percent of their degrees in the liberal-arts (as opposed to professional) fields, he is also led to exclude as really "professional colleges" no fewer than 317 of them, thus proposing that the total universe of private liberal-arts colleges be more than halved, reduc-ing the number to a total of 212.[44]

While not everyone would agree with this particular exercise in reclassification,[45] it does draw attention to the progressive opening up of a gap between colleges in the Liberal Arts I and II categories, as well as the degree to which, under the pressures of a rapidly shifting marketplace, the bulk (it seems) of the institutions we are accustomed to thinking of as liberal-arts colleges, having moved heavily into the business of prevocational education, have been nudged also into the comprehensive sector. But the gap in question (or something close to it) has long been evident in dimensions of collegiate life other than the curricular. When Trow and Fulton analyzed the data generated by the Carnegie faculty survey of 1969 with a view towards finding out how research activity was distrib-uted across the various institutional sectors of the higher educational system, they found that while there was something of a division between the so-called research and teaching institutions, it lay not between the universities with a substantial commitment to graduate education and the four- and two-year colleges but rather between the universities and top tier of four-year colleges on the one hand and the less highly selective four- and two-year colleges on the other. In this they noted, as in other matters, that a veritable "fault line" runs between the "high quality" four-year colleges and the rest, with those "high quality" colleges showing "levels of research activity. . .that in sheer rate of publication are close to that of the lesser universities, and markedly higher than those of the great majority of four- and two-year colleges."[46]

A similar fault line, though one running this time right through the center of the Liberal Arts I sector, showed up almost a quarter of a century later (1994–1995) in two studies of rather different type. In the first of these (a very "hands-on" effort), Robert McCaughey investigated teaching and research activities pursued by the humanities and social science faculties at some two dozen of our leading Liberal Arts I colleges, which, he concluded, were representative of a group probably no larger than three dozen. While these faculty members differed from "[research] university faculty in accepting that the primary mission of their employing institutions" was that of teaching undergraduates, he found also that they claimed "to see no contradiction between their personal identities as scholars and their institutional responsibility to be effective undergraduate teachers." Using external publication and scholarly citation counts for the faculty under study and measuring their levels of activity against that of a control group composed of more than seven hundred full-time faculty in the same disciplines at three of our major research universities (Columbia, Princeton, and Yale), he came to the conclusion that scholarly activity among this group of liberal-arts faculty is substantially greater than has usually been assumed on the basis of the Carnegie surveys for liberal-arts faculty in general. A quarter of them, it turns out, perform at levels of scholarly activity typical among their colleagues at Columbia, Princeton, and Yale, and, of these, half perform "above those levels." Finally, having gone on to compare the "externally generated scholarly ratings" of the faculty in his study with "evaluations of their individual teaching performance" generated by their home institutions, he found a correlation between scholarly engagement and teaching effectiveness that was "positive at a level that is statistically significant."[47]

McCaughey's conclusions, moreover, should be brought into contact with (and, indeed, throw considerable light on) one of the most interesting findings emerging from a study of "institutional climates" recently conducted by Alexander Astin and others at UCLA that involved a balanced sample of approximately two hundred universities and colleges of all levels of selectivity. Having distinguished between sets of factors that together can be taken to indicate the strength of a given institution's "student orientation," on the one hand, and "research orientation," on the other, they drew a series of conclusions, of which three may be mentioned here. First, they found that of the ten institutions that fell into both the top 10 percent in research orientation and the bottom 10 percent in student orientation, all (not surprisingly) were research universities. Second, that of the eight institutions that were in the bottom 10 percent in research orientation but the top 10 percent in student orientation, all were non-selective, residential liberal-arts colleges falling into the Liberal Arts II group in the Carnegie categories. Again, there is nothing counterintuitive about that. Third, that of the eleven institutions that ranked high on *both* research and student orientation, all were private, highly selective liberal-arts colleges from the Liberal Arts I sector, several belonging, in fact, to the group studied already by McCaughey.[48]

A measure of further disaggregation, then, is clearly called for if one is to come to terms adequately with the changing nature of professional life even in the tiny, liberal-arts college sector of the American academic universe. A century ago, the great *condottieri* of the university "revolution" in America were notably condescending towards the institutions characteristic of this sector—what one of them dismissed as "a regime of petty sectarian colleges." Thus David Starr Jordan, president of Stanford, confidently predicted that with time "the college will disappear, in fact, if not in name. The best will *become* universities, the others will return to their place as academies."[49] A century later, however, his prediction has proved to be incorrect. While they no longer dominate the American higher educational scene, they are far from having been nudged into the world of secondary education—from which, in any case and *pace* Jordan, they had not emerged in the first place. Nor have they *become* universities—or, at least, not universities as he understood that term. They remain instead what they have always been, direct lineal descendants of the single-college universities that, in the fifteenth and sixteenth centuries, had emerged in Spain, Scotland, and Ireland. They remain, that is to say, small universities devoting themselves exclusively to under-graduate instruction,[50] representing a distinctive strand in American higher education and constituting the institutional arena where about 8 percent of American academics now pursue their professional careers.

As a group, these colleges have succeeded in maintaining a proudly consistent commitment to the central importance of effective teaching, and they appear (as a group still, though differentially so) to provide conditions of work conducive to a comparatively high degree of career satisfaction and positive faculty morale. As we have seen, however, it appears that the group is now becoming segmented, with the bulk of the Carnegie Liberal Arts II group being tugged by market forces into the orbit of the Comprehensive sector, and a smaller segment of the Liberal Arts I group (perhaps a fifth) being drawn towards the research university sector—or at least, and as McCaughey puts it, experiencing a change that has led their faculties to effect "a partial convergence with the faculties of research universities in their professional identities and the level of their scholarly activities."[51]

A hundred years ago, and again in the heady boom years of the 1960s, that change might well have presaged the impending transformation of some of these institutions into small research universities. But that, I would predict, is unlikely to be the case either under present conditions or in the foreseeable future. Fiscal pressures, the burden of placing graduate students in a bleak job market, a slowly dawning recognition of the fact that these colleges already provide a comparatively privileged setting for both teaching and research, the recovery of a sense of heightened institutional status in the academic world at large, the stirring at last on the broader professional scene of "a renewed fondness for undergraduates whose pleasure in the material [being taught] is not dimmed by anxiety about our ability to get them a good job teaching it"[52]—all of these things conspire to blunt the edge of any lingering temptation to reach out for the equivocal grandeurs of "university status." Instead, the future for these institutions, and for those privileged to teach at them, is likely to involve the pursuit of a more distinctive mission: not simply the successful combination of the teaching and scholarly imperatives that has already proved itself so fruitful, but also, and beyond that, the more self-conscious cultivation of the type of "integrative" scholarship that has already established (as Kenneth Ruscio has demonstrated) a distinguishing presence among their faculties. It is a type of scholarship more broadly interpretative in its aspirations, more consciously linked to classroom needs, more accessible to student understanding and even, in some of its dimensions, to student involvement; a type of scholarship responsive, in effect (if also, interestingly, *avant le propos*), to Ernest Boyer's call for a more inclusive understanding of what academics have in mind when they speak of "research."[53]

The profession at large, I would suggest, may well have something important to learn from the commitment to this sort of scholarship, from the rather special institutions whose ethos encourages it, and from the modalities of academic life prevailing at those institutions. There are, after all, forms of significance other than the merely statistical.

ENDNOTES

[1]Burton R. Clark, "Listening to the Professoriate," *Change* XVII (September-October 1985): 36–43; Burton R. Clark, ed., *The Academic Profession: National, Disciplinary, and Institutional Settings* (Berkeley and Los Angeles, Calif.: University of California Press, 1987), esp. "Conclusions," 371–398; Nathan O. Hatch, ed., *The Professions in American History* (Notre Dame, Ind.: University of Notre Dame Press, 1988), esp. "Introduction," 1–13 and Laurence Vesey, "Higher Education as a Profession," 15–32.

[2]See especially Clark, ed., *The Academic Profession.*

[3]Robert Dingwall and Philip Lewis, *The Sociology of the Professions: Lawyers, Doctors and Others* (London: Macmillan, 1983), 23–26.

[4]See Guy Neave and Gary Rhoades, "The Academic Estate in Western Europe," in Clark, ed., *The Academic Profession,* 211–270 (focusing on the situation in France, Germany, the Netherlands, and Scandinavia); also Clark's introduction in ibid., 6–7.

[5]Vesey, "Higher Education as a Profession," in Hatch, ed., *The Professions in American History,* 15, 20.

[6]Carnegie Foundation for the Advancement of Teaching, *A Classification of Institutions of Higher Education: 1994 Edition* (Princeton, N.J.: Carnegie Foundation for the Advancement of Teaching, 1994), x, 3–5, 25–28, counting institutions in the Research Universities I and Baccalaureate (Liberal Arts) Colleges I categories.

[7]And those teaching in the latter schools now appear to constitute a majority of the faculty at American research universities—thus Sydney Ann Halpern, "Professional Schools in the American University," in Clark, ed., *The Academic Profession,* 304, 326. Halpern bases this claim on data furnished by the National Center for Education Statistics.

[8]I refer here to the distinction in the Carnegie institutional categories between "Masters (Comprehensive) Colleges and Universities" and "Baccalaureate (Liberal Arts) Colleges." Among the baccalaureate institutions it was the comprehensive universities and colleges, and such other four-year institutions as the state colleges, that saw the sharpest, most continuous, and most distressing declines in arts enrollments after the early 1970s. Cornell and Swarthmore, for example, saw only the most modest fluctuation between 1954 and 1980 in the percentage of arts and sciences degrees conferred. At Ball State University, on the other hand, where the arts and sciences share of degrees awarded had risen between 1954 and 1970 from 2.5 to 29.9 percent, that share had fallen back dramatically by 1986 to 13.3 percent. I draw these figures from the careful analyses by William G. Bowen and Julie Ann Sosa, *Prospects for Faculty in the Arts and Sciences: A Study of Factors Affecting Demand and Supply: 1987–2002* (Princeton, N.J.: Princeton University Press, 1989), 45–65 and Appendix A, 187–190; also Sarah E. Turner and William G. Bowen, "The Flight from the Arts and Sciences: Trends in Degrees Conferred," *Science* CCL (26 October 1990): 517–521. For a summary of the general enrollment picture conveyed by these studies and other statistical sets and analyses, see Francis Oakley, *Community of Learning: The American College and the Liberal Arts Tradition* (New York and London: Oxford University Press, 1992), 78–83.

[9]Cited in Bruce A. Kimball, *The "True Professional Ideal" in America: A History* (Cambridge, Mass., and Oxford: B. Blackwell, 1992), 230, 266. The whole discussion, on pp. 198–325, is pertinent.

[10]Professional income, which reached a high point in 1913, declined in value thereafter relative to the compensation received by the average worker but recovered considerable ground in the 1960s, only to slide off again in the 1970s and early 1980s. See Kimball, *The "True Professional Ideal" in America,* 198–325, and Howard R. Bowen and Jack H. Schuster, *American Professors: A National Resource Imperiled* (New York and Oxford: Oxford University Press, 1986), chap. 6, 80–112 (this chapter is contributed by W. Lee Hansen).

[11]Thus Joan Gilbert, "The Liberal Arts College: Is It Really an Endangered Species?" *Change* XXVII (September-October 1995): 37. Cf. Turner and Bowen, "The Flight from the Arts and Sciences," 517–521.

[12]See nn. 10, 44, and 47.

[13]For some observations on this aspect of the recent critical commentary, see Oakley, *Community of Learning,* 105–136.

[14]Frederick Rudolph, *The American College and University: A History* (New York: Vintage Books, 1965), 47, 486; Carnegie Foundation for the Advancement of Teaching, *A Classification of Institutions of Higher Education,* x.

[15]Walter P. Metzger, "The Academic Profession in the United States," in Clark, ed., *The Academic Profession,* 124. The 1960s alone, then, saw almost as many new academic positions created as had the three centuries and more since the founding of Harvard College. Everett Carll Ladd, Jr., and Seymour Martin Lipset, *The Divided Academy: Professors and Politics* (New York: McGraw-Hill, 1975), 1–2, Table 1. Their figures are drawn from *Historical Abstracts of the United States* (1960), 210 and *Statistical Abstracts of the United States* (1973), 731 and are "global" ones, including visiting and temporary faculty.

[16]Susan H. Russell et al., *Faculty in Higher Education Institutions: 1988* (Washington, D.C.: US Department of Education, 1990), Tables 2.1, 2.2; 9–10, xviii–xix. The initial data from the 1993 study are reported in *Faculty and Institutional Staff: Who Are They and What Do They Do?,* 1993 Study of Postsecondary Faculty (Washington, D.C.: US Department of Education, 1996), Table 1, 9. See also the "Technical Notes," 19, where it is acknowledged that whereas the 1988 survey "was limited to faculty whose regular assignment included instruction, the faculty universe for NSOPF-93 was expanded to include anyone who was designated as faculty, whether or not their responsibilities included instruction, and other (non-faculty) personnel with instructional responsibilities."

[17]Russell et al., *Faculty in Higher Education Institutions: 1988,* Tables 2.1 and 2.2; 9–10. Note that in breaking its data down by institutional sector, this survey employs nine categories: public research, private research, public doctoral, private doctoral, public comprehensive, private comprehensive, liberal arts, public two-year, and "other." While these categories lack the precision and full range of the Carnegie classifications and are not fully aligned with them, they are often close enough to permit useful (if rough) comparison.

[18]Ibid., Tables 2.7, 2.1, 2.3, 2.4; 9–15.

[19]Ibid., Table 2.5; 13.

[20]Ibid., Table 4.1; 45. See also 39–40.

[21]Ibid., Table 4.3; 47. See also 41, 91.

[22]Ibid., Table 4.1; 45. See also 40.

[23]Ibid., Tables 4.4 and 4.6; 44 and 50. See also 41–43 and 91.

[24]Ibid., Tables 3.1 and 3.3; 25 and 28. See also 19–22 and 91.

[25]Ibid., Tables 3.7 and 3.8; 33–34 and 23–24.

[26]Thus, for example, between 1988 and 1993, the overall percentages for minority faculty had increased as follows: Asian, from 4 to 5 percent; black, from a little over 3 to 5 percent; Hispanic, from 2 to 3 percent. The figure

for Native Americans had still not moved over the 1 percent line. See *Faculty and Instructional Staff*, Figure 1 and Table 1, pp. 2, 9. Similarly, between 1987 and 1994, the overall, cross-institutional average for women in the full-time contingent edged up undramatically from 27 to 31.6 percent. See "The Annual Report on the Economic Status of the Profession: 1994–95," *Academe* LXXXI (March-April 1995): 27 (Table 14). For the equally modest (if complex) changes in the number of hours faculty are spending in the classroom, see Arthur Levine, "How the Academic Profession is Changing," in this issue of *Dædalus*.

[27]For the questionnaires distributed in 1969 and for tabulations from the weighted data generated by the survey, see Ladd and Lipset, *The Divided Academy,* Appendix A and C, 315–328, 341–369. Results of the 1989 survey are tabulated in Ernest J. Boyer, *Scholarship Reconsidered: Priorities for the Professoriate* (Princeton, N.J.: Carnegie Foundation for the Advancement of Teaching, 1990), Appendix A, 85–126. In addition, see Martin Trow and Oliver Fulton, "Research Activity in American Higher Education," in Martin Trow, ed., *Teachers and Students: Aspects of American Higher Education* (New York: McGraw-Hill, 1975), 39–83; Everett Carll Ladd, Jr., "The Work Experience of American College Professors: Some Data and an Argument," *Current Issues in Higher Education* AAHE (1979): 3–12; Bowen and Schuster, *American Professors.*

[28]As Trow and Fulton indicate, referring to Talcott Parsons and Gerald Platt, *The American Academic Profession: A Pilot Study* (Washington, D.C.: National Science Foundation, 1968). For a summary statement that also folds in some more recent data, see Francis Oakley, *Scholarship and Teaching: A Matter of Mutual Support,* ACLS Occasional Paper, No. 32 (New York: American Council of Learned Societies, 1996). The data thus far released from the 1993 National Study of Postsecondary Faculty add nothing to the picture on this matter.

[29]Boyer, *Scholarship Reconsidered,* Appendix A, Tables A-26, A-19, A-23.

[30]For the 1969 figures, see Ladd and Lipset, *The Divided Academy,* 348–349 and 352–353. Cf. the "Technical Notes" in Appendix B of Boyer, *Scholarship Reconsidered,* 127, for the differences between data collection in 1969 and in 1989.

[31]Bowen and Sosa, *Prospects for Faculty in the Arts and Sciences,* 16–17; see especially Figure 2.1 and Table 2.1. Note that the authors view the 1987 age distribution as "more normalized." Ibid., 127. *Three Thousand Futures: The Next Twenty Years for Higher Education,* Final Report of the Carnegie Council on Policy Studies in Higher Education (San Francisco, Calif., and London: Jossey-Bass, 1980), 25. As of 1992, 8.1 percent of the full-time faculty contingent fell below the age of thirty-five and 4.5 percent above the age of sixty-five. See *Digest of Educational Statistics: 1996* (Washington, D.C.: US Department of Education, 1996), Tables 222, 232.

[32]There are some problems with the comparability of the 1963 and 1988 numbers. I draw the 1963/1980 contrast from *Three Thousand Futures,* 82, where the basis for the count is not indicated. The figures reported in Russell et al., *Faculty in Higher Education: 1988,* Table 2.5, 13 (which are broken down, however, into full-time and part-time) give the following

approximate counts: (a) Faculty at liberal-arts colleges—full-time, 1 in about 12.5; part-time, 1 in 13.5; (b) Faculty at two-year colleges—full-time, 1 in 5.3; part-time, 1 in 2.

[33]That is, the decline between 1970–1971 and 1983–1984 "was so great that it eliminated entirely the gains in real salaries that had been achieved in the 1960s." See Bowen and Sosa, *Prospects for Faculty in the Arts and Sciences,* 145–147, and especially Table 8.1, for detailed comparisons with other occupations. Cf. Bowen and Schuster, *American Professors,* chap. 6, 80–112, and the *Digest of Educational Statistics: 1996,* Table 229, p. 243.

[34]Thus Christopher Lasch, *The New Radicalism in America (1889–1963): The Intellectual as Social Type* (New York: Knopf, 1965), x; cited in Kimball, *The "True Professional Ideal" in America,* 316.

[35]Bowen and Schuster, *American Professors,* 132, Table 7-5, which reveals that other professions and national institutions had likewise experienced a significant loss of public esteem.

[36]These survey data are reported in "Trendlines—The Faculty: Deeply Troubled," *Change* XVII (September-October 1985): 31–34.

[37]For these figures and judgments, see Bowen and Schuster, *American Professors,* chap. 8, 137–162.

[38]Boyer, *Scholarship Reconsidered,* Appendix A, Tables A-32 and A-36, though a further 13 percent agreed "with reservations" with the former assertion and a further 8 percent concurred with the same qualification in the latter.

[39]See Philip G. Altbach and Lionel S. Lewis, "Professional Attitudes—An International Survey," *Change* XXVII (November-December 1995): 53, Table 3. "As a result of this survey," the authors claim, "we now for the first time have comparable data about the attitudes and activities of the academic profession in 14 countries." Ibid., 51.

[40]Ibid., 51 and 57.

[41]Ibid., 52.

[42]Boyer, *Scholarship Reconsidered,* Appendix A, Tables A-3, A-6, A-7, A-11, A-12, A-13, A-18, A-23, A-32, A-35, A-37, A-39, A-40. In their 1983–1984 study, *American Professors,* 140, Bowen and Schuster had similarly found excellent conditions of work and continuing high faculty morale at the four more selective Liberal Arts I campuses they visited, though the situation at the Liberal Arts II campus in their sample was apparently less satisfactory.

[43]*A Classification of Institutions of Higher Education: 1994,* xi and xiii, Tables 1 and 3. Interestingly enough, the Carnegie Classifications for 1994 (ibid., xiv, Table 4) reflect (largely, I assume, because of some reclassification of institutions into the Baccalaureate College category) a modest reversal of the trend, listing a total of 637 institutions—i.e., 17.7 percent of the overall institutional total educating some 6.9 percent of the overall student population.

[44]David W. Breneman, "Are We Losing Our Liberal Arts Colleges?" *The College Board Review* (156) (Summer 1990): 16–21, 29; *Liberal Arts Colleges: Thriving, Surviving, or Endangered?* (Washington, D.C.: Brookings Institution, 1994), esp. chap. 1, 1–19, and Appendix A, 138–161.

[45]Though we may assume that it was skepticism about the viability of the Liberal Arts II category that had earlier led Bowen and Sosa to combine the Comprehensive II and Liberal Arts II institutions into the unified category of Other Four-Year Institutions—see their *Prospects for Faculty in the Arts and Sciences,* 191–192.

[46]Trow and Fulton, "Research Activity in American Higher Education," in Trow, ed., *Teachers and Students,* 49 and nn. 13, 74, and 79. Note that in classifying institutions they do not use the Carnegie categories but divide them into three broad categories: universities, four-year undergraduate colleges, and two-year colleges. They then break down both the university and college categories (on the basis of differential quality) into three further classes designated as high, medium, and low. They set forth the grounds for these distinctions in Appendix A, 366–370.

[47]Robert A. McCaughey, *Scholars and Teachers: The Faculties of Select Liberal Arts Colleges and Their Place in American Higher Learning* (New York: Barnard College, 1995), esp. ix, 41–46, 92–93, 103–105.

[48]Alexander W. Aston and Mitchell J. Chang, "Colleges that Emphasize Research and Teaching: Can You Have Your Cake and Eat It Too?" *Change* XXVII (September-October 1995): 45–49. Among the eleven "high-high" colleges listed, Carleton, Smith, Swarthmore, and Williams were part of the group studied by McCaughey.

[49]Quoted in Frederick Rudolph, *The American College and University: A History* (New York: Vintage Books, 1965), 68, 330, and 443 (italics are mine), where he also draws attention to similar and widely shared contemporaneous appraisals by President Harper of Chicago and Professor Burgess of Columbia.

[50]See George Makdisi, *The Rise of Colleges: Institutions of Learning in Islam and the West* (Edinburgh: Edinburgh University Press, 1981), 228–230; cf. "On the Origins and Development of the College in Islam and the West," in Khalil I. Semaan, ed., *Islam and the Medieval West: Aspects of Intercultural Relations* (Albany, N.Y.: State University of New York Press, 1980), 22–49.

[51]McCaughey, *Scholars and Teachers,* iii.

[52]David Damrosch, *We Scholars: Changing the Culture of the University* (Cambridge, Mass. and London: Harvard University Press, 1996), 169.

[53]For a fuller statement, see Oakley, *Community of Learning,* 152–157. Cf. Kenneth P. Ruscio, "The Distinctive Scholarship of the Selective Liberal Arts College," *Journal of Higher Education* LVIII (2) (1987): 205–222; David Davis-Van Atta, Sam C. Carrier, and Frank Frankfort, *Educating American Scientists: The Role of the Research Colleges* (Oberlin, Ohio: Oberlin College, 1985), and David Davis-Van Atta and Sam C. Carrier, *Maintaining America's Scientific Productivity: The Necessity of the Liberal Arts Colleges* (Oberlin, Ohio: Oberlin College, 1986)—these are reports of conferences on these issues convened at Oberlin in 1985 and 1986 by Carleton, Franklin and Marshall, Reed, Swarthmore, and Williams Colleges and attended by representatives of some fifty leading liberal-arts colleges. For Boyer's plea concerning the nature of research at our institutions of higher education, see his *Scholarship Reconsidered,* esp. 18–25, 53–64.

Walter E. Massey

Uncertainties in the Changing Academic Profession

THERE IS NO DOUBT that the academic profession, like most institutions of higher education, has changed substantially over the past decades and since the end of the Cold War and that it is undergoing substantial changes now. However, the future outcome of these changes is still uncertain. The present situation might be labeled as a state of dynamic flux in which the end results are still undetermined. The theme of this essay concerns some of the uncertainties in the changing academic profession. These uncertainties are caused by circumstances, conditions, and forces that are often external to the academic community, although some are generated internally. In many instances, the external and internal conditions and forces are closely linked and cannot be neatly divided into different categories.

I will discuss three explicit external forces: 1) changing demographics and the debate over affirmative action and diversity; 2) the role of the federal government, along with that of private industry; and 3) the revolutionary advances in technology. Internally, there are a number of forces that are promoting change. Here, I refer to what might be seen as various "reform movements," although "reform" may not adequately capture the nature of the proposed changes in many instances and the term "movement" is perhaps too grandiose. These efforts have several different, but overlapping, objectives. A common feature is a focus on the need for colleges and universities to educate students in a broader perspective by inculcating into the curriculum such con-

---

Walter E. Massey is President of Morehouse College.

cepts as service learning, values education, and moral, ethical, and personal development.

I will discuss how these various forces may affect institutions of higher education and the degree to which these forces create an environment of uncertainty within the academic profession. The United States has perhaps the most diverse set of institutions of higher education in the world, and therefore it is impossible to speak of "American higher education" as a monolithic uniform enterprise. I have chosen, therefore, to focus on three categories of institutions: the major research universities,[1] "second-tier" doctoral-granting institutions,[2] and undergraduate liberal-arts colleges (primarily private institutions).

DEMOGRAPHICS, AFFIRMATIVE ACTION, AND DIVERSITY

One of the most striking changes in higher education over the past three decades has been in the racial, ethnic, and gender composition of colleges as well as in the age groups of individuals at various institutions. The overall number of college-age youths attending an institution is not increasing and in fact has decreased slightly, due primarily to a decline in the participation of white students (in particular, white males). Since 1990, the number of white students decreased by 5 percent.[3] The number of African-Americans increased by 16 percent between 1990 and 1995, with the Hispanic population growing a significant 40 percent during the same period and by over 100 percent over the last decade.[4] But African-Americans and Hispanics still fall behind whites in terms of the rates at which they enter college from high school. The gap, however, has been narrowing. Among so-called minority students, enrollment in colleges and universities has increased by almost 30 percent since 1990 and by over 65 percent in the decade from 1984 to 1995.[5] The increase in enrollment among African-American students is primarily within the historically white institutions. Currently, only about 16 percent of African-American college students are enrolled in what are called the "historically black colleges and universities" (HBCUs).[6] In the 1960s, the majority of black students were enrolled in these historically black institutions. This is a dramatic change, especially since it has occurred in only one generation.

The policies, laws, and attitudes that led to this shift in enrollment from historically black to predominantly white institutions in the 1980s are now being debated again, with equal vigor if slightly less rancor. The passage of Proposition 209 in California and the decision of the regents of the University of California to discontinue all affirmative-action programs within the university system have attracted most of the attention on these issues. The Fifth Circuit Court decision in the Hopwood case, however, has had perhaps a more immediate effect in Texas with respect to the admission of blacks and other minorities into institutions of higher education. Within the higher education community, the various arguments for and against affirmative action differ somewhat from those of a generation ago. The arguments in the 1960s were focused primarily on providing equal opportunity for access. Current debates go beyond that and focus on the educational benefits of having a diverse student population and faculty. The various arguments for and against affirmative action, diversity, and equal opportunity in many cases lend themselves to confusion, overlap, and misunderstanding, which tend to frustrate meaningful arguments and exchanges of views.

As a principal participant in the University of California discussions, debates, and indeed arguments leading up to the regents' decision and the passage of Proposition 209, and now as the president of a historically black college in what was one of the most segregated states in the nation a generation ago, I have a particular, though not necessarily privileged, perspective on these issues.

As noted above, the value and necessity of affirmative-action programs in higher education is now argued from a somewhat different perspective than it was in the 1960s and early 1970s. The primary goal of affirmative action in the 1960s was to ensure that minority students, primarily black students at that time, were not denied equal opportunities for access to institutions of higher education. Beyond the access issue was the recognized need for support mechanisms in colleges to help these students make up for past years of deficiencies in their education. It was recognized that an "affirmative" activity to reach out and identify black students, not to mention faculty and staff, who could succeed in previously white institutions was a necessary part of this effort. Also, it was argued that an increased presence of black students in white institutions would add to the educational experience of whites and might have a positive effect on the way in which courses were taught, though that was not the principal and certainly not the overriding justification for affirmative-action programs.

Today, a major argument for affirmative action in higher education is not just as a mechanism to right past wrongs, or to provide equal access, but as a tool to achieve "diversity." "Diversity"—a mix of students of different racial, ethnic, and social backgrounds— is regarded as an educational asset, a condition that enhances the educational experience of all students. Affirmative action in this context benefits whites as well as African-Americans, Hispanics, and other minorities. Therefore, it is argued that affirmative action, as a method of achieving diversity, is no less important for the nation at the present time, and may perhaps be even more important, than it was in the 1960s.

Those who differ with this concept and argument do so from varying perspectives. There are those who would accept the fact that diversity in colleges and universities is indeed an academic asset, a worthwhile goal, and hence has widespread benefits. However, they also argue that using affirmative action in the admissions process, that is, using race or ethnicity as a significant factor in the process of determining who should enter college, is an inappropriate way to achieve the goal of diversity. They argue that it stigmatizes those who are its beneficiaries by implying that such students would not have been admitted on their "own merits" and are really less than capable of succeeding at the institution.

Second, it creates antagonisms between groups—those who are beneficiaries of preferential treatment and those who are not. Such antagonisms mitigate any meaningful interaction that may occur between the two groups. The result, they contend, is that real diversity is not achieved, if one defines diversity as substantive interaction, exchange of ideas, and an appreciation of one another's culture, background, and history. These opponents note that meaningful interaction between *individuals* from different backgrounds, and not between groups, is necessary for substantive positive results to come out of having a diverse student body. Such interaction is most likely to occur in an environment where people are seen as individuals, not as representatives of particular racial or ethnic groups, and in an environment where everyone feels that they have been and are being judged, evaluated, and rewarded because of individual personal characteristics and achievements. This will only occur, they say, when preferential treatment based on group identity is ended. Affirmative action in this sense, they argue, is inimical to a goal of establishing truly diverse campuses.

Others who oppose the use of affirmative action to achieve diversity contend that diversity itself is an inappropriate or unachievable goal for institutions to seek. They say that diversity as a concept is too vague and ill-defined to be a useful tool for setting social policy. Does it simply mean having students (and faculty) from different racial and ethnic groups on the same campus? In the same environment? In the same classes? Or does it require some in-depth level of social interaction between individuals from different groups? Does it require structured experiences whereby students learn to understand and appreciate different ethnic and racial cultures? These critics also question whether there is sufficient evidence to support the hypothesis that having a diverse student body does, in fact, enhance the education of all students on such campuses.

One of the great uncertainties affecting the future of higher education is which of these views is likely to prevail. At present, there seems to be a majority opinion that diversity is a positive aspect of a college experience and is a goal worth pursuing, even if affirmative action as we now know it and practice it must be changed, modified, "mended," or possibly ended.

In a recent survey in the state of Washington concerning opinions about diversity on college and university campuses, more than 70 percent of the respondents agreed that "diversity efforts benefit campuses and students," and more than three-quarters expressed a view that "a diverse student body does have positive effects on the education of all students." Nearly 80 percent agreed with the statement that "the changing characteristics of America's population make diversity in education necessary." However, beyond the admissions area and with respect to the curriculum, more than half (52 percent of those responding) believed that "focusing on various cultures and histories would create divisions and conflicts."[7]

The leaders of higher education institutions and the prominent educational associations have argued very strongly and publicly for the continued use of affirmative action in efforts to achieve diversity. An advertisement in the *New York Times* signed by all of the university presidents who belong to the Association of American Universities,[8] as well as statements made by the American Council on Education (ACE) and other organizations, gives very strong evidence that colleges and universities will most likely continue their efforts to achieve and maintain a diverse student population in spite of potential, and actual, changes in the laws.

One can make a case, however, that affirmative action in admissions to colleges and universities and various support programs in existence for blacks, Hispanics, and other minorities have other benefits that will justify their continuation, even beyond the goal of creating a diverse college environment. Certainly, the increased number of minorities, and blacks in particular, in professional fields such as medicine and law as well as in science and engineering has been tremendously enhanced over the past three decades by affirmative-action programs. And the contributions these individuals in various professions make to the nation is an argument in and of itself to be used on behalf of affirmative-action programs. To those who maintain that the nation has reached a point where blacks, Hispanics, and others would enter college and graduate and professional schools at the same rate in the absence of affirmative action, the evidence from California and Texas is certainly to the contrary.

In the 1997–1998 incoming class at the University of Texas Law School, a school that has been one of the preeminent and predominant educators of black lawyers, there are only three African-American students who have stated an intent to enroll, down from over thirty in the previous entering class. The University of California, Berkeley, Law School announced that "if current figures hold up, enrollment of blacks...would decline to one next fall from twenty the year before...."[9] And one is already seeing similar results at the undergraduate level at the University of California. With the exception of Asian-American freshman applicants, other minority freshman applications have declined for the past two years.[10]

Admittedly, it is too soon to predict the long-term effects of these changes in California and Texas, and perhaps the various outreach programs that are intended to replace affirmative action in California, and other approaches being contemplated in Texas, will counteract these downtrends. But, for the near term, it certainly appears that these changes will have a major negative effect on the participation rates of blacks and Hispanics in colleges and universities in those two states.

To what degree the students who were not admitted to law school in Texas and California or to undergraduate programs at the University of California have chosen to go elsewhere for similar programs is not clear. If one contemplates the implications of abolishing or seriously constraining affirmative-action programs nationwide, it seems clear that it will severely curtail the number of blacks and Hispanics who will pursue undergraduate degrees as well as professional and graduate degrees.

It is not only students who are affected by the outcome of the debates over affirmative action and diversity efforts; faculty composition will probably be affected even more so. In the faculty area, the gains made by minority professors are not as substantial as those made by minority students. Faculty in predominantly white universities are still overwhelmingly white, although there have been some gains made by blacks, Hispanics, and especially Asians over the past two decades. The 1996–1997 ACE Report on Minorities in Higher Education indicates that faculty of color (African-Americans, Hispanics, and Asian-Americans) increased by almost 44 percent during the decade from 1983 to 1993 compared with just over a 6 percent increase for whites; but even so, faculty of color still account for only about 12 percent of full-time faculty and about 9 percent of full professors, and significant numbers of these are in two-year institutions.[11]

The relatively poor job market for new faculty does not suggest that these numbers will increase dramatically in the near future. Minority Ph.D.s are thought to have an advantage in this market because colleges and universities are motivated to diversify their faculties for many of the reasons cited above. While this may appear to be true from a few highly publicized cases of visible minority scholars lured from one institution to another, a recent study supported by the Ford and Spencer Foundations does not support this myth. This study shows that for minority faculty, there were no advantages in being a member of a minority group, and indeed in some cases minority Ph.D.s have substantially fewer offers of employment than other individuals from the same or similar institutions. As the director of the study noted, "This contention [that because so few faculty of color are in the graduate pipeline, they are highly sought after] is a gross overstatement."[12]

These debates and their outcomes are likely to affect different institutions in different ways, and I will comment later on my views of how the three sets of institutions (research universities, liberal-arts colleges, and "second-tier" graduate universities) are likely to be affected and how they are likely to respond.

THE FEDERAL GOVERNMENT/PRIVATE INDUSTRY

The influence of the federal government on colleges and universities remains very strong. The largest portion of direct funding of research in academic institutions, about 60 percent of all such funding, still comes from the federal government. Although the percentage of academic research funded by the federal government has decreased over the past two decades relative to that coming from industry and other sources, it still remains the largest source of support; in some fields, particularly the physical and life sciences and engineering, the federal role is overwhelming.[13]

It is generally accepted that the end of the Cold War as well as other changes in federal government policy and public attitudes mean that federal funding for research in universities will not grow in the foreseeable future at the rate that it has over the past two decades, and certainly not at the rate of the past four decades.

The approximate 3 percent increase proposed for the R&D budget in federal agencies this year is generally deemed to be positive, since the indications were that even such a modest increase would not be forthcoming. However, long-term budget projections, connected with deficit reduction targets, show little or no real growth in funding in the major R&D agencies; in some areas there may actually be a decline.

The federal government's role extends beyond direct funding of research into numerous other areas. The indirect costs associated with research funding play an important role in the institutional support of research universities receiving such funds. Changes in policy that reduce the amount of funds that can go to indirect costs also greatly affect these institutions.

The current administration's emphasis on higher education is providing an even more visible role for the federal government, and perhaps an even more influential one. Financial aid is one of the most important areas of interest. Pell grants, subsidized loan programs, and now the proposed tax credit for tuition expenses are extremely important to students and middle-income families in particular. The level of funding of these federal programs greatly affects the ability of minority students to attend college, especially the college of their choice. Data from 1992–1993 show that approximately 40 percent of all minority students receive some form of federal financial aid, compared to 28 percent of white students.[14]

Even beyond the federal government's direct and indirect financial support of research, financial aid, and other programs, various rules, laws, regulatory issues, and policies also have a great effect on universities and colleges. The current debate over the interpretations of Title IX has involved a number of major institutions. Health and safety rules, applied not just to campus operations but to research and teaching laboratories, add to the cost of teaching science and conducting research. And the Americans With Disabilities Act (ADA) has an enormous impact on colleges and universities.

This is not to imply that the role of the federal government in the future will be necessarily negative. The increased attention to higher education, both in the executive branch and in Congress, may well lead to a reinvestment in our colleges and universities or to the passage of laws that are more favorable to these institutions. Senator Phil Gramm (Republican, Texas) has proposed the National Research Investment Act of 1997, which would "double the amount of federal investment in basic science and medical research over the next ten years."[15]

The level of federal funding for R&D, the position of the federal government on various regulatory issues, and the amount of financial-aid support will likely in the future, as in the past, be determined politically in a context that includes considerations that go well beyond higher education. The perceived need and commitment to achieve a balanced federal budget and growing priorities in other areas like heath care, social security, and continuing support for defense will make the uncertainties in this area a continuing concern for higher education.

Policies and priorities of the private commercial sector are affecting institutions of higher education. In many areas, the role and

policies of the federal government are juxtaposed with or correlated to the role of industry. The increased involvement of the
industrial sector with research universities in the past decade and
a half began in the early 1980s with the passage of the Bayh-Dole
Act and the perception of threats from Japan and Germany in
areas of technology development and high-technology industries.
Encouraged by federal agencies such as the National Science Foundation (NSF), the Department of Commerce, and the National
Institutes of Health (NIH), various cooperative research and development programs between universities and industry have grown
considerably. Direct funding of academic research and development by industry has tripled during this period, although it still
represents only about 7 percent of the total university funding.[16]

As the federal government's support of research has declined
relative to other areas, university faculty and administrators have
been more aggressive in seeking relationships with and support
from the private sector. State and local governments have been
supportive of such efforts. Many states have created their own
programs to encourage university/industry interaction; notable
examples are the Edison Program in Ohio, the Benjamin Franklin
Partnerships in Pennsylvania, and the Economic Development Institute of Georgia. State and local governments, while in many
cases reducing appropriations for higher education, view colleges
and universities not only as sources of educated individuals but as
sources of direct economic benefits, such as through the start-up of
new companies and advising and supporting local industry.

The private industrial sector may affect higher education in
another, more direct way in the future—as a direct competitor. As
companies have assessed their need for an educated and trained
work force, they have devoted more effort to their own in-house
training and education programs. Initially, they focused more on
entry-level workers and designed programs to teach them basic
skills. Now, they are devoting more efforts to their skilled, educated work force. The rapid changes in technology as well as in
management principles and approaches require ongoing educational activities and what some companies call continuous education. In fact, it is likely that American industry spends more on
training and educating their work force than colleges and universities combined spend on educating its students.

Motorola Corporation is a prime example of what the future may hold for many companies. What was once a department of training has evolved over the years into Motorola University. This institution provides training and education not just for Motorola employees but for companies and universities around the nation and the world, and it has a joint degree-granting program with the Kellogg School of Management at Northwestern University. What was once the General Motors Institute of Technology, primarily a vocational institution, is now the GMI Engineering and Management Institute (no longer associated with General Motors), a degree-granting private undergraduate and graduate institution.[17]

Some of the motivation for investment by companies in in-house education grows from a need for the continual upgrading of skills even among the best-trained engineers and scientists. But some of the motivation also comes from a differing industrial perspective on the best way to educate individuals, especially engineers and scientists, for the future industrial workplace. The highly focused disciplinary orientation of graduate institutions is seen by some to be increasingly less appropriate for the needs of modern industry. The recent National Academy of Scientists/COSEPUP Report on Graduate Education addresses this issue and stresses the need for broader and more diverse experiences for graduate students as part of their research, education, and training in order to prepare them for changing employment opportunities. The recently announced grant by the Olin Foundation to establish an engineering school cites the same argument. On June 6, 1997, the Olin Foundation stated that "the curriculum [at the new engineering college, Olin College] will emphasize active learning, student research, integrated studies and communication skills as well as experience working in teams."[18]

The interaction between universities (especially research universities) and industry is likely to continue and grow. Many companies that have traditionally operated large in-house basic research laboratories have phased these out over the past several years and are looking more toward partnerships with universities as a way of having access to new knowledge. And, as noted, universities see a mutual benefit from these relationships as a result of declining federal funds for research and development.

What is not as clear is the degree to which the educational programs in universities will be changed as a result of the private sector's concerns or through these interactions. The response of some universities to the Olin Foundation's announcement, however, is an indication that attention is being paid to the concerns of private industry.

TECHNOLOGY

There is general, if not uniform, agreement that one of the greatest forces affecting the future of colleges and universities will be advances in technology, not only in the educational process, but in management and administrative areas as well. But there are numerous uncertainties in this area. Technology has already made a significant difference in the way research is conducted in universities, and it is beginning to affect, in very positive ways, the educational process of teaching and learning. In many cases, it is the promise and anticipation of what technology can do in the future that is now affecting attitudes and ideas about how we can teach and learn, even though the full effects of these technological changes are not yet with us. Many institutions and faculty have already begun new experimental approaches to teaching and learning using distance learning, Intranet and Internet connections, CD-ROM, and other technologies. The educational community is very much involved in a discussion and debate about the roles of faculty and students in this new anticipated environment. Some institutions have replaced experimental laboratories with computer-simulated laboratory experiments. Libraries are being reconfigured to enhance access to electronic information resources rather than books. And networking between institutions is allowing courses not only to be shared between students at different institutions but taught by faculty at different institutions.

Technology will raise issues that may threaten the traditional roles of colleges and universities. Nontraditional institutions have taken advantage of technological developments to provide the kind of education, information, services, and learning experiences that traditionally have been the almost exclusive domain of colleges and universities. For-profit institutions such as the University of Phoenix as well as specialized data bases and information sources available via the Internet have become increasingly popular.

"Faculty stars"—individuals who are nationally or internationally recognized as being experts in their field, or who are very popular lecturers and speakers—are now making their services available to audiences far beyond the walls of their local institutions. And in many instances, these faculty members are pursuing these ventures not through their home institutions but through other entities such as those mentioned above. This raises a question about the relationship between faculty members and their home institutions, and how exclusive and mutually loyal this relationship should be.

Technology is also allowing information to be created and disseminated more and more easily. For universities and colleges, the question of quality control will arise and is already a concern in some sectors. Term papers are now readily available via services on the Internet and college students are reportedly using such services instead of writing term papers on their own. But beyond that, there is little control over the reliability of the information students and faculty access through the Internet. Astrologists or creationists may develop as impressive a web page with information on the origins of the universe as can be developed by the National Science Foundation, the Smithsonian, or NASA. It is unclear what kinds of mechanisms or processes will allow the discrimination of the reliable from the ridiculous. The expanding use of technology will offer new ways and many opportunities to enhance the educational process in institutions of higher education but will also carry with it potential pitfalls that will require increased diligence by faculty in our colleges and universities.

FORCES INTERNAL TO HIGHER EDUCATION

The internal forces affecting change within higher education are as strong as the external forces, and in many cases it is difficult to distinguish whether or not the various forces are internal or external. There are various "reform movements" that emanate from a number of sources. These "movements" have several different, but quite often overlapping, objectives. The American Association of Higher Education (AAHE) is sponsoring a Forum on the Faculty of the Future, which is looking at new reward structures, job definitions, and work assumptions for faculty. The primary areas of emphasis are new definitions of scholarship and research and a broadening of the criteria by which faculty are judged in their development. One example is the idea that more emphasis should be put on the application of knowledge, in addition to the dissemination of knowledge (teaching) and the discovery of knowledge (research). Another is to recognize, in the reward structure, that individual faculty members may appropriately devote more or less time to each of these activities over the course of a career.

The Southern Association of Colleges (SACS), along with other accreditation bodies, has emphasized assessment outcomes and measurements as major factors in judging whether or not institutions meet standards for accreditation and reaccreditation. "Measurables," as they apply to student and faculty development, together with what is termed "institutional effectiveness" are major features in the accreditation process for SACS. Colleges and universities, it is argued, ought to be able to demonstrate and document that they are achieving the goals espoused in their mission statements. In particular, the value added to student development should be measurable. Much of this approach is related to continuing concern with the status of undergraduate education, and not just in our major research universities. Increasingly there is also concern about the effectiveness of undergraduate education in our liberal-arts colleges, institutions where it had been mostly assumed that undergraduate education was being carried out in a highly effective manner. However, with more undergraduate institutions hiring faculty who in the past might have gone to research universities, some detect a possible danger of the "research ethos" infiltrating undergraduate liberal-arts institutions, to the extent that their teaching missions might be adversely affected.

Along with other organizations, Campus Compact, "a national coalition of college and university presidents committed to helping students develop the values and skills of citizenship through participation in public and community service,"[19] has put a great deal of emphasis on encouraging colleges and universities to develop service learning in their curricula. Service learning involves students having an experience-based component to classroom teaching. This is closely aligned with the values-development movement, where the moral, ethical, and personal development of the student assumes as important a role as his or her intellectual development. Most of the organizations, foundations, associations, and study groups addressing or promoting these various issues are also very much concerned with institutional governance. Governance and decision-making in colleges and universities seem to be inextricably intertwined with these various reforms. Projects supported by the Pew and Kellogg Foundations have suggested substantial changes in the way faculty are involved in governance and decision-making policies.[20] The underlying assumption is that current faculty governance systems are among the major obstacles to reform in higher education. And, as noted above, graduate education is also being reexamined.

Let me now comment on how I see these factors affecting three sets of institutions: research universities, liberal-arts colleges, and second-tier doctoral-granting universities.

MAJOR RESEARCH UNIVERSITIES

The major research universities in the United States have generated the knowledge that has led to rapid progress in many areas of society, certainly in areas of science and technology. The knowledge generated by the faculty in these institutions has been instrumental the creation of entire new industries in the past four decades—computers and communications, biotechnology, microelectronics—as well as in rapid advances in other fields. And these institutions have been the source of many of the faculty who have gone on to teach and do research in undergraduate colleges and other universities around the country, and indeed around the world. If these institutions appear to be more conservative in their attitudes towards change, it is understandable because they have proven so successful in the mode of operation in which they presently exist. Caution in making radical changes in how these institutions operate is probably reasonable public and institutional policy.

In considering how the issues of changing demographics and concern with diversity will affect these institutions and how they will respond, it is useful to distinguish between the public and private universities. The public universities will most likely be forced to change policies and practices sooner, as has already been demonstrated in California and Texas. But the private universities could also be affected if the ruling in the Fifth Circuit Court (the Hopwood case) is taken to the Supreme Court and upheld. The Attorney General in Texas has already ruled that the decision applies to private colleges and universities in Texas as well as to public institutions. Research universities will most certainly try other means to pursue diversity if the traditional affirmative-action approaches are ruled to be illegal and inappropriate. Outreach efforts, programs that are economically based, and targeted recruitment to schools or areas with high minority populations are some of the programs already being put into place, especially in California, and they are being planned elsewhere as well. It is unclear how successful these programs will be. They certainly will take time to implement, which means that there will be a period in which enrollment of minorities in these institutions will be drastically affected. In my opinion, these programs will not be as effective in enrolling the numbers of minority students that present affirmative-action programs have attained.

There is at present a clear commitment to affirmative action from the leaders of these institutions as a means to achieve diversity on their campuses. The statement by the presidents of the AAU universities, statements by the American Council on Education, and other national organizations attest to this fact. However, the faculty on these campuses have yet to be heard from with the same degree of unanimity and forcefulness. At the University of California during the debate and discussions leading up to the vote by the regents, the faculty senates were by no means unanimous with respect to the issue of affirmative action. And many faculty around the country, especially members of groups such as the National Association of Scholars, support the regents' decision, in general are opposed to affirmative action, and are also among those who question the concept of diversity as an appropriate institutional goal. In an essay in the *Chronicle of Higher Education,* Professor Martin Trow from the University of California at Berkeley offered an explicit challenge to the presidents and chancellors who signed the AAU statement, questioning whether university presidents and chancellors have the right to speak for their institution on such issues.[21]

My assessment is that these institutions are genuinely committed to the values of a diverse student body and a diverse faculty, and they will continue to pursue such goals, even if the changes in the laws make doing so more difficult. In developing new approaches, they can set standards for the rest of higher education just as they have set standards in other areas of scholarship and research.

The greatest negative effect if they are forced to change their practices, however, could well be in the area of faculty recruitment, hiring, and development. Although the Fifth Circuit decision primarily addresses admissions practices and policies, the regents' policy at the University of California addresses *all* affirmative-action programs, except those that are specifically mandated by the federal government. One program that was affected immediately, TOPS (Target of Opportunity Program), was designed to recruit minority and female faculty. Programs designed for postdoctoral and graduate fellowships were also affected. If the major research universities are stifled in their ability to increase the number of minority graduate students and faculty, it will have a serious deleterious effect on all universities who rely on these institutions as a source of their faculty.

Major changes in the policies of the federal government and certainly any changes in funding for research and development affect these institutions most of all, because they receive the vast majority of federal R&D funds. However, as long as peer review prevails in the allocation of federal R&D dollars, these institutions will still receive the majority of such support. They could be affected more if there are changes in the criteria for the allocation of federal funds, such as geographically targeted or programmatically targeted allocations, some of which are likely to happen as the competition for federal funds becomes more intense. The large universities that I have called the second-tier doctoral-granting institutions have faculties who are very competitive in many areas, and they also possess political support that can affect federal policies for the distribution of research and development funds.

The major research universities, however, have already begun to anticipate the probability of a decrease in the growth of federal R&D support. They have instituted programs to build stronger relationships with industry and partnerships with the national laboratories and other research entities. They have emphasized the commercialization of intellectual property and have established close ties to state governments and state agencies. They have also been responsive to the concerns of the industrial sector with respect to the training of their graduate students. University-industry and faculty-researcher exchanges are more allowable, as are internship-like experiences for graduate students in industry under the auspices of the National Science Foundation and other federal agencies. Joint research projects between industry and these universities have become more common, and practically every major research university has put forth more visible efforts to demonstrate the contributions they make to the nation, their state, and their local communities. Most of the contributions highlighted are in the areas of economic development—spin-off companies, consulting with industry, and as a source of talent for industry. But they have also become more visibly involved in such activities as precollege education.

The major research universities will affect the use of technology as much as they will be affected by it. These institutions have invented and originated much of the technological revolution. They will be at the forefront in using technology for research and instruction. They have the resources and the talent to exploit technology for the best practices, and the younger faculty and graduate students in these institutions will probably lead the way in infusing technology throughout the institutions. These universities can and hopefully will be a positive force in enhancing the educational resources available to other institutions by sharing access to their libraries, offering specialized scientific equipment and experiments that can be accessed remotely, and through access to their faculty, who are in most cases the leading experts in their particular areas.

It is unclear to what degree the various reform efforts will be absorbed into the major research universities. Some of these activities are already taking place at Brown, Stanford, and other research universities that are part of Campus Compact. The America Reads program initiated by President Clinton has attracted a number of major research universities, and almost all are involved in some outreach efforts to high schools and elementary schools as well as school reform efforts. Criticisms about course offerings at the undergraduate level have also led to more attention being paid to this area. In 1991, the University of California at Berkeley implemented the American Cultures Breadth Requirement, which focuses on American identity and experiences that are shaped by constituent cultural traditions.[22] The Hewlett Foundation supports a project on liberal education in research universities that has involved some of the major institutions, and a growing number of young faculty, female faculty, and minority faculty are attracted to some of the reform efforts. For example, the Presidential Young Investigators, a highly prestigious group of young researchers identified and supported by the NSF, issued a report in 1992 calling for more emphasis on teaching, diversity, and other efforts that are consistent with the recommendations of the reform movements. And, even within such research-oriented entities as the Science and Technology Centers supported by the NSF, there has been increasing emphasis put on such issues as enhancing diversity, outreach to high schools, and changing the graduate experience to be more accommodating to women, especially women with families. The theme for the National Conference of Black Physics Students held at the Massachusetts Institute of Technology in March of 1997 was "Physics: The Possibilities Are Endless," with the content of the conference emphasizing alternate careers for physics graduates and the need for changes in the way physicists are educated.

So major research universities are certainly being affected and are accommodating and encompassing many of the ideas being put forth by the reform movements. But the fundamental character of these institutions is unlikely to change dramatically and probably should not. There will be a continuing need for a set of institutions to be at the forefront of research and scholarship, to have a major emphasis on graduate training for research and teaching careers in universities, and to provide a strong disciplinary-based mode of inquiry. These are the places where new disciplines are most likely to be invented as a result of interdisciplinary activities. They also need to be the continuing source of the very best faculty for other institutions in the nation. The primary question is how many of these institutions does the nation need or can it afford?

A report of the President's Council of Advisors on Science and Technology addressed this question and concluded that, given the expected level of federal funding and the need for new faculty and graduate training in the foreseeable future, we are close to the point of having too many universities that aspire to be major research institutions.[23] Such views are not greeted enthusiastically by the second-tier universities, as I will discuss later.

LIBERAL-ARTS COLLEGES

These institutions, the majority of them privately supported, are less affected than the major research universities by the ongoing debate over diversity and by the changes in demographics. Except for a very few, the pressure on admissions is much less than in the major research universities, and the admissions criteria are traditionally much broader. They are not primarily in the business of producing future faculty members or researchers, and so are able to take into account a wider range of criteria in the admissions process. They are also much less in the public eye with respect to these issues. The absence of professional schools and graduate programs, which in many cases are the sources of controversy in admissions, also makes them less visible.

Moreover, the growing competition among these institutions means that they will welcome good minority students who are not admitted to or choose not to attend Berkeley, the University of Texas, and other institutions that may find themselves having to institute different admissions policies. Thus, some of these institutions, and in particular a subset of the historically black liberal-arts colleges, may ironically benefit from the changes in policy at the larger majority universities.

The liberal-arts colleges will also be less affected than the major universities by changes in federal funding for research and development. However, they are greatly affected by changes in other federal policies that address higher education. The area of financial aid is one where there is the greatest dependence, but such regulatory issues as the ADA, health and safety issues, and Title IX (with respect to nondiscrimination in the funding of athletic programs) are all very serious matters for these institutions. They, in many instances, lack the financial resources of the major institutions to be able to respond to changes in federal policies without seriously affecting their educational programs, resulting in higher costs to students. This is a problem for all institutions, but it is particularly exacerbated by the relatively smaller resources of liberal-arts colleges (although there are some notable exceptions to this description). These colleges are more sensitive to and more affected by changes in policies emanating from the Department of Education than from the NSF, NIH, or NASA. For this reason, there is a great interest among these schools in the Higher Education Reauthorization Act, as opposed to debates on the future of R&D funding.

For the liberal-arts colleges, technology, properly used and accommodated, can and will be a valuable asset and resource. However, it also poses a number of challenges. Among the greatest is the fact that adapting to and implementing the use of technology is extremely costly and requires expertise and resources (technological, infrastructural, and human) that are not always readily available at these institutions. There is great opportunity, but there is also the prospect that some will lag behind, if not be left behind, in the technological revolution. The potential for remote access to resources at major universities, laboratories, and public agencies such as the Library of Congress, the Smithsonian Museum, and others, and the ability to share resources among themselves and other institutions, is an exciting prospect for these colleges. The use of technology can help to reduce the costs of scientific laboratories and specialized equipment purchases; having access to faculty and experts at other institutions can reduce the need for expertise in every area in which the college has academic offerings. Used appropriately, technology will allow students at the liberal-arts colleges to have experiences that in the past were only available to students in the major research universities. But the possibility of "haves and have-nots" emerging among this set of institutions is much more likely than among the major research institutions.

These are the schools at the leading edge of the reform movements, and they are among the first to adopt and put into practice many of the recommendations that come from these various movements. They see these directions as a way to distinguish themselves from other, large institutions and to find a market niche in the increasingly competitive world of higher education. Coupled with the use of technology, there is an opportunity for distinctiveness at the local level without sacrificing student and faculty access to mainstream scholarship and pedagogy. The New American College envisioned and advocated by the late Ernest Boyer,[24] if it emerges, will likely emerge from within this group of institutions.

SECOND-TIER DOCTORAL-GRANTING UNIVERSITIES

The second-tier doctoral-granting universities appear to be the most vulnerable to changes in federal policies for the support of research and development, and in particular to decreasing support from the federal government. These institutions will find it increasingly difficult to move into the top ranks. The report of the President's Council of Advisers on Science and Technology addressed in more detail the conditions and issues these institutions will face—decreases in the rate of federal funding and in the rate of growth of faculty hiring, leading to a need for fewer graduate students and perhaps graduate departments in some areas. And there will be increasing competition from the smaller liberal-arts colleges for some of the better students.

Here again it is useful to distinguish between the public and private institutions in this category. The public institutions, especially those in states where they are the "flagship" institutions or serve a very large number of students, will have the advantage of state and local support. As states and local communities increasingly recognize the value of having an excellent university in their midst, these institutions will continue to receive resources and support. An example of this is the current discussion in the state of Kentucky. The governor has made it part of his agenda to have the University of Kentucky move into the first ranks of major research universities, and he has called for the investment of hundreds of millions of dollars in new faculty and new areas of research.

In the state of Georgia, support goes even further through the HOPE Scholarship Program, which provides free tuition for any resident of Georgia to any public institution in the state if the student achieves a certain grade-point average in high school. This program has already had a positive effect on the ability of the University of Georgia, Georgia Tech, and other public institutions to recruit some of the best students who in the past would have gone out-of-state to more prestigious universities.

In areas characterized by a strong industrial community, there is a recognition that universities have great value, and support is coming from this sector. The privately supported universities in this second-tier group will not have the same advantages that the public universities have with respect to support from the state, and they will be under more pressure to reexamine their mission and to focus more on particular areas of strength. This is already in evidence at Rochester University and Syracuse University.

However, the second-tier institutions also have an opportunity to take advantage of the present job situation and hire excellently educated faculty who are not able to find positions at the top research institutions. Among some of these institutions there is also a realization that it is not necessary to emulate the top research universities in order to be successful. The University of Illinois at Chicago is defining itself as a major urban university, although it still competes with the Urbana campus in terms of quality of research.

In many ways, these institutions have been more open and responsive to changes in demographics than either the major research universities or the liberal-arts colleges. The largest number of graduate degrees granted to African-American students are from this set of institutions, not the top research universities. In undergraduate programs, these universities tend to provide more access to local students at much lower costs than the liberal-arts colleges or the major research universities, and they are proving to be attractive to minority students.

In the area of technology, these institutions face the same issues and challenges as the major research universities and the small liberal-arts colleges, but they also face the same opportunities.

A SPECIAL NOTE ON HISTORICALLY BLACK
COLLEGES AND UNIVERSITIES (HBCUs)

It would require an entire article to discuss historically black institutions in depth, but the forces affecting the other institutions addressed above affect these institutions in many of the same ways though differently in some important respects. There are approximately 107 HBCUs, of which thirty-nine are members of the College Fund/UNCF. These institutions enroll approximately 16 percent of all African-American students in higher education. Of 1992–1993 bachelor's degree recipients, about one-third of African-Americans received their degrees from HBCUs.[25] Among African-Americans, 9.7 percent of all doctoral degree recipients attended HBCUs, and HBCUs awarded 15.9 percent of all first professional degrees to African-Americans.[26] HBCUs still play a very important role in American higher education.

Perhaps more than any other group (excluding the top research universities), the ability of these institutions to maintain strong programs and prosper in the future is dependent upon policies of the federal government. The HBCUs are greatly affected by federal policies, not because of the support of research and development, but primarily through financial-aid and other types of programs targeted towards these institutions, such as the Title III federal programs. A large percentage of students in these institutions (as much as 80–100 percent at some) are heavily dependent on federal financial aid in order to support their education. The institutions themselves depend on the federal government for institutional support in terms of upgrading their infrastructure, in particular their technological infrastructure. Seemingly small changes in federal policies or federal budgets (such as an increase or decrease in the Pell grant or the amount of money available for subsidized loans) can have a significant effect on these institutions. Their resources are much more limited than the predominantly white small liberal-arts colleges and certainly the major universities.

The issue of changing demographics and the debate over diversity and affirmative action also affects the HBCUs. Some of the best of these institutions academically may become more attractive alternatives for African-American students who are not admitted or who choose not to attend universities in California, Texas, and other states where policies may change. In fact, one can imagine a renaissance among some of these institutions due to their ability to recruit a larger number of excellent students and faculty who may not wish to be at institutions where they perceive the atmosphere to be less welcoming than it has been in the past. This is only likely to occur in those HBCUs that can provide a similar level of academic quality as the majority white institutions.

The changes in law and public policy will affect the public HBCUs in a different way than the private ones. Many of the southern states, where most of the public HBCUs are located, are under various court mandates or self-imposed policies to invest more resources into those institutions. One is likely to see in the future an increasing difference of programs and mix of students on the campuses of the public HBCUs as opposed to the private

HBCUs. There is a deep irony in the various court decisions being made with respect to affirmative action in higher education—HBCUs in Alabama and Mississippi are under various court orders to increase their efforts to recruit white students, while in Texas the majority white institutions are now under court orders to restrict or eliminate their affirmative-action programs to recruit more minority students.

The effects of technology on these institutions will be much greater than perhaps on any other group, except for some of the small liberal-arts colleges. They are as a whole much further behind in implementing technology into their educational and administrative activities. The cost factor is much more important, as is the availability of human talent to implement programs and train faculty and staff in the use of the new technologies. The dangers of falling behind are much more serious here, and the prospect of there being "haves and have-nots" is much more likely.

The ability to link with other institutions will be very important to this set of schools; if implemented appropriately and in a timely way, technology can be one of the greatest assets in maintaining the strength of these institutions, for the same reasons cited above for the small liberal-arts colleges.

The various reform movements are already finding a receptive audience among many of these institutions. In many respects, the principles and approaches espoused by the reform movements are quite compatible with the historic missions of the HBCUs; a commitment to service, priority for community involvement and outreach, focus on the individual student, concern about ethics and values, and an overwhelming commitment to teaching and working with students of all academic backgrounds are things these institutions have been doing throughout their history. This is not to say that they have been uniformly successful in all of these areas, but the philosophical underpinnings of many of the notions put forth by Ernest Boyer for the New American College and other reform movement spokespersons are things that are very compatible with the traditions and missions of these institutions.

SUMMARY

As noted in the beginning, this is a period of great uncertainty for the academic profession. A number of changes are taking place, and I have tried to address only three: the role of the federal government as well as that of industry; changing demographics and the debate over diversity; and the technological revolution. It is my opinion that these forces will affect different institutions in varying ways, and I have only commented on three sets of institutions, along with the HBCUs.

Overall, I think the future will see more differentiation among institutions of higher education, for some of the reasons noted above. The need to reexamine missions, to focus and adapt to these changing forces and circumstances, is imminent. This could be a very healthy scenario for the nation and for higher education as an enterprise. Certainly, having more institutions with differing missions, goals, and educational experiences will offer students of various backgrounds and ages more options for their education, and technology will allow a greater degree of commonality and uniformity across institutions. These positive outcomes will be enhanced if differences among institutions are not automatically translated into differences in quality and if excellence is accepted and judged in different ways for different institutions. Along similar lines, a healthy differentiation among institutions could be inhibited by attempts to apply a uniform set of criteria to measure institutions, as is happening in the growing number of such popular rankings of colleges and universities as *US News and World Report* and others.

Periods of great change can be unsettling and may be seen as threats or opportunities; higher education is not immune to these feelings. However, we have reason to be optimistic about the future of American higher education. One of the great strengths of our system of higher education has been its great diversity, not in terms of students on campuses, but in terms of the different types of institutions. As with any organism, the ability to adapt to change and evolve is proportionate to the complexity of the organism. American higher education is certainly diverse and also complex.

ENDNOTES

[1] I have defined "major research universities" as those that are traditionally within the top twenty in terms of ranking by the National Academy and in terms of research funds from the federal government—those that are widely recognized as being the best of their kind in the world.

[2] I have defined the "second-tier doctoral-granting universities" as those that are below the top twenty as measured by the various rankings of graduate schools from the National Academy and in terms of research funding from the federal government.

[3] American Council on Education, *Minorities in Higher Education, Fifteenth Annual Status Report* (Washington, D.C.: American Council on Education, 1997), 78.

[4] Ibid.

[5] Ibid.

[6] Ibid., 76–79.

[7] "Voters Support Campus Diversity Efforts," *Higher Education & National Affairs,* 5 May 1997, 5.

[8] *New York Times,* 14 April 1997.

[9] Peter Applebome, "Affirmative Action Bar Transforms Law Schools," *New York Times,* 2 July 1997, A10.

[10] Fall 1997 undergraduate applications to the University of California, Office of Student Academic Services.

[11] American Council on Education, *Minorities in Higher Education, Fifteenth Annual Status Report,* 33.

[12] Darrell Smith, "Faculty Diversity When Jobs Are Scarce: Debunking the Myths," *Chronicle of Higher Education,* 6 September 1996, B3.

[13] *1996 Science and Technology Pocket Data Book* (Arlington, Va.: National Science Foundation, 1996), 2.

[14] Department of Education, Office of Postsecondary Education, Washington, D.C.

[15] The National Research Investment Act of 1997.

[16] *1996 Science and Technology Pocket Data Book,* 11.

[17] "Tradition of Excellence," GMI Engineering & Management Institute, Office of Admissions.

[18] F. W. Olin Foundation News Release, New York, 6 June 1997.

[19] *Campus Compact: A Season of Service* (Providence, R.I.: Campus Compact, 1997), 1.

[20] Robert Zemsky, "The Lattice and the Ratchet," *Policy Perspectives* 2 (4) (June 1990).

[21]Martin Trow, "The Chiefs of Public Universities Should be Civil Servants, Not Political Actors," *Chronicle of Higher Education,* 16 May 1997, A48.

[22]"American Cultures at the University of California at Berkeley," University of California at Berkeley, Public Information Office.

[23]*Renewing the Promise* (Washington, D.C.: PCAST, 1992).

[24]Ernest Boyer, *Scholarship Reconsidered* (Princeton, N.J.: Carnegie Foundation for the Advancement of Teaching, 1990).

[25]Michael T. Nettles, ed., *The African American Education Data Book, Volume I: Higher and Adult Education* (Fairfax, Va.: Frederick D. Patterson Research Institute of the College Fund/UNCF, 1997), 283.

[26]Ibid., 79.

Patrick M. Callan

Stewards of Opportunity:
America's Public Community Colleges

MERICA'S PUBLIC COMMUNITY COLLEGES enroll almost half of all undergraduates in higher education's public sector.[1] Universally perceived as the first way station on the road to social mobility, they are at the leading edge of educational opportunity. Millions of Americans and hundreds of communities benefit from their convenient locations, wide range of programs, and open admission policies. What are these community colleges? For many people, including more than a few in academe, they are terra incognita. The most impressive fact about them is their magnitude: some 1,036 publicly supported community colleges enroll over 5.3 million students. Equally impressive, although less obvious, is their diversity, a diversity so great that it defies almost any attempt at generalization. But typically—although there is no typical community college—the community colleges are two-year schools with three primary missions: 1) general education equivalent to the freshman and sophomore years at a four-year college or university; 2) vocational and occupational training; and 3) community service. Over time, and across and within states, these colleges vary widely in the emphasis given to each of these missions. Nevertheless, the faculty commitment to teaching is strong and pervasive, whether it be English 101, computer technology in vocational training, or conversational French for footloose suburbanites.

Although their origins are in the early years of the twentieth century, today's public community colleges are products of post–World War II America. Only after about 1960 did they become the

---

Patrick M. Callan is President of the Higher Education Policy Institute.

95

primary instrument for the expansion of college opportunity. An analogy here is appropriate: After the Morrill Act in 1862, the land-grant colleges expanded the very definition of higher education, providing opportunities for a new population and extending the curriculum to the practical and applied. Likewise, a hundred years later, the community colleges have expanded prior conceptions of what constituted higher education and its students. And, like the land-grant colleges, the community colleges grew and flourished in an era of economic transition and were nurtured by democratic, egalitarian, and political impulses.

Generalizations about community colleges based on national— or even state—statistics have little applicability to individual institutions. These colleges remain true to their local origins. They are *community* colleges in reality as well as name, as diverse as the towns, cities, and neighborhoods that they serve. Governors and legislators, particularly those in our most populous states, sometimes inappropriately treat all community colleges in their states as if they were virtually identical. They find the task of tailoring laws to meet the needs of the many different members of so diverse a group to be beyond easy solution. Nor, I have found, is there an easy approach for those who write about community colleges; I can only promise to try to avoid too much oversimplification.

THE COLLEGES, THEIR FACULTY, AND THEIR STUDENTS

Of the country's 2,640 public higher education institutions, 604 are four-year colleges and universities and 1,036 are community colleges. Of the 11.1 million students, some 5.8 million, including those in graduate programs, are enrolled in four-year institutions and about 5.3 million are in the community colleges, some in academic programs, others in occupational training.[2] The large number of community colleges is not surprising, for many states have had the goal of a community college within commuting distance of every citizen. In contrast, few states need—or can afford—more than one major research university.

After World War II higher education expanded in an almost phenomenal fashion, and the community colleges contributed a major share of this growth. As William Friday, longtime and distinguished president of the University of North Carolina, once commented, four-year colleges had previously been located "up isolated, little hollows" where the students would be sheltered from worldly temptations. In the last half of this century, however, the community colleges were brought to the people, the people responded, and the colleges grew in numbers and students. Financial considerations played a part in this growth: Local support in most states initially reduced the burden on state general funds, and low or no tuition attracted students who could not otherwise afford to leave their homes, families, or work.

The many patterns of funding and governing the community colleges—as many as there are states—are difficult to squeeze into useful categories. Two broad, relatively recent trends can be discerned. First, most colleges now rely much more heavily than in the past on state funds and student tuition. Originally, the community colleges were funded in the same manner as the public schools, with largely local support supplemented by state funds, and without tuition. State funds now provide the greatest share both nationally (39 percent) and in forty-two states. Nationally, revenue from tuition (20 percent) now slightly exceeds local funding (18 percent), and in four states the colleges receive the largest share of their support from it. The higher the tuition, of course, the greater the adverse impact on access for those who are most dependent on the colleges.[3] Second, like the four-year colleges and universities, the community colleges are now much more likely than in the past to be part of a statewide or multicampus system. However, even though they are part of a system, most community colleges have some form of local board.

The apparent shift of both funding and governance from the local level to the state does not necessarily, I believe, justify sounding an alarm about creeping centralization. Nothing in my experience, having visited a variety of states, suggests that most community colleges are any more amenable now than they ever were to taking direction from outside their local community.

The Faculty

The number of faculty members in the public community colleges—now about 290,000—has roughly tripled over the past twenty years.[4] Their average, nine-month salary of $41,000 in 1993–1994 was some 25 percent less than the pay at public universities and 11 percent less than that at other public four-year institutions. Sixty percent of community-college faculty hold a master's degree, and, as might be expected in a teaching institution, fewer than 16 percent hold doctoral or professional degrees. At approximately 66 percent of the community colleges, the faculty are covered by a collective bargaining agreement, in contrast to 55 percent of the four-year institutions at which their counterparts teach. Ninety-two percent of community-college faculty believe that teaching effectiveness should be the primary criterion for the promotion of faculty, contrasted to 22 percent of their research university counterparts.

Although they have administrative responsibilities similar to those of their counterparts at four-year campuses, community-college faculty are highly unlikely to engage in research or other scholarly activity. Eighty-one percent consider teaching to be their principal activity, and they report spending far more time teaching than do four-year college faculty. Alexander Astin found that more than three-fourths of the community-college faculty teach more than twelve hours of classes per week, contrasted with only about one-third of four-year college faculty and about 10 percent of those at universities. A similar percentage believe that creating a positive undergraduate experience is a high or very high priority for the community colleges, compared to 55 percent at public universities.

Community-college faculty are more likely to be part-time instructors than are their counterparts in the public, four-year institutions. The part-time status of community-college faculty has increased steadily over the years. Part-time faculty made up 38.5 percent of two-year college instructors in 1962; by 1971 this number had increased to 40 percent, and by 1974 to almost 50 percent. Today, 65 percent of community-college faculty are part-time. It is difficult to tell whether this high proportion of part-time faculty bodes well for the future. One would have to examine each college separately to assess its prospects. There would appear to be two major benefits from the great number of part-time instructors. The first, as every budget officer knows, is that they are less expensive than full-time instructors, for they have few benefits, enjoy little in the way of office space, and, on a class-hour basis, are paid less than their full-time colleagues. In addition, their part-time status and lack of job security makes them expendable when programming or funding shifts occur. Their contributions to institutional flexibility do not, however, afford much benefit to the part-time faculty members. Being poorly paid can mean teaching at more than one college to garner a living wage. Nor is the part-time faculty member an unqualified asset to the college itself; inexpensive and expendable, he or she is unlikely to participate in college affairs, committee activities, curricular development, and academic counseling.

The Students

Community colleges draw their students from a much different population than do four-year institutions, and student characteristics strongly suggest the importance of these institutions for college opportunity:

1) With an average age of twenty-nine, community-college students are generally older than those in the four-year colleges and universities. Thirty-five percent are under twenty-one years of age, in contrast to 42 percent of four-year college students. And 36 percent are thirty years of age or older, in contrast to 23 percent of those at four-year campuses.[5]

2) Some 47 percent of undergraduates at community colleges are employed for thirty-five or more hours per week, in contrast to 27 percent of those at four-year colleges. At the same time, about the same percentage of students at both types of institutions are not employed at all.[6]

3) Community colleges enroll roughly half of the students in higher education who come from minority or ethnic backgrounds— for example, 45 percent of African-American students, 52 percent of Hispanic students, and 56 percent of Native Americans.[7]

4) Of students at the community colleges, 40 percent are from families with incomes of less than $30,000 a year, in contrast to only 28 percent of first-year students at four-year colleges and universities.[8]

A college's geographic location is usually a critical determinant of the characteristics of its students. A college in a major city is much more likely than one "up a little hollow" to have a large and diverse student body, with a high proportion of older, part-time, and minority students. Many of these urban colleges also face the same inner-city problems that trouble the public schools—problems that can range from youth gangs to students' lack of preparation or motivation. But whether large or small, urban or rural, community colleges share a common history.

A BRIEF HISTORY: GROWTH AND OPEN ACCESS

In their common history, the community colleges are the newcomers on the higher education block; the first public two-year institution was established in 1901. Early growth was, and to some extent still is, influenced by the two older neighbors, the public schools and the four-year colleges and universities. And, throughout this century, the community colleges sought—and still seek—to define and redefine their multiple missions to reflect the needs of their many constituencies. It is quite impossible, of course, to do justice here to their rich history, but a brief historical background (albeit heavily reliant on others[9]) seems necessary.

In 1901, the initial two years of college-level work were first offered at a Joliet, Illinois, high school in response to urgings of William Rainey Harper, president of the University of Chicago, who promised Joliet students advanced standing at the University. Others followed his lead—for example, David Starr Jordan at Stanford and Alexis Lange at Berkeley in California. These and other leaders of major universities seem to have had mixed motives: a laudable motive to widen educational opportunity coincided with a wish to control university enrollment by relegating freshmen and sophomores to the high schools. At their inception, the two-year colleges' role was defined by others—by the public schools of which they were a part and by the four-year institutions that, to a greater or lesser extent, dictated their curricula.

This early role-definition by others has been a mixed legacy. Both the public schools and the four-year colleges and universities have cultures that offer coherence to their institutions, faculty, and students. For the public schools, concepts of child and adolescent development are pervasive. At the four-year campuses, scholarly activity and research, institutionalized in disciplinary departments, underlie the intellectual culture. Neither culture is really appropriate for the community colleges, whose faculty, as others suggest, "are beset by uncertainties and torn by ambiguities in a professional role that wavers somewhere between traditional college professors and traditional high school teachers."[10] This problem of ambiguity and uncertainty is one to which I will return, for it is not confined to the faculty alone.

In 1925, some forty-seven two-year colleges were departments of high schools and governed by public school boards. Growth over the first twenty-five years had hardly been phenomenal. The colleges were widely dispersed, isolated in their local communities, and had the primary mission of transferring students to a four-year campus. The American Association of Junior Colleges (AAJC), founded in 1920,[11] sowed the seed of a national presence, and its officers were early proponents of expanding the colleges' occupational training efforts.

By 1950, the colleges began to have their own governing boards and were universally termed "junior colleges." During the Great Depression, between 1932 and 1939, their enrollment almost doubled: states found the colleges an economical alternative to four-year institutions, and students found them an alternative to joblessness. A widely read 1932 report of the Carnegie Foundation for the Advancement of Teaching helped them gain a national identity as a distinct sector of higher education.[12] This report urged the massive diversion of students from college transfer programs to those for occupational training, attempts that met with indifferent success. Students and their parents saw a four-year college education as an ultimate goal and resisted attempts to block the open admissions and transfer route to social and economic mobility.

By 1970, the "junior colleges" had become "community colleges," in part because this was proposed in the 1948 "Truman Report."[13] More substantively, I believe, that report authoritatively stated the case for broad and equal educational opportunity that has set the direction of American higher education—at least until now. The report urged an imperative, that "free and universal access to education, in terms of the interest, ability, and need of the student, must be a major goal in American education." The community colleges were central to the report's plan for expanding opportunity, and their extensive development was recommended. Population growth, the baby boomers, and an expanding job market were influential. Equally important, a national consensus supported full development of human talent, and this consensus fueled both the expansion of American higher education generally and the explosive increase in both the number of and enrollment at community colleges. Between 1950 and 1970, the number of community colleges more than doubled, and enrollment increased from 217,000 to 1,630,000. As returning veterans and the subsequent baby-boom generation dramatically increased demand for college, the role of the community colleges as an "open door" for entry to the four-year institutions reemerged. In 1971, the Carnegie Commission on Higher Education reported that community colleges were being established at a rate of one a week. The colleges embraced the call for wider access. In this postwar period, a growing number of students were older and less affluent than those of the prewar years.

Enrollment has continued to grow; between 1969 and 1994 community-college enrollment increased by some 174 percent, contrasted with 47 percent for four-year institutions. Today, in 1997, "community colleges" retain their name but are increasingly characterized as "comprehensive community colleges." The major emphasis of the colleges has shifted from the transfer function to vocational training. Between 1970 and 1990, the number of associate degrees awarded in occupational fields increased from 43 percent of all degrees to 63 percent, and the number in academic fields decreased accordingly. Recent years have seen state governments, business, industry, and private foundations increase their financial support for vocational programs. At the same time, the two primary missions of academic and vocational education seem to have been eroded in what may be the colleges' excessive zeal to be all things to all people. In part, this zeal could be attributed to the desire to educate new or previously neglected populations, such as displaced housewives, ethnic minorities, immigrants, and older adults. Also, the colleges needed to maintain enrollments to obtain state financial support. A report by the Carnegie Commission on Higher Education, headed by Clark Kerr, may have had some influence. The report, *The Open Door Colleges: Policies for*

Community Colleges, favored a comprehensive model for the colleges, one that would offer "a variety of educational programs, including transfer education, general education, remedial courses, occupational programs, continuing education for adults, and cultural programs designed to enrich the community environment."[14] Changes in the nature of the job market were another factor. More than semantics was involved in subsuming "technical" and other occupational programs under an umbrella of "career education" to encompass both two-year and four-year education—the colleges now find themselves educating older students with baccalaureate degrees who are seeking either new careers or advancement in their present ones.

As the end of the century approaches, the community colleges are undoubtedly a success. Collectively they are now clearly an integral part of American higher education, and most are, or aspire to be, "comprehensive" institutions. Individually, however, the colleges have not yet resolved questions about their particular institutional identity. Overly enthusiastic response to community needs has sometimes blurred the line between vocational training and avocational recreation. Resources are strained at many colleges by the needs of older students and, particularly, those of students from public schools of declining quality. Pressure from their local communities for them to be a social and cultural resource confuses and complicates full realization of primary educational missions. The community colleges have given America a new dimension of what constitutes higher education in this country. They have become a national presence and asset but remain a uniquely local phenomenon. A few, but not many, resemble traditional, four-year liberal-arts colleges. A few, but again not many, resemble specialized technical institutes. Most combine the functions of both, often with the added responsibilities of teaching, for example, English as a second language, citizenship, and—under contract with business or industry—highly specialized skills. The colleges, their faculty, and their students now face the uncertainties of demographic, economic, and technological change. Can they continue to meet the challenges of change as they did in the past?

ENVIRONMENTAL CHANGE: POLITICAL AND EDUCATIONAL RESPONSE

The future always brings surprises. Often, the problems that we had expected to be so troublesome happily disappear, only to be replaced by others that we did not foresee. Fully aware of the risks of predication, I believe that America's commitment to career opportunity and college access will be sorely tested by emerging societal change. Three such changes—demographic, economic, and technological—will require response by the community colleges. The colleges have successfully adjusted and adapted to change in the past, but their options will be more limited in the coming years. I will look first at the changes and then at the options for response.

Demographic Change

Population growth and the increasing number of potential students must be placed high on the list of external forces likely to shape the future of American higher education generally and that of community colleges in particular. Nearly half of all states are experiencing explosive growth of elementary and secondary school enrollments at this time.[15] In about half of the states, enrollments after elementary and high school are projected to increase by 30 percent or more over the next fifteen years; this will place the greatest demand on state higher education systems since the baby-boom cohorts of the 1960s and 1970s.

The gross numbers and projections tell only a part of the story. Many of the states with the fastest-growing populations are those whose young citizens most dramatically reflect the increasingly heterogeneous American ethnic profile. The potential pool of the next generation of college students is the most diverse in higher education's history. It may also be the poorest. The proportion of children in poverty is high in many of the states that expect the greatest growth in absolute numbers and ethnic diversity.

Many of these states, including California, Florida, Texas, and Washington, are among those most reliant on community colleges for both initial access to four-year colleges and for postsecondary occupational training. In California, overall college enrollments are projected to increase by some 24 percent—over 455,000 students—over the next decade with 76 percent of these, almost 348,000 students, to be accommodated by the community colleges. In Florida, the forecast is for 106,000 new students, of which some 65,000 are projected for the community colleges.

Economic Change

Predicting the economy presents greater uncertainties than does demography. The labor market remains volatile, even as the American economy continues to grow and unemployment falls. Demand for retraining and upgrading of skills is likely to intensify during both good and bad economic times, and preparation for second and third careers is becoming commonplace. Moreover, in the global information economy, education and training beyond high school have become necessary conditions for jobs and careers that permit Americans a middle-class standard of living.

Today's public-sector economy is quite different, however, from the one that supported the heyday of community-college growth in the 1960s and 1970s. This earlier age of expansion overlapped with a period of large and rapidly growing state and local budgets—the largest and most rapid in the nation's history. Beginning in the early 1950s, this boom period only ended with the taxpayers' revolt of the late 1970s, an end symbolized by California's Proposition 13. In contrast to that era, the next tidal wave of students will arrive at a time of fiscal constraints on state and local governments. Tax limitation measures will be only one factor in this new fiscal environment. The uncertain impact of federal devolution of responsibilities to the state and local levels is likely to absorb state funds, and it will be the rare state in which higher education does not face intensified competition with other public services. The community colleges have relatively low costs. They are an efficient channel in targeting public financial resources for lower division and occupational instruction without increasing other expenditures, such as those for residential facilities and research. Yet even with these cost advantages, the sheer volume of additional students, along with the financial constraints and competition, will, I believe, generate strong pressure for greater productivity and efficiency.

Technological Change

Computers and related electronic wonders (I still find them wonders) offer potential for extending opportunities without major investments in bricks and mortar. They promise a greater sharing of educational programs and resources and can increase cost effectiveness by the selective substitution of technology for physical plant and personnel. In its interactive forms, electronic technology offers alternatives that are more active and collaborative than most conventional classroom and lecture instruction. And it can make learning more individual by tailoring the pace and level to each student. The almost limitless reach of electronic communication and interaction can also make geographic and political boundaries obsolete. The fiefdoms contained by state lines and local community-college districts will be increasingly permeable by public and private competitors.

Technological advance carries the possibility—or threat—that states will bypass traditional institutions completely, including community colleges. John S. Daniel, vice chancellor of the Open University in the United Kingdom, has recently described eleven "mega-universities" throughout the world (none currently in the United States) that serve over 100,000 degree-seeking students through distance learning, doing so at costs far below even those of the community colleges.[16] The nascent Western Governors University incorporates several characteristics of these institutions, including the separation of assessment and credentialing from instruction—an essential element of distance education, and one that is likely to increase the visibility of learning outcomes in our country. These alternatives and others that may emerge can become increasingly attractive investments to political leaders if the existing array of institutions—particularly community colleges, where most of the demand will initially come—are perceived as unable or unwilling to use the possibilities inherent in technologies to respond to emerging societal needs.

Four Options for an Uncertain Future

Educating more students without commensurably more money may leave the states and the colleges with a set of four difficult choices. Three of these have long been arrows in the quivers of college administrators: raise tuition, limit enrollments, or increase productivity by conventional means. The fourth would also increase productivity but would be a departure from traditional practice. All have advantages and disadvantages, but, on balance, the fourth appears to hold the best chance for maintaining the community colleges' place at the leading edge of college and career opportunity.

Option one, raising tuition significantly, could, given the low income of so many of the new students, have a significant, adverse impact on access by pricing many students out of participation. A massive increase in need-based student financial assistance would temper the impact, but funding this assistance would require a major public policy commitment to aid needy students. Option two, maintaining enrollments at current levels—or at whatever levels can be supported at the current expenditure per student—would necessarily reduce access while the population is growing.

Options one and two are unlikely to be politically sustainable. Tuition levels and access can be highly salient issues in state capitols. Many states that raised tuition sharply in the early 1990s had, by the middle of the decade, been forced by adverse public reactions to impose freezes on tuition increases. California's experiment with steep tuition increases and enrollment reductions, for example, provoked a public backlash that sent elected officials and higher education leaders running for cover. Public demands for access and affordability reflect a growing awareness that a middle-class standard of living requires education and training beyond high school. My colleague, Arthur Levine, may be correct in his assertion that state and federal policymakers have little appetite for further expansion of access. I agree that recent developments appear to cast doubt on the viability of the historical commitment to access—for example, the current federal priority of financial relief for middle-class students and for the institutions that serve them; the growing hostility of policymakers towards remedial instruction; and the lack of state interest in developing performance indicators for budgeting that are related to equity. All of these suggest an environment in which the community-college role as an "educational safety net" may be jeopardized.

I do not, however, believe that the American public is likely to tolerate a wholesale rolling back of educational opportunity. "Nearly eight out of ten Americans (79 percent) are convinced that high school graduates should go to college 'because in the long run they will have better job prospects.' An even larger percent (89 percent) feel that society should not allow lack of money to prevent a qualified and motivated student from getting a college education."[17] The community colleges will remain the first and last resort of the economically and educationally disadvantaged—those least served by other sectors of higher education, those seeking second educational chances, the casualties of economic dislocation, and, most recently, the clients of reformed public assistance programs.

Because these colleges are public institutions, dependent on governmental support, their ability to respond to the needs of a growing population relies on a state and national commitment to educational equity and economic opportunity. Yet just to maintain opportunity (as measured by participation rates) at current levels in the face of population increases will require that the colleges serve more students. Pressure on states to contain costs will intensify with increasing demands for access and the growing fiscal needs of other state services. In the high-growth states particularly, additional public investment will be required to maintain or increase access. It is not likely, however, that this support will be at a rate equal to the current costs per student. Only a combination of state support and productivity improvements can respond to the pressures of growth and state financial constraints.

Option three would raise productivity through the conventional means—larger classes, for example, or higher student-faculty ratios, or greater proportions of lower-paid faculty, particularly part-timers. Some community colleges may have the flexibility to make such adjustments. But the wholesale adoption of these approaches as the *principal* strategy for addressing enrollment demand would ultimately undermine educational effectiveness. Unfortunately, option three is the least palatable to community-college faculty but may be the most politically attractive to state legislators and governors, if, that is, the colleges have not already taken the initiative suggested in option four. The attraction of option three is that it would provide access to "something" for all applicants who are eligible and motivated, even if the "something" is the educational equivalent of an industrial assembly line. This option is also more politically appealing than the first two because it would have an impact on fewer people.

Option four would also improve productivity but would do so by developing and implementing alternative approaches to conventional, classroom-based instruction. Unlike option three, this scenario cannot be mandated by government but instead requires the participation and leadership of the colleges and their faculty. These approaches would produce equal or superior student learning at the same or lower costs. They would rely on better educational use of student time; taking full advantage of the potential of electronic technology to extend the instructional reach of faculty; more effective use of the existing physical plant rather than investing in more bricks and mortar; and assessment of student learning as the basis for awarding degrees and credentials. Assessment would permit efficiency to be measured by student accomplishment—learning outcomes—in contrast to conventional input measures, such as staffing ratios, number of full-time faculty, or cost per credit hour. In recent years there have been many calls for such an instructional "revolution" in teaching and learning, all based upon these and similar principles, and all shifting the emphasis from lectures and classrooms to assessed learning outcomes and redesigned instructional processes that support student learning.[18]

Can the community colleges undertake such a transformation? They have distinct advantages, the greatest of which may be that teaching, learning, and access are their unequivocal missions. The colleges have been the nation's primary instrument for the expansion of educational opportunity, first to young high school graduates and then to adults of all ages, part-time students, and many others. They have often been on the cutting edge of innovation in American higher education—particularly with respect to the diversity of the students they have served, scheduling, instructional sites, and academic calendars. In these ways, the community colleges have shown great flexibility in organizing educational programs around the needs of their students; they have been less organized around the preferences of educational "providers" than most campuses in the four-year sector. In their methods of instruction, however, the community colleges have been less innovative, and, in common with the rest of higher education and the public schools, they rely heavily on the traditional, teacher-centered classroom and the lecture. This largely unexamined adherence to traditional teaching practice represents a major obstacle to significant improvement of teaching and learning. The reluctance to stray from well-traveled roads may be reinforced by faculty unionization to impede, for example, the adoption of electronic technology for both distance and campus instruction. And resistance to change is particularly in evidence when instructional change involves selective substitution of capital for labor.

CONCLUSION

There are few, if any, indications that American society will have less need for the educational services provided by public community colleges in the early twenty-first century than it has had in the late twentieth century. To the contrary, demographic and economic shifts portend growing needs for collegiate programs for the baccalaureate-bound; for technical and occupational training for employment; for the upgrading of knowledge and skills; for broad accessibility to develop the nation's human talent; and to promote equity and opportunity. These are necessary conditions for the preservation and enhancement of democratic values and institutions into the next century. And no sector of American higher education is better positioned than the community colleges for a world that will be characterized by relentless and simultaneous pressure for opportunity, educational quality, and cost effectiveness. The ability of community colleges to address these societal demands will depend on continued public commitment and on the adaptive capacity of the colleges. The fundamental challenge to the colleges will be developing and nurturing an intellectual culture undergirded by systematically rigorous attention to adult learning; to instructional contexts and methods that will best produce learning in a heterogeneous student population; and to the assessment of knowledge and skills derived from learning.

Almost by definition, community colleges challenge the conventional wisdom that correlates quality with *institutional* characteristics, not student *accomplishment*—that is, with "inputs" such as selective admissions, high levels of expenditure, and prestige derived from research reputation and institutional venerability. These measures are simply not applicable to the community colleges that, by design, were deliberately established as the primary institutions of mass higher education. The logic of mass education, and particularly of open admissions, leads inexorably to a concept of quality based on educational outcomes and assessment of added educational value. Absent such concept, accessibility often becomes a perceived substitute for quality, with a consequent erosion of public confidence and absence of essential information for educational improvement. Building, refining, and applying this concept of quality is the unfinished agenda of the community colleges in the twentieth century, and it is the indispensable condition for the radical transformation in teaching and learning that community colleges and their faculties must lead if they are to maintain and enhance their relevance and their capacity to serve society in the twenty-first century.

ENDNOTES

[1]Discussion of private two-year colleges is not within the scope of this essay.

[2]*Chronicle of Higher Education Almanac* 43 (1) (1996): 17.

[3]LaVergne Rosow, "The Working Poor and the Community College," *Phi Delta Kappan* (June 1994): 797.

[4]For information about community-college faculty, I relied on J. Lombardi, "The Ambiguity of Part-Time Faculty," in J. Lombardi and A. M. Cohen, eds., *Perspectives on the Community Colleges: Essays* (Washington, D.C.: American Council on Education, 1992), 51–67; Henry Allen, "Faculty Workload and Productivity in the 1990s: Preliminary Findings," in *NEA Almanac of Higher Education* (Washington, D.C.: National Education Association, 1996), 27–28; Alexander Astin, *The American College Teacher* (Los Angeles, Calif.: Higher Education Research Institute, 1991); American Association of Community Colleges, *Pocket Profile Community Colleges, 1995–96* (Washington, D.C.: American Association of Community Colleges, 1996); and *The Condition of the Professoriate* (Princeton, N.J.: Carnegie Foundation for the Advancement of Teaching, 1989).

[5]US Department of Education, National Center for Higher Education Statistics, *Digest of Education Statistics 1966* (Washington, D.C.: US Department of Education, 1966), Table 173.

[6]US Department of Education, National Center for Educational Statistics, National Postsecondary Student Aid Study, Washington, D.C., 1992.

[7]American Association of Community Colleges, *Facts About Community Colleges* (Washington, D.C.: American Association of Community Colleges, 1997).

[8]Michael S. McPherson and Morton Owen Schapiro, "Are We Keeping College Affordable? Student Aid, Access, and Choice in American Higher Education," paper prepared for the Princeton Conference on Higher Education, 21–23 March 1996, Table 7.

[9]See Steven Brint and Jerome Karabel, *The Diverted Dream: Community Colleges and the Promise of Educational Opportunity in America, 1900–1985* (New York: Oxford University Press, 1989); and Dale Tillery and William L. Deegan, "The Evolution of Two-Year Colleges Through Four Generations," in William L. Deegan, *Renewing the American Community College: Priorities and Strategies for Effective Leadership* (San Francisco, Calif.: Jossey-Bass Publishers, 1988). I would note that I do not entirely agree with the conclusions these authors draw from their respective historical accounts.

[10]Dennis McGrath and Martin B. Spear, *The Academic Crisis of the Community College* (Albany, N.Y.: State University of New York Press, 1991).

[11]See Robert Pedersen, "The St. Louis Conference: The Junior College Movement Reborn," in *Community College Journal* (April-May 1995): 26–30.

[12]The report, "State Higher Education in California," is discussed at length in Brint and Karabel, *The Diverted Dream,* 47–52.

[13]President's Commission on Higher Education, *Higher Education for American Democracy: A Report of the President's Commission on Higher Education* (New York: Harper & Row, 1948).

[14]The Carnegie Commission on Higher Education, *The Open Door Colleges: Policies for the Community Colleges* (New York: McGraw-Hill Book Company, June 1970), 17.

[15]Richard W. Riley, *A Back to School Special Report: The Baby Boom Echo* (Washington, D.C.: US Department of Education, 21 August 1996).

[16]John S. Daniel, *Mega-Universities and Knowledge Media* (London: Kogan Page Limited, 1996).

[17]A comment on the national data can be found in John Immerwahr with Steve Farkas, "The Closing Gateway: Californians Consider Their Higher Education System," a report by the Public Agenda Foundation for the California Higher Education Policy Center, San Jose, Calif., September 1993, 19.

[18]See, for example, D. Bruce Johnstone, "Learning Productivity: A New Imperative for American Higher Education," in William C. Barba, ed., *Higher Education in Crisis: New York in National Perspective* (New York: Garland Publishing, Inc., 1995), 31–60; and Robert Barr and John Tagg, "From Teaching to Learning—A New Paradigm for Undergraduate Education," *Change Magazine* (November-December 1994): 13–21.

Patricia J. Gumport

Public Universities as Academic Workplaces

P UBLIC UNIVERSITIES HAVE LONG BEEN CENTRAL to the success of the national higher-education enterprise, pursuing distinctive missions while responding to changing societal expectations to expand and diversify their functions. In recent years, however, a number of decision makers and opinion-shapers—federal and state legislators, educational officials, citizens' groups, and others—have generated external pressures on public universities, including vocal cries to reduce costs, explicit calls for accountability, demands for greater attention to undergraduate education, and wider scrutiny of faculty productivity. While these pressures have also affected private colleges and universities, cumulative pressure from the states on public universities has prompted the latter to search for new revenue sources and redesigned delivery systems. Within this political and economic climate, it is essential to consider how the challenges facing public universities today may fundamentally affect the lives of faculty within them. The importance of such a task is made clear when it is recalled that among the diverse institutional settings within which American faculty work, public universities employ the largest proportion of the US academic profession of any sector in the higher education system.[1]

For over a decade, interested observers have expressed concern that the post–World War II decades of academic opportunity, financial support, and public esteem for faculty have waned, making universities less desirable workplaces.[2] For the most part, observers have focused on the changing mix of expectations and

Patricia J. Gumport is Associate Professor of Education at Stanford University.

113

resources for faculty, noting declining economic conditions and conflicting messages about how faculty should spend their time.

Contemporary discourse on the problems plaguing public higher education reaffirms these concerns, as academic organizations are criticized for their inherent inefficiency. Faculty are increasingly cast as either the problem, characterized as unproductive and self-interested, or as the obstacle to the solution, with norms for shared governance rendering faculty participation ineffective—or, at worst, obstructionist. The degree to which such unfavorable conceptions of faculty have become widespread is striking; so, too, is the extent to which, simultaneously, a new style of academic management has become more legitimate. Particularly in public universities, these two perceptions have become mutually reinforcing. The locus of control for decision making is shifting away from departments and their faculties and toward various state-level actors and university spokespersons, who continually assert the need for even greater managerial flexibility to make a wide range of difficult resource allocation decisions, including those with educational implications.

This trend is significant because, among other reasons, it runs counter to expectations that faculty bring to their workplaces. Across fields of study, generations of academics have been socialized in the ideal of shared governance or, stated more pragmatically, the right to active participation or at least consultation in academic decisions. Against this background, it seems inevitable that today's public universities will disappoint and that tomorrow's will ultimately disillusion the faculty, as well as those holding in view society's long-range investment in public universities. I share these concerns and accordingly use this essay as an opportunity to reflect on possible futures, fully aware that doing so is tantamount to proceeding along an untested limb that may duly be pruned in light of emerging case-study and national data. These reflections are offered in the spirit of considering how public universities may be sustained as economically, organizationally, and intellectually viable and attractive places for academic work.

The approach used here will first provide a historical context by portraying in broad brush strokes the wider social forces that have reshaped the mission, finance, and governance of public universities. Against this backdrop, it will then be possible to examine how, in the contemporary climate, nonfaculty actors have been reshaping expectations for the conduct of faculty work in ways that are potentially detrimental to the intellectual environment of public universities.

HISTORICAL PRECEDENTS FOR CHANGE AND LESSONS OF INSTITUTION-BUILDING

Faculty have not always been active participants in steering dramatic macro-level changes in the mission, finance, and governance of public universities. Rather, decades of institution-building have encompassed an interplay of social forces that encouraged public universities to adapt their missions alongside increasingly complex environmental demands and public expectations.[3] Thus, any discussion of the changing character of public universities as academic workplaces must explain how the expansion and diversification of university functions have emerged from federal and state government initiatives that encouraged campus leaders to embrace new opportunities. While the inducement of federal and state funding has been critical in shaping how higher-education institutions respond to changing societal needs, the enormous challenge of coordinating efforts by various federal, state, and campus actors has overshadowed the concomitant shifts in expectations for faculty work in those settings.

Federal Initiatives

Since the middle of the nineteenth century, the national government's interest in higher education has been an enduring, formative presence in public colleges and universities, even though the states hold principal responsibility for them. This is especially true for public universities, which for the most part are chartered, financed, and governed as state entities.[4] The federal government has on several occasions enacted legislation to support the expansion of the states' public higher-education institutions and enrollments.

The earliest and most visible comprehensive federal initiative for public universities was the Morrill Act, passed in 1862.[5] While the intrastate politics and institutional struggles that often underlaid land-grant designation are worthy of detailed analysis in their own right, the Morrill Act had two specific consequences that shed light on how government initiatives have shaped public higher education. First, it contributed to an unprecedented diversification of the missions of public colleges and universities. Second, the act marked the creation of a symbolic and substantive national commitment to facilitate higher education's pursuit of a federally guided agenda. The distribution of federal financial resources to the states had three primary aims: democratization, to increase access to higher education; manpower training, to develop vocational/technical skills and liberal education; and applied research, to benefit the people of the states that built land-grant institutions (and, by extension, the national interest).

Over the next several decades and well into the twentieth century, additional federal legislation extended the basic concept of the land-grant idea. With World War II came the recognition of a need for highly trained personnel and the development of sophisticated technology for national defense. Higher-education institutions positioned themselves as a suitable home for some portion of these activities. Sponsored research altered the very structures and mission of public universities, nurturing a growing interdependence between research, graduate education, and undergraduate education. Federal support became fuel for growth as funds were delivered through research (especially in science-oriented fields, and directed by mission-oriented agencies), as well as through emerging student- and institutional-aid mechanisms. The postwar surge of federal initiatives (such as the GI Bill, the National Defense Education Act of 1958, and the Higher Education Acts of 1963 and 1965) contributed to the further evolution of state institutions. Embracing the national interest in open access and expanded enrollments, even state teachers' colleges broadened their functions.

Relying on funds promoting democratization, work-force training, and research, public-university leaders and their growing faculties developed more extensive programs of undergraduate education and, in some institutions, expanded into graduate education and scientific research to seek competitive advantage across the disciplines. University leaders were encouraged by external actors to elaborate these commitments to institution-building. Clearly, public institutions depended upon public appropriations, and in turn the public expected these campuses to expand the scope of their activities into multipurpose institutions.

Concern Over the Locus of Control

Yet, even as national funds were essential to facilitate this expansion (and thus were welcomed by the states), universities and state governments alike were concerned that reliance on federal assistance might compromise the integrity or threaten the autonomy of public universities.[6] Was the federal government to be benevolent patron or demanding paymaster? Were public universities to adapt to whatever federal opportunities arose or to plan for and initiate reforms themselves? Could states establish unified planning and coordination of higher education or would they establish a system of decentralized budgeting, program review, and authority over university operations in which intrastate campuses would compete with one another? Would the federal government, the states, or the campuses determine public university missions, programs, and structures?

In spite of the acknowledged benefits of post–World War II expansion, waves of fiscal constraint hit all levels of the system by the mid-1970s. State and campus leaders became aware of the enormous revenues needed to support the huge institutional structures that had emerged—funding for research, for instrumentation and facilities, and for financial assistance to students. Deliberations about competing priorities and strategies for resource allocation in an uncertain economy dominated higher-education policy arenas; this theme is echoed in discussions among state and campus leaders today. Increasingly concern was focused on the worry that the interest of the federal government in higher education appeared to be waning or was, at best, contingent. The solution for public universities was to develop a plurality of funding sources (including revenue from private sources) and to design strategies for directly contributing to economic development at the local, state, and national levels.[7] Campus leaders constructed these activities as not only a legitimate extension of land-grant purposes, but also a prudent and even a necessary approach to sustain the enterprise in a turbulent context.

Valuable Lessons

As institutional purposes evolved in tandem with external funding sources, a number of valuable lessons become clear in retrospect. In over a century of public university institution-building, substantial changes in mission, finance, and governance practices in turn had changed the organization of academic work and authority, leading primarily to the predominance of academic stratification and bureaucratic coordination. This relationship between changing institutional purposes, work environments, and expectations for faculty members foreshadowed the dramatic expansion in the range of faculty roles and workplace experiences in the contemporary era. As such, the lessons linking institutional purposes and the university-as-workplace over a hundred years demand careful consideration.

The first lesson is that federal higher education initiatives and priority-setting at the macro level have made an enormous difference to public universities and the faculty within them. The federal government has decisively stimulated the extent and nature of state commitments to higher education. Incrementally and without centralized coordination, new and diverse initiatives increasing the availability of public funds expanded the revenue base for universities—while at the same time creating future dependence on, and institutional vulnerability to, resources beyond state appropriations. As campuses sought to evolve from a primary mission of instruction into "federal grant universities,"[8] their reliance on federal funds both to fuel academic R&D imperatives and sustain student financial assistance was a dominant concern. Public universities continue to find themselves vulnerable to changes in levels of federal funding for higher education, to say nothing of indirect funding shifts that have been passed down to the state level (such as health care and social services), and thus they compete with higher education for state appropriations.

A second and equally sobering lesson is that over the past few decades concerns about institutional autonomy have shifted from worry about a domineering federal presence to more explicit tensions between public universities and their state governments. State governments have, of course, had a dominant presence in funding and coordinating the work of public universities. This presence is constitutionally derived and legitimated as a necessary safeguard of the public interest. States have granted to academic institutions varying degrees of substantive autonomy to determine their institutional goals and procedural autonomy to designate the means by which institutions will pursue such goals.[9] As states recognized that the unchecked expansion of missions and programs of the heady post–World War II years might not be in their best interests, statewide coordination efforts sought the voluntary cooperation of higher-education institutions. An elaborate set of structural mechanisms—from academic program approval and program review to central purchasing, line-item budgets, and pre-audits of expenditures—mediated between public institutions and their state legislatures.[10] However, these statewide coordination mechanisms opened the door to attempts by a number of state agencies to control and consolidate academic programs in the 1980s and early 1990s.

A third lesson focuses on the diverse institutional settings that emerged for public higher education. As external initiatives prompted mission differentiation, campuses took on different primary functions and resources such that the public sector came to include flagship research universities and doctoral-granting institutions, comprehensive state colleges and universities, and community colleges. Unquestionably, variation in public universities as academic workplaces to some extent parallels mission differentiation. At elite public universities the expectation is for faculty to engage in a mix of undergraduate, master's, and doctoral instruction as well as research, while at state colleges and universities the expectation is for primarily undergraduate and master's instruction. This general characterization gives way, however, when we look more closely at the faculty in each of those settings; it is not necessarily the case that the segmented market for public higher education is characterized by parallel differences in faculty goals, work styles, authority, and attitudes.[11] This is due in part to the professional socialization for teaching and research imprinted upon faculty members from their doctoral education. As new generations of faculty carry their Ph.D.s to nonelite institutional settings, they may bring a wider range of professional aspirations than is expected—or appropriate—in their academic workplace. Thus, while the public sector is highly differentiated by mission, faculty orientations in those settings may be highly diverse as well.

A fourth lesson to be drawn from this historical overview of institution-building is a marked distinction between "haves" and "have-nots." The competition for resources and status has reinforced academic stratification on several levels. In the push for competitive advancement, not only have public institutions been ranked relative to one another, but it has become commonplace to have rankings within any given university campus. Academic units have become characterized for their value as differential assets in the quest for institutional upward mobility, in particular for their revenue-generating capabilities.[12] Although universities have long claimed to have comprehensive coverage across academic fields, on any given campus there are distinctive programmatic strengths that enhance its reputation and position with respect to competitive markets—be they for students, for faculty, or for research. As public funding fluctuated, it quickly became apparent that the revenue-generating capability of a unit can serve as a valuable corrective. Since resource differences across academic departments have in part been compensated for by cross-subsidization, the potential for a program to raise revenue for the entire institution adds another factor in deliberations over which academic programs are most central to university missions.

A final lesson concerns the evolution of shared authority—the drift of authority upward, especially in large public systems, and the tension between managerial and academic temperaments.[13] The ideal of interdependence among faculty and administrators is historically rooted in the need for effective coordination of an increasingly complex organization. The rationale for mixing professional and bureaucratic authority grew out of two major changes in the nature of academic work: the specialization of faculty, and the rise of bureaucratic coordination. The growing ranks of faculty became increasingly specialized, such that their primary expertise as educators was located in departmentally based domains of curriculum, instruction, peer review, and research. Faculty asserted their professional autonomy by controlling standards for entrance and promotion, as well as standards of work. Faculty participated in a variety of governing structures, such as committees and the academic senate. To compensate for the faculty's specialization and the segmentation of academic work, administrative positions were established to centralize key functions of fiscal oversight, assume standardization across units, and link the university with (or buffer it from) external actors. Effective sharing of authority between faculty and administrators rested on a key premise of shared goals and values, a premise increasingly tested as collective bargaining by faculty became visible in public higher education in the decades of the 1960s and 1970s. Although faculty in elite public universities tended to see unions as inappropriate to their situation, faculty at other levels of public higher education tended to look more favorably at collective bargaining arrangements for their potential to safeguard job security and the terms of academic work.

These complex arrangements for sharing authority have been further complicated by the expanding managerial presence of non-academic administrators. Particularly in the past twenty-five years, these actors have become more visible in sheer numbers and in expenditures for their functions, even as higher education has entered an era of selective investment after the seemingly limitless first century of planning for growth.[14] Responding to uncertain economic and political climates as well as to state-level demands for cost containment and efficiency, these administrators have come to assume a central mediating role. Their functions have been both to read the environment and to position the institution and its programs amidst changing enrollment projections, antici-pated state allocations, and changing academic markets for re-search and economic development. A growing tension has ensued, however, as this evolving jurisdiction reflects an intermingling of budgetary and academic matters. Moreover, if specific circumstances of the day were construed as a crisis, traditional academic gover-nance structures could be (and have been) legitimately bypassed in favor of swift, centralized decision-making. Increasingly, this ma-neuver has come to be a celebrated alternative to faculty participa-tion and existing governance arrangements, presumed to be too time-consuming or inescapably tainted by self-interest. Thus, deci-sion-making affecting even the academic domain has moved out of departments, as all-important resource allocation and restructur-ing decisions have come to be made by university administrators and external (state-level) actors. The increased centrality of these actors can in part be accounted for as a necessary organizational adaptation in which managerialism filled a vacuum of inactivity that stemmed from faculty specialization and the segmentation of academic work.

CONTEMPORARY CHALLENGES AND UNIVERSITY RESPONSES

Further evidence has accumulated in the past few decades that these early lessons retain significance for today's public universities as academic workplaces. External pressures are demanding shifts of emphasis within an already wide-ranging set of institutional commitments, rather than taking on new purposes. Public universities are today beset by persistent vulnerability, as their legitimacy and even their means of operation still depend upon political and economic resources from the wider environment. Responding to an array of challenges that have been at times contradictory as well as expensive, university managers and their governing boards have attempted to respond to shifting demands in ways that have tangible consequences for the context and conduct of faculty work.

Before describing those consequences, though, we must first consider three interrelated yet distinct features that have become prominent in this contemporary landscape. The first is decidedly economic. For nearly three decades, public universities have faced a mix of financial concerns, including unpredictable funding fluctuations from major revenue sources, unfavorable economic conditions (e.g., inflation, recession), operating costs increasing faster than inflation, and intensifying admonishments from students, parents, and legislatures to control costs. Within the past decade the biggest unanticipated hit came from state budgets, as appropriations fell substantially below budget projections that campus leaders had relied upon in the prior two decades of strategic planning. The gap between budget projections and financial realities heightened the economic pressure on public universities.[15] The reasons underlying reductions in state funds to higher education are many; they include recession in state economies and the devolution of federal programs, especially medical-services programs, to state and local governments. As states wrestle with a new mix of competing budgetary priorities, financial reductions to public universities have been justified to the wider public for their reputed impact of making these institutions more accountable.

Interestingly, the shortfall in state appropriations to public higher education was not accompanied by a reduction in state involvement in determining university purposes and practices. Across the country, many public universities have received clear messages to heed new market signals. They have been told, by means of legislation and exhortation, to prepare for undergraduate enrollment increases in the coming decades; to improve access; to enhance the quality of undergraduate education; to offer academic programs that will better match employment opportunities and expectations; and to offer demonstrable progress in institutional performance, including cost-effectiveness, the assessment of student learning, and faculty productivity. The tenor of these demands has been characterized by an insistence on two guiding principles. The first is that the university cannot and should not be buffered from the market; it will not be permitted to shield vestiges of inefficiency and irrelevance once protected by the trump of academic autonomy. The second is to view functioning like a business in a competitive context as the one acceptable avenue toward self-improvement. Taken together these two principles may be seen as a political challenge, under the pressure of which public universities and their faculties have themselves become "in play" in the political arena. In today's climate, they must prove themselves entities worthy of continued investment according to new measures of effectiveness. Against this shared backdrop, public institutions have varying degrees of political clout to withstand state legislative pressure; while alumni loyalty may help cushion some campuses, others do not have that currency to draw upon.

These economic and political features of the contemporary landscape are conjoined in a third dynamic—the expectation that public universities will raise their own revenue through tuition and fees, sponsored research funds, auxiliary enterprises, fund-raising, collaboration with industry, and so on. Given this expectation, faculty work comes to be viewed as an institutional resource that can be assessed in terms of the extent to which it contributes to improved institutional performance along such dimensions.

Indeed, public universities are seeking a plurality of funding sources now more than ever. At the same time, acknowledging the financial impossibility of pursuing all things equally well, they have had to question whether they can afford to try to be all things to all people. For example, it is a formidable challenge to lower costs while simultaneously improving access to and the quality of undergraduate education, while still competing for national R&D funds. Working together with their governing boards, university managers have coped with this mix of institutional pressures by devising cost-cutting initiatives alongside a series of revenue-generating strategies. These have ranged the gamut from salary freezes and hiring freezes to early-retirement incentive programs; dramatic tuition increases (along with policies for high tuition/high aid); not filling faculty vacancies; reducing and contracting out selected services; consolidating and closing academic programs; cutting expenditures on libraries, maintenance, and instructional equipment; mounting aggressive campaigns for private fund-raising; restating the institution's record of public service to the state; and innumerable instances of administrative and academic restructuring in response to general and specific legislative mandates.[16]

Among the more visible and controversial practices, three initiatives by the University of California in the mid-1990s exemplify the potential of such cost-cutting and revenue-generating strategies to reshape the character of public universities: early-retirement incentives, differential tuition, and contracting out (or "outsourcing") certain academic programs. Thousands of professors (approximately two thousand "ladder" faculty) in the University of California chose to retire early in three waves of such voluntary retirement programs. While the consequences are as yet unclear, some departments on University of California campuses were affected by losses on two levels: a large number of vacancies to be filled on an ad hoc basis, and the loss of senior faculty with years of institutional memory. A second initiative saw the establishment of fee surcharges for selected professional schools. As a supplement to regular fees, the professional school fee surcharge opens the way for charging differential fees in other programs throughout the university. Such fees would presumably be set based on proximity to markets for human capital development; their existence could greatly reduce cross-subsidization by allowing selected schools to retain the additional fee income. The third initiative has been the selective outsourcing of academic programs. As a move toward cost-effectiveness, the University of California has proposed to disestablish and outsource selected academic programs to extension and community colleges. Thus far introductory Spanish has been proposed for such a move, and other elementary language courses, along with elementary levels of mathematics and writing, have been considered. The thrust of the idea is to export courses off-campus to achieve cost savings and streamline administrative operations. At a deeper level, of course, initiatives to outsource selected academic programs illuminate changing beliefs about what a university ought to look like, calling into question the appropriateness of private-sector models of adaptation for higher education.

EXPECTATIONS FOR FACULTY WORK

As public universities respond to these contemporary economic and political challenges, changes in institutional practices directly alter the expectations of faculty work. The revised expectations, which come from a mix of initiatives by legislative bodies, statewide coordinating boards, governing boards, and university leaders, are intended not only to raise revenue but, at a deeper level, to rethink the purpose of public universities—seeing them now as delivery systems. Seeing public higher education in this way brings three themes to the fore.

One prominent theme is the directive from state legislatures to improve undergraduate education, which has been translated into a directive to spend more time on undergraduate teaching. This directive comes in the context of a national emphasis on "putting students first."[17] In some public universities, teaching loads have been increased, small graduate programs have been closed, and faculty have been told not to spend too much time with graduate students.[18] In other public universities, faculty are told to recommit their time and attention to undergraduates while simultaneously being urged to actively pursue government research grants and university-industry collaboration. The emphasis on undergraduate education raises the question of whether merit-pay criteria or promotion and tenure criteria will be revised correspondingly. Moreover, while this orientation is part of an organizational approach to "redeploy faculty resources," there are significant and at times painful tradeoffs in making this shift.

A second and related theme is the expectation that some means of assessing faculty performance and productivity will be established. Such procedures have been developed in the context of demonstrating institutional performance and productivity, with new means to document teaching (e.g., evaluations, portfolios, peer review) for annual reviews. Numerous additional mechanisms are used to assess contributions to both undergraduate education and research, and the bureaucracy is poised to assemble data, from student credit hours by faculty and department to publication activity and research grant awards. Of course, that which is quantifiable is preferable to those who keep and analyze such centralized data. To date, the several types of data have not been considered equally in promotion and tenure decisions, which rely more heavily on national, peer-reviewed assessments of productivity rather than local reputations. This chasm between expectations and rewards is striking.

A third theme shaping the new expectations of faculty work is the ability to justify academic programs on the basis of their contributions to the state's economic development, a function that is increasingly regarded as falling within the university's service mission. On many campuses, academic program review is now a regular exercise; even if a unit is not undergoing program review at a given moment, evidence demonstrating how the program or the faculty member contributes to the state's economy is encouraged, if not expected.[19] When the time comes for selective reinvestment among academic programs, the close-to-the-market programs appear to be thriving, while those programs that appear less relevant are weakened.[20] At the same time, public universities are asked to search out and serve a new clientele—the adult learner, those in the workplace, and those at a distance. A restratification of academic programs is emerging in this light, laden with implications for intensifying differential status within the faculty.

The cumulative effect on faculty of these shifts in the academic workplace is substantial. A strong case could be made that the absence of faculty input into these revised expectations is appropriate. It is entirely possible that faculty did not want to deal with such issues, preferring the administration to be a buffer while faculty engage in their core academic functions and students study, leaving managers to respond to the challenges rather than mobilizing the entire campus community for input. However, as university managers and governing boards have been at the forefront of responding to contemporary challenges and repositioning their institutions, nonfaculty actors have also taken on the role of speaking for the institution in discussions of how much time faculty should teach, what and how faculty should teach, and how administrators can enhance faculty teaching. Whether by design or by default, traditional faculty governance structures have been bypassed in formulating these expectations—prompting us to consider how faculty have come to be characterized in the academic workplace.

CONCEPTIONS OF FACULTY AT WORK

The cumulative effect of these challenges is a substantial reconceptualization of faculty work—indeed of faculty obligations—by management. Faculty have been constructed as a significant management challenge. Seen in quite new ways, faculty are employees, potential revenue sources, resources to be redeployed, and competitors rather than colleagues.

As public universities have been pressured to become more like businesses, university managers have become the major reshapers of the academic workplace. If administrators have become managers and spokespersons for the institution, faculty have become more like employees in a setting that emphasizes the need to meet performance expectations.[21] Faculty are not exempt from being given revised or additional workloads, or being told how to spend their time (teaching or research, teaching undergraduates or graduate students) and which programs to devote their energy to. Annual performance reviews for all ranks of faculty document how faculty spend time and what they produce. The new style of academic management regards the notion of a professionally self-regulating and autonomous faculty, if it ever existed, as no longer affordable, let alone appropriate for state employees. In addition to the evaluation of teaching performance, there is a more comprehensive surveillance of academic work, including requests from campus administration to report office hours, consulting activities, and time spent out of town. If faculty are employees, an interesting question is raised—for whom do they work? The administration, the state, their students, the public? In any case, this approach treats faculty as workers who need to be monitored rather than as professionals who are trusted to work according to internalized standards.[22]

In addition to treating faculty more like employees, such an approach holds that faculty contributions can be measured in terms of the revenue they generate. In an instrumentalist approach, faculty work can be divided into measurable components with demonstrable production. As data on individuals are aggregated to the departmental level, faculty members can be accounted for by such measures as number of courses taught, student credit hours per term, research dollars brought in, and publications produced. Of course, these dimensions are valued differently across campuses within the public university sector, as faculty in lower-prestige settings earn their keep through student full-time equivalents (FTEs), while faculty in flagships earn their keep through grant-getting and publication activities. Within this performance paradigm, institutional service (such as committee work) and community service (such as promoting town-gown relationships) have been devalued as a way for tenured faculty to spend their time—and have thus been deemed to be something from which nontenured faculty should be protected. As this set of criteria is gaining currency, it is possible that the domain of faculty work will expand to reflect new sources of revenue. On the horizon, in addition to the technology-transfer activities in which knowledge is applied for economic development in local, regional, and state needs, new markets are emerging for intellectual property from teaching (e.g., courseware, videos for distance education).[23] Whether this arena of potential revenue will benefit the individual faculty member or the institution will likely be determined through negotiations between faculty and those administrators whose duties have come to include knowledge management.

Along with the performance-assessment approach, the new academic management paradigm regards faculty as competitors rather than colleagues. The organization and its workers are seen as atomistic—reduced to a set of discrete operating units that have expenditures and revenues as well as production (e.g., student FTEs, degrees awarded), thus opening a unit's performance to cost-benefit analyses. Departments are units that spend and raise funds within fiscal constraints and are thus liabilities or assets for the organizational balance sheet. There is not much room here for the notion of a scholarly community. As mentioned earlier, stratification among academic units is not new. However, today's stratification further challenges a sense of the organization as a collectivity. In addition to eroding the ethos of campus as an academic community or the faculty as a scholarly community, the atomistic approach incidentally works against the likelihood that faculty will perceive themselves as employees with a shared interest, which is the basis of solidarity in collective bargaining.

It is no surprise that the division of academic labor among faculty reflects not only different types of work but also what has come to be differently valued and differently compensated work. As university managers have applied the ideas of "theorists" like Drucker and Champy, with attendant prescriptions for reengineering, organizational units and their employees come to be seen as resources to be rearranged, downsized, or streamlined in the name of efficiency and repositioning the organization for survival. Practices of cross-subsidization that were once taken for granted are jeopardized in this more competitive ethos—even as unit leaders engage in a tug-of-war to retain revenue from fee income or research overhead and managers seek to protect their all-important discretionary resources. Dominant concerns of actors in the organization become guarding concentrations of capital, worrying about bigger salary differences across and even within academic units, and protecting programs from being dismantled or outsourced. In this context, it is difficult to keep central the notion that we are engaged in an educational enterprise. Moreover, if faculty were characterized as unduly individualistic before this climate, one can only imagine how such a climate will exacerbate a survival-of-the-fittest orientation.

Finally, a key consequence for faculty is that they are considered resources that need to be redeployed for the institution to improve its delivery of educational services. Facing competitive pressures, flexibility in organizational redesign is paramount. A well-known fact of academic organizations is that the bulk of resources is intractable, since it resides in faculty salaries. Seen from this perspective, inflexibility is cemented by tenure—the ultimate buffer from the market. It is not surprising that there is now widespread discussion of eliminating tenure and creating alternatives to tenure. Of course, scrutiny of tenure may not be explicitly stated as distrust (i.e., that tenure serves as a cloak for incompetence); instead, it is rooted in a managerial paradigm that seeks the flexibility to shift resources in response to short-term demands. The preferred approach to faculty hiring becomes one of filling vacancies with part-time faculty. As retirements occur, we are apt to see a greater proportion of part-time faculty, thus shifting a substantial proportion of the teaching function to another layer of academic personnel.

In addition to creating more of a disparity between the academic "haves" and "have-nots," this shift has implications for governance: Will part-time faculty have greater involvement as organizational members? Or, conversely, will the ranks of faculty who can participate in faculty governance over time be diminished—thereby leaving more decision-making power in the hands of full-time administrators? In either case, at the risk of stating the obvious, "redeployment" of faculty resources may invoke a visceral objection, offending the academic sensibility with this military imagery. Although uncomfortable, it is nonetheless necessary to consider this as a change over time in the nature of faculty recruitment. Perhaps a different analogy can illuminate the shift: Formerly managed like a zoo, the organization sought to add new exhibits. When a lion died, the tendency was to replace it with another lion. In the past few decades, with reduced availability of resources to purchase distinctiveness, a vacancy signaled the opportunity to use those resources to obtain an exotic beast, a star who could enhance the organization's reputation. The increased reliance on part-timers, however, signals a shift: rather than establish permanent exhibits, the zoo becomes dominated by short-term appearances of various rare and not-so-rare animals that can capture the interest of zoo visitors and yet be quickly dismantled by zookeepers and owners when interest dwindles. In the name of flexibility, this use of resources is not inherently bad for business; whether it is appropriate for public universities is another matter.

CONCLUSION

This essay has reflected on public universities as academic workplaces. As institutional purposes have evolved alongside external demands, so have expectations for faculty work. In the contemporary era, faculty have come to be understood as a management challenge, rather than as professionals who are integral to the reshaping of the enterprise. Focusing on public universities, the contention here is that the end of the twentieth century is a defining moment in which the character of the enterprise is being reshaped. It is no longer reasonable to assume that universities will sustain their commitments to comprehensive field coverage regardless of a department's demonstrated relevance and revenue-generating potential. No longer able to succeed by means of additive or steady-state solutions, public universities are responding to external pressures to shift concentrations of resources and capital. Nonfaculty actors are at the forefront of critical decisions about what will be eliminated and what will be protected, as well as the basis on which these decisions will be made. Faculty not only have a right to participate in this reshaping, they have a responsibility to do so. Failure to participate will not stop the process; it will only render them outside of the process.

When I reflect on my choice to become a faculty member, I hear a faint echo that faculty are the heart and soul of an institution. If this is still the case, I wonder what kind of heart and soul the institution of tomorrow will have. Who will the faculty be? Who will make the critical academic decisions? What contexts will foster academic work such that faculty can educate and nurture future generations of citizens, workers, scholars, and ideas? Short-term adaptations may prove to be short-sighted, jeopardizing what is in the long-term public interest. I worry that faculty are missing an opportunity to insert themselves into the conversation among those who claim to speak for the public interest.

In this political and economic climate, institutional autonomy and professional autonomy vis-à-vis self-governance have been recast as a luxury that public universities cannot afford. This is a profound change in stance. Autonomy in the past was a professional obligation, one that was tied to high ideals—a trust in academic expertise, a commitment to disinterested inquiry, as well as a point of departure for fresh thinking about that which is not currently valued. Will those ideals simply be dismissed as mythical, nostalgic, or an entitlement for the few? Must faculty entirely abandon the notion of being buffered from the market? Will faculty internalize a conception of themselves as employees, competitors, revenue-generators, and redeployable resources? And what educational consequences will result?

If faculty in public universities want the privilege of mulling over their ideas for teaching, of reading and writing, will they have to remove themselves from their workplaces to get it? Will the preferred route be to take themselves out of those institutional settings, and will this reflect a further differentiation between "haves" and "have-nots"? Will the academic labor force become increasingly segmented within larger economic and political structures such that only an elite few can claim alignment with that academic calling? Even within the public-university sector, we are likely to see differences. Higher-prestige campuses, especially the state flagships, generally have more political clout to withstand state legislative intervention due to alumni loyalty, while the lower-prestige institutions do not.

Faculty must realize that the contemporary arena of institutional repositioning is at least as much about political positioning between competing interest groups, both within and outside their workplaces. To speak of mutual trust and cooperation is pie-in-the-sky thinking. Perhaps faculty should be delighted that the public still views higher education as a key to the future, as a means of individual upward mobility, providing socialization and citizenship as well as work-force training and economic development. But given that public interest comes with scrutiny and demands for accountability, it is incumbent upon the faculty to insert themselves into the conversation and do a better job of explaining what they do.[24]

Obviously, there are many remaining unanswered questions about the future of the American academic profession and the future of public universities. In examining the nexus of these two turbulent areas, I yearn for better footing. Perhaps faculty themselves can provide some of that. My hope is that faculty, together with their administrative spokespeople, can make the case that there is something worth preserving that is being rendered obsolete by today's managerial paradigm and performance metric. I am not making a case to preserve academic ideals that now seem nostalgic, nor am I calling for faculty participation in a way that is tantamount to making a case for waste, which would be politically indefensible and imprudent in tough economic times. My call is simple and timely. I want faculty to listen to external pressures but to be ardent in their advocacy of intangible but essential values. The public university has immeasurable societal values; it nurtures people and their ideas. Faculty, who have expertise in academic matters, must not be silenced. Otherwise they may one day soon find themselves in a very different institution, or perhaps even outside it altogether.

ACKNOWLEDGMENTS

This essay was informed by my research in the sociology of knowledge and the study of higher education. I wish to thank the authors in this volume for a helpful conversation about this essay; Robert Berdahl, Marc Chun, Sandra Faulkner, Stephen Graubard, and Daniel Julius for thoughtful comments on a draft; and Marc Chun and Brian Pusser for valuable research assistance. The writing of this essay was supported, in part, by the National Center for Postsecondary Improvement, under the Educational Research and Development Center program, agreement number R309A60001, CFDA 84.309A, as administered by the Office of Educational Research and Improvement (OERI), US Department of Education. The findings and opinions expressed herein do not reflect the position or policies of OERI or the US Department of Education.

ENDNOTES

[1]In order to draw some parameters for this essay I focus on public universities, which are 12 percent of US higher-education institutions, enroll 35 percent of the students, and employ approximately 50 percent of the half-million US faculty. My reflections are not intended to describe the broader population of public institutions that extends to two-year and baccalaureate-only-granting colleges, although I do want to note that the broader sector employs 70 percent of US faculty, about 40 percent of whom are unionized. Carnegie Foundation for the Advancement of Teaching, *A Classification of Institutions of Higher Education* (Princeton, N.J.: Carnegie Foundation for the Advancement of Teaching, 1994); US Department of Education, "Faculty and Instructional Staff," Washington, D.C., fall 1992; and Dan Julius, ed., *Managing the Industrial Labor Relations Process in Higher Education* (Washington, D.C.: College and University Personnel Association, 1995).

[2]See, for example, Ann Ausin and Zelda Gamson, *Academic Workplace: New Tensions, Heightened Demands,* ASHE-ERIC Higher Education Research Report No. 10 (Washington, D.C.: Association for the Study of Higher Education, 1983); Philip Altbach, "Problems and Possibilities: The American Academic Profession," in Philip Altbach, Robert Berdahl, and Patricia Gumport, *Higher Education in American Society,* 3d ed. (Amherst, N.Y.: Prometheus, 1994); Robert Blackburn and Janet Lawrence, *Faculty at Work: Motivation, Expectation, Satisfaction* (Baltimore, Md.: Johns Hopkins University Press, 1995); James Fairweather, *Faculty Work and Public Trust* (Boston, Mass.: Allyn and Bacon, 1996).

[3]See Burton Clark's insightful account of system evolution in "The Problem of Complexity in Modern Higher Education," in S. Rothblatt and B. Wittrock, eds., *The European and American University Since 1800* (Cambridge: Cambridge University Press, 1993). For an account of the contemporary scene, see Patricia Gumport and Brian Pusser, "Restructuring the Academic Environment," in M. Peterson, D. Dill, and L. Mets, eds., *Planning and Management for a Changing Environment* (San Francisco, Calif.: Jossey-Bass, 1997).

[4]As exceptions, public universities in California and Michigan have constitutional autonomy that empowers their Boards of Regents to a greater extent than governing boards in other states.

[5]The Morrill Act stipulated that public lands (30,000 acres) be apportioned for sale by the states, with the proceeds used to promote higher education for the industrial classes, thus making the Morrill Act instrumental in establishing land-grant institutions in each state. Between 1862–1870, thirty-seven states developed land-grant universities. These were either existing state institutions that adapted their missions or entirely new institutions. Some historians have argued that although the Morrill Act was clearly a sign of national commitment to higher education, it originated and gained momentum from grass-roots constituencies of industrial and agricultural interests, especially those located in the northeast. Roger Williams, *The Origins of Federal Support for Higher Education* (University Park, Pa.: Pennsylvania State University Press, 1991).

[6]Concern over the uneasy partnership was articulated by Robert Berdahl in his landmark book *Statewide Coordination of Higher Education* (Washington, D.C.: American Council on Education, 1971). Berdahl advised that state planners be astute in coordination and incorporation of federal assistance, so that they not simply follow federal financial inducements when the best interests of the state would have dictated otherwise. A similar concern was expressed by Babbidge and Rosenzweig in wondering if the federal government was "inducing States or institutions to do what it wanted," or whether federal assistance was there "to help States and institutions do better or more of that which they are already doing, or to help them do at all that they would like to do but cannot afford to do." Homer Babbidge and Robert Rosenzweig, *The Federal Interest in Higher Education* (New York: McGraw-Hill, 1962).

[7]For a critical examination of the rationale that higher education should be supported for its contributions to economic development, see Sheila Slaughter, "From Serving Students to Serving the Economy: Changing Expectations of Faculty Role Performance," *Higher Education* 14 (1) (February 1985): 41–56; Sheila Slaughter and Edward Silva, "Towards a Political Economy of Retrenchment: The American Public Research Universities," *Review of Higher Education* 8 (1985): 295–318; and Henry Etzkowitz, "Entrepreneurial Scientists and Entrepreneurial Universities in American Academic Science," *Minerva* 21 (2/3) (1983): 198–233.

[8]The phrase was coined by Clark Kerr in his 1963 classic. Clark Kerr, *The Uses of the University,* 3d ed. (Cambridge, Mass.: Harvard University Press, 1982).

[9]Berdahl's distinction is found in *Statewide Coordination of Higher Education.*

[10]See Lyman Glenny, *Autonomy of Public Colleges: The Challenge of Coordination* (New York: McGraw-Hill, 1959). In *Statewide Coordination of Higher Education,* 13, Berdahl foreshadowed the likelihood that the state role would change. At the time, he characterized it this way: ". . .given the current need for expansion of both the number and types of programs, the probable state role is that of traffic cop for new programs rather than destroyer of existing ones. Of course, there is always the danger that, under conditions like those in the depression-ridden 1930s, states may again react by forcing severe cutbacks in current programs." Even in the 1990s Berdahl retained a cautious watch, noting that state

coordinating bodies have not yet reached the partnership potential he had foreseen for them two decades earlier. "Public Universities and State Governments: Is the Tension Benign?" *Educational Record* 71 (1) (Winter 1990): 38–42.

[11]This point is nicely developed in Kenneth Ruscio's chapter, "Many Sectors, Many Professions," in Burton Clark, ed., *The Academic Profession* (Berkeley and Los Angeles, Calif.: University of California Press, 1987). In reference to Gouldner's classic distinction, Ruscio argues that cosmopolitan as opposed to local orientations are not so neatly evident today. Alvin Gouldner, "Cosmopolitans and Locals: Toward an Analysis of Latent Social Roles," *Administrative Science Quarterly* 2 (March 1958): 281–306.

[12]Patricia Gumport, "The Contested Terrain of Academic Program Reduction," *Journal of Higher Education* 64 (3) (May-June 1993): 283–311.

[13]See Burton Clark, *The Higher Education System* (Berkeley and Los Angeles, Calif.: University of California Press, 1983); and Ruscio, "Many Sectors, Many Professions."

[14]Patricia Gumport and Brian Pusser, "A Case of Bureaucratic Accretion: Context and Consequences," *Journal of Higher Education* 66 (5) (September/October 1995): 493–520.

[15]It is ironic that demands have increased in the face of reduced funding to the point that public universities are increasingly characterized as "state-assisted" rather than "state-supported" institutions. National data on declining state appropriations reveal that between 1980 and 1993 state funding for public universities and colleges fell just under 10 percent. Between 1986 and 1992, state general fund appropriations saw a reduction in dollars allocated per student enrolled. Between 1981 and 1993, total government funding as a percentage of all revenue sources for higher education declined almost 10 percent. For annual updates of funding changes, see the annual *Chronicle of Higher Education Almanac* and US Department of Education, National Center for Education Statistics, IPEDS Finance Surveys.

[16]Public higher education has been directed to restructure administratively and academically, with general mandates in states such as Arizona and Florida, while a more specific legislative mandate to restructure occurred in Virginia in 1994. See Terrence MacTaggart and associates' work on restructuring governing systems in North Dakota, Massachusetts, Alaska, Minnesota, and Maryland in Terrence J. MacTaggart, *Restructuring Higher Education* (San Francisco, Calif.: Jossey-Bass, 1996).

[17]For example, see the report by the Kellogg Commission on the Future of State and Land-Grant Universities, "Returning to Our Roots: The Student Experience," April 1997.

[18]In response to a restructuring mandate and uniform guidelines in a 1994 General Assembly Act as well as the criteria given by the State Council on Higher Education in Virginia, restructuring at the University of Virginia exemplifies some of these changes. Faculty across all departments are expected to be more productive, a message expressed even more precisely as "The faculty, with 1,500 more students to teach, will have to be 13 percent more productive," in *Targeting Excellence: A Tracking Report* (1995). The report also explains that faculty

members whose research funding and interests have declined have been assigned additional courses; and in one department (history) all faculty now serve as undergraduate advisors. At the same time, faculty across all departments face new performance evaluation procedures, with a mandate that teaching be considered in the annual review of each faculty member. Accompanying this discussion of how to ensure that faculty teach more undergraduates and teach them better is an admonishment that graduate students should not consume a disproportionate share of faculty time. In an interesting note of irony, the progress report states that some 20,000 hours of faculty, staff, and student time went into the year-long effort to prepare the report.

[19]Examples abound of department-based efforts in the face of being targeted for elimination, such as at the University of Oregon in the early 1990s, as well as institution-wide efforts to do so in 1997. See *Partnership Illinois* by the University of Illinois and *Partners for Progress* by the North Dakota State University System.

[20]See Sheila Slaughter, "Retrenchment in the 1980s: The Politics of Prestige and Gender," *Journal of Higher Education* 64 (3) (May/June 1993): 250–282; Sheila Slaughter, "Criteria for Restructuring Postsecondary Education," *Journal for Higher Education Management* 10 (2) (Winter-Spring 1995): 31–44; and Sheila Slaughter and Larry Leslie, *Academic Capitalism: Politics, Policies, and the Entrepreneurial University* (Baltimore, Md.: Johns Hopkins University Press, 1997).

[21]Of historical import on the conception of faculty as employees or managers, it is crucial to note the Supreme Court ruled faculty positions as managerial in the Yeshiva decision. In spite of this ruling, faculty have gained bargaining status in public colleges and universities as employees. Of course, it should also be noted that employees can be highly professionalized, as is evident with musicians, dancers, and others organized according to more of a crafts-union analogy. See Julius, ed., *Managing the Industrial Labor Relations Process in Higher Education.* Of related interest, within a workplace model that sees administrators as managers and faculty as workers, students become mere consumers.

[22]Of course, this may be part of a broader societal trend in which a logic of accountability is imposed on other professions as well. See the argument offered by Gary Rhoades, *Managed Professionals* (Albany, N.Y.: SUNY Press, forthcoming).

[23]Patricia Gumport and Marc Chun, "Technology and Higher Education: Opportunities and Challenges for the New Era," in Philip Altbach, Robert Berdahl, and Patricia Gumport, eds., *American Higher Education in the 21st Century: Social, Political, and Economic Challenges* (Baltimore, Md.: Johns Hopkins University Press, forthcoming).

[24]See Levine's compelling editorial on this point. Arthur Levine, "Higher Education's New Status as a Mature Industry," *Chronicle of Higher Education,* 31 January 1997.

R. M. Douglas

Survival of the Fittest?
Postgraduate Education and the
Professoriate at the Fin de Siècle

LATE IN 1989, AS A NEWLY MATRICULATED STUDENT in the Ph.D. program in history at Brown University, I attended a lecture at which William G. Bowen, the former president of Princeton, was the featured speaker. Dr. Bowen had come to Brown to promote his book, *Prospects for Faculty in the Arts and Sciences,* which set out four possible models of the requirements of colleges and universities for full-time faculty members over the next quarter-century.[1] Although he was careful to emphasize that his models were not predictions but rather projections of existing trends, Dr. Bowen nonetheless offered an encouraging vision of the future. Even the most pessimistic of his scenarios suggested that from 1997 onwards, demand in all fields for new Ph.D.s would exceed supply, with by far the greatest shortages arising in those traditional Cinderella disciplines, the humanities and social sciences. Nor was this favorable situation likely to be affected in any significant way by changes in employment patterns among existing faculty, including—as did in fact occur soon afterward—the abolition of compulsory retirement.[2] Walking home after the lecture, I congratulated myself on my good fortune in coming to the United States to join what was clearly poised to become one of the most dynamic growth industries of the late twentieth century.

By the time I graduated in May of 1996, there was little sign of this long-predicted hiring boom. Instead, the academic job market had declined alarmingly from even the mediocre levels of the previous decade. With the onset of the recession of the early 1990s, state

---

R. M. Douglas is Visiting Assistant Professor of History at Colgate University.

137

funding for higher education was either frozen or reduced in real terms, and the most damaging cuts fell on the sectors of the academic economy whose requirements historically have had the greatest impact on the demand for new professors—the public university systems of California and New York. Although the generation of university teachers hired during the great expansion of the 1950s and 1960s did, as predicted, begin to retire in the 1990s, in many cases the positions they had occupied disappeared with them. Retrenchment by state governments, whose impact was also felt by private institutions, coincided with a steady increase above the rate of inflation in the cost of higher education and a greater readiness on the part of legislators to question, and even to regulate, what colleges and universities do with the money they receive. The cumulative result of this confluence of adverse trends has been perhaps the deepest depression of this century in academic employment, rivaling in its severity even the post-Vietnam-era slump that gave rise to the so-called lost generation of unemployed Ph.D.s in the 1970s. At present, tenure-track vacancies in history attract an average of 105 applications, many of them from candidates of superb quality and considerable experience;[3] in less-favored fields like English and philosophy, many times that number of applications for a single position is commonplace.

Misfortune for some, of course, is usually associated with opportunity for others. The principal beneficiaries of this situation have been the smaller and less well-known colleges, which are now able to pick and choose from long lists of desirable candidates.[4] Institutions that ten years ago might have confined their recruiting efforts to the immediate region are conducting nationwide searches, while vacancies advertised locally are in any event becoming de facto national searches thanks to the proliferation of electronic bulletin boards and web sites. Schools unwilling to contemplate the outlay involved in hiring a full-time instructor, moreover, can find a ready supply of well-qualified individuals willing to work without benefits or security as adjuncts, often for as little as $1,500 per course.

The dismal condition of the would-be academic at the moment, then, uncannily parallels the "surplus woman" problem of mid-Victorian England. Condemned to what one contemporary described as a state of "educated destitution" by the shortage of suitable occupations[5] and obliged to eke out a penurious and uncertain existence as a teacher—virtually the only form of employment for which she was qualified—the Victorian spinster more often than not experienced working conditions so harsh that "either health fails, or, which is of as great importance, the geniality of the mind gives way."[6] In like manner today the newly qualified Ph.D. of either sex—the latter-day analogue of the "distressed," or downwardly mobile, gentlewoman—is all too likely to wind up in one of the few walks of life whose practitioners are exploited as thoroughly and unashamedly as the nineteenth-century governess or in which working conditions remain as relentlessly Dickensian— the university adjunct. For those individuals finding themselves in this precarious position, the observation of the Victorian social commentator J. D. Milne remains as applicable today as it was in the case of their counterparts a century and a half ago:

> ...prevented from mingling her regard in much that is of vital importance to the well-being of mankind, and from undertaking many duties to which she feels naturally called—there is entailed upon her a constant sense of alienation from society, and the still more oppressive sense of a purposeless existence.[7]

Notwithstanding the growing globalization of the economy, it is unlikely that we will be able to solve our problem as the Victorians solved theirs—the wholesale export of the affected group to the colonies. Instead, various solutions have been canvassed to deal with the superabundance of "surplus" faculty, ranging from the opening of new avenues of employment (retraining Ph.D.s in the humanities and social sciences for positions outside the academy) to curbs upon supply (the wholesale elimination of Ph.D. programs). Since the latter expedient is both simpler and cheaper than the former, it is not surprising that it should be the first to be resorted to. Thus in December 1995, the Ohio Board of Regents discontinued funding for six of the state's eight doctoral programs in history, arguing that it was futile to spend public money on the training of prospective academics when only one graduate in four from these programs was able to secure employment at a four-year institution. Although this decision was much criticized by faculty members at the "downsized" universities and elsewhere, it did have the salutary effect of focusing attention on the question of what doctoral education in the humanities was, or ought to be, for. The defenders of the axed programs contended that graduate training is good in itself, inasmuch as it contributes to the personal development of those who undertake it as well as the development of knowledge within the disciplines. They further pointed out that graduate students make a significant contribution to higher education while working as teaching assistants, and that many doctoral recipients who do not find a place within the academy carry useful skills into a wide array of other fields, ranging from secondary-school teaching to the civil service. To these arguments the Board of Regents replied that doctoral programs exist primarily to provide their graduates with a professional qualification enabling them to find academic employment; measured by this yardstick, the institutions concerned were demonstrably failing in their mission.

That the advancement of knowledge is itself a sufficient justification for graduate education is an admirable ideal. Nevertheless, there is no question that the overwhelming majority of students who enter Ph.D. programs in the humanities do so to equip themselves for academic appointments and that large numbers of them are falling short of their objective. The situation would, of course, be worse still if recommendations like Dr. Bowen's in 1989 for a considerable expansion of postgraduate education in the arts and sciences had been adopted; not for the first time, one may be thankful for the invincible inertia of the academy.[8] But for newly qualified Ph.D.s at the outset of their academic careers, and even more so for those now entering the graduate schools with the intention of becoming university teachers, the familiar landmarks of the professional career are disappearing into thin air. In this new environment, traditional formulae for entry to and advancement within the academy no longer appear to apply. What then are the implications for postgraduate education if, as seems to be the case, the standard career path of the newly fledged academic—hired directly from graduate school to a tenure-track position, publication of the dissertation, and securing of tenure—is tending to become the exception rather than the rule?

By far the most important change in recent years for those contemplating a career as a professor in the humanities is the reality that the process of qualification has become a more formidable undertaking than was the case even fifteen years ago. For

Ph.D.-seekers in history, the mean time-to-degree—that is, the number of years between completion of the baccalaureate and acquisition of the doctorate—rose from 9.22 years in the quinquennium ending in 1980 to 12.21 years in the similar period ending in 1992—a one-third increase in little more than a decade.[9] To a far greater extent than the primary degree, therefore, the Ph.D. represents a vast and growing investment of time and money, if to the actual cost of tuition, fees, and living expenses is added the loss of so many years of earning potential. So heavy has the financial burden become that the wholly self-supporting doctoral student is now a vanishing breed, a development formally recognized by many universities in making the award of financial aid a condition of continued enrollment beyond the first year. This more stringent process of selection does not, however, appear to have had any appreciable impact on the length of time taken by students to complete their degrees, and the roots of the problem must lie elsewhere.

One factor that undoubtedly has had a major impact has been the changing pattern of postgraduate funding since the 1970s. It should come as no surprise to anyone that there is a strong correlation between the availability of financial aid—and its type—and the likelihood that the doctorate will be completed within a reasonable time frame.[10] In recent years, shrinking financial-aid budgets have driven many graduate schools not only to curtail the amount of aid offered to students but, concomitant with measures to cut back on full-time faculty numbers, to replace fellowship support with assistantships.[11] One consequence of this shift has been a reduction in the amount of time Ph.D. candidates can devote to their research, with the result that they are likely to have made less progress than in the past towards their degrees by the time their institutional funding has been exhausted. Furthermore, even in the dwindling number of universities that have retained fellowships as the primary form of postgraduate support, few Ph.D. candidates can expect to be supported by their institutions throughout the entire period of their studies, obliging them to rely upon external funding to make up the shortfall.[12] Thus, timely completion of the dissertation has increasingly become a question of whether one is successful in winning foundation grants to supplement an increasingly thinly spread level of university-based funding. It need hardly be said that this situation discriminates heavily in favor of students from elite institutions that historically have attracted a disproportionate share of such prizes and whose mean times-to-degree are significantly lower than those from less-prominent graduate schools.[13]

For students who are unsuccessful in these competitions, the outlook is distinctly disheartening. They must confront the prospect of being thrown upon their own resources in the fourth or fifth year of study, a stage at which few will be close to completion. Once that point has been reached, the range of alternatives effectively narrows to three: drop out; self-finance one's studies by taking out loans; or attempt to continue work on the dissertation while holding down a job elsewhere, usually as an adjunct. In my experience, the second of these options is the most likely to be chosen (for reasons that are readily apparent, none but the most determined among those who pursue the third ever succeed in completing their degrees). Having already invested so heavily in their studies, however, many who find themselves in this position feel they have no option but to stay the course, often accumulating in the process a level of debt equivalent to a fair-sized mortgage. For some, this burden of indebtedness ultimately becomes unsustainable, forcing them out of the academy. The same set of circumstances, on the other hand, can also produce the phenomenon of the perennial graduate student. Because federally guaranteed loans do not fall due until their holders graduate, heavily indebted students have a strong incentive to defer taking their degrees so as to avoid demands for repayment they have no hope of meeting until they obtain employment. This strategy, however, has shortcomings of its own. Of late it has become much more common for employers to demand that the Ph.D. be in hand at the time of application, whereas formerly the degree was not required until the appointment was actually made. Advanced doctoral candidates can, therefore, find themselves in a catch-22: precluded from applying for positions until they graduate but unable to graduate until they secure a position.

Considered cold-bloodedly, lengthening times-to-degree resulting in higher attrition rates in graduate school might be regarded as a kind of self-regulating solution—albeit an appallingly wasteful and inhumane one—to the "surplus Ph.D." problem. Contrary to what might be expected, however, it appears that the seemingly open-ended prolongation of graduate studies in recent years is closely correlated with the precarious state of the academic economy and in particular with students' perception that it is wiser to continue working on their dissertations until such time as they can present as highly polished a document as the job market now seems to demand. As a comparison of the bibliography of a representative dissertation of the 1990s with one from a manuscript written in the 1960s will show, the completion of a Ph.D. in the humanities today typically requires a more exhaustive, and expensive, foundation of research than was considered necessary in the past. The more recent document is likely to be based upon a wider range of primary sources, often spanning several countries, and to involve the utilization—or, at any rate, the citation—of materials derived from more than one discipline. It is an open question whether this trend toward more extensive research in graduate school necessarily translates into higher scholarly standards, or whether the more reflective scrutiny of a smaller amount of source material might not yield no less satisfactory results than work based upon a mass of what may be half-digested data. Nevertheless, the realities of the marketplace now dictate that to pass muster with employers, a dissertation requires a much more elaborate compendium of research than was the case a generation ago. Likewise, the pressure to have published one's work—or at least have a book contract in hand when launching oneself upon the job market—is more intense at present than at any time previously. This, in turn, has obliged aspirant professors, at an earlier stage of their careers, to frame and carry out their research projects in such a way as to meet the requirements not only of their advisers and committees but, perhaps more importantly, of commissioning editors of university presses.

It may be thought that these are, if anything, positive and wholesome developments. Certainly, too many dissertations in the past have been designed as exercises in research technique rather than to make definite contributions to knowledge; and it is entirely to the good that graduate students be conscious from the outset of the need to address their work to a wider audience than the three or four members of their dissertation committees. Nor is there anything wrong in itself with a shift in the direction of more thoroughgoing and comprehensive research. But if the imperatives of the market are to dictate what constitutes an "acceptable" level of achievement in graduate school, as to some extent they must, it is difficult to see how, given the current state of the academic economy, the trend towards ever-lengthening times-to-degree can be reversed or even halted. The more competitive the market becomes, the greater employers' expectations of the new Ph.D.s they hire will be, and the greater the temptation among students to remain in graduate school until they are in a position to meet those expectations. Such pressures are undoubtedly contributing to the trend for new entrants to the profession to be virtually middle-aged by the time they commence their academic careers. In 1994, the average age at which Ph.D.-recipients in history were conferred with their degrees was 35.3 years—a figure that will do little to alter the demographic profile of a profession where more than a third of the practitioners in the humanities are already over the age of fifty-five.[14]

It appears, then, that at present the academy has a built-in preference for precocity in terms of scholarly production, rather than for those individuals whose research, however valuable, is of a character that will not bear fruit in the form of publications until some years after their appointment.[15] There is a real danger, however, that the perception that the most important work of one's career is what one does in graduate school will come to exercise an undue influence on the selection not only of dissertation topics but even fields of specialization. Towards the end of my own post-graduate career, I was struck by the number of students who had just entered the program and were anxiously seeking guidance from their elders as to the "hot" areas of study, offering the best chances of eventual employability. This was, of course, a difficult question to answer, inasmuch as the "hot" field at any given moment, being by definition the one most relevant to current concerns, is also likely to prove the most evanescent. Nevertheless, that such factors should be uppermost in the minds of graduate students at the outset of their studies is an ominous development: for if it is hard to predict the "hot" field of the future, the "cold" field of the present—measured not by scholarly vitality but by the prevailing level of demand for its practitioners—is all too readily identifiable.[16] Should current circumstances persist, and in the absence of any countervailing influences, economic pressures may eventually come to play as great a role in determining the agenda of research in the humanities as they already do in the social and physical sciences.

One might, nevertheless, hope that focusing on such bottom-line considerations will at any event cause the academy to become more responsive to the growing demands of its principal "consumers"—i.e., students and parents—for a greater emphasis upon undergraduate teaching, the university professor's primary function. Unaccountably, this remains the one aspect of his or her duties that is not taught systematically in graduate school. Instead, unsupervised teaching assistants are expected to learn by doing, from whatever examples they have drawn—in many cases, from the negative—from their own experience as students, or after receiving the dubious benefit, at the more conscientious institutions, of a one- or two-hour teaching "workshop." In light of this level of preparation, it is perhaps remarkable that the overall standard of teaching is as high as it is—although, as doctors are said to bury their mistakes, I fear that all too often I ended up flunking mine. But it is easy to imagine the carnage that would ensue if medicine were taught in the same manner as university teaching; that it is not may provide an indication of the relative importance we accord the two endeavors.

There is, however, little likelihood that the situation will change under present circumstances. At a university at which I interviewed some time ago, a member of the search committee revealed that to reduce the avalanche of applications it had received to manageable proportions, the committee had fixed the possession of a book contract as its "opening bid" for those who would be called to an initial interview. The institution in question was an inner-city commuter school offering associate and baccalaureate degrees along with a small master's program, virtually all of whose students required one or more remedial courses to qualify them for regular college-level coursework and in which more than a third of matriculants entered without being able to read at the tenth-grade level. From my own, admittedly limited, perspective, it appeared that the needs of such an institution called for the hiring of an especially skilled and dedicated teacher with experience in the special problems affecting nontraditional students, and that the possession or otherwise of book contracts was at best a secondary consideration. But research records being more readily measurable and comparable than teaching ability—competence in which is not a requirement for the doctorate, in any case[17]—it is unsurprising, and perhaps inevitable, that they should continue to be used as the primary criterion for evaluation. There is, therefore, little reason to hope that the current glut of qualified candidates, in and of itself, will do very much to raise the profile of undergraduate teaching within the academy.

In one respect, the tightening academic economy is likely to have a beneficial effect. As institutions and colleges seek to consolidate positions and scale back departments, those who have been broadly trained in a variety of fields or disciplines will be far better positioned than the individual capable of teaching not much more than the subject of his or her dissertation.[18] To the extent that this trend counterbalances the hyperspecialization and fragmentation of the academy, it can only be welcomed, although it is hard to see how the current demand for interdisciplinarity can be satisfied without further prolonging the time taken to complete the Ph.D. (unless, to paraphrase Brendan Behan, we are to train faculty to be illiterate in two disciplines rather than one).

Taken as a whole, though, the general outlook for aspiring academics does not afford much basis for optimism. It would be pointless, as well as unnecessarily alarmist, to speak of a "crisis" afflicting would-be professors—although there are thousands of unemployed or underemployed Ph.D.s who might well think otherwise. Rather, it is necessary to recognize the extent to which the operation of *laissez-faire* is tending to channel the professoriate of the future in directions that serve neither their own interests nor those of the academy as a whole. As constituted at present, the process of preparation for an academic career combines the rigors of a forced march with the unpredictability of a lottery. Among those who survive this process of unnatural selection and actually secure positions, scholarly ability and stamina can certainly be said to play a large part—although not so much, perhaps, as good fortune.

Social Darwinism, however, is no more satisfactory as an organizing principle for academic society than it is for the wider world. If it should prove to be the case that the higher-education sector is merely undergoing a cyclical downturn, albeit one of particular severity, there is nothing to be done but wait for the laws of supply and demand to restore a condition of relative normalcy. But if—as at this juncture seems much more probable—the academy is in fact undergoing a radical restructuring, the effects of which will remain with us for the foreseeable future, it will be necessary to reexamine the place of the Ph.D. within that new environment. In doing so, we would be unwise to assume that potential recruits to the academy will continue year after year to flock into the graduate schools "like ghetto kids hoping to make the NBA," as one observer has felicitously remarked.[19] The rewards of scholarly life, intangible though they might be for the most part, have always been sufficient to attract into the profession an adequate supply of talented and dedicated professionals, devoted to their craft and to the diffusion of knowledge. But it is unrealistic to suppose that the academy will always be able to count upon the availability of such resources. The increased militancy of graduate students on many campuses, demonstrated most recently in the Yale teaching assistants' strike, is at bottom a protest against the precariousness of their employment prospects, now that the expectation of upward mobility no longer exists to compensate for the trials of the academic apprenticeship. Although such manifestations will probably become more widespread, a very real possibility is that prospective postgraduates will simply fail to come forward, especially as those members of the current cohort of Ph.D.s who succeed against the odds in finding positions communicate the reality of the situation to their own promising students. While present conditions persist, it is simply irresponsible to encourage even the brightest undergraduates to consider a career as a university teacher. Given the lengthy gestation period of new Ph.D.s, however, there is no guarantee that the oversupply of the present will not after all give rise to a shortage of faculty—or the right kind of faculty—ten or fifteen years in the future.

Unless we are, then, to face the prospect, continued indefinitely, of a series of infrequent booms and increasingly acute slumps, there seems to be an obvious need for the graduate schools themselves to make a coordinated effort at a national level to determine the academy's actual requirements for new faculty and how these might best be met. There are at present in this country some two hundred institutions offering Ph.D.s in the humanities, each of which remains a little universe unto itself. Historically, the immense diversity implied in a postgraduate sector on this scale has been the greatest strength of American doctoral education. That diversity is now being threatened, on the one hand, by a series of market-driven trends whose combined effect appears to be working towards the production of a research-oriented "one size fits all" Ph.D. and, on the other, by the danger that state legislatures will adopt the precedent set by the Ohio Board of Regents and carry out their own rough-and-ready reconstruction of graduate education. Should such initiatives become widespread, as they inevitably will in default of any attempt by the academy to put its own house in order, there is every reason to believe that the brunt of any cutbacks will be borne by the lesser-known and less well-established programs, leaving the elite research institutions even more firmly in possession of the field. The implications of a development of this sort for the social, and perhaps also the intellectual, diversity of the professoriate are disquieting.

The only viable alternative I can see to downsizing by legislative fiat, however, is for the postgraduate sector collectively to take action on its own account. To be effective, any coordinated effort could only be conducted on a voluntary basis: the more extreme and, in some cases, coercive expedients that have recently been proposed to deal with these problems are clearly impracticable as well as undesirable.[20] One possibility might be to reexamine the function of the master's degree, with a view towards restoring its position as a "gatekeeping" credential for the doctorate—much as the M.Phil., a one- or two-year research degree, serves at present in the Irish postgraduate system. Another, for which there seems to be an undeniable case, is for graduate schools to enable applicants at the very least to make informed choices about the potential hazards they are undertaking by providing in a standardized format information on each institution's attrition rate, mean and median time-to-degree, and success in placing its graduates in academic and other employment.

The scope for cooperation and collaboration between graduate schools is obviously much wider than these examples. But even if such efforts did not go beyond the realm of a more efficient exchange of information between the various institutions than currently takes place through the medium of the Council of Graduate

Schools, there is much useful work to be done. An investigation of the reasons behind most graduate students' need to take much longer to complete the doctorate than the five years assumed by most universities for funding purposes, for example, could lead to a valuable debate on the existing structure of the Ph.D. as well as the cost-effectiveness of admitting and half-supporting thousands of students who will never take their degrees.[21] Similarly, an inquiry into the relevance of the skills learned in graduate school to the tasks professors are actually required to carry out, especially in those institutions where research is not emphasized, might shed light on the utility of the doctorate as a teaching credential.[22] It is, of course, entirely possible that the conclusion ultimately extracted from studies like these will be that the current system is working well or that, however imperfect, it remains the best of all possible worlds. But armed with this knowledge, the postgraduate sector would be in a better position than at present to resist the depredations of downsizers, or at least to ensure that the voices of academics as well as accountants are heard when hard decisions have to be made.

Graduate schools have a dual mandate to be responsible to the institutions as well as the individuals they serve. As nurseries of the professoriate of the future, it is appropriate and requisite for them to concern themselves not only with the fate of their own graduates but the academic profession as a whole. The present moment seems an especially propitious time to examine how well its needs are being served in this regard.

ENDNOTES

[1]W. G. Bowen and J. A. Sosa, *Prospects for Faculty in the Arts and Sciences: A Study of Factors Affecting Demand and Supply, 1987 to 2012* (Princeton, N.J.: Princeton University Press, 1989).

[2]Ibid., 158.

[3]This figure is for 1995. R. B. Townsend, "Studies Report Mixed News for History Job Seekers," *Perspectives* 35 (3) (March 1997): 8.

[4]A distinct impression of universities being spoiled in terms of choice is conveyed by the lengthening list of desirable professional and personal characteristics that many employers now feel justified in demanding of potential employees. Thus one southern state institution, advertising a tenure-track

position in American history in 1995, required candidates to submit, *inter alia,* "documented evidence of collegiality."

[5]B. R. Parkes, *Essays on Women's Work,* 2d ed. (London: Strahan, 1866), 73.

[6]J. D. Milne, *Industrial and Social Position of Women in the Middle and Lower Ranks* (London: Chapman and Hall, 1857), 131.

[7]Ibid., 19–20.

[8]Even without purposeful action to increase enrollments, admissions to Ph.D. programs in the humanities rose significantly in the late 1980s and early 1990s. The most plausible explanation of this phenomenon is that holders of liberal-arts baccalaureate degrees, facing a constricted job market during these years, sought refuge from the recession in the graduate schools.

[9]National Research Council, *Research-Doctorate Programs in the United States: Continuity and Change,* ed. M. L. Goldberger, B. A. Maher, and P. E. Flattau (Washington, D.C.: National Academy Press, 1995), 714.

[10]R. G. Ehrenberg and P. G. Mavros, "Do Doctoral Student Financial Support Patterns Affect their Times-To-Degree and Completion Probabilities?" *Journal of Human Resources* 30 (3) (June 1995).

[11]For details of this shift in patterns of support, see W. G. Bowen and N. Rudenstine, *In Pursuit of the Ph.D.* (Princeton, N.J.: Princeton University Press, 1991), 91–98.

[12]A notable exception can be found at Washington University in St. Louis, which recently began to provide support for six years to all entrants to its doctoral program and to cap admissions at the number it could afford to maintain at this level. The results so far have been striking: a reduction of the mean time-to-degree from 9.8 to 7.4 years and a fall of 30 percent in the attrition rate after the first year. "'Small is Beautiful' for its Ph.D. Programs, Washington U. Decides," *Chronicle of Higher Education,* 21 March 1997.

[13]Of the twenty top-ranked history programs in the National Research Council's 1992 study, fourteen had mean times-to-degree lower than ten years. This was the case at only one of the bottom-ranked twenty. Goldberger, Maher, and Flattau, eds., *Research-Doctorate Programs in the United States,* 361, 364–365.

[14]"Survey Finds More Ph.D.'s, Less Success in Job Market," *Perspectives* 34 (4) (April 1996): 11–12.

[15]This "front-loading" of research expectations may also help explain why junior scholars are markedly less committed to the defense of tenure than their elders. In an environment in which a portfolio that might have sufficed to earn its holder consideration for tenure a decade ago is now merely the prerequisite for a realistic chance at a tenure-track position, the entire question is apt to take on an air of faint unreality.

[16]One would, for example, require an uncommon level of fortitude—or perhaps a private income—to contemplate a career in ancient history or American diplomatic history at the present time.

[17]Some institutions, it is true, do state in their regulations that Ph.D. candidates must demonstrate a satisfactory level of teaching ability before being permitted to graduate. But it is almost unheard of for students to be denied a degree on that ground alone. In some of this country's most prestigious graduate schools, moreover, Ph.D. candidates are neither required nor permitted to teach undergraduate courses.

[18]As always, it is possible to have too much of a good thing. A recent advertisement by a Midwestern public university optimistically invites applications from persons qualified to teach "advanced courses in Russian history and Europe since 1815, as well as Middle East and/or world history since 1945. . .[together with] world civilization and U.S. history introductory surveys, interdisciplinary general education courses, and classes for distance education." Another, at a four-year institution in the south, seeks individuals with "a Ph.D. in European history and qualifications for teaching British, European, Asian, African, and Latin American history."

[19]Professor Thomas D. Parker, Boston University, quoted in *American Demographics* 19 (1) (January 1997): 45.

[20]Such suggestions include measures to purge "dysfunctional" tenured faculty from the academy and the selection for closure (according to criteria that remain somewhat obscure) of existing doctoral programs as well as a ban on the creation of new ones. See C. Nelson, "Lessons from the Job Wars: What is to be Done?" *Academe* 81 (6) (November/December 1995).

[21]It is estimated that graduate students are, depending on the method of calculation, between three and six times as costly to the institutions training them as an equivalent number of undergraduates. B. R. Clark, *Places of Inquiry: Research and Advanced Education in Modern Universities* (Berkeley, Calif.: University of California Press, 1995), 150.

[22]A critique of the existing format of the research-doctorate has recently been offered in Louis Menand's "How To Make the Ph.D. Matter," *New York Times Magazine,* 22 September 1996. Whatever may be thought about the merits of his proposed reform—the reconstitution of the doctorate as a three-year taught degree—this is a question on which investigation and debate are long overdue.

The biggest changes since 1945 fall under the rubric of demographics: there is now a much larger and, more importantly, a far more diverse professoriate. Greater roles have been taken by women and African-American scholars in setting intellectual agendas, both in the domain of race and gender studies and more generally. Academic culture has in a sense been de-Europeanized. Although European ideas, models, and traditions remain predominant, even for those who challenge them, they are no longer transparent. They are interrogated and contextualized. The most energetic, even aggressive, work in literature, history, anthropology, and cinema studies is now exploring other cultures and the notions of "difference" and "otherness."

Although the culture wars continue, the theory wars have concluded. There are signs that a reengagement with history is underway, which promises a more dialogic (and fruitful) relation between theory and history in the humanities and social sciences. One sees this development in literature within the broad array of critical practices comprehended, some more historical than others, under the rubric "The New Historicism." In the social sciences, despite and to some degree in reaction to the imperial quest of rational-choice theorists for a simplified and unified social science, there is a renewed interest in institutional approaches and more complex models in economics and political science.

Thomas Bender

From "Politics, Intellect, and the
American University, 1945–1995"
Dædalus 126 (1) (Winter 1997)

Eugene Goodheart

Reflections on the Culture Wars

OVER ONE HUNDRED YEARS AGO, when the Industrial Revolution was transforming the face, if not the soul, of England, John Henry Newman delivered a set of lectures on *The Idea of a University* in which he characterized the habit of mind formed by a liberal education as one of "freedom, equitableness, calmness, moderation and wisdom."[1] For the post-Enlightenment mind, the progress of knowledge assumes the increasing specialization of the disciplines, a counterpart to the division of labor in the industrial sphere. Newman anticipated being called reactionary in advocating a reversal of the principle of the division of labor in defense of the liberal mind. For him, however, it was not a case of either/or. Without denying a place to the division of labor in the scholarly universe, he was properly fearful that the precious habit of mind formed by a liberal education would be lost in the triumph of the separate disciplines, and he was determined to champion its cause.

Specialization, particularly in the natural sciences, has accelerated since Newman's time, and the gulf between the sciences and the humanities is wider than ever. But that is not where the main threat to the liberal mind, now beset by its own internal conflicts, lies. It is not that disciplines do not speak to each other, as Newman feared. On the contrary, assumptions from one discipline often migrate to other disciplines and produce an interdisciplinary mind-set—like the assumptions that tradition and innovation are opposing forces and that objectivity is an illusion. Tradition has come to be seen as the dead hand of the past, an obstacle to the

---

Eugene Goodheart is E. M. Gross Professor of Humanities at Brandeis University.

153

acquiring of new knowledge. The case against the appeal to objectivity is more complicated. It reflects a view that each of us sees the world within the limitations of a particular point of view and that it is an imperializing presumption to claim that my or anyone else's view is objective truth. It follows then that the claim to objectivity often conceals the particular interest of a group (class, race, etc.) that controls or has controlled the way we know the world.

Against established ways of knowing, various identity groups have emerged. Hitherto marginally represented in society at large and in the academy (women, gays, blacks, and other constituencies), they have proposed new *theoretical* perspectives on matters of politics, social institutions, gender relationships, sexual preference, and the experience of literature. Theory itself has come to be identified with these new perspectives, and those who have resisted them have sometimes taken a position against theory. The real divisions or conflicts are not so much between disciplines as within the disciplines themselves. The subject of this essay is the battle being waged over assumptions like the ones mentioned above (tradition versus innovation, objectivism versus perspectivism), with the intention of casting a skeptical eye on the way the oppositions have been formulated. As I hope to show, the very terms with which the battles have been fought not only distort the issues at stake but guarantee that nothing fruitful can emerge from these battles.

I.

In *The Origins of Literary Study in America,* Gerald Graff and Michael Warner remind us that controversy has always been a vital part of academic life. What we have today is not controversy but war. The villains in this drama, Graff and Warner would have us believe, are traditional custodians of culture who foster a mystified "pastoral conception of the humanities as an 'overlay' of values which is to humanize the otherwise fallen realm of work and practical affairs.... It conveniently masks the fact that the humanities have always been a site of conflict and have never been immune to the incursions of industrialism."[2] In Graff and Warner's account, the traditionalists who hold this view become violent in their defense against the demystifiers. "What makes the current fulminations against the recent direction of literary studies so useless is that they are finally complaints about the presence of disagreement."[3] As the title of his recent book, *Beyond the Culture Wars,* tells us, Graff wants to get beyond warfare. Yet his own formulations reflect the pressures of combat. He favors the kind of debate that he says has characterized the profession of the humanities from its very beginnings and at the same time denies the validity of disagreement to those who conceive the profession differently. Are all the complaints against the demystifiers of the pastoral conception of the humanities "fulminations"? Could they not be described as disagreements? In Graff's scenario, to unmask the pastoral tradition is to disagree, to defend it is to fulminate. (I leave aside the question of whether "the pastoral conception of the humanities" is an accurate representation of the views of those who are the targets of demystification.)

"War" is somewhat hyperbolic with respect to events *within* the academy. The antitraditionalists have pretty much won the day. There are strong discontented academic voices, but they are a distinct and by no means united minority. I have in mind critics like Harold Bloom, Frank Kermode, and Robert Alter. The scholarly work in the new dispensation has become routine and, as we might expect, has lost some of the polemical edge that it had when in its insurgency. If there is war, it is being waged for the most part between those inside and those outside the academy. William Bennett, Dinesh D'Souza, and Hilton Kramer are among the nonacademics who attack the academy and are themselves objects of attack.

Graff and Warner are right to describe the current situation as one in which adversaries do not respectfully disagree with each other. "Fulmination" is not far off the mark in representing the tenor of many cultural encounters, but they are unfairly partisan in attributing the fulminations mainly to the conservative side. The fact is that cultural radicals as well as conservatives often substitute contempt for argument. Fruitful debate can occur only in an atmosphere of mutual respect between adversaries, and this can be achieved only when the arguments on either side deserve respect. It is not that one or another of the opposing views that define the current conflict (e.g., between universalists and multiculturalists, objectivists and anti-objectivists, defenders of the canon and critics of the canon) is intrinsically disreputable. There are admirable and less admirable expressions of each of the views. If the debate is to provide illumination, the antagonists must respond to the strongest possible formulations of their adversaries' views.

Graff characterizes stereotypically the older male professor's "defense of universality" as having "once put generations of students to sleep." In his illustration, the old male professor turns out to be a female nonprofessor, namely, Lynne Cheney, former head of the National Endowment for the Humanities, whose use of "threadbare phrases" such as "what it means to be human" or "to know joy and find purpose nonetheless; to be capable of wisdom and folly" can "become interesting again" only when they are "challenged by the likes of a young feminist professor."[4] Lynne Cheney's phrases may be threadbare, but in identifying these phrases with an argument for universalism, one is hardly doing justice to the possibilities of such an argument. Any serious quarrel with universalism must engage its most distinguished exponents: if not Plato, Descartes, and Kant, at least those in the intellectual tradition they inspired. A benefit of taking on a strong adversary is that your ideas may be challenged and strengthened in the process.

Another benefit is the discovery of the weaknesses and limitations of your own view. The encounter with a strong adversary becomes an exercise in self-criticism. In his essay on Coleridge, John Stuart Mill, the Benthamite, examines conservative social and political thought, not to affirm the superiority of liberalism, but to learn what conservativism in its most impressive formulation can teach liberals. The impulse in Mill to do so derived from his perception of a radical deficiency in the mind-set of his mentor. Bentham "failed in deriving light from other minds."[5] During his mental crisis, Mill became painfully aware of the limitations and inadequacies of his own understanding as well as of his emotional constitution. From this discovery, he concluded that self-criticism should be the basis for intellectual formation. Learning becomes a struggle with oneself, a willingness to think against oneself.

The very idea of a culture war is inimical to a model of education as self-criticism (for that is what Mill's essays on Bentham and Coleridge propose). A warrior acquires weapons to achieve victory. In the cultural sphere, the weapons of choice are words and ideas. The cultural warrior attends to the words and ideas of his adversaries, not to learn from them, but to discover those weaknesses that he can then exploit to his own advantage. Attack and defense becomes the dominant cultural style. The very formulation of the issues that divide adversaries guarantee that they will not listen to each other. Even Graff, who can be a generous and fair expositor of ideas, effectively disenfranchises the side to which he is not sympathetic by the way he states its basic terms.

Consider, for example, his conception of the opposing forces in the academy. On one side is a fixed tradition; on the other, innovation and novelty. "The modern university has from the very beginning rested on a deeply contradictory mission. The university is expected to preserve, to transmit and honor our traditions, yet at the same time it is supposed to produce new knowledge."[6] And elsewhere Graff and his collaborator Michael Warner speak of "the authority of tradition [as lying] in its being inherited rather than assembled through debate, its defining values as axiomatic. Historically, professional literary criticism has found itself between the opposing needs of constructing debatable hypotheses, on the one hand, and preserving a normative heritage, on the other."[7] The view that there is an inherent opposition between tradition and new knowledge (hence making the mission of the academy contradictory) rests upon the assumption that tradition is a fixed or petrified corpus and cannot be the source of new ideas.

In a recent article in *Civilization,* David Damrosch makes a similar distinction between "the preservation and transmission of culture" and "the production of knowledge," which until recently has corresponded to a distinction between the humanities and the sciences. Preservation and transmission are uncritically conflated so that transmission becomes a mere repetition of the past rather than what it is, a mediation of the past in the new circumstances of the present. Every mediation effects a change by giving the cultural past a new look, if it does not actually transform it, in which case the distinction between transmission and the production of knowledge collapses. Damrosch associates the production of knowledge with a "skeptical, analytic mode."[8] It is not clear how a respectful and even reverent interpretation of a text, for example, that adds to other interpretations is to be distinguished from a skeptical or analytic approach in terms of the production of knowledge. What is there in skepticism that is intrinsically the source of new knowledge? One can imagine a skepticism about new approaches that obstructs the advancement of knowledge.

The opposition between tradition and innovation is imported from the sciences, where ignorance of the achievements of the past does not constitute an obstacle to scientific discovery. The model of the sciences does not apply to the humanities, where discoveries are of a different order and where indeed discovery in the sense of "the production of new knowledge" may not be an apt characterization of humanistic study. As David Bromwich remarks, "Scholarly discovery in the humanities does now and then produce new knowledge. That is only one of the interesting things it does. It may also (by a fresh arrangement of facts) help to create the intuitions of a whole generation. And it may (by a stroke of interpretative acuteness) serve as a stimulus to further discovery or as an incitement to thinking."[9] It is something of an irony or paradox that the model of science should be imported into the humanities at a time when the scientific ideal of objective knowledge has become the object of a radically skeptical mistrust in the humanities.

Tradition entails both change and continuity. Within it, arguments occur about its meaning, and new conceptions of its significance arise. Neither the Marxist nor the Freudian tradition is a fixed legacy of the figure who inspired it. T. S. Eliot, the most conservative of modernists, understood the relationship between tradition and the individual talent as a dialectic between change and continuity. Even "making it new" already has a tradition, as Harold Rosenberg pointed out in an essay in which he coined the phrase "the tradition of the new." Tradition, as conceived by Graff and Damrosch, resembles the view attributed to William Bennett by Peter Brooks: "an inherited body of knowledge—itself embodying certain transcendent 'values'—which has assumed fixed form and should be preserved and transmitted, by teachers and scholars, with fidelity and reverence." Brooks, it seems to me, is much closer to the reality of tradition when he speaks of it as "a historically contingent, a historical culture formation, based on readings, interpretations, discriminations performed by people and cultural institutions in historical time." The view of tradition as fixed "represses the fact that traditions not only shape individual interpretations but are themselves the product of interpretation."[10]

If both sides were understood to have different stakes in tradition, the debate would take on a quite different cast. The cultural radical might find his own view enriched by attending to his tradition. The conservative would be compelled to affirm what is alive in his sense of tradition. Nothing new and worthwhile can be produced without having its source in some tradition. As Tzvetan Todorov puts it, "The goal of a humanist, liberal education is to form minds that are simultaneously tolerant and critical. The method employed to attain this goal is the mastery of a particular tradition."[11]

"Tradition" is not the only misunderstood term in the culture wars. Just as tradition has been opposed to innovation, objectivity has been set against perspectivism, with the first term representing a conservative view and the second term a radical or liberal view. Objectivists are universalists who affirm a common culture; perspectivists are multiculturalists who champion diversity. A stranger to the conflicts might find it odd that the cultural Left has identified itself with an anti-universalist view. It was after all one of the founders of modern conservatism, the reactionary Joseph DeMaistre, who said that "there is no such thing as *man* in the world. I have seen, during my life, Frenchmen, Italians, Russians, etc. But as far as *man* is concerned, I declare I have never in my life met him; if he exists, he is unknown to me."[12] Ideas of objectivity, universality, and commonality—the legacy of Enlightenment progressivism—have by an irony of history become objects of Leftist suspicion. They are seen as ideological masks to justify the particular interests of the dominant culture.

Anti-universalism, anti-objectivism, anti-essentialism are now the shibboleths of a movement, requiring no thought. "As with most colleagues I respect," writes a distinguished member of the profession, "my antis are impeccable: I am anti-foundationalist, anti-essentialist, anti-universalist, and I do not believe in the possibility of that view from nowhere that gets one beyond contingency."[13] This is an unreflective declaration of party affiliation. It is also a misconception of the adversary view. Foundationalism is not a matter of getting somewhere from nowhere. On the contrary, it is the anti-foundationalist who begins from nowhere. Apparently, respect for colleagues depends not upon their quality of mind but rather upon their position in the political-cultural spectrum. There is even an implication of disrespect for thinkers of the caliber of Descartes, Kant, and Chomsky. It should be noted that the anti-universalist view has not gone unchallenged on the Left. In his recent book, *The Twilight of Common Dreams: Why America is Wracked by Culture Wars,* Todd Gitlin points out the disastrous political and social consequences of a militant identity politics.

> For the Left as for the rest of America, the question is not whether to recognize the multiplicity of American groups, the variety of American communities, the disparity of American experiences. Those exist as long as people think they exist. The question is one of proportion. What is a Left without a commons, even a hypothetical one? If there is no people, but only peoples, there is no Left.[14]

I would emend the last sentence to say: there is no humanity.

The disreputable status of objectivity, as it plays itself out in the current debates, is in my view a result of the tendentious manner in which the term is understood. Even such a prized work as Peter Novick's *That Noble Dream: The "Objectivity Question" and the American Historical Profession* formulates "the question" in such a way that it becomes hard to understand how a sophisticated intellectual can subscribe to the objectivist view. Here is Novick's sympathetic description of the anti-objectivist challenge in the 1960s.

> In one field after another distinctions between fact and value and between theory and observation were called into question. For many, postures of disinterestedness and neutrality increasingly appeared as outmoded and illusory. It ceased to be axiomatic that the scholar's or scientist's task was to represent accurately what was "out there." Most crucially, and across the board, the notion of a determinate and unitary truth about the physical or social world, approachable if not ultimately reachable, came to be seen by a growing number of scholars as a chimera.[15]

Novick writes as a historian, and his account accurately reflects distinctions made by others, but he accepts them uncritically. Value-laden statements allow for objectivity. A person is not prevented from objectively pursuing injustice by his passion for justice. Disinterestedness in a judge is a means of rising above prejudice to discover the truth and administer justice. And one may believe in the possibility of objectivity without believing in "the notion of a determinate and unitary truth," just as one can be a perspectivist and hold the view that statements can be judged objectively from a particular point of view as true or false. (Perspectivism and objectivism are not necessarily opposed, as Novick suggests elsewhere in his book.[16]) Objectivity has unfortunately become the sign for a cluster of ideas (absolute or unitary truth, value-neutral fact, perspective-free observation) that is not entailed in the idea of objectivity.

The fact is that objectivity or the appeal to it is inescapable in any forum in which ideas are argued and debated.[17] If that were not the case, the intellectual enterprise would be impossible. Since disagreements could never be overcome by an appeal to fact or reason, why would one bother to engage in reasoned debate? (Novick himself implicitly claims objectivity for himself when in his introduction he speaks of his "even-handedness" and "detachment," as he must if he means to be persuasive.[18]) The anti-objectivist view begins with the truth that objectivity is difficult to attain; it leaps illicitly to the conclusion that it is an impossible and undesirable ideal, undesirable because objectivity is confused with the authoritarian implications of absolute truth. This is a paradoxical conclusion in light of the fact that the suppression of the search for objective truth is a feature of tyranny. The rulers of Oceania in George Orwell's *1984* perpetuate their rule by denying potential rebels and dissidents access to the facts of both the past and the present that would expose the lies and corruption of the rulers. The truth of Orwell's insight into the connection between objective knowledge and freedom is, of course, confirmed not only by the most egregious examples (Nazi Germany and the Soviet Union) but by tyrannies everywhere. One can only speculate about the insensitivity of postmodern theory, the theory of the cultural Left, to this fact. Could it be that the very freedom of our society makes it possible for it to be taken for granted and for a condition of that freedom to be disparaged?

I am sure that Richard Rorty, the most forceful contemporary philosopher of the anti-objectivist view, would quarrel with my account of it. As a passionate advocate of solidarity, he appreciates the need for common understanding and would substitute intersubjectivity for objectivity. "[W]e deny that the search for objective truth is a search for correspondence to reality, and urge that it be seen instead as a search for the widest possible intersubjective agreement."[19] And how would this agreement be achieved without having recourse to objective appeals to reality when necessary? The subject of the essay from which I have just quoted is academic freedom and its philosophical suppositions. "Philosophers on my side of the argument think that if we stop trying to give epistemological justifications, and instead give sociopolitical justifications, we shall be both more honest and more clearheaded. We think that disinterested, objective inquiry would not only survive the adoption of our philosophical views but survive in a desirably purified form."[20]

I am not sure what it means to give "sociopolitical justifications," apart from displaying your party credentials to the like-minded and demonstrating how your words and actions serve a particular cause. How this would serve disinterested, objective inquiry is not at all clear. Given Rorty's view that objectivity is an illusion, it seems intellectually irresponsible to appropriate its language for his view and then to assert that he has purified objectivism, when in fact he has undermined it. (Rorty's idea of social-political justification is a benign version of Foucault's idea of knowledge and power as seamlessly connected. Unlike Rorty, Foucault dispenses with the idea of disinterestedness altogether.)

I am less concerned to score points against Rorty than to show how difficult, if not impossible, it is for even the most persuasive of anti-objectivists to escape the claim of objectivism. Instead of confronting the claim, they avoid or displace it from the question of how we know the world to struggle politically. Here is Evelyn Fox Keller agreeing with Rorty:

> Rorty is right: invocations of epistemology are beside the point; indeed, they are simultaneously misleading and counterproductive. The crisis we face today is real enough, but it has far less to do with arguments about the locus or status of ontological Truth than it has to do with current social, political, and economic realities. Terms like "objectivity" and "PC" have become weapons in the social, political, and economic struggles in which we are all embedded.[21]

Though Keller wants to get beyond the culture wars, her very formulation of the issues is a contribution to the combat. By capitalizing Truth, she illicitly identifies the objectivist conceptions with absolutist views of truth. By enclosing "objectivity" and

"PC" in quotation marks, she makes clear who the culprits are. There is no acknowledgment in the passage that the words enclosed in quotation marks may be weapons on the other side. She does acknowledge that she is embedded in the struggles but gives little indication about what part she plays.

Postmodernism is the covering name given to identity politics (the politics of race, gender, sexual preference, and class). Perspectivism (that is to say, anti-objectivist, anti-universalist theory) provides its epistemological basis, but it claims to be more than a particular theory. Having inherited the authority of theory from poststructuralism (in particular, deconstruction), postmodernist advocates construe all attacks on their cultural theory as attacks upon theory itself. Here again we have a case of a tendentious formulation of the issue.

But first we need to acknowledge the truth in the charge. Some critics write from a bias against theory, a bias that goes as far back as Matthew Arnold, who mistrusted all systematic thinking in the humanities and emphasized the importance of flexibility and suppleness in the exercise of the critical intelligence. For T. S. Eliot, the one needful thing was intelligence, and F. R. Leavis toward the end of a long career that was decidedly hostile to theoretical reflection about literature finally found what might be called an antitheoretical theory congenial to his own views. The work of Michael Polanyi, mediated through Marjorie Grene, gave Leavis what he wanted— a conception of knowledge (Polanyi called it "tacit") that allowed for the play of intuition in criticism.

The current heirs of Arnold, Eliot, and Leavis tend to be English critics like Denis Donoghue and Christopher Ricks, who advocate the cultivation of theory-free reading zones in which the local pleasures and meanings of the text become manifest.[22] But in our theoretical age, even they cannot avoid a confrontation with theory. As the theorists legitimately claim, no one can perform, whether consciously or not, an intellectual task without assumptions and implications that have a theoretical bearing. Even Leavis felt obliged to reflect about what he was doing as a critic. This of course does not mean that critics are obliged to subscribe to a theory, or, as one says nowadays, "theorize" the practical work that they do. They may legitimately want to resist a theoretical formulation of their work to preserve a sense of freedom, flexibility, and complexity. A *conscious* employment of theory can be stultifying; what distinguishes an untheoretical criticism is the personal voice of the critic, assuming of course that the critic has a personality. Postmodern theory, disbelieving in the integrity of the subject (i.e., the self), has effectively exorcised the personal voice. The postmodern critic enters a discourse in which his prose becomes stylistically indistinguishable from other practitioners of the discourse. It is the discourse, not the person, that writes.

Not all critics of current theory are hostile to theory per se. What some find distressing is the lack of sophistication and rigor in the theorizing and an obscurantist idiom that often conceals it. Writing apropos of the Sokal affair (in which a physicist at New York University, Alan Sokal, submitted an article on science that parodied the idiom of postmodern theory to editors of a postmodern journal, *Social Text,* who took it seriously enough to publish), the philosophers Paul Boghosian and Thomas Nagel deplore "the sloppy and naive quality of what passes for philosophical argument and. . .the central role that such argument has been meant to play."[23] Apparently it is enough for a writer to use the jargon of a particular ideological discourse fluently to impress the community of discoursers that something is being said—or at least to prevent them from seeing through the nonsense. The Sokal affair also exposed the embarrassing bad faith of the postmodern editors of *Social Text,* who placed on Sokal the responsibility for their failure to tell the difference between a genuine work of scholarship and a parody of it. The real issue for philosophical critics like Boghosian and Nagel has to do not with whether "doing theory" is worthwhile but with the value of what passes for theory. For them the question is not whether to theorize or not to theorize; they are questioning the character and quality of the theory.

The culture wars have been largely waged within the provinces of the humanities and, to a lesser extent, the social sciences—over different conceptions of the disciplines. The problem of miscomprehension between science and the humanities, addressed by C. P. Snow in his little book on *The Two Cultures* decades ago, has undergone a significant development. Snow argued that humanists were woefully ignorant of and indifferent to scientific knowledge. Postmodern theorists, as if in belated response to Snow, have renewed the science/humanities conflict by calling into question fundamental tenets of scientific knowledge—the possibility of objective knowledge and its progressive character. On the one hand, "science studies" under postmodern sponsorship try to undermine what the postmoderns see as the complacency of the scientific community about the objective and progressive character of scientific knowledge. On the other hand, scientists and philosophers of science have been provoked both by anti-objectivist arguments and by the crudity of their formulation. Often obscurantist, postmodern rhetoric asserts the impossibility of objective truth (lower- as well as uppercase) without the fine-grained engagement with the issues that mark the work of professional philosophers trained in the analytic school. Postmodernist theories have been largely unchallenged because *rigor* in theorizing is not sufficiently cultivated within the humanities, so it is always a salutary event when those who have some knowledge about theory making respond to the theories.

The effect of misleading and tendentious formulations of the issues is to disenfranchise one side or another from the debate by making it impossible to say certain things that should be said. This is particularly the case in matters that are more directly political than epistemological. For instance, ideology critics have a field day exposing colonialist motives and motifs in texts and institutions. Those who wish to defend these texts and institutions are at a distinct disadvantage. Who would want to defend a demystified imperialism? The usual tack is to deflect the charge of imperialism by denying its presence or relevance or minimizing its significance. What is off-limits is any effort to show the benefits of colonialism. I recall a meeting with a Marxist-leaning Indian foreign exchange professor where he expressed contempt for Western scholars of what is called subaltern studies, who regularly denounce imperialism and its legacy in India and elsewhere without knowing the actual facts. It was the Brahmins, not the English colonialists, who maintained the caste system; it was the English colonizers who created educational opportunities for the Untouchables. According to this Indian professor, the departure of the English did not improve the lot of the Untouchables or, for that matter, those on the lower rungs of the caste system. On the contrary, their conditions have worsened. Truth is not served in denying the facts, nor is imperialism served in expressing them.

How did the current situation arise? The story has been told again and again of the sixties radicals who established themselves in the academy in the seventies and eighties and transformed their activism into theories of interpretation. Having lost the political battles in the early seventies (the general society and its politics grew increasingly conservative), they transferred their energies to the academic arena. Texts in the humanities became the terrain on which political battles were to be fought. Literary works were now read not for their artfulness or wisdom but for their ideological motives.

The opposition in the academy proved to be less formidable than the conservative force of society in general and its political structures. The intellectual and moral passion that had created the New Criticism, for example, was spent, and scholars of English literature were running out of subjects. Structuralism, deconstruction, and ideology critique focusing on race, gender, and class generated a new energy and excitement in the academy. It encountered little opposition because the scholarly establishment lacked the conviction of the insurgents. What I am describing did not occur everywhere in the academy. I suspect that many institutions of higher learning in the country did not experience an academic transformation and that there are still places where the older traditions of teaching prevail. But the transformation did take place in the leading institutions that have a disproportionate influence not only on academic but also on cultural life generally. Occurrences at Yale or Johns Hopkins or Duke capture the attention of the mass media and shape the perceptions of a large section of the population about what is occurring in the academy.

What explains intellectual intolerance in and outside the academy is the politicization of academic discourse. If politics occupies the entire space of discourse, you are no longer required to persuade others of the rightness of your views by appealing to reason (i.e., logic and evidence). Indeed, you cannot hope to persuade the other side because of the assumption that what determines the opposing view are interests, hidden or open, that are not amenable to reason. Intellectual exchanges become disdainful rhetorical encounters in which each side affirms itself without the prospect of common agreement. Differences between the like-minded can be adjudicated (i.e., among cultural conservatives or among cultural radicals); but between opposing sides reasonable exchange is very difficult, if not impossible, precisely because "sociopolitical" rather than "epistemological justification" (Rorty's phrases) is the order of the day. Academic intellectuals are no longer required to justify knowledge; they need only tell us what they believe.

II.

In my own discipline of literary studies, ideology critique rules the roost. It is a species of the hermeneutics of suspicion and one of the sources of the culture war. There is nothing more aggressive than the effort to demystify the supposed illusions of others. As I have written previously, "Real debate or dialogue becomes impossible, because the ground between demystifier and antagonist is not the problematic nature of truth [or an uncertainty about where the truth lies], but the difference between truth and illusion. The person who claims to know the truth and is *certain* that others with an opposing view are the captives of illusion is a potential despot."[24] Here is a paradox: those who possess this certainty about the illusions of others usually call themselves anti-foundationalists, anti-essentialists, and anti-universalists. And they are suspicious of all claims to objectivity. So where does their certainty about the mystifications of others come from? Apparently from a conviction about the moral superiority of their side in the cultural and political struggles. If mystification conceals motives of domination, then the moral task of criticism is to unmask these motives.

Unlike perspectivists who tend toward skepticism about all claims to objectivity, ideology critics equivocate on the question of objectivity. They would claim it for their demystifications but at the same time share with perspectivists a sensitivity to the partiality and self-interestedness of all points of view. Ideology critique can be a valuable activity if it knows its limits, discriminating between what requires and what does not require demystification. In contemporary practice in the academy, it has become an imperial obsession with disastrous consequences.

One casualty of this obsession in literary study is the virtual disappearance of the practice of aesthetic criticism. Even some scholars who ally themselves with the ideology critics share a sense of loss or discomfort. Here is the testimony of George Levine in an introduction to a book entitled *Aesthetics and Ideology:*

> This book and this introduction have required that I face directly my own anxieties about what my passion for literature will seem like to the critical culture with which I want to claim alliance.... Beginning this book with the language of the affective, the sublime, the aesthetic, I hoped to rescue from the wreckage of the mystified ideal of the beautiful the qualities that allowed for such rich ambivalences. Eliot is anti-Semitic and worse. Arnold is both statist and snob. I wouldn't be without the writings of either of them. That, I recognize, puts me and this book under suspicion.[25]

The passage, I think, reveals more than Levine intends. What are we to make of allies who suspect the motives of a literary critic who employs the language of the affective, the sublime, the aesthetic? Levine's "anxieties" about taking an aesthetic stance in the presence of his ideologically motivated colleagues are so strong that he cannot avoid compromising his formulations about a "very small breathing space [why very small?] of free play and disinterest"[26] to the point of virtually conceding the futility of the effort.

> There must be a distinction between aspiration to some impossible ideal disinterested stance, and the effort to resist, in certain situations, the political thrust of one's own interests in order—in these situations—to keep open to new knowledge of alternative possibilities and to avoid the consequences of simple partisanship.... Even if the Arnoldian and Bloomian ideal of intellectual free space is merely utopian and ultimately a mystifying and disguise of actual power, the notion that the university is not or should not try to be fundamentally different from partisan political institutions is merely absurd.[27]

One might wonder to the contrary: Is it not absurd to try to rise above the fray (i.e., "partisan political institutions") if the ideal of intellectual free space is mystification? If you wish to make a case for an aspiration to disinterestedness, it is self-defeating to characterize the object of the effort as "impossible," "ultimately mystifying," and a "disguise of actual power."

This is the place to say something about the contentious phrase "political correctness." Quarrels abound about whether it exists, the extent to which it exists, its content if indeed it does exist, and to whom it applies. My understanding of PC is that it does not or should not apply to the content of a position or theory but rather to the way it is expressed. Evelyn Fox Keller is right to resist the "easy invocation of PC as shorthand for postmodernism, social constructionism, feminism and multiculturalism,"[28] for it is possible for those who adhere to these doctrines to be open to criticism and to refrain from imposing their views on others. It is also true that those who attack postmodernism may have their own brand of political correctness that they seek to impose on others. Neoconservative critics often display a close-minded vehemence that belies their claim to disinterestedness. Extreme versions of a doctrine on whatever side of the cultural or political spectrum tend to breed an ethos of political correctness, and their effect may be disproportionate to their actual constituency. These versions have a way of haunting moderate and reasonable expressions of, for instance, postmodernism, as Levine's anxieties suggest.

Political correctness implies intimidation, for it places the offender outside the pale. Of course, it is always possible that the experience of PC is illusory and paranoiac, that it does not correspond to the facts of the case. But the evidence seems compelling when those with sympathy for a particular view find problems with it and experience fear or anxiety that they may offend those who hold the view unambivalently.

What is remarkable about a number of the essays in the Levine anthology is the defensiveness with which the claim of the aesthetic is articulated. Ideological suspicion haunts even the best of the essays. Thus Peter Brooks in a fine essay entitled "What Happened to Poetics?" cites a passage from a prominent New Historicist in which he asks literary scholars to make a choice between two models of study: "Critical research and teaching in the Humanities may be either a merely academic displacement or a genuine academic instantiation of oppositional social and political praxis." Brooks's response is admirable, but not unexceptionable.

> The terms in which the choice is posed create a kind of academic melodrama, of the disempowered professional wimp versus the macho resistance hero. Even if we want to align ourselves with the latter, and want to refuse definitively the notion of the critic as a

genteel belated Victorian preaching sweetness and light, we may find that his version of the choice plays into the hands of our enemies, and seriously undermines our ability to speak of literature with any particular qualifications for doing so.[29]

The contrast of styles between Brooks and the New Historicist alone should make it clear whom we are to trust. There is little to add to Brooks's incisive characterization of the false choices posed. But it is dismaying that the incisiveness is marred by a wholly unnecessary concessiveness—"even if we want to align ourselves with the latter [the macho resistance hero]." Why, after what Brooks shows us to be false in the New Historicist's formulation, should we want to align ourselves with the latter? And why the concern about "playing into the hands of our enemies"? In citing a different passage from the same hapless critic, Brooks remarks that "one senses that this is material to hide from the eyes of such as Lynne Cheney or Hilton Kramer or Dinesh D'Souza, or other recent critics of the academic humanities, since it so readily confirms their intemperate view that the academy has become a conspiracy of aging Sixties radicals made only slightly dangerous by the fact that their prose can't shoot straight." If it confirms their view, how intemperate is it? This is culture war anxiety.

It may seem captious and ungrateful for me to fault Brooks for what is generally an excellent essay. But it is precisely Brooks's excellence as a critic that makes the reader wonder about the allies he has chosen. There are reasons for him not to associate himself with Cheney, Kramer, and D'Souza, but what are his reasons for allying himself with the crude demystifiers of the aesthetic? With such friends, who needs enemies? (Levine, as I have shown, seems caught in a similar bind.) The only explanation can be that in a state of war one feels that one must choose sides, and there are apparently only two sides to choose from.

The quarrel or tension between ideology and aesthetics bears directly on the possibility of objectivity, for aesthetics in its classic formulation (e.g., Shaftesbury, Kant, Schiller) makes a claim for disinterestedness. As Jerome Stolnitz remarks, summarizing the aesthetic tradition, we perceive beauty when it is the object of a "disinterested and sympathetic attention. . .and contemplation for its own sake alone [as in] 'the look of the rock,' the sound of the ocean, the colors in the painting."[30] Ideology critics have challenged the claim of disinterestedness on grounds that have to be taken seriously. If all our activities are interest-driven, the plausible view of Nietzche and William James among others, we cannot at the very least be complacent about assuming the existence of disinterestedness. But again we have the problem of how the issue is formulated. What do we mean by interest and disinterest? Ideology critics tend to see interest in its class or group-bound sense as serving the self or the constituency of which the self is a part. But interest can also be directed toward the cause of justice and the interests of humanity and in that sense can be conceived as aspiring to a value-laden disinterestedness. Disinterestedness, understood in this way, is uncommon, but possible.

In construing interest in the narrow self-interested sense, the ideology critics focus on the social, political, and economic conditions in which certain views arise. The question then becomes what to make of a knowledge of those conditions. Does it demystify the aesthetic theory of Shaftesbury to know that it arose out of a sense of personal "displacement" and "self-division" following upon the English Revolution?

> Henceforth it would be impossible for nobles to inhabit an aristocratic *Lebensform* regarded in the old, pre-seventeenth-century way as altogether natural, normative and problematic.
>
> Such nobles as Shaftesbury, whose family had risen to power and eminence on the dangerously volatile currents of the Restoration, would thereafter occupy a sphere of contingency and human construction where their status, titles, and house of assembly would conceivably be abolished anew, where the nobles recognize themselves at a deep level as now suffering the sufferance of the people.[31]

This passage describes the circumstances in which Shaftesbury conceived a utopia of aesthetic contemplation, freed of the contingencies of [his] social existence; it does not discredit his ideas. It may be true, as the writer of the passage argues, that "Shaftesbury's double displacement first of the political onto the ethical and then of the ethical onto the aesthetic would effectively obscure in later years the ideological role of his writing in assisting to legitimate the Whig consensual polity."[32] But Shaftesbury's work influenced the work of Kant, Schiller, and the Victorian social critics (it informs Arnold's conception of culture) and cannot be *reduced* to "Whig consensual polity."

I have cited Linda Dowling, whose short and excellent book *The Vulgarization of Art: The Victorians and Aesthetic Democracy* (an essay of only one hundred pages) exemplifies what is admirable, but rare, in ideological interpretation. Her account of the conditions under which aesthetic ideas arise illuminates their motives but does not cause her to prejudge the value of those ideas. Her view of the ideas themselves is complex. She appreciates their character as a moral critique of the constitution of society, particularly in her discussion of Schiller's *On an Aesthetic Education of Man.* Her engagement with the ideas is philosophical rather than ideological when, for instance, she follows Alasdair MacIntyre in his view of how Shaftesbury's "rejection. . .of the traditional Aristotelian ideas concerning the essential nature and telos of human beings [and his reliance on 'the natural passions of the individual'] makes it henceforth impossible to supply anything like a traditional account of the virtues."[33] Dowling's work, influenced by current ideological concerns in the academy, displays the possibility of disinterestedness that is the occasion for her discussion.

There are lessons to be drawn from her account of the aesthetic tradition. From its very beginnings, there has been a tension between its emphasis on distinction (hence its elitism) and its ambition to become the spiritual basis of democracy, an expression of the *sensus communis,* in Shaftesbury's phrase. This tension is evident in Arnold's aristocratic conception of cultural distinction, on the one hand, and his view of culture as a force that wishes "to do away with classes," on the other. Arnold wanted to democratize society on his high cultural terms. But democracy cannot exist without the consent of the people, who are formed by a mass culture and who may not be "in communication with the realm of transcendental value"[34] where beauty can be found or who may find beauty in sources other than the transcendental realm (popular culture, for instance). If the aesthetic sense is to have the power not only to express beauty but transform social reality (Schiller's view), it can only do so with the consent of the people, otherwise it would become another form of tyranny. We in the academy are the heirs to this unresolvable tension, which may not be an undesirable condition so long as we understand that it cannot be resolved. The canon will always be under pressure, at once resistant and accommodating to change. The danger arises when the tension turns into a war in which adversaries try to resolve it one way or the other.

So long as this tension remains unresolved, debate will persist. I do not foresee (nor do I think desirable) a return to a time, largely imaginary, when the professional imperative was the contemplation of the aesthetic qualities of a work of art, exclusive of political, historical, and moral considerations—of the sort recently advocated by Harold Bloom in *The Western Canon.* But I would hope to see a recovery of the practice of aesthetic criticism as well as a more generous conception of what constitutes politics and history in the literary academy. Right now political and historical perspectives tend to be the possession of the cultural Left.

Politics in and of art need not be the object of the demystifier's eye, searching for motives of domination. In our democratic age we should be able to appreciate what is valuable in the imagination of an aristocratic conception of life in the works of the ancient Greek poets or the spiritual aspirations in the religious imaginations of Dante and Milton. It is not history or politics that is inimical to the artistic imagination but tendentious and impoverished conceptions of history and politics.

We should also be able to recover an idea of culture that provides a vantage point to criticize what is corrupt and degraded in contemporary political and social life. The new discipline of cultural studies promotes ideological criticism of what is seen as the pretensions of high culture. The cause of high culture has been largely taken up by neoconservatives outside the academy whose stridency often gives it a sectarian coloration that compromises its spirit. Left and Right provoke stridency in each other. Robert Hughes neatly sums up the current situation: "Radical academic and cultural conservatives are now locked in a full-blown, mutually sustaining *folie a deux,* and the only person each dislikes more than the other is the one who tells them both to lighten up."[35]

* * *

The argument in this essay represents an ongoing effort on my part to reenfranchise certain ideas that have become disreputable in the humanities: objectivity, disinterestedness, tradition, and aesthetic appreciation. I think their loss of credit is a misfortune for the academy. They are or should be the common possession of scholars of whatever political or cultural persuasion—Left, Right, or Center—which is not to say that it is a bad thing for these ideas to have been put under the kind of pressure that forces a reformulation and strengthening of them. To agree on their necessity in intellectual exchange is not to agree about everything, but it may create the possibility of overcoming the current academic Balkanization in which one seeks the comfort zone of the like-minded or prepares to do battle with the enemy.

ENDNOTES

[1]John Henry Newman, "Knowledge Its Own End" in John Henry Newman, *The Idea of a University* (London: B. M. Pickering, 1852).

[2]Gerald Graff and Michael Warner, *The Origins of Literary Study in America* (New York: Routledge, 1989), 8.

[3]Ibid., 13.

[4]Gerald Graff, *Beyond the Culture Wars: How Teaching the Conflicts Can Revitalize American Education* (New York: Norton, 1992), 52.

[5]John Stuart Mill, "Bentham," in Gertrude Himmelfarb, ed., *Essays on Politics and Culture* (Gloucester, Mass.: Petersmith, 1973), 92.

[6]Graff, *Beyond the Culture Wars,* 7.

[7]Graff and Warner, *The Origins of Literary Study in America,* 11–12.

[8]David Damrosch, "A Past We Can Live With," *Civilization* (April-May 1997): 77.

[9]David Bromwich, *Politics By Other Means: Higher Education and Group Thinking* (New Haven, Conn.: Yale University Press, 1992), 106.

[10]Peter Brooks, "What Happened to Poetics?" in George Levine, ed., *Aesthetics and Ideology* (New Brunswick, N.J.: Rutgers University Press, 1994), 11.

[11]Tzvetan Todorov, "Crimes Against Humanities," *The New Republic* (3 July 1989): 30.

[12]See Stephen Holmes, *The Anatomy of Antiliberalism* (Cambridge, Mass.: Harvard University Press, 1993), 14.

[13]Levine, ed., *Aesthetics and Ideology,* 11.

[14]See Todd Gitlin, *The Twilight of Common Dreams* (New York: Metropolitan Books, Henry Holt & Co., 1995).

[15]Peter Novick, *That Noble Dream: The "Objectivity Question" and the American Historical Profession* (New York: Cambridge University Press, 1988), 523.

[16]See ibid., 596.

[17]See Alan B. Spitzer, *Historical Truth and Lies About the Past* (Chapel Hill, N.C.: University of North Carolina Press, 1996).

[18]Novick, *That Noble Dream,* 12, 14.

[19]Richard Rorty, "Does Academic Freedom Have Philosophical Presuppositions?" in Louis Menand, ed., *The Future of Academic Freedom* (Chicago, Ill.: University of Chicago Press, 1996), 21.

[20]Ibid., 27.

[21]Evelyn Fox Keller, "Science and Its Critics," in ibid., 211.

[22]See Denis Donoghue, "The Joy of Texts," review of *The Pleasures of Reading in an Ideological Age,* by Robert Alter. *The New Republic,* 26 June 1989, 17.

[23]*Lingua Franca* (July/August 1996): 60.

[24]Eugene Goodheart, *The Reign of Ideology* (New York: Columbia University Press, 1996), 19.

[25]Levine, ed., *Aesthetics and Ideology,* 11.

[26]Ibid.

[27]Ibid., 14.

[28]Keller, "Science and Its Critics," in Menand, ed., *The Future of Academic Freedom,* 204.

[29]Brooks, "What Happened to Poetics?" in Levine, ed., *Aesthetics and Ideology,* 158.

[30]Jerome Stolnitz, *Aesthetics and the Philosophy of Art Criticism* (Boston, Mass.: Houghton Mifflin, 1960), 34–35.

[31]Linda Dowling, *The Vulgarization of Art: The Victorians and Aesthetic Democracy* (London and Charlottesville, Va.: University of Virginia Press, 1996), 4.

[32]Ibid., 13.

[33]Ibid., 10.

[34]Ibid., 61.

[35]Robert Hughes, *The Culture of Complaint: The Fraying of America* (New York: Oxford University Press, 1993), 79.

At the other end of our disciplinary spectrum, in English literature, M. H. Abrams also recalls his prewar Harvard education and uses it as a baseline for charting the transformation of his discipline. In the eclectic undergraduate courses of the 1930s, a loose historicism prevailed, sometimes arid, sometimes rich and rewarding in individual perspectives. It was the graduate program, however, that left young Abrams most dissatisfied. It was freighted with two anachronistic legacies of the nineteenth century's aspirations to *Wissenschaftlichheit*: on the one hand, historical linguistics and positivistic philology ("distinctly unexciting"); on the other, a false comprehensiveness, and excessive demand for "coverage" of the history of English literature. Abrams directs our attention, however, to what was absent from the offerings in English literature: any focus on criticism. Only one lone voice at Harvard—that of an outsider to the university, I. A. Richards—raised the claims of critical analysis as the central task of literary study. Abrams never became an orthodox adherent of the New Criticism that came to power in English departments in the 1950s. Yet his pathbreaking work, though historical, was a history of *criticism*—the subject he felt to be most lacking in Harvard's English department in the 1930s. His book, *The Mirror and the Lamp*, mediated that passage from philological and positivistic historical scholarship to the primacy of criticism in literary study that marked the postwar years.

Carl Schorske

From "The New Rigorism in the
Human Sciences, 1940–1960"
Dædalus 126 (1) (Winter 1997)

Charles Bernstein

A Blow Is Like an Instrument

I shall not see—and don't I know 'em?
A critic lovely as a poem.
> —*Dorothy Parker*

LAST SPRING I WENT TO A TALK by Stanley Cavell at Books & Company in New York City (just a few months before that great independent bookstore permanently closed its doors). A crowd of perhaps fifty people gathered in the upstairs space of the store to hear the distinguished philosopher talk about Hollywood melodramas of a bygone era. The question period that followed Cavell's initial presentation was characterized by a mix of erudition and over-the-top enthrallment in these films, both by Cavell and the audience members. While I had seen some of the films being discussed, I had only the haziest recollection of any of the details being pored over by the group, as if they were a familiar part of a shared culture of those participating—a culture I also shared with them, but had fallen out of, at least to a degree. Toward the end, someone asked Cavell to talk about *Platinum Blonde,* and in the course of his remarks he noted that in the film Marlene Dietrich sings both in a gorilla costume and in a white tuxedo; he said that one of the questions the film raised is whether the Dietrich figure could appear in these ways and still be taken for a responsible mother. I heard this question as reflecting on what Cavell himself—this year's president of the professional organization of academic philosophers—was doing: Can you do philoso-

---

Charles Bernstein is David Gray Professor of Poetry and Letters and Professor of English and Comparative Literature at the University at Buffalo, State University of New York.

177

phy in a gorilla suit or a white tuxedo and still be responsible to the profession and to the activity of philosophy (which is not the same thing)?

Stanley Cavell is no guerrilla warrior in the trenches of the canon wars. And his suits, while tailored, tend to be blue or gray. Nonetheless, what counts for him as an activity of philosophy, at least in this instance, is barely recognizable in terms of the ostensible subject matter of his talk. Because what is philosophical about his project is not the content but his mode of thinking, by which I don't mean a set of philosophical issues that he applies to a discussion of the subject but rather an attitude of inquiry, a manner of listening, a mode of recognizing what is significant and proceeding from there to identifying networks of significance. So the answer to the question "Can philosophy still be philosophy if it is performed in a gorilla suit or a white tuxedo?" is that philosophy can only be philosophy if it acknowledges the suits it is wearing and also that these suits are not (only) what are issued to us in central casting but (also) ones that we fashion and refashion ourselves.

There are no core subjects, no core texts in the humanities, and this is the great democratic vista of our mutual endeavor in arts and letters, the source of our greatest anxiety and our greatest possibilities. In literary studies, it is not enough to show what has been done but what it is possible to do. Art works are not just monuments of the past but investments in the present, investments we squander with our penurious insistence on taking such works as cultural capital rather than as capital expenditure. For the most part, our programs of Great Books amount to little more than lip service to an idea of Culture that is encapsulated into tokens and affixed to curricular charm bracelets to be taken out at parties for display—but never employed in the workings of our present culture. Ideas are dead except when in use. And for use you don't need a preset list of ideas or Great Works; almost any will do if enactment, not prescription, is the aim.

I often teach works that raise, for many students, some of the most basic questions about poetry: What is poetry? How can this work be a poem? How and what does it mean? These are not questions that I especially want to talk about nor ones that the works at hand continue to raise for me. Whatever questions I may have of this sort I have either resolved or put aside as I listen for quite different, much more particular, things. My own familiarity with the poetry I teach puts me at some distance from most students, who are coming to this work for the first time. And yet when I overcome my resistance and engage in the discussion, which I often find becomes contentious and emotional, I am reminded that when a text is dressed in the costume of poetry, that (in and of itself) is a provocation to consider these basic questions of language, meaning, and art. Inevitably, raising such questions is one of the uses of the poetry to which I am committed—that is, poetry marked by its aversion to conformity, to received ideas, to the expected or mandated or regulated form. These aversions and resistances have their history. They are never entirely novel nor free of traditions, including the traditions of the new; that history is nothing less than literary history. But the point of literary history is not just that a selected sequence of works was created, nor that they are enduring or great (or deplorable and hideous), nor that they form part of a cultural fabric of that time or a tradition that extends to the present. All that is well and good, but aesthetically secondary. The point, that is, is not (not *just*) the transcendental or cultural or historical or ideological or psychoanalytic deduction of a work of art but how that work plays itself out; its performance, not (just) its interpretation. But as history is written by the victors, so art (as a matter of professional imperatives) is taught by the explainers.

It need not be so, for we are professors and not deducers: our work is as much to promote as to dispel, to generate as much as document. I am not—I know it sounds as if I am—professing the virtue of art over the deadness of criticism, but rather the aversion of virtue that is a first principle of the arts and an inherent, if generally discredited, possibility for the humanities.

I suspect part of the problem may lie in the way that a certain idea of philosophy as critique, rather than art as practice, has been the model for the best defense of the university. I don't say critique as opposed to aesthetics, but critique without aesthetics—that is, the sort of institutionalized critique that dominates the American university—is empty, a shell game of Great Books and Big Methods, full of solutions and cultural capital, signifying nothing.

While I lament the lack of cultural and historical information on the part of students, I also lament the often proud ignorance of contemporary culture on the part of the faculty. Poetry and the arts are living entities in our culture. It is not enough to know the work of a particular moment in history, removed from the context of our contemporary culture; such knowledge risks being transmitted stillborn. Just as we now insist that literary works need to be read in their sociohistorical context, so we must also insist that they be read into the present aesthetic context.

I do not suggest that the (contemporary) practice of poetry should eclipse literary history (as, for a time, the contemporary practice of analytic philosophy eclipsed the history of philosophy). I do believe, however, that literary history or theory that is uninformed by the newly emerging forms of poetic practice (which is a professional orthodoxy) is as problematic as literary criticism or literary history uninformed by contemporary theoretical or methodological practices (a professional heresy). I realize that my insistence on the aesthetic function of poetry and the significance of contemporary literature for literary studies has an odd echo with some of the tenets of the New Critics. But I point this out mainly to debunk the dogma that works that "create linguistic difficulty and density and therefore make meaning problematic" have remained, or were ever, the center of attention of literary studies from the New Critics until the present, as Catherine Gallagher recently suggested.[1] As far as English literary studies of this century is concerned, *The Waste Land* and *Ulysses* have had to bear most of the weight of this claim. But these cease to be difficult texts insofar as they are fetishized as Arnoldian tokens of "bestness," a process that replaces their linguistic, aesthetic, and sociohistorical complexity with the very unambiguous status of cultural treasure; in any case, they have not been contemporary texts for well over half a century. Despite the homage, "difficult" or "ambiguous" literature has not, as a rule, meant teaching disorienting or unfamiliar works of literature to college students, and especially not works that challenged the professor's critical or ideological paradigms or were written in unfamiliar or disruptive dictions, dialects, or lexicons. Rather, it has meant turning a narrow range of designated difficulties into puzzles that are resolvable by checking off the boxes on the "Understanding Poetry" worksheet while rejecting ways of reading poetry that do not produce "understanding" but rather response, questions, disorientation, interaction, more poems. In fact, if you look at the anthologies of English and American literature that have been used in humanities classes over the past fifty years, you will see that if "difficulty" is a criteria at all, it is as likely to be one for the exclusion of a work as for its inclusion—a tendency that has only accelerated in recent years as "accessibility" and moral uplift have taken on both a political and pedagogic imperative. In the end, despite their defense of difficulty, the New Critics were primarily responsible for defanging radical modernism and enthroning its milquetoast other, High Antimodernism (a reference to their own work certainly, but one that also brings to mind the work they abjured). Moreover, as Gallagher accurately points out, the New Critics and their heirs actively discounted much of the demotic, folk, vulgar, idiosyncratic, ethnic, erotic, black, "women's," and genre poetry for which its methods were inadequate. This is not, I would insist, because this work was not ambiguous or difficult enough but because it posed the wrong kind of difficulties and ambiguities.

The academic profession is not a unified body but a composite of many dissimilar individuals and groups pursuing projects ranging from the valiantly idiosyncratic to the proscriptively conventional. As several of the studies in this volume attest, most of the popular generalizations about what professors do or do not do are unsupported by facts. For example, it turns out that, as a whole, professors work very long hours, generally beyond anything required of them. Moreover, the studies in this collection underscore the fallacy of focusing on the number of classroom hours a professor teaches, since this leads to a fundamental misrepresentation of the nature of academic work. It would be as if you measured the work of a lawyer only by the hours spent in her client's presence, or the work of a cook by how long it takes to eat his soufflé, or the work of a legislator by the number of pages of legislation he or she has written. Yet comparable misrepresentations of the academic profession are having dire consequences, most specifically in abetting the increase in nontenured part-time employment that is eroding not only the working conditions of the university but the quality of education that universities can provide.

Misinformation feeds on misinformation, so it is particularly unfortunate that political expediency has encouraged many of those who speak in the name of the university to abandon any vision of the radically democratic role the university can, but too often does not, play in this culture. That is to say, tenure and academic freedom are valuable not because they provide job security to individual faculty members but because they serve the public good. There is no conflict between the public interest and full-time tenured employment: short-term cost savings cannot justify the long-term economic folly of compromising one of the most substantial intellectual and cultural resources this society has created. The question is not whether our society can afford to maintain the intellectual and cultural space of the university at present levels but whether it can afford not to.

The greatest benefit of the university is not that it trains students for anything in particular, nor that it imbues in them a particular set of ideas, but that it is a place for open-ended research that can just as well lead nowhere as somewhere, research that is wasteful and inefficient by short-term socioeconomic standards but practically a steal as a long-term research and development investment in democracy, freedom, and creativity—without which we won't have much of an economic future, or the one we have won't be worth the flesh it's imprinted on. At its most effective, the university is not oriented toward marketplace discipline and employment training but rather toward maximizing the capacity for reflection and creativity. When it is most fully achieving its potential, university classes are not goal-oriented or preprofessional but self-defining and exploratory. Attempts to regulate the university according to market values only pervert what is best and least accountable about these cultural spaces. We cannot make education more efficient without making it more deficient.

Arthur Levine, in this issue, suggests that we imagine our relationship to our constituents on the model of a bank's relationship to its depositors. With a bank, you deposit something you have already acquired; with education, you are seeking to acquire something you do not already have. For at its best, education delivers nothing—it enables, animates. That is, the information imparted is embedded in an interaction. Information stripped of this interaction is largely inert: it is as if you are given the data base but not the software to use it, or, perhaps more accurately, you are given the data and the software but not the tools to question the collection method, reframe the categories, or collect new data. Let the buyer beware: the new "consumer-oriented" education may be cheap, but it also may not be worth very much.

The university I envision is more imaginary than actual, for everywhere the tried and sometimes true pushes out the untried but possible.

Within the academic profession, fights are often intramural, as new disciplinary and methodological projects threaten older ones, the new and old both claiming to be the victims of unprecedented dogmatism, bad faith, and a lack of intellectual or cultural values. In literary studies, these conflicts tend to be among three different conceptions of the field. One group defines literary studies in terms of its traditional subject matter, that is, the literary works that have traditionally served as the principal object of study in the field. This group maintains relative consensus among its constituents. A second group accepts the idea of the field as defined by its subject matter but proposes a new range of subject matters—from works underrepresented in traditional literary study to works that challenge the very idea of the literary. There is consensus among the constituents of this second group on broadening the subject matter of the field but, necessarily, no consensus on exactly what the new subjects should be. A third group consists of those who define the field primarily in terms of a particular method of analysis, critique, or interpretation. There is little consensus among the constituents of this third group, since the approaches adopted are often seen to be mutually exclusive. No doubt many in the profession are, to varying degrees, sympathetic to all three of these conceptions of the field.

The danger for the academic profession is not that one side or another will "win"—that the new barbarians will become the old boys or the traditionalists will block innovation. Rather, the problem is the idea that consensus should prevail. Manufacturing consent always involves devaluing or excluding that which does not fit the frame. What I value is not temperance but tolerance, for an insistence on temperance can mark an intolerance not only of the intemperate but also of unconventional—or unassimilated—forms of expression. We do not need to agree—or even converse—so long as we tolerate the possibility of radically different approaches, even to our most cherished ideas of decorum, methodology, rationality, and subject matter. The university that I value leaves all of these matters open, undecided—and not just open for debate, but open for multiple practices. The point is not to replace one approach with another but to reorient ourselves toward a kind of inquiry in which there are no final solutions, no universally mandated protocols. The point is not to administer culture but to participate in it.

In discussions about the state of the university, complaints about "tenured radicals" abound. I am more worried about tenured smugness and tenured burnout. While I respect the authority of scholarship, I reject the authoritativeness of any prescribed set of books, methods, experts, or standards. The problem is not that there has been too much reform but that there has hardly been any at all: the content has shifted, but this reflects demographic changes more than ideological ones; the structure of authority remains the same. Given the passionate engagement with their research of most of the graduate students I know, the often deanimating mandates of perceived professional success are the surest symptom of the problem. From the time they enter graduate school, the intensity, commitment, and creativity of the young scholar is routinely reoriented toward a cynical professional wiliness that emphasizes who it is opportune to quote or what best fits market prospects, rather than what the young scholar is most capable of doing or what best suits her passions or aesthetic proclivities. The profession, panicked by the market and temperamentally conservative (even in its apparently nonconservative guises), seems bent on shaping young scholars in its own image rather than encouraging the production of new and unexpected images. In these circumstances, professors—sometimes unintentionally, sometimes with the best intentions—often seem less inclined to offer themselves as aids to the young scholar's research than to act as living roadblocks.

While specialization is appropriate for a scholar's own work—and there is nothing more sublime about the university than those obsessive scholars who seem to know everything about a specific subject, writer, or period—specialization is too often projected onto students at large, as the same few books get taught over and again while the vast wealth of new books and old books remain "outside my field" (why not take a walk on the adjacent fields from time to time?). The problem may well be that many professors do not feel they have the authority to teach or supervise work in which they do not have expertise. I suppose imagining I have no expertise at all may be my greatest advantage: I can consider teaching or discussing almost anything if a student makes a compelling proposal for its necessity. My subject is contemporary poetry, but I find that it stretches from there to almost anywhere—by which I mean to say that whatever time students have in the university, in college or graduate school, should be a time of indiscriminate, prodigal, voracious reading and searching: *one text must lead directly to the next.* Against the mandated, hypotactic, rationalized logic of conventional syllabi, I suggest we go a-vagabonding; let our curriculums spin out into paratactic sagas. I propose we focus less on adducing the meaning of a homogenous sequence of works and more on addressing the relation of a heterogeneous series of works (Li Po next to Oulipo, "Jabberwocky" with Newton's *Optics*). Nor is this another appeal to interdisciplinarity, which assumes the form of the constituent disciplines that are already established and carefully preserves their distinctness through the process. Indeed, I have come to realize that poetry is one of the most intradisciplinary topics in the humanities, but this is because poetry already—since well before Lucretius—potentially encompasses all the disciplines of the humanities.

I realize my approach will not be to everyone's taste, nor do I wish to impose my sensibilities on the academic profession at large. What I ask for is greater tolerance for such approaches in a university that allows for the multiple and even the incommensurable, not just in its theories but in its practices.

It is not that I overstate my case; I am making a case for overstatement.

This wild adventure in learning is surely what inspired many of us to make the arts or humanities our calling, yet we lose the passion as we go from this adventure in texts to administering culture by the teaspoon. And this is very like what we do when we imagine our graduate programs primarily in terms of vocational training in narrowly predefined fields rather than as opportunities for open-ended research, centers for the study of the arts, lavish emporiums of further thinking. Does anyone doubt that we deaden the potential of future research and future teaching with our cramped, vocational/preprofessional disciplinary fantasies? And what a travesty, in particular, this training for jobs that do not even exist— though we all must do everything we can to reverse the pernicious trend toward poorly paid adjunct work in place of full-time, tenured employment. Yet I must disagree with those who, with great probity, advise that we reduce graduate programs to make them conform more precisely to the job market, so as to avoid overproduction of Ph.D.s. Rather, we should welcome into our graduate programs those whose goal is not to have the same job as their teachers but who, for a number of reasons, want to take one, two, or five years, modestly funded in exchange for some teaching, to pursue their studies, in ways that they must be primarily responsible to define.

And what of academic standards? Are not these the dikes that protect us from the flood of unregulated thought? Or are they like the narrow Chinese shoe that deforms our thinking to fit its image of rigor? When I examine the formats and implied standards for peer-reviewed journals and academic conferences, they suggest to me a preference for lifeless prose, bloated with the compulsory repetitive explanation of what every other "important" piece on this subject has said. Of course, many professors will insist that they do not subscribe to this. The point is not what any one of us does but rather the institutional culture we accept. It seems to me that the academic culture of the humanities places more emphasis on learning its ropes, on professional conformity, than it does on any actual research, writing, thinking, or teaching by the people who make up the profession. Indeed, it doesn't really matter what constitutes this conformity; the distinction being made is in an important sense antipathetic to substance. This is the chief function of anonymous peer review: to ensure not quality nor objectivity but compliance.

Anonymous peer reviewing enforces prevalent disciplinary standards, especially standards about the tone or manner of an argument, even while permitting the publication of a wide range of ideas—as long as the ideas are expressed in the dominant style. While it might seem that anonymous review would encourage greater textual freedom, in practice the submission of an anonymous article to multiple anonymous readers ends up favoring work that comes closest to conforming to accepted norms of argument and writing style—indeed, such a procedure is one of the best ways to determine what these norms are. Of course, it's no big surprise that institutions perpetuate their institutional styles. But perhaps what may make what I am saying sound—to some in the profession—exaggerated is that I find it deplorable that the academic profession is, well, too *academic*. Maybe this is because I am more accustomed to the form of cultural exchange and production found among poets and through independently produced "small press" books and magazines, which seems more vital and more committed to the values often ascribed to the academic profession—that is, more committed to fomenting imagination than controlling imagination—than the academic profession itself. The academic profession has a lot to learn from such communities of independent artists and scholars. I also feel that the academic profession has an obligation to provide a sanctuary for the arts, especially in a period of devastating cuts in government support for them.

What I object to is disciplinarity for the sake of disciplinarity and not in the service of inquiry. Too often, the procedures developed by the academic profession to ensure fairness and rigor end up creating a game that rewards routinized learning over risk. Blind peer reviewing, like its cousins standardized testing and evaluation, may be an advantage when it comes to discouraging preferential treatment for individuals, but the price it often pays for this is bolstering preferential treatment for the most acceptable types of discourse and fostering the bureaucratization of knowledge production. Anonymous peer review, like standardized testing and uniform assessment, encourages blandness and conformity in the style of presentation and response, leading those whose futures are dependent on such reviews and evaluations to shy away from taking risks with their writing styles or modes of argument or ideas. The policy is to reward the best test-takers but not necessarily the most engaging or culturally significant achievements. The result is that academic prose, like the career patterns it reflects, tends to avoid animation in favor of caution and to defer exuberance in favor of interminable self-justification and self-glossing that is unrelated to the needs of documentation or communication, research or teaching. I am not saying there is no place for anonymous peer reviewing but that there is far too much deference given to a system that in trying to eliminate one kind of bias actually institutes another kind. In contrast, not enough recognition is given to those activities pursued by members of the academic profession that question the rules of the game, that champion rather than adjudicate, that see universities as places for wild questions and not just for the prescribed answers.

Emphasis on conventional testing is antithetical to an aesthetically charged encounter with art. Testing students on their ability to memorize names or dates or on their skill at identifying passages taken out of context encourages them to focus on mastering information rather than on reading literary works: the two goals are in opposition.

The best way to describe how I teach is by calling it a reading workshop, for I am less concerned with analysis or explanations of individual poems than with finding ways to intensify the experience of poetry, of the poetic, through a consideration of how the different styles and structures and forms of contemporary poetry can affect the way we see and understand the world. No previous experience with poetry is necessary. What is more important is a willingness to consider the implausible, to try out alternative ways of thinking, to listen to the way language sounds before trying to figure out what it means, to lose yourself in a flurry of syllables and regain your bearings in dimensions otherwise imagined as out of reach, to hear how poems work to delight, inform, redress, lament, extol, oppose, renew, rhapsodize, imagine, foment. . . .

The stigmatization of the poetic and the aesthetic in writing is a foundational component of the judgment of academic prose, to the detriment of students and teachers alike. As something of a prank—call it empirical research—I submitted my essay "What's Art Got to Do With It: The Subject of the Humanities in the Age of Cultural Studies,"[2] which was written as the keynote speech for the annual convention of the Northeast Modern Language Association, to *PMLA,* since I was aware that the flagship publication of the profession welcomes talk about poetic function as long as one does not actively engage in poetic acts. That is, I knew that the recent publication committees of *PMLA* might support some of what I said "in theory" but not in practice, never as a writing practice. I mention this not because *PMLA* is an important place of publication for a poet or essayist but because its attitudes set a tone of conformity and hypocrisy that governs the profession and sharply delimits the possibilities for the writing styles of graduate students and untenured faculty—that is, the groups most likely to do innovative work. And the reason for this is that the accrediting and legitimating function of the literary academy rests not on a particular subject matter or political view or methodology but rather on the domination over the form of expression. In short, legitimation lies in the control of the means of representation.

Consider, for a start, *PMLA*'s statement on the form for readers' reports that says submissions are to be evaluated for "importance of the subject, originality of thought, accuracy of the facts, clarity and readability of style. . . ." Readability of style? *PMLA*? Compared to what? Importance of the subject? That phrase is expected to be understood only in the narrowest professional sense, that is, in terms of the concerns of specialization and scholarly detail that in most other contexts would argue against the "importance of the subject" of most *PMLA* articles but should not, I would contend, undermine their legitimate place in this publication. For the *PMLA* of the 1990s to hold onto "originality" as a criterion, given the decisive eroding of that concept in articles it has sponsored, suggests the problem to which my irritable charge of "hypocrisy" gives vent. I suppose I am naive enough to believe that bad faith does not have to be mandated. So the "clarity" of which the editorial policy statement speaks becomes, in this context, an entirely disciplinary affair, an empty marker of legitimation that confers value on outmoded and indefensible principles of writing.

Both *PMLA* readers rejected my essay without qualifications— and I suspect few of you who have gotten this far in this essay will wonder why. One rejection, anonymous, says that the essay "is provocative" but "not appropriate for *PMLA*. I would suggest the author rewrite it—tightening it up, clarifying the argument—for submission elsewhere." The essay should be rejected because it 1) "lacks focus," 2) has an "inconsistency of tone," 3) "is disjointed, loose, in need of revision to make it more 'punchy.' The reader wonders at times what the point is." And 4) "Many readers will consider self-indulgent the author's reference to writing his essay 'lying down on the couch, the pad propped up by my knee.'" (As I write this I am standing upside down floating over Manhattan in a helium balloon.) The referee goes on: "The author makes intriguing assertions, with sweeping generalizations, which he or she does not support with any evidence. In order to convince the reader that he or she is not simply expressing eccentric opinions on literary matters, the author ought to explain in greater depth the reason for which he or she has come to a particular conclusion." I *am* expressing eccentric opinions on literary matters, without *PMLA*'s brand of "clarity" and "evidence": eccentric, indulgent, disjointed, loose, inconsistent—and proud. But evidently not punch drunk, though I do wonder what articles in recent issues of *PMLA* the professor finds stylistically "punchy." While it is easy to poke fun at this sort of *Elements of Style* fundamentalism, such a constrained approach to reading has dire effects in the classroom, where it alienates students from writing and reading. That is something our culture cannot afford.

The other rejection, signed by Richard Ohmann, a prominent progressive whose critical work on the English profession I admire, makes a witty reply suggesting that it is not so much that the essay is "not recommended for *PMLA*" but that "*PMLA* is not recommended for this essay." (I quote Professor Ohmann with his permission.) Still, Ohmann thinks I am being unfair to cultural studies, which may be true, but fails to register that the essay subsumes cultural studies in a much broader polemic out of which many individual practitioners of cultural studies come out ahead. Indeed, I imagine my poetry and essays are themselves forms of cultural studies. Ultimately, the reviewer, famous for his own sharp and useful critiques of the academy in decades past, feels that my essay falls outside "the academic humanities" since it does not "refer specifically to texts, generalize about them, construct an historical framework of analysis, all that academic stuff." He concludes, "I don't think the author wants to write this kind of article. I'd go for the aphorism and provocations and some other venue." I feel like a dancehall performer in *Gunsmoke* being thrown out of town by Marshal Dillon: "That may be awright for Paree or SoHo but we don't cotton to that around here." "But,

Marshal, I have as much right to be in this territory as you, and so maybe I just won't mosey along!"

The men on the hill, they say, "learn the rules, *then* break them." I like to "think the reverse" whenever possible and even if not: break 'em enough times you won't have to learn 'em, or the rules will have changed, or you will change them, or make up your own rules and don't follow those either; anyway whose rules are they?, I didn't see the signs, musta missed them in the duststorm; or, as we say in Medias Res (Medias Res, Nevada)—rope 'em and then learn 'em, shoot 'em and then cook 'em (chop up fine before marinading indefinitely), float jerkily and carry a Bic pen at all times, where aim I?, is this my fear / or did I just step into the public sphere?, are you there Mordred?; Give me your tired tuxes, your tattered nabobs of oligarchy yearning to Keep that Smut Off the Net, Thank you Senator Exon the open spaces around here were scaring me, how many syllables can you fit on the head of a pin cushion? What's that spell, Mario? Who are you calling a verse? That's not what I meant y'all, not what I meant at all.

In contrast to the sciences, in the humanities we shrink from teaching difficult or hard-to-grasp material in a desperate, self-defeating effort to make literature and art accessible. From an educational point of view, it might be better to insist that what is inaccessible or impossible to grasp is exactly what needs to be taught in our schools. This is why I feel that, despite all the attention to radical changes in the humanities, we have not changed nearly enough. The focus on teaching representative and expressive works, where representation and expression are understood in an almost entirely unrelated sense, shows a continuity from the 1890s to the 1990s. If the earlier phase of humanism marked literature as expressive of mankind, the new humanism of identity politics condemns the universalization but adopts the underlying structure: literary works are expressive or representative of not mankind but particular subsets of human beings (by means of which their basic humanity shines forth). The almost total absence of poetry from primary and secondary school curriculums certainly suggests the problem. Light fiction seems to be the best vehicle for the new humanism, and if poetry comes into the picture at all it is almost surely going to be sincere, sentimental, instructive, and uplifting. This entails reading poetry not for its aesthetic values—which is to say, as aesthetic construction—but as moral sentiment or else recognizing that as moral discourse poetry will often seem inaccessible, immoral, without values, decadent.

Moreover, I can't help but feel that the unwillingness to teach difficult or challenging or unconventional work is based less on good intentions than on condescension—the false belief that students are not smart enough to understand anything other than the most artless art. (Just between you and me, it turns out that lots of students get enthusiastic about much of the poetry that most high school and college English teachers have long since redlined but are bored to tears by the poetry of uplift foisted on them.)

SHORTY PETTERSTEIN INTERVIEW [LENNY BRUCE]

How would you compare the kind of music you play with a, how would you compare that with art, you know, what kind of art, artistic...?

Man, like I think Art blows the most, I mean, uh, he came with the band about three years ago, man, dig, and, uh, like, he was a real, uh, you know, small-town cat—and I mean he was swinging, man, but he was a small-town cat. And I mean he started to blow with us and he was real nut, you know, cool....

What would you advise the young artist, the young musician, to do? Would you advise him to get an academic education or strive immediately for self-expression?

Well, man, I mean, I'm a musician, dig. And I mean to me the most important thing is that you should blow, you know.... If a cat wants to blow and he wants to blow, and, uh, then he's got to have a scene where he can blow.

That would apply to the artists playing horns and wind instruments, they would have to blow. What about those, for example, who are playing string instruments? Or would you say, how's the picture there?

Well, I mean, you know, it's, uh, pretty much all the same, man. A blow is like an instrument, you know.

At the *Dædalus* authors' conference, where a small group of us met to discuss the essays in this volume, I responded to some disorientation, not to say disappointment, about my essay by noting that it could be understood as a series of discontinuous remarks, more performance than treatise. One response to this comment was to assume that I had admitted to a major flaw in my argument. My point was quite the contrary, but the response goes to the heart of the issue. The arts and sciences of this century have shown that deductive methods of argument—narrow rationalizing—hardly exhaust the full capacity of reason. Induction and discontinuity are slighted only at the cost of slighting reason itself. There is no evidence that the conventional expository prose that is the ubiquitous output of the academic profession produces more insights or better research than nonexpository modes. There is no evidence that a tone of austere probity, rather than one that is ironic or raucous, furthers the value of teaching or inquiry. It may be true that standard academic prose permits dissident ideas, but ideas mean little if not embodied in material practices, and for those in the academic profession, writing is one of the most fundamental of such practices. Writing is never neutral, never an objective mechanism for the delivery of facts. Therefore, the repression of writing practices is a form of suppressing dissidence—even if it is dissidence, I would add, for the sake of dissidence.

So while my attitude towards the academic profession is highly critical, I want to insist that one of the primary values of such a profession results from its constituents challenging authority, questioning conventional rhetorical forms, and remaining restless and quarrelsome and unsatisfied, especially with the bureaucratization of knowledge that is the inertial force that pulls us together as a profession. Which is to say: *The profession is best when it professionalizes least.* As negative as I am about the rhetorical rigidity of the academic profession, a comparison with journalism, corporate communications, or technical writing will show that these other professions police their respective writing styles far more completely than the academic profession. That is why it is vital to raise these issues about rhetorical and pedagogic practices, because universities remain one of the few cultural spaces in the United States in which there is at least the potential for critical discourse, for violation of norms and standards and protocols.

For the destination is always staring just out of view, and all the signs are flashing "access denied." I make meaning of the failure to arrive, for so often it is a breaking down of the chain of sense that lets me find my way. A way away from the scanning over and over of what went wrong—the failure of community that may, in flits and faults, give way to conversation. I start with the senselessness of the world and try to make some sense with it, as if words were visceral and thoughts could be tolls. It's the loss, I want to say, I don't know *of what*—but not to find either (neither voice nor truth: voicings, trusts).

As something of a trickster myself, I probably enjoy literary hoaxes more than most. So 1996 was an exceptional year, with two exemplary forgeries proving nearly opposite points, at one level, but together confirming an instability of judgment that I think we would be better to savor than lambaste.

I actually had the occasion to meet **Alan Sokal** at a party not very long ago. I mentioned my devotion to **Ossian, Orson Welles,** and **Ern Malley** (Australia's greatest poet), but I'm afraid Professor Sokal looked back at me rather blankly. (Not to worry, I'm used to that.) It seemed I was not the first to aestheticize his twenty minutes of fame, and he was not amused: What academics took seriously in the humanities was patent nonsense, and he had hoped to wake people up to the problem. (I'm afraid this rather proved to me that he really doesn't understand the distinction between *différence* and *jouissance,* as he boasts in his "shocking" exposé in *Lingua Franca* in which he reveals his hoax.) For me, a hoax really needs no justification, so his explanations are rather like chocolate icing on a cheesecake; but then, I may be one of the few people he has spoken to who actually finds contemporary literary theory not patently nonsensical enough. (I keep my copy of **Edward Lear** in my breast pocket at all times.)

For those who may have missed l'Affaire Sokal: I salute your resolute unworldliness. My daughter reacted to me in much this way when I professed not to know that **Dennis Rodman** had made a public appearance in drag ("But I thought he was a basketball player?"). My first impression when I saw the article on page one of the *New York Times* about Sokal's, um, intervention was that surely Sokal and **Andrew Ross** of *Social Text* (which published

Sokal's faux-footnote-laden discussion of gravity as a social construction), who are both professors at New York University, had conspired to pull a fast one on the *Times* in an effort to get them to focus on issues in which both of them are interested: the discourses (legitimate and illegitimate) of science and the relation of science to ideology, but also poststructuralism to empiricism and literary theory to politics. (The closest the *Times* could otherwise come to treating this topic would be in a review of *Mars Attacks,* if it was turned over to a second-string reviewer.) That still seems like the best explanation for the whole affair, and I am all for getting the principals to let it all hang out on a segment of the **Howard Stern** show on cable television's E! station. Now as for Ross, the first time I met him, many years ago, the topic quickly turned to **Hugh MacDiarmid** (who has written some very great poems on science) and, to his eternal credit, Ross went on to recite several stanzas from *A Drunk Man Looks at the Thistle,* MacDiarmid's magnificent poem in Scots dialect (or Scotsbonics, as it is now known). In any case, I personally believe that even the social is not a social construction, but then what do I know? But as **Dick Clark** once said, "I never let my personal beliefs enter into anything I do."

In *Gravity and Grace,* Simone Weil does imagine gravity as a social—not construction, but—*fact*. It's not enough to recognize that Weil's gravity and Newton's are mutually informing; we also need to acknowledge that, without grace, gravity will get you every time, pull you down into the mud and keep you there until you choke on bad faith and rotten apples (not to say Macs). And doesn't Habermas, in *Knowledge and Human Interest,* make the very useful distinction between scientific knowledge, which allows for prediction and control, and dialogic or hermeneutic knowledge, which allows for interpretation and reflection? Are we destined to constantly reinvent the centipede or stumble into hubris? Sokal insists despite what he imagines to be a chorus of detractors that the "external world" really exists. The internal world exists too. But either assertion is really beside the point. The point is what we are going to do about it, and who and how we are going to tell.

But I mentioned two hoaxes, right? Let's see, oh yes, here it is, I definitely said two. The second hoax took place over a period of a few years in a number of poetry magazines, including *Conjunctions, American Poetry Review,* and *Grand Street.* Translations of the work of a Japanese poet, Araki Yasusada, began to appear, with the explanation that Yasusada was a survivor of the atomic bombing of Hiroshima who had died a few years ago. The work was interesting, quite unexpected in its style from the little most of us knew about postwar Japanese poetry, and somewhat resembled the poems of Jack Spicer (a happy similarity, so far as I was concerned). Only it turned out that the work was by an American, not a Japanese, and some of the editors who published it felt betrayed and duped. One said he would not have published it if he knew the actual authorship, and this, of course, seems the reaction the forgery set out to provoke. Is the work valuable as poetry because it is authentic in its witness? Is the poem only worth publishing because it is a poem by a survivor? Is the poet's identity or autobiography more important than the poem? Does the value of poetry now primarily rest in conveying cultural information rather than in aesthetic exploration (including the exploration carried out by the forgery)? Is this just another example of white male *ressentiment* (assuming, as the incident encourages us to assume, that the real author is a white male)? Were the editors Sokaled or Rossed?

HE'S SO HEAVY, HE'S MY SOKAL
  after Danny Kaye and Milton Schafer

        Please, please don't Sokal me
        Sokal the baby, Sokal the priest
        But don't, don't Sokal me
        I'm laughing so hard I could cry

        If I Sokaled you
        You wouldn't like it
        You wouldn't approve
        If I Sokaled you
        You'd Sokal so hard you would split

        O, O let go of my 'no'
        It isn't so funny you goof
        Oh, no I've misplaced the sunny
        Stop or I'll fall up through the roof

But please, please don't Sokal me
Sokal the baby, Sokal the priest
Sokal your mother, Sokal your brother,
Sokal some other guy
But don't, don't Sokal me
I'm laughing so hard I could sigh

Cut it out now, cut it out now!
I'm historicized, I can't take it anymore!
Come on, beat it, get out of here!
You're symptomizing me!
I'm practically reified!

Wait until I get you, you piece of...
Cut it out 'cause I'm getting sore

And please, please don't Sokal me
Sokal the baby, Sokal the priest
Sokal your father, Sokal your sister,
Sokal some other guy
But don't, don't Sokal me
I'm laughing so hard I could cry

The status of dialect, or nonstandard English, is another politically charged issue for the academic profession. Indeed, the issues raised by the controversies that rage around standardized language go to the heart of the ideology of education and the kinds of language practices sanctioned by the academic profession. At the same time, the controversy illustrates the either/or thinking that, as I have suggested, also plagues discussions of issues such as the core curriculum, academic standards, and objectivity.

In the most visible form of the conflict, Black English is reviled by the conservative mainstream as deformed English and celebrated by Afrocentrics as the mother tongue. What is sanctified as ordinary for one group is derided as spurious by the other. The very ordinariness of Black English is what makes it seem of self-evident value to its speakers—and rightly so—but this ordinariness is a red herring to conservatives, because it is not ordinary to them. The problem is that there is no one ordinary language but many ordinary languages. All languages are social constructions—Black English as much as standard English. In this case, there is para-doxical conflict between the ordinary and the conventional, between dialect and the standard, between the normal and the spoken, between the intelligible and the vernacular. It is the ordinary versus the really ordinary. Conventional, standard English derives its authority from being perceived as the normal, the intelligible, and also the transparent. "It must be ordinary, because it's what I understand." Dialect, however, casts the conventional or standard as artificial or other or learned or imposed ("it's not my ordinary") while sometimes claiming to be authentic or natural or spoken.

In this situation, the academic profession finds itself caught in a double bind that turns it against itself, for authenticity and normalcy both misconceive the dynamic and essentially rhetorical or trop(e)ical social fact of language. Black English is just as rich a language as standard English, just as valid (all languages are equally valid). The point is not to go from fetishizing (or naturalizing) the standard to fetishizing (or naturalizing) the authentic, but to acknowledge the multiple possibilities, and different social valences, of language and to recognize that the ordinary lies not in any one type of language but in the between.

The most salient values of the university are reflected by the fact that it is the largest and most vibrant noncommercial quasi-public space in the United States. The bright idea of managers and politicians to adopt commercial decision-making on campus is almost always an erosion of the immutable value of the institution, destructive beyond measure.

Yet it is no longer taken for granted that immersion in the literature, art, and philosophy of the past and present has any practical benefit for society, and this too often has had the perverse effect of making those who remain convinced respond with a narrow, and often shrill, insistence on the necessity of one list or another of treasured or representative works that must be taught (since we cannot ensure that they will be read or understood). The boat is sinking, and we spend our time debating which pieces of furniture ought to go into the main dining room instead of fixing the leaks. But the value of the noncommercial space of the university is independent of any particular work or method, no matter how much any one of us loves the works or methods we have chosen to profess, for the values taught are reading values: critical thinking, reflection, social and bibliographic contexts of meaning, and the relation of forms, styles, dictions, and genres in determining what any work has to say. For most students, who come out of media-intense but breathtakingly narrow cultural confines, distance learning and large lecture classes, while efficient on a cost-per-student basis, are ineffective. Teaching in our culture at this time is more than ever a labor-intensive activity. It requires prolonged engagement with individual students: gauging their reactions and responding to each one, individually. The answer is never in the technology—audiovisuals, web connections, and books included—but in how we learn to use these technologies.

My commitment is to public education: the education of the public at large and an education about the public, how it is constituted. Yet we are writing off our large public institutions of learning with the cynical assumption that graduates of such colleges have no practical need for the sort of open-ended education in the arts and sciences that most of us in the humanities support. "I never learned anything in college, so why should they?" Indeed, from a corporate point of view, having too many people in the work force who think too much may be detrimental if they are to end up in dead-end jobs that require little thought. Such ideas are fundamentally antidemocratic, of course; they are the breeding ground for a passive and malinformed citizenry that is unable to make sense of the complex issues that confront the nation. What price do we have to pay for an informed citizenry, one that can understand the complex multiplicity of American culture, that can read into events and not simply register them as a series of fated accomplishments? What sort of investment are we willing to make in the intellectual and cultural development of our citizens so that we can remain, as a country, innovative, vibrant, socially responsible? How can we prepare ourselves for the unexpected, the difficult, the troubling events that are sure to lie ahead for all of us? Will we spend billions for defense while begrudging any money spent on what we are defending? The great experiment in mass education is not even a hundred years old; it has had virtually no downside. That we teeter on abandoning this commitment now is a testament to a smallness, a lack of generosity, and a contempt for noncommercial values that can only make us poorer—not only culturally, but economically.

I open the door and it shuts after me. That is, the more I venture out into the open, the more I find it is behind me and I am moving not toward some uninhabited space but deeper into a maelstrom of criss-crossing inscriptions. The open is a vanishing point—the closer I get to it, the greater the distance from which it beckons. And I begin the journey again.

ENDNOTES

[1]Catherine Gallagher, "The History of Literary Criticism," *Dædalus* 126 (1) (Winter 1997): 140.

[2]"What's Art Got to Do With It" was published in *American Literary History* and anthologized in *The American Literary History Reader,* ed. Gordon Hutner (New York: Oxford University Press, 1995) and in *Beauty and the Critic: Aesthetics in an Age of Cultural Studies,* ed. James Soderholm (Tuscaloosa, Ala.: University of Alabama Press, 1997).

Jay A. Labinger

The Science Wars and the Future of the American Academic Profession

I T IS ALL TOO EASY TO BE PERPLEXED about the state of health of academic institutions in the United States. On the one hand, observers proclaim this to be "the golden age of the American university,"[1] and it would be hard to disagree based on any sort of objective measure, such as the competition for admission to selective institutions or the net influx of foreign students. Subjectively, the positive public image of the American university also seems to be holding.[2] At the same time, a steady stream of jeremiads fills the shelves at bookstores and libraries, lamenting the catastrophic failure of American higher education to carry out its intended functions and portraying American colleges and universities as places where students go to have their minds closed and their spirits killed by tenured radicals engaged in a giant professorial scam.[3] It is difficult to read such books without feeling like we are doing *something* wrong.

The status of the natural sciences is similarly confusing. Feedback in the form of student demand is no less positive than in other disciplines. Predictions that by now we would not be producing enough scientists to replace the increasing numbers of retirees from academic positions show no signs of coming true. American scientific research continues to lead the world in most fields, by any objective or subjective measure. While a good deal of scientific research goes on outside the universities (in contrast to the majority of scholarly work in other disciplines), surely this

---

Jay A. Labinger is Administrator of the Beckman Institute at the California Institute of Technology.

201

leadership is due in very large part to the academic component.[4] Nonetheless, academic scientists sense that all is not well. The most obvious sign is pressure on research funding. It is telling that the latest federal R&D budget, which barely (if even) keeps up with inflation, is being celebrated as a "significant achievement" compared to what *might* have happened.[5] Issues on which scientists may think they have the most authority slip completely out of their jurisdiction and become topics of debate in Congress and the media. For instance, what is the proper balance between fundamental and applied research? How widespread is the problem of scientific fraud, and what can/should be done about it? What are the consequences of the increasing proportion of industrial sponsorship of academic research as well as the burgeoning entrepreneurial behavior of academic scientists? Is the potential for conflict of interest significantly dangerous? There are many more questions.

These lurking problems are mostly specific to the natural sciences. Do the more general problems of the university apply to science as well? The critics tend to draw a line between science and the rest of the university, excluding scientists from the most virulent attacks (aside from the universal complaint of slighting teaching at the expense of research). But if, *as scientists,* we take any comfort from this partial exculpation, it must be balanced against the implicit criticism of our roles as members of the academic profession. Science is portrayed as a completely separate enterprise in academe, with little interaction or even mutual awareness between it and the other disciplines. The implications of the departmental structure of American universities, and the conflicting demands of disciplinary versus institutional loyalty, have been discussed before,[6] but now the consequences are presented in a particularly dire light. As described by Allan Bloom, "The scientists have had less and less to say to, and to do with, their colleagues in the social studies and humanities. The university has lost whatever polis-like character it had and has become like the ship on which the passengers are just accidental fellow travelers soon to disembark and go their separate ways."[7]

In this context, recent developments in the relationship between science and the other disciplines must seem supremely ironic. Scholars in the social sciences and humanities are increasingly looking to the sciences for subjects to study, and scientists are increasingly becoming aware of this work—but does this mean that we are finally beginning the work of lowering the barriers? Apparently not: according to the reactions of (some) scientists, we are dealing with a trend that looks much more like a cross-border invasion than a cross-boundary collaboration. And this trend has been characterized as a potentially serious threat, both to science and to the academy. In this essay, I will briefly summarize the history and substance of what have come to be known as the science wars, offer a recommendation for a more charitable view of science studies by scientists, and try to assess their potential for affecting, both for good and ill, the future of the scientific enterprise and the academic profession.

A BRIEF CHRONICLE OF THE SCIENCE WARS

Arguably, the person who has had the greatest influence on scholarly titles in recent years (since the invention of the colon, perhaps?) is George Lucas. A search of the computerized catalogs of two modest university collections (Caltech and the Claremont Colleges) yielded well over fifty books, all published since the appearance of *Star Wars* in 1977, with the word "Wars" in their titles—*Aspirin Wars, Car Wars, Erotic Wars, Gene Wars, Memory Wars, Mind Wars, Sperm Wars, Time Wars,* and so on—not even counting individual articles.

And now we have "science wars." The phrase (probably derived from "culture wars") has become popularized, primarily by a special issue of the journal *Social Text* (more on that shortly). But what are they about, and who are the forces on each side? Basically, these are turf wars. Can those who are not professional, trained, practicing scientists speak to what science is about and how it works, or do scientists remain the sole authorities on these issues? In antebellum times (say, before the 1960s) scientists were largely unthreatened by nonscientists studying science. History of science tended to be primarily of a celebratory nature, while philosophy of science was viewed by scientists as, well, philosophy—not about anything *real*.

But things have changed, and the publication of Thomas Kuhn's *The Structure of Scientific Revolutions* in 1962 is often identified as a key factor in that change. Of course, there is a long tradition of inquiry into the nature of knowledge. But Kuhn's work, perhaps granted an extra measure of authority by his credentials as a physicist, served for many to legitimate the notion that scientific knowledge is not a simple and rational consequence of "the way the world really is," and it led to a number of alternative approaches to the study of science over the next decades. Perhaps the first systematic one was the "Strong Program" initiated at Edinburgh in the early 1970s, which constituted a sociological treatment of scientific knowledge. Such studies of science are centered around the concept of social constructivism—that scientific facts are constructed by the activities of scientists and are not just sitting out there in nature, waiting to be picked up.

Since then an extensive body of science studies, from a variety of viewpoints—social, cultural, linguistic, feminist—has burgeoned. These vary widely in many aspects—commitment to realism or relativism, respect for or hostility towards the scientific enterprise, and others—and it would be both misleading and unfair to try to capture them all in a simple description. They do call into question the traditional view of what science is about and how it works, though, and it would not be at all surprising for them to provoke at least some sense of disturbance among scientists. Nonetheless, for a long time (until around 1990) there was little evidence that scientists paid much attention to these movements. If we represent the science wars as a Lucasian film trilogy, the appropriate title for the first reel would be *The Mouse that Roared.*[8]

Scientists began taking notice in the early 1990s, and for this second phase we can use one of Lucas's titles: *The Empire Strikes Back* is a very apt description of the responses that started showing up in print. The first significant attacks, focusing on the social constructivist school, were incorporated in books published in 1992 by physicist Steven Weinberg and biologist Lewis Wolpert.[9] In 1994 the battle lines were drawn for all to see. An account of a heated debate between Wolpert and Harry Collins, a sociologist of science, at a meeting of the British Association for the Advancement of Science appeared in the (London) *Times Higher Education Supplement,* while an anticonstructivist meeting of the National Academy of Scholars was featured in US papers such as the *Boston Globe.* But the main event so far—the grand declaration of war— was the book *Higher Superstition* by biologist Paul Gross and mathematician Norman Levitt,[10] which examined a number of areas of study and concluded that they constitute a general movement that is hostile to science, arrogant in its assumption of competence, and aimed at overthrowing scientific authority. As a sequel, the authors organized a meeting of the New York Academy of Sciences in 1995 entitled "The Flight from Science and Reason."[11]

The targets of these attacks began regrouping and put forth an organized defense of their positions in the aforementioned special issue of *Social Text,* which appeared in 1996.[12] However, the defenders unknowingly harbored a detractor. An article by physicist Alan Sokal, entitled "Transgressing the Boundaries: Towards a Transformative Hermeneutics of Quantum Gravity,"[13] was accepted for this special issue. Simultaneously with its publication, Sokal revealed that his article was a parody, deliberately crammed with as much nonsense as possible and submitted to test whether the hoax would be detected.[14] Inevitably, it was this aspect of the issue—what has come to be known as the Sokal Affair—that received all the attention. Letters and op-ed pieces, both praising and criticizing Sokal, filled the *New York Times* for weeks and continue to echo in a wide range of scholarly and popular media, most visibly in a recent issue of *Newsweek.*[15]

A FEW NOTES FROM A WAR CORRESPONDENT

I first became interested in science studies about five years ago. The suggestion that barriers between science and the other academic disciplines are detrimental to the health of the university seemed accurate to me; I was also dissatisfied with the demarcation between my own professional pursuits—then strictly scientific—and my extracurricular interests. Some of my initial reading forays into social studies of science proved quite intriguing but also disappointing, because the authors exhibited little apparent interest in attracting scientists to their work and often indulged in rhetoric that could not help but provoke some scientists to antagonism, even if unintentionally. I expressed some of these thoughts in an article, which was published in *Social Studies of Science* along with a set of responses.[16] By and large the latter were quite positive, recognizing the need for developing dialogue between the two camps.

I was dismayed, therefore, by the outbreak of war signaled by the appearance of the Gross and Levitt book and its call for scientists to change their attitude towards science studies from benign neglect to active combat. While perhaps few have yet rallied to that banner, some in prominent positions have done so. For example, in a guest editorial in *Chemical & Engineering News* (the weekly organ received by all members of the American Chemical Society), Allen Bard, editor of the prestigious *Journal of the American Chemical Society,* opined: "Scientists should also confront the sociologists and philosophers at their institutions who are attacking the foundations of science. Presumably, tenure decisions and promotions at universities are based on scholarship, and academic scientists must take an interest in the academic decisions in other departments on campus. This is not a question of academic freedom, but rather one of competency."[17] I did say that I hoped to see more interactions between different disciplines, but that is not quite the sort of thing I meant.

Is this really about an attack on the foundations of science? And can scientists simply dismiss such work as incompetent? Obviously I cannot address the full range of topics; *Higher Superstition* alone criticizes four major groups (so defined on the basis of getting an entire chapter to themselves)—social constructivism, postmodern literary and cultural criticism, feminist criticism, and radical environmentalism—along with several smaller movements, and other writers have still-longer hit lists. But I would like to comment briefly on one aspect, social constructivism, and argue for a much more positive interpretation of what (some of) these science studies are trying to do.

The bare idea that scientific knowledge is socially constructed may be fleshed out in a number of ways, ranging from the mild position that social factors *affect* scientific practice—even Gross and Levitt find that perfectly acceptable[18]—to the extreme view that the laws of nature *themselves* are socially determined, caricatured by Sokal's invitation to those who so believe to try transgressing those laws from his twenty-third floor apartment. A philosopher (*not* a social constructivist) has offered a more moderate statement:

> The deep point of the sociological critique is that the social forces
> that operate in this modification of practice—the rules for consensus

shaping, the conversations with peers, the training process and broader socialization within a larger community—may be sufficiently powerful that the effects of nature are negligible.[19]

This has been given a much more vivid voice: "The natural world in no way constrains what is believed to be." Most scientists would, I believe, reject this version, as indeed do many in the science studies world as well. Susan Haack, a philosopher, writes for example, "Bad sociology of science is thus *purely* sociological, whereas good sociology of science, acknowledging the relevance of evidential considerations, is not."[20] Noting the possibility of "bad good sociology of knowledge"—sociology done poorly though taking the right approach—she charitably (and symmetrically) recognizes the possibility of "good bad sociology"—that studies based on a purely sociological perspective could nonetheless yield valuable results. But she insists that any such accomplishment would be mostly by chance.

I propose a different perspective, one that starts from the *correct* version of the above quote: "The appropriate attitude for conducting this kind of enquiry is to assume that 'the natural world in no way constrains what is believed to be.'"[21] That is quite different: it represents the "social is all" view as a methodological starting point, not an ideology or a conclusion. In this sense, what Haack calls bad sociology is not denying the relevance of nature but simply bracketing it out of consideration, in order to focus on the social. And certainly such a research strategy should not seem foreign to any scientist, as Haack herself points out: "What is distinctive about inquiry in the sciences is, rather: systematic commitment to criticism and testing, and to *isolating one variable at a time....*"[22] Granting that there is a social dimension to the scientific endeavor—without necessarily specifying its magnitude—and that it is worthy of scholarly examination, then a social constructivist approach can be viewed as just one possible experimental design strategy, and one that may not be so unreasonable according to traditional scientific standards.

Certainly a constructivist approach is not the *only* strategy, and I have argued for its shortcomings elsewhere.[23] Furthermore, it must be acknowledged that many (most?) of those engaged in science studies would refuse to concede either the nonuniqueness or the incompleteness of their approaches; it is also true that they are often prone to making flamboyant rhetorical claims that offend those who are committed to any sort of realist position. So it is not surprising that this particular battleground is one of the main sites where the science wars are fought. But perhaps a small shift of perspective can allow us to fit it within our traditional understanding of scholarly—even experimental—work and to recognize the possibility of obtaining useful insights even though we may not like the starting premise.

I believe a number of projects in cultural and literary criticism of science (usually attacked under the blanket term of postmodernism, which may make up in convenience some of what it lacks in definition) may be similarly reconstituted, although a detailed discussion would be out of place here. We are living in a world that is completely permeated by science and its products; it seems perfectly understandable that many who are not practicing scientists nonetheless feel the urge to bring their own professional expertise to bear in the attempt to make sense of this scientific world.

Now, nothing I have said so far should be taken as denying that *some* science studies are incompetently done, or are motivated by a clearly hostile stance, or exhibit tones that might be reasonably characterized as arrogant. Bad work (whether "bad good" or "bad bad" by Haack's criteria) is always with us.[24] It also must be admitted that rigorous criteria for deciding whether a piece of work is good or bad are hard to come by. For this reason, Sokal's "prank," which has been lauded by some and condemned by others, seems to me quite appropriate. We need some kind of assay, and Sokal has provided an *experimental* one (note the title of his *Lingua Franca* article). Complaints about betrayal of trust and the like are beside the point; we would like assurance that the system is capable of distinguishing between sound work and garbage, and the results of this particular experiment were less than encouraging.

Nevertheless, I hope that scientists would recognize that much of the work that has been characterized as attacking the foundations of science may actually be part of the same project, viewed on the largest scale, that they themselves are engaged in. Compare Dudley Herschbach's mountain-climbing metaphor for science:

It is vital to have some scientists willing to explore unorthodox paths, perhaps straying far from the route favored by consensus. By going off in what is deemed the wrong way, such a maverick may discern the right path. Hence in science, it is not even desirable, much less necessary or possible, to be right at each step.[25]

THE (PRESENT AND) FUTURE OF THE SCIENCE WARS

We need a title for the third reel of the science-wars epic. From the point of view of science, *Much Ado About Nothing* may well be the most appropriate. There is little or no evidence that the "assault" on science and reason has had any measurable effect on science itself, dire proclamations like the following (from a philosopher, not a scientist) notwithstanding:

> In Feyerabend's view, science is a religion, for it rests on certain dogmas which cannot be rationally justified. . . . Because most scientists can't justify their methodology, Feyerabend's claims have gone largely unanswered. As a result, Feyerabend's position has become prominent in both academia and the public at large. This has arguably led not only to the rise of pseudoscience and religious fundamentalism, but also to a shrinking pool of scientific jobs and research funds.[26]

There may well be a shrinking pool of scientific jobs and research funds, but is it because the public at large (or Congress at small) has taken Feyerabendism to heart? I think not. The countersuggestion that scientists blame science studies for their plight rather than confronting the true culprits—the end of the Cold War and consequent reductions in defense-related research and the deficit-induced pressure on budgets for science[27]—is also off the mark. Science is undergoing change because it is entering a no-growth regime, simply because it cannot grow anymore. Derek da Solla Price was one of the first to note that the scientific endeavor has been growing exponentially and continuously for several centuries. Using the number of scientific journals as a quantitative measure, he discovered fairly smooth exponential growth, with a doubling period of about fifteen years, throughout the entire period from 1750 to 1950. Clearly such growth could not continue indefinitely—without making everyone in the world a scientist, it cannot continue much at all past the present—and this enforced demographic transition is more than enough to account for the strains on the scientific community.[28]

If I might digress for a moment, the growth of academe shows very similar behavior. Figure 1 plots the number of faculty in US academic institutions from 1880–1980.[29] The exponential growth is, again, remarkably smooth, persisting through all the changes in emphasis and historical events during that century. If these data are representative, they do not reflect common wisdom, such as: "It is obvious. . .that the intrusion of the federal government into higher education since the end of World War II. . .[made] for an expansion of the professoriate to a size almost inconceivable when the United States dropped its atom bombs over Japan."[30] There is no corresponding deviation in the graph. Furthermore, the growth rate—a doubling period of about sixteen years—is almost identical to that determined for science by Price. Is there some innate institutional growth rate operating here? In any case, clearly academe has reached or is about to reach an impenetrable ceiling just as science has, and doubtless some of the current upheaval should be ascribed to that same cause.

Figure 1. Number of Faculty in US Academic Institutions, 1880–1980

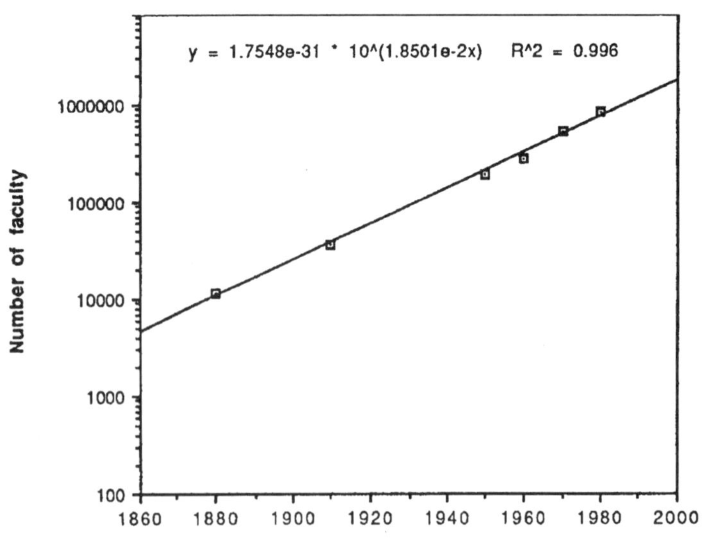

So if science is not really threatened, why is there so much agitation? Sokal has proposed that these are primarily *civil* wars within the other disciplines:

> Finally, *within* academia and the left, this affair tapped into a pre-existing pool of consternation and resentment among non-postmodernist academics in the humanities and social sciences (of which I, as a scientist, was largely unaware). It's this latter factor that has kept the affair going—in the form of innumerable forums, colloquia and debates—in academia.[31]

I think that is fairly accurate. At the "Flight from Science and Reason" conference, the majority of participants were nonscientists, as Paul Gross points out,[32] and some of the most virulent attacks came from that group (see below). My own (mostly anecdotal) experience is also consistent with this interpretation. Very few practicing scientists have yet become aware that anything is happening at all. If I mention to a colleague that I am writing on the "science wars," the inevitable response is, "What is that?"; and when I gave a talk on the topic to a group of inorganic chemists last summer (when the Sokal affair was still going strong in the newspapers), exactly one hand went up (in an audience of nearly one hundred) when I asked who had read or even heard of the Gross and Levitt book. (A "science wars briefing" in a recent issue of *Nature* may help to raise scientific awareness.[33])

Furthermore, I have seen no documentation for the claim that antiscience attitudes have diffused into the general public. A 1995 NSF-funded poll showed not only that the popular attitude towards science is strongly positive but, more importantly, that the level of support has remained essentially constant since the surveys began in 1979.[34] If the "postmodern attacks" on science were having any significant impact outside academe, surely one would expect *some* downward trend during this period.

What about the impact within academe, then? Beyond the sound and fury, is anything tangible happening? This is the question of greatest relevance to our concern about the academic profession. I have little data, but there are a few intriguing cases, most notably in the form of two scholars who were not hired at the Princeton Institute for Advanced Studies.

About six years ago an offer of a position at the Institute to a prominent social scientist, Bruno Latour, was in the works, but scientists at the Institute objected. Frank Wilczek, a particle physicist, commented:

> Roughly speaking, this school [of science studies] takes the techniques anthropologists have used to study preliterate cultures—going in without preconceptions and observing—and applies [these methods] to science. That is clearly inappropriate in the study of modern science. You can't make sense of the endeavor without reference to what it is about. It is a human endeavor and scientists have all the human motivations, but ultimately the test is a confrontation with reality.[35]

As I have mentioned earlier, it is not at all clear to me that observing without preconceptions is an inappropriate method. Even if one agrees (as I do) with the last phrase of Wilczek's quote, the key word there is "ultimately." Nonetheless, the offer was withdrawn. At the time, the event did not attract much general attention. Now history has repeated itself, with the overturning of an appointment to historian of science Norton Wise; this time the controversy has spilled over into the academic world at large as a new battle in the science wars.[36]

How might the evolution of the science wars play out in academe? I can imagine two distinct (but by no means mutually exclusive) scenarios. Continuing with our movie title schema, I will call the first of these the *I'm Gonna Git You Sucka!* scenario. Recall the suggestion, cited earlier, that scientists should monitor tenure decisions in other departments. That has been amplified and expanded, as in the following two remarks (both from philosophers) from the New York Academy of Sciences meeting:

> Walk a few steps away from the faculties of science, engineering, medicine, or law, towards the faculty of arts. Here you will meet another world, one where falsities and lies are tolerated, nay manufactured and taught, in industrial quantities. . . . This fraud has got to be stopped, in the name of intellectual honesty. . . . Let them do that anywhere else they please, but not in schools; for these are supposed to be places of learning. We should expel the charlatans from the university. . . .[37]

> The sole remedy at our disposal is to quarantine the antiscience brigades and inoculate the rest of the population against them. This requires that those who know something about science—I mean scientists—will have to devote some of their energy to systematic confrontation with the enemies of science....[38]

A disturbing aspect of these diatribes, beyond the apocalyptic tone, is the implication that a number of movements, each comprised of many scholars with widely ranging goals and methods, can nonetheless be linked together as the "antiscience brigades." This is a strategy of "unite and conquer" that avoids the need to treat an individual case on its own merits when guilt by association can be imposed instead. In the Wise case several commentators (including Wise himself) suggested that this was the main factor in his rejection, as he is not generally considered to be as controversial and "far out" within the field of science studies as Latour.

A quote from Gross and Levitt, if stated less stridently than the above, offers an even more threatening proposition:

> The humanities, as traditionally understood, are indispensable to our civilization and to the prospects of living a fulfilling life within it. The indispensability of professional academic humanists, on the other hand, is a less certain proposition.... If, taking a fanciful hypothesis, the humanities department at MIT (a bastion, by the way, of left-wing rectitude) were to walk out in a huff, the scientific faculty could...patch together a humanities curriculum, to be taught by the scientists themselves...[that] would be, we imagine, no worse than operative.... The notion that scientists and engineers will always accept as axiomatic the competence and indispensability for higher education of humanists and social scientists is altogether too smug.[39]

There are many possible comments—such as, what should we make of Gross and Levitt's accusation of arrogance on the part of humanists and social scientists in light of the last quote?[40]—but let the obvious one suffice: if these polemics are translated from the realm of rhetoric to that of action, the potential for destroying the quality of life in the academic profession seems virtually limitless.

But there is, I would like to believe, an upside potential as well. If it is true that the rigid and near-universal separation between science and other disciplines has been and is undesirable, is it possible that the science wars could be converted from a wedge, to separate them further, into a bridge (forgive the overused metaphor), to rejoin them? This might be the *Terms of Endearment* scenario. Collaboration, or at least more mutual awareness, between scientists and those engaged in science studies may provide a mechanism whereby each side can get a better idea of what their opposite numbers are up to.

I do not mean to pretend that this is going to be easy to achieve. To begin with, as has often been observed, the practice of science readily consumes all the time that is granted to it. It is quite understandable that the majority of academic scientists, especially young ones struggling for tenure, would feel that devoting any fraction of that time to matters outside their mainstream research— even if they were interested in doing so—could not be justified.[41] And of course the structure of academe only reinforces that conclusion: it rarely offers much in the way of rewards for such interdisciplinary pursuits, or even for critical examination of one's own discipline.

At the same time, a scientist making exploratory moves in the direction of science studies can encounter indications that the welcome mat may not be out. These include some of the examples of rhetorical excess alluded to earlier, which can make it difficult to focus on possible joint agendas, as well as what seem to be explicit rejections of the desirability of cross-boundary interactions, such as:

> The social epistemologist should engage in what ethnomethodologists call "participant observation" of scientific practices. In other words, she should learn to ply her trade in the presence of those whose company she is most likely to loathe.[42]

> The opinions of scientists about science studies are not of much importance. . . . The vision we develop of science does not have to resemble what scientists think about science, any more than the understanding a physician has about the inner workings of my body must resemble what I feel of it.[43]

But we should not make too much out of rhetoric—especially out of individual soundbites. People say different things at different times and places, as chemist Dudley Herschbach noted at the

New York Academy of Sciences meeting,[44] and many of those engaged in science studies, including the last two quoted above, have elsewhere expressed interest in reconciliation. Indeed, there are examples of productive interactions between scientists and those who study science, even though the hostilities get all the press. So perhaps the barriers are not insurmountable.[45]

What is to be gained by striving to surmount them? First and foremost, as already indicated, is the reversal of the fragmentation of the university. If we agree that sharp disciplinary separation is not beneficial to the health of the academic profession, such moves are essential. Beyond that, I believe there are potential advantages for science studies and science alike. I have argued elsewhere that science studies would benefit from collaborations with practicing scientists, while the latter might well find that some of the ideas introduced and elaborated by science studies give them new and stimulating insights into the way they do their work.[46] The intersection of science and public policy is an obvious locus for productive interactions as well.

One topic of particular relevance to the academic profession is science education. Science studies can claim to have debunked the idealized model of science that Philip Kitcher has termed "Legend,"[47] but I expect that any practicing scientist has already learned that lesson from his experience. (That may in part explain why some scientists are little impressed by science studies.) The *teaching* of science, on the other hand, is usually thoroughly imbued with Legend, from beginning surveys for non-science majors all the way up through graduate courses. This was brought home to me a few years ago, reading the student evaluations of an advanced course I taught on catalysis. For such a course, which covers primarily recent and still-ongoing work, I like to present a good deal of the material in case-study mode. That is, I might describe some of the first experiments on a given topic, explain how they led to a certain conclusion, then show how later work changed the interpretation, and so on. A number of students did not care for this at all. "It's too confusing," one evaluation read. "Why can't you just give us the facts?" I found this response rather surprising, especially from graduate students who would shortly be going out into the real world and engaging in that sort of process themselves. On reconsideration, perhaps it is not so surprising if the majority of their education has led them to view science as the unproblematic generation of facts—a view that is not significantly changed until they enter into the actual practice of science. Herschbach has experienced this as well:

> Many students [in introductory science courses] have told me about a disheartening syndrome: the questions and problems seem to have only one right answer, to be found by some canonical procedure. The student who does not quickly grasp the "right" way, or finds it uncongenial, is soon likely to become alienated from science.... Nothing could be further from what actual frontier science is like.[48]

I would make a similar argument concerning the science we teach to those who are *not* going to become scientists: why should they be taught according to a model that we do not take seriously? As noted earlier, many scientific critics are worried about the negative impact of science studies on the public image of science.[49] If the more extreme versions of relativism/constructivism were to be accepted as common wisdom, that certainly *would* be disastrous; but I see little or no evidence that there is any significant danger of that happening. On the other hand, an overly idealized public understanding of how science works is also dangerous: when science (inevitably) fails to live up to the ideal, there will always be the possibility of disenchantment and backlash. Two of my Caltech colleagues have argued convincingly that such misunderstanding is a major factor in much of the recent agitation over scientific "misconduct."[50] Perhaps, in teaching science, the addition of a dose of science studies might be beneficial.[51]

In closing, I would support the above-cited call for scientists to pay some attention to their colleagues outside of science—but not as a confrontation of enemies. No doubt there *are* some enemies out there; but if, as argued here, they pose little real threat to science, the time and energy required would be much more profitably expended in a positive engagement—to the possible benefit of science and science studies, as well as the highly probable benefit of the academic profession—than in escalating the science wars to the next level of bellicosity.

ENDNOTES

[1]See Thomas Bender, "Politics, Intellect, and the American University, 1945–1995," *Dædalus* 126 (1) (Winter 1997): 1–38; and references cited therein.

[2]See Kenneth Prewitt, "America's Research Universities under Public Scrutiny," in Jonathan R. Cole, Elinor G. Barber, and Stephen R. Graubard, eds., *The Research University in a Time of Discontent* (Baltimore, Md.: The Johns Hopkins University Press, 1994), 203–217.

[3]Allan Bloom, *The Closing of the American Mind* (New York: Simon and Schuster, 1987); Page Smith, *Killing the Spirit: Higher Education in America* (New York: Viking, 1990); Roger Kimball, *Tenured Radicals: How Politics Has Corrupted Our Higher Education* (New York: Harper & Row, 1990); Charles J. Sykes, *ProfScam: Professors and the Demise of Higher Education* (Washington, D.C.: Regnery Gateway, 1988).

[4]In a recent assessment of scientific research output, based on citation analysis, the United States, the United Kingdom, and Canada came out with unexpectedly high ratings compared to France and Germany—both countries with strong science traditions and reputations. The author suggested this might be due to the preponderance of research in universities in the former group versus dedicated research institutes in the latter: the university may be a better environment to foster high-quality research. Robert M. May, "The Scientific Wealth of Nations," *Science* 275 (1997): 793–796. Alternatively, of course, it may just be that citation analysis does not really tell us very much about quality.

[5]Andrew Lawlor, "Smoother Road for R&D Spending?" *Science* 275 (1997): 916–919.

[6]See Walter P. Metzger, "The Academic Profession in the United States," Tony Becher, "The Disciplinary Shaping of the Profession," and Kenneth P. Ruscio, "Many Sectors, Many Professions," all in Burton R. Clark, ed., *The Academic Profession: National, Disciplinary, and Institutional Settings* (Berkeley, Calif.: University of California Press, 1987). Of interest in this regard is a recent survey reporting that 77 percent of US academics considered affiliation with their academic discipline to be very important, while only 36 percent felt the same about institutional affiliation: Ernest L. Boyer, Philip G. Altbach, and Mary Jean Whitelaw, *The Academic Profession: An International Perspective* (Princeton, N.J.: The Carnegie Foundation, 1994), 80.

[7]Bloom, *The Closing of the American Mind,* 350.

[8]Recalling the 1959 movie in which the leaders of a small, impoverished nation devise a plan to declare war on the United States and lose, thus ensuring future prosperity; unfortunately they schedule their invasion for a holiday, and it goes completely unnoticed.

[9]Steven Weinberg, *Dreams of a Final Theory: The Search for the Fundamental Laws of Nature* (New York: Pantheon, 1992); Lewis Wolpert, *The Unnatural Nature of Science: Why Science Does Not Make (Common) Sense* (London: Faber & Faber, 1992).

[10]Paul R. Gross and Norman Levitt, *Higher Superstition: The Academic Left and Its Quarrels with Science* (Baltimore, Md.: The Johns Hopkins University Press, 1994).

[11]The proceedings were subsequently published: Paul R. Gross, Norman Levitt, and Martin W. Lewis, eds., *The Flight from Science and Reason* (New York: New York Academy of Sciences, 1996).

[12]*Social Text* 14 (Spring/Summer 1996), reprinted with the addition of a number of articles (and the deletion of one—Sokal's) as Andrew Ross, ed., *Science Wars* (Durham, N.C.: Duke University Press, 1996).

[13]The text of this article, as well as a number of commentaries and many links to related work, may be found at <http://weber.u.washington.edu/~jwalsh/sokal>.

[14]Alan D. Sokal, "A Physicist Experiments with Cultural Studies," *Lingua Franca* (May/June 1996): 62–64.

[15]Sharon Begley, "The Science Wars," *Newsweek* (21 April 1997): 54–57.

[16]Jay A. Labinger, "Science as Culture: A View from the Petri Dish," *Social Studies of Science* 25 (1995): 285–306; and following articles.

[17]Allen J. Bard, "The Antiscience Cancer," *Chemical & Engineering News* (22 April 1996): 5.

[18]Gross and Levitt, *Higher Superstition,* 43–44.

[19]Philip Kitcher, *The Advancement of Science: Science Without Legend, Objectivity Without Illusions* (Oxford: Oxford University Press, 1993), 162.

[20]Susan Haack, "Towards a Sober Sociology of Science," in Gross et al., *The Flight from Science and Reason,* 259–265.

[21]H. M. Collins, "Son of Seven Sexes: The Social Destruction of a Physical Phenomenon," *Social Studies of Science* 11 (1981): 33–62.

[22]Haack, "Towards a Sober Sociology of Science," 261 (my italics).

[23]Labinger, "Science as Culture."

[24]There is a rule to this effect, known as Sturgeon's Law. When challenged that 90 percent of science fiction is crap, science fiction author Theodore Sturgeon freely agreed, but countered that 90 percent of *anything* is crap. I cite this not in support of the magnitude he proposed but simply as a reminder that judging a whole by a few of its more egregious parts can be highly misleading.

[25]Dudley R. Herschbach, "Imaginary Gardens with Real Toads," in Gross et al., *The Flight from Science and Reason,* 11–30.

[26]Theodore Schick, from a paper given at a conference titled "Science in the Age of (Mis)Information," sponsored by the Committee for the Scientific Investigation of Claims of the Paranormal, as reported in the *New York Times,* 7 July 1996.

[27]See, for example, Dorothy Nelkin, "The Science Wars: Response to a Marriage Failed," in Ross, *Science Wars,* 114–122.

[28]Derek da Solla Price, *Little Science, Big Science. . .and Beyond* (New York: Columbia University Press, 1963). See also David L. Goodstein, "Scientific Elites and Scientific Illiterates," *Engineering & Science* 56 (Spring 1993): 23–31; John Ziman, *Prometheus Bound: Science in a Dynamic Steady State* (Cambridge: Cambridge University Press, 1994); Rodney W. Nichols, "Federal Science Policy and Universities: Consequences of Success," in Cole et al., *The Research University in a Time of Discontent,* 271–298.

[29]Data from Metzger, "The Academic Profession in the United States," 124.

[30]Stephen R. Graubard, "The Research University: Notes Toward a New History," in Cole et al., *The Research University in a Time of Discontent,* 361.

[31]Alan D. Sokal, posted on an e-mail discussion list, 12 December 1996. A similar view is suggested in John R. Searle, "Rationality and Realism, What Is at Stake?" in Cole et al., *The Research University in a Time of Discontent,* 55–83.

[32]Paul R. Gross, Letter to the Editor, *Chronicle of Higher Education,* 20 October 1995, B3.

[33]*Nature* 387 (22 May 1997): 331–335.

[34]Andrew Lawlor, "Support for Science Stays Strong," *Science* 272 (31 May 1996): 1256.

[35]David Berreby, ". . .that damned elusive Bruno Latour," *Lingua Franca* (September/October 1994): 24

[36]Liz McMillen, "The Science Wars Flare at the Institute for Advanced Study," *Chronicle of Higher Education,* 16 May 1997, A13.

[37]Mario Bunge, "In Praise of Intolerance to Charlatanism in Academia," in Gross et al., *The Flight from Science and Reason,* 96–115.

[38]Barry R. Gross, "Flights of Fancy: Science, Reason, and Common Sense," in Gross et al., *The Flight from Science and Reason,* 79–86.

[39]Gross and Levitt, *Higher Superstition,* 242–243.

[40]One might counter with a diploma form suggested by a scientist in 1955: "The Johns Hopkins University certifies that John Wentworth Doe does *not* know anything but Biochemistry. Please pay no attention to any pronouncement he may make on any other subject, particularly when he joins with others of his kind to save the world from something or other. However, he worked hard for this degree and is potentially a most valuable citizen. Please treat him kindly." Cited in John C. Burnham, *How Superstition Won and Science Lost* (New Brunswick, N.J.: Rutgers University Press, 1987), 251. Presumably the truth lies somewhere in between?

[41]On the other hand, it might be noted—admittedly, rather cynically—that as scientists find it increasingly difficult to obtain full funding for mainstream research, the possibility of engaging in some (relatively inexpensive) part-time work at the borders of science may start to look more attractive.

[42]Steve Fuller, *Philosophy, Rhetoric and the End of Knowledge* (Madison, Wis.: University of Wisconsin Press, 1993), 311.

[43]Bruno Latour, Letter to the Editor, *The Sciences* (March/April 1995): 6–7

[44]Herschbach, "Imaginary Gardens with Real Toads," 15.

[45]A reviewer wondered whether the increasing numbers of women and minorities who become practicing scientists might make a difference, since their viewpoints play prominent roles in critiques of science. Again there is little hard data, but my impression is that the (lack of) awareness of science studies is essentially the same among these groups as for scientists in general.

[46]Labinger, "Science as Culture."

[47]Kitcher, *The Advancement of Science,* 3–10.

[48]Herschbach, "Imaginary Gardens with Real Toads," 17.

[49]Concern for the public image of science does not necessarily imply respect for those who try to do something about it, as Gould pointed out in his eulogy for the late Carl Sagan. Stephen Jay Gould, "Bright Star Among Billions," *Science* 275 (1997): 599.

[50]James Woodward and David Goodstein, "Conduct, Misconduct and the Structure of Science," *American Scientist* 84 (September-October 1996): 479–490.

[51]A similar argument was offered in a recent editorial in *Nature.* "Science Wars and the Need for Respect and Rigour," *Nature* 385 (1997): 373. See also Henry H. Bauer, *Scientific Literacy and the Myth of the Scientific Method* (Urbana, Ill.: University of Illinois Press, 1992).

Cheryl B. Leggon

The Scientist as Academic

T O UNDERSTAND THE SCIENTIST AS ACADEMIC in today's university environment, it is important to understand the sociohistorical contexts of the scientific and academic professions in the United States. Science is as much a profession as medicine and law. And like medicine and law, it has made a social contract with the larger society. This contract is possible because the scientific community has convinced the public and state legislatures that it is devoted to public service.[1] The key stipulation of this contract is that scientists will exercise control over the community of science. The questions subject to their control include such fundamental matters as who is trained to do science; how scientists are trained and by whom; and how—and by whom—scientists' professional conduct is regulated. The rationale underlying this stipulation is that only scientists are qualified to evaluate science and other scientists, because science is based on a specialized body of knowledge. What distinguishes science (and other professions) from nonprofessional occupations is that at both the macro and micro levels "knowledge is the basis for the power that is the basis for professional status."[2] One recurring theme in the relationship between the community of scientists and the larger society is that science has established itself as the means by which the larger society is able to achieve its goals. The essence of the social contract between science and American society is summed up well by historian David Noble:

> The control over science by scientists—the hallmark of the postwar pattern—is increasingly becoming the control over science by the

---

Cheryl B. Leggon is Associate Professor of Sociology at Wake Forest University.

221

science-based corporations that scientists serve and sometimes own or direct. The issue here has little to do with the fanciful contrast between "basic" and "applied" research, and even less with the struggle to defend "pure" research against external controls. The issue, rather, has always been—and continues to be—control by whom, and to what end?[3]

Since World War II, science and scientists have been held in high esteem by American society. In 1957, the Soviet launch of *Sputnik* served as a catalyst—reaffirming the importance of science and technology for defense and space research, obviously, but also for other kinds of scientific inquiry. That this is true is most clearly demonstrated by the fact that funds from the defense and space agencies generously supported university researchers—especially engineers. Between 1960 and 1968, total federal spending on research and development increased by an average of over 5 percent per year, in real terms.[4]

Science was viewed as the means to a better standard of living for all. The broad popularity of this belief was reflected in the advertising slogans of two major US corporations: "better living through chemistry," and "progress is our most important product." The decades of the 1950s and 1960s were a golden age for higher education and science in the United States. Scientists were more influential then than ever before in US history. Science's public popularity and acclaim were epitomized by *Time* magazine selecting fifteen scientists as its collective men (*sic*) of the year for 1961, stating that "science is at the apogee of its power."[5]

This heady environment began to change during the mid-1960s, as the broader society became increasingly willing to scrutinize the scientific community and insist that it be more accountable and demonstrate the social relevance of its research through specific measures of progress in such areas as highway safety, crime, poverty, and urban decay. This trend intensified during the Nixon administration, which imposed the largest cuts in the science budget since the end of World War II. Part of this change in the esteem for science can be attributed to the lessening of Cold War tensions during the early 1970s years of détente, which brought a reduction in the emphasis placed on research funding. Part can be attributed to the public's realization that the scientific products of the postwar decades were not uniformly beneficial—a realization heightened by such high-profile disasters as Three Mile Island and Love Canal.[6] Since the mid-1980s pressure has increased in Congress to shift national attention away from basic science and toward science with technological applications able to bolster declining American economic competitiveness.[7]

Over the last half century, there have been major changes in the way science is done. Perhaps foremost among these has been the greater scale and complexity of the questions science is addressing—which has, inevitably, brought about the blurring of disciplinary boundaries within the natural sciences in general, and between the so-called hard and soft sciences in particular.[8] Also significant is the rise of multi-investigator, multi-institutional programs to focus on costly problems. Revolutionary advances in computing and communications technology have also transformed all scientific fields.[9]

In assessing the significance of these and other dynamic trends, it must be kept in mind that the current status of the social contract between scientists and the broader American society is still fundamentally the result of the scientific community's enormous and myriad achievements on behalf of the nation's safety during World War II. The terms of the postwar, peacetime contract between scientists and the larger society were first articulated in a report entitled "Science: The Endless Frontier," issued by Vannevar Bush, the director of the wartime Office of Scientific Research and Development (OSRD). There is no consensus on the origin of this report. Some, including Bush himself, attributed its origin to a conversation between Bush and President Franklin D. Roosevelt. According to this version, Bush expressed concern about support for science after World War II; Roosevelt, in reply, requested a report to respond to this concern. Others, such as Oscar M. Ruelhausen (general counsel of OSRD), attributed the origin of the report to an influential government lawyer, Oscar S. Cox. Cox wanted to adopt the administrative technique developed by OSRD for defense in peacetime.[10] Despite the lack of consensus on the origin of "Science: The Endless Frontier," there is consensus that the report was written in a highly charged political context—the growing debate over how the federal government "should advance science for the general welfare in peacetime."[11] Significantly, this report linked the fortunes of science to those of the government: "Since health, well-being, and security are proper concerns of government, scientific progress is, and must be, of vital interest to the government."[12] The report acknowledged and gave official sanction to the unchallenged right of the scientific community to manage its own affairs. This meant that the government agreed to let the scientific community decide how funds were allocated and the scientific assessment of their use.[13] The definitive characteristic of this contract was that scientists controlled science—how it was done, by whom, and under what conditions.

During the 1970s, corporate America revived the view that investment in basic research was an essential prerequisite for the nation's economic prosperity. "Science's return to political favor, after its period in the wilderness during the Nixon presidency, had started in the mid-1970s under President Ford and had rapidly gathered some steam under [President] Carter."[14] Governmental funding for basic research expanded significantly at the end of the Ford administration; federal support for science rose to an all-time high. Not incidentally, the number of institutions in the United States offering doctoral programs increased significantly during the 1970s and 1980s; this trend continued into the 1990s. In 1970 there were 173 institutions awarding doctorates; in 1987, there were 213; and in 1994, 236.[15]

These changed circumstances were the backdrop for a revision of the terms of the social contract between scientists and society in the 1980s. Under the Reagan presidency major changes in science policy occurred; the private sector assumed a dominant role in setting the agenda for the public funding of science. One key aspect of this was a fundamental change in perspective on the part of the scientific community. The paradigm of the scientist as independent scholar, motivated solely by the pursuit of knowledge for knowledge's sake (and, hence, unconcerned about the eventual utility of one's research), was overtaken by a new model of the "savvy," cost-conscious, bottom-line oriented, entrepreneurial researcher. This shift affected academic institutions decisively. David Dickson, an authority on the new politics of science, has argued that the social responsibilities of scientists were redefined as "the need to help private corporations achieve their economic and political objectives."[16]

As universities' basic research agendas have become increasingly affected by corporate needs, the gap between what is considered basic research and what is regarded as applied commercial development has narrowed. This, in turn, has established a range of new relationships between academe and the private sector.[17] Foremost among these arrangements is the use of university scientists as private consultants, a trend particularly pronounced in biotechnology. These new relationships have also resulted in a growing convergence of interests between academe and industry, the most important among which is shared opposition to nonscientific control of the production and application of scientifically generated knowledge. In similar, if not unexpected fashion, both industry and academe favor increased government funding of basic science and the university infrastructures needed to perform it.

The far-reaching result of this new relationship between academe and industry is that it has fundamentally changed the norms of science. Consider, for example, the dramatic shift in how members of the scientific community view the norm of open communication among scientists. Nearly twenty-five years ago the eminent sociologist of science, Robert Merton, described this norm as "communism," because of its overarching presumption that all intellectual property was held in common by the community of scientists.[18] But as scientists have increasingly found it possible to realize individual profit from their roles as researchers or consultants, they become reluctant to discuss their findings openly in the laboratory and at professional meetings for fear that a colleague might capitalize financially on them. Needless to say, such a view strikes at the very heart of the time-honored norm of the open communication of ideas, fundamental to Western scientific development for centuries. Moreover, this barrier to open communication disrupts relationships among research workers. Graduate students are affected insofar as it may influence the choice of problems selected for their work. A related effect is a "faculty brain drain" resulting from university faculty members leaving academic positions to pursue the same research in a commercial setting where they realize greater benefits. There can be no question that the scope of this trend is already such as to jeopardize the ability of many universities to train a new generation of research workers.[19]

WHO ARE THE NEW SCIENTIST-ACADEMICS?

It is important to note that the professional experiences of the scientist as academic vary along key dimensions. One dimension encompasses the differences among the fields that comprise the natural sciences, differences in such basic considerations as how, and under what conditions, science is done. For example, biology and chemistry require an extensive infrastructure of laboratories, equipment, and staff; mathematics does not. Similarly, differences can be found among the natural sciences regarding the extent to which a discipline has been able to convince the larger society of its importance to the nation's future; this varies considerably across disciplines, and within a discipline over time.

The dimension of greatest interest to sociologists is the setting or type of institution within which the scientist as academic works. Institutions of higher education differ in terms of whether the institution is private or public, two-year or four-year, religious-affiliated or not, exclusive or inclusive in its admissions policies, has a large or small teaching load, a greater or lesser focus on research, adequate or inadequate funding, and similar consider-ations. Still another source of difference is whether the institution is dedicated to certain historic objectives—e.g., historically black colleges and universities (HBCUs), women's colleges, and institu-tions serving predominantly Hispanic communities. In turn, these differences contribute to variations in working conditions among higher-education institutions. For example, the scientist as aca-demic working in an HBCU with a heavy teaching load has less time for research than his or her counterpart working in a research institution with a lighter teaching load.

One of the most important dimensions along which professional experiences differ is stage in career. In today's university, it is useful and possible to distinguish between two groups of scientists: those heading toward the end of their career and those at the beginning. Such a distinction is necessary simply because the pat-tern of career experiences is profoundly different for these two groups. Because it is the "new" scientists who find themselves bearing the brunt of much of science's current problems, they are the focus of this discussion.[20]

A recent study uses data from a 1992 faculty survey to create a demographic profile of the American professoriate.[21] This study operationally defines the new scientists as the group of full-time faculty members who were in the first seven years of their career at the time of the survey, having been hired during the years from 1986 to 1992. These new scientists comprised a little more than one-third of the 482,963 full-time faculty members employed in teaching positions in the fall of 1992. Compared to their senior colleagues, these new scientists were more likely to be women, somewhat more likely to be members of minority groups, and less likely to be foreign-born.

More recent studies show that women comprise more than 40 percent of the new-faculty generation but only 28 percent of the senior faculty. Women's rising graduate enrollment and men's falling graduate enrollment in science and engineering (S&E) has increased women's share of graduate S&E enrollment to 38 percent.[22] Further, these differences are field specific. Men are concentrated in fields in which total enrollment is decreasing—notably, mathematical and computer sciences, physical sciences, and engineering. Women, by contrast, are concentrated in fields in which total enrollment is stable or increasing—for example, the biological sciences. Women are newcomers to engineering as well; while in 1970 women accounted for less than 1 percent of earned bachelor's degrees in engineering, in 1991 they accounted for almost 16 percent.

Newly hired women outnumber newly hired men at both liberal-arts and community colleges, yet they are only one-third of the new hires at doctoral institutions.[23] Women continue to have difficulty getting tenure in general, and particularly at the most prestigious research institutions. Nationwide, almost one-fourth of the tenured faculty are women; by contrast, at elite research universities, the proportion is a little better than one-tenth.[24] The irony is that the rhetoric of such institutions suggests a far more substantial effort to appoint outstanding women to their faculties.

Women on faculties are less satisfied with their positions than their male colleagues. This is not surprising in light of reported differences in working conditions between female and male faculty. Compared to their male colleagues, women are more likely to work in part-time rather than in full-time positions; to earn lower salaries; to be found in the lower professorial ranks; to have higher teaching loads and more committee and advising assignments; and to work in less prestigious institutions.[25]

Almost 17 percent of the new-generation faculty members were members of minority groups, as compared to 11 percent of the senior professors. The proportion of minority professors among the US professoriate increased at a glacial pace from 9 percent in 1989 to about 10 percent in 1995–1996.[26] However, it is important to note that the category "minority groups" includes Asian Americans and that as a group Asian American men made the biggest gains among the new-generation group.[27] These gains are attributable, in part, to the fact that Asian American professors tend to work in fields that pay more, such as the physical sciences and engineering. According to a report on faculty job satisfaction, compared to their white counterparts, minority faculty are less likely to be tenured; are concentrated in lower academic ranks and have greater teaching loads; and often feel they encounter prejudice, discrimination, and a continuing climate of racism.[28]

New-generation faculty members are less likely than their senior colleagues to have been born in the United States. According to "The American Faculty in Transition: A First Look at the New Academic Generation," a recent study by the National Center for Education Statistics, approximately one-quarter of the new-generation scholars were not US-born, compared to less than 16 percent of their senior colleagues. Moreover, this increase is attributed largely to the shift in the natural sciences, in which about 75 percent of the junior scientists were US-born as compared to 86 percent of the senior scientists.[29] This is consistent with trend data showing that between 1985 and 1995 the number of non-US citizens earning doctorates in the United States doubled, accounting for almost two-thirds of the growth in doctorates during that ten-year period.[30] More than 70 percent of non-US citizens earning doctoral degrees from US universities specialized in the life sciences, physical sciences, and engineering. In 1995, non-US citizens accounted for 32 percent of all Ph.D.s, 45 percent of those in the physical sciences and 60 percent of those in engineering. The issue of the numbers and proportions of US-born Ph.D. recipients in the sciences is important in the context of the argument that the weak job market in the sciences is partially attributable to the increased hiring of non-US scientists by US institutions. Recent data support this argument. The percentage of non-US Ph.D.s staying in the United States after graduation has increased from 54 percent in

1985 to 65 percent in 1995. During that ten-year period, the number of non-US Ph.D.s with employment commitments at graduation increased by 30 percent, while the number seeking work or postdoctoral study grew by more than 250 percent. Moreover, the number of non-US Ph.D.s seeking work or study at the time of graduation increased from 32 percent in 1985 to 43 percent in 1995. According to a recent summary of earned doctorates, "a disproportionate share of those still seeking work or study at graduation are non-US Ph.D.s."[31]

Overall, 45 percent of the new-generation faculty members have been hired by research and doctoral institutions, 24 percent by master's institutions, 19 percent by two-year colleges, 8 percent by liberal-arts colleges, and the rest by other institutions. These percentages vary by gender, race, and ethnicity. It is noteworthy, for example, that "just over 46 percent of all full-time female academics at research institutions have been in academe for seven years or less."[32] Asian Americans are concentrated on the faculties of research institutions. Over one-third of Latino and Native American faculty work at two-year colleges; the corresponding figure for their white colleagues is 23 percent.

Not surprisingly, a greater percentage of the senior professors than of new-generation faculty are tenured or in tenure-track positions. Regardless of gender and ethnicity, new faculty members are taking longer to land full-time faculty appointments than did their mentors. In addition, new faculty members are twice as likely as their mentors to work in an employment sector outside of postsecondary education. In sum, the career paths for new-generation faculty members appear to be different from those of the senior faculty. The latter's career path was usually from doctorate to postdoctorate to full-time position; the former's path is from doctorate to a series of postdoctorate positions and *perhaps* to full-time positions. The chance that a new science Ph.D. will be able to secure permanent full-time employment in academe is dropping every year. This is an inevitable result of an increase in the growth of poorly paid, temporary jobs in academic science and the decline of full-time, tenured positions.[33]

MAJOR ISSUES FACING THE SCIENTIST AS ACADEMIC

Results from a 1995–1996 survey on race and ethnicity in the American professoriate indicate that "All scholars, regardless of race, complained that they were feeling more stress than they did in 1989. Time pressures, lack of personal time, and household responsibilities weighed heavily on them, and women felt more burdened than men."[34] The Internet, not surprisingly, is one medium being used to help scientists deal with stress. An electronic bulletin board called the Young Scientists' Network (YSN) has developed into a vehicle through which young scientists can share their professional problems and solutions, and commiserate with each other.[35]

Several major factors influence the career of the new scientist as academic in today's university: 1) increased competition for funding and jobs; 2) growth in the number of untenured academic science jobs; 3) technological developments; 4) change in academic priorities; and 5) the adequacy of traditional graduate school training to prepare students for the contemporary job market.

Increased competition for both funding and jobs can be attributed to one factor—that there are too many Ph.D.s in science in the United States. In 1995, the number of new Ph.D.s reached a record high of 41,610, including 7,913 in the life sciences, 6,806 in the physical sciences, and 6,623 in the social sciences.[36] A smaller proportion of Ph.D.s in 1995 than before reported definite postgraduation commitments.

That the academic job market is unable to absorb these new science Ph.D.s is supported by statistics from a survey of those who earned doctorates.[37] Of those with definite commitments, a smaller proportion of Ph.D.s planned to be employed and a larger proportion planned postdoctoral study than previously. Among both US citizens and permanent residents receiving doctorates between 1975 and 1995 and having postgraduation commitments in the United States, the percentage of those committed to work in academe increased slightly for fields in the physical sciences (from 40.6 to 41.5 percent) but decreased somewhat for those in the life sciences (from 58.5 to 53.3 percent). In those same two decades, the percentage of doctorate recipients with postgraduation commitments to industry or self-employment within the United States increased for both the physical sciences and the life sciences.

A study by the Committee on Science, Engineering, and Public Policy (COSEPUP) of the National Research Council noted that 16 percent of all 1993 chemistry Ph.D.s were looking for work the summer after graduation, as were 14 percent of new physics Ph.D.s. In 1994, 14 percent of new mathematics Ph.D.s were looking for work after graduation.[38] In light of these data, it is remarkable that for almost a decade there has been a debate among those in the scientific community about whether there are too many science Ph.D.s.[39]

The sheer number of science Ph.D.s is partially responsible in turn for the overall trend toward a decline in the numbers of scientists obtaining grants since the 1960s. Indeed, actually obtaining funding for a research-grant application now depends on achieving rank scores consistently at the "outstanding" level; "above average" is no longer sufficient to obtain favorable consideration.[40] Although increased competition for research funding affects both men and women, it affects women disproportionately for the simple reason that more women than men are in the junior ranks, a stage in their career at which research funds are most difficult to obtain.[41] Of course, from the perspective of the employing institution, grants give a scientist a dual advantage; the ability to win grants increases both an individual scientist's stature within his or her department and the clout of the department within the university.[42]

New-generation scientists can be divided into two broad groups. The first consists of the many who must work in postdoctoral or temporary research positions for years because they cannot find jobs. The second group consists of those who find jobs but cannot, because of their relatively junior status, find the funding for their research. For example, a 1995 report from the American Chemical Society stated that "suitable permanent employment" was not readily available for 250 (or 12 percent) of the 2,100 Ph.D.s in chemistry awarded annually.[43] This is significant when placed in the context of the 1993 unemployment rates of 2 percent for recent Ph.D. recipients and 1.6 percent for all scientists and engineers.[44] Moreover, the proportion of S&E Ph.D.s employed by academe has fallen from 51 percent in 1977 to 43 percent in 1991.[45]

Also compelling is the qualitative evidence of a glut of science Ph.D.s. While some members of the US scientific community debate whether there might be a shortage of Ph.D.s, young scientists' professional experiences tell them that the opposite is true. These experiences range from anecdotes about having to take a series of postdoctoral positions because full-time positions were scarce to the many cases in which there are several hundred applications for one teaching job. One of the self-proclaimed purposes of the Young Scientists' Network is to inform the public that young scientists are *not* in short supply, but that they are being forced out of science because they cannot find jobs.[46]

Three things can be done to improve the Ph.D. science job market: reduce the supply of Ph.D. scientists, increase the demand for them, or both. The supply can be reduced by cutting down on the number of students accepted into Ph.D. programs—an unlikely outcome for at least two reasons. First, allocations of resources to academic departments are usually based on student enrollments; thus, departments face an unambiguous disincentive to exercise self-limitation. Second, graduate students are a source of labor for both teaching and research. Hence, increasing the demand for science Ph.D.s—perhaps by redesigning graduate programs to impart a broader range of marketable skills—seems a more realistic way to improve the job market.

The increase in competition for both jobs and funds has caused major problems for the young academic scientist. Current conditions in the science job market in the United States result not only in unemployment and underemployment but also frustration, anxiety, and disrupted family and personal lives. For example, anecdotes abound regarding young scientists who have put marriage plans on hold "indefinitely" because of the uncertainty in the American science job market. Although this is problematic for all scientists, it is particularly acute for female scientists who must also deal with the "three-clock" problem: "a woman must synchronize her biological clock, her career clock, and her partner's career clock."[47] A partner's career clock often has a significant impact on the careers of female scientists because they are far more likely than male scientists to be married to another scientist. A partner's career impacts the female scientist in other ways as well. For example, she may choose her graduate institution based on its geographic proximity to her partner's place of graduate study or work instead of its fit with her professional interests. In turn, this affects the quality of the institution at which she will be able to receive her first full-time, post-Ph.D. employment. Thus, the ramifications of personal life choices for female scientists are not only short-term and long-term, but cumulative.

Although permanent full-time positions are at a premium, postdoctoral positions in science have increased 63 percent from 1982 to 1992 (an increase in absolute numbers from 15,000 to 24,000).[48] The growth in untenured academic science jobs can be attributed to two factors. First, increasing pressures on college and university budgets encourage institutions to cut labor costs wherever possible—and to be more hesitant in committing to individuals through tenure.[49] Second, the overproduction of Ph.D.s in many disciplines results in increasingly fierce competition for both research funds and the relatively few full-time positions available.

Both part-time and nontenure-track positions entail major disadvantages for the academic scientist's career. These disadvantages include low salaries, little job security, low or no benefits, no voice in institutional governance, and limited opportunities to write grants in order to begin independent research. Perhaps the most pernicious aspect of these positions is the stigma attached to them. This stems from a time when full-time jobs were more plentiful and those in part-time positions may have been thought to be less qualified or less committed to their jobs than the full-timers. In years past, many such part-time positions were held by women—consequently, the issue of part-timers came to be seen as a "woman's issue." If women are still affected by the part-time stigma, some degree of equality may be found in the fact that the stigma has begun to affect men as well, such that it has now been redefined as a "young scientist's issue."[50] Ironically, perspectives toward these postdoctoral part-time positions held by postdocs themselves and the academic employers they hope to attract are polar opposites. Postdocs and part-timers generally view these positions as a way to enhance their resume and "get a foot in the door" of full-time employment. To the contrary, employers view those positions as indicators of someone whose career does not merit a full-time faculty position. Indeed, there seem to be two separate employment tracks stretching across the landscape of academic institutions—one for full-time faculty and the other for part-time faculty. Movement from the part-time to the full-time track is rare.

Computer and other communication technology have the potential to exert a profound effect on the career of the scientist as academic in many ways. First, both e-mail and fax technologies have enhanced the research process by speeding the exchange of data among researchers. With these technologies, geographic distance need no longer place limits on who collaborates with whom—thus giving rise to a virtually limitless number of new communities with which the scientist as academic can affiliate. Historically, professionals have been part of two basic communities: the institution in which they work, and the community of fellow professionals outside their workplace. The myriad additional communities made possible by advances in communications technology could have significant implications for determining the community or communities with which the scientist as academic chooses to identify. A new model in the business world uses technology to link people, assets, and ideas in temporary organizations called virtual offices to perform a particular task. Can we not already point to a parallel to this in the sciences, as technology links people, assets, and ideas in temporary organizations called virtual universities?[51]

Not only is technology transforming how research is done, it is also transforming how teaching is—or will be—done. The increasing use of technology by faculty results from a combination of push and pull factors. The pull factor is that the technology is improving and becoming more user-friendly. The push factor is that many students enter college experienced in using the technology—often more experienced than some members of the faculty.[52] Some teachers already make extensive use of the World Wide Web for several reasons: it is user friendly; it enables them to provide more current information to their students on a real-time basis; and it offers the ability to integrate multiple media.[53] Of course this is not meant to imply that most faculty use this technology in their classes at the present; indeed, my guess is that most do not. Nevertheless, some Web enthusiasts envisage a transformation so pronounced that the professor will become more of a coach or facilitator than a teacher, in an environment of hands-on, user-paced, technology-based instruction. The ramifications of trends in instructional technology for the faculty member have not been thought through at all comprehensively. For example, having students communicate with their professor by e-mail means that the professor must sit at the keyboard and respond to each e-mail message. The simple fact that this changed mode of communication with students can be time-consuming must be taken into account in assessing the professor's work load and performance.

During the decade of the 1950s there occurred a shift in academic priorities from teaching/research/service to research/teaching/service. This shift suggests that research has grown in importance at the expense of service and teaching. For many reasons—not the least of which is the decrease in funding for academic research—some argue for the need to restore teaching to its former primary position. This does not mean teaching "old" disciplines in new ways. For example, some academic mathematicians contend that both the approach and content of university mathematics are dangerously out of synch with the needs of both students and industry.[54] Usually, the professor writes problems on the board and then proceeds to solve them for a freshman calculus class consisting of two hundred or more people. Some contend that this old pedagogy is partially responsible for the drop in the number of students who express an interest in mathematics. They argue that it is also responsible for the truism in the mathematics community that the half-life of mathematics students is one year—i.e., that as a group of students progresses in college, half the mathematics students leave the field each year.[55]

In the United States, the traditional model for graduate education in the sciences is organized around intensive research experience.[56] During the 1950s and 1960s, posts in academic science expanded tremendously, and the subsequent growth in demand for university teaching and research staff provided graduate students with a seemingly inexhaustible source of jobs and options. Consequently, students became oriented toward careers in academic science. Some members of the American science community have suggested that this model is inappropriate for the needs of the contemporary job market, in which there is a paucity of tenured and tenure-track academic positions. Many institutions are "over tenured" and have few if any slots available. Graduate education programs need to be revamped to better prepare students for career paths other than the traditional one leading to academe. For example, Anne C. Petersen, former deputy director of the National Science Foundation, suggests that "the Ph.D. should be construed in our society more like the law degree. A lot of people go to law school with no plans to practice law."[57]

A recent report, "Reshaping the Graduate Education of Scientists and Engineers," suggests that doctoral education must change to have a broader training focus, preparing people for careers outside academe.[58] Some institutions have already begun to do this. For the past four years, the physics department at the Massachusetts Institute of Technology has exposed graduate students to alternative careers through a series of seminars scheduled during the winter break. These seminars feature physicists who are management consultants, patent lawyers, and business owners. Northwestern University's department of biochemistry, molecular biology, and cell biology uses an interdisciplinary approach to subtly introduce graduate students to alternative careers. In 1994 the department stopped offering its own Ph.D.s and instead created an Interdepartmental Biological Sciences Program. This program includes biochemistry, molecular biology, cell biology, as well as civil engineering. In the same vein, at the University of Colorado graduate students can broaden their training by completing one of six interdisciplinary programs in science—such as environmental policy.[59] The University of California at Berkeley has a seminar series on biotechnology companies for graduate students in the biological sciences and business; this series was proposed by a group of graduate students. Finally, the University of Michigan's chemistry department plans to offer during the 1997–1998 academic year a graduate course to teach workplace skills, such as writing a clear and concise memorandum, that students can use anywhere.[60]

Several factors must be taken into account to understand the situation of the scientist as academic today. First, we must think of ways to help graduate science education programs meet the needs of both the Ph.D. scientist and the contemporary job market. Perhaps graduate programs in science could include components to teach Ph.D. scientists how to look for a job and how to market themselves. This could be done through a "professional seminar" walking students through the steps of preparing a research proposal, a book prospectus, or similar necessary techniques. This would also include teaching students how to negotiate the terms of their employment—regardless of the potential sector of employment. Most important, we need to think of ways for graduate programs to broaden their focus in order to prepare students for careers other than those in academe. This is particularly important in light of a recent finding that "employers complain that new Ph.D.s are often too specialized for the range of tasks that they will confront and that they have a difficult time in adapting to the demands of nonacademic work."[61]

Second, graduate schools should not be the only ones concerned with broadening the focus of graduate education; funding agencies should share this concern. For example, one scientist at the National Institutes of Health is working on funding programs to offer other tracks to Ph.D.s in the biological sciences, such as science administration (proposal and grant reviewers).[62]

Finally, the community of scientists—teachers, researchers, policy analysts, administrators, and program evaluators—needs to take responsibility for educating the public about science. A major source of the intensified competition for both jobs and research grants is inadequate funding, itself in large part a result of the shrinking constituency of science in the broader society. As one recent commentator has averred, "Research is a public service. . .and the current system for academic research is not responding effectively to social change."[63] Secretary of Health and Human Services Donna Shalala has expressed the point well: "If science is to thrive, every citizen must be an active constituent of science."[64] This is especially important insofar as the public, long since having left behind its unquestioning admiration for the scientific endeavor, seems increasingly to view scientists' quest for knowledge as "a prodigious appetite for more money and more growth that cannot be sustained."[65] Since the ultimate source of government funds is the public, strategically it seems prudent to educate the public about the value of science and scientific research. Members of the scientific community cannot escape asking themselves, "Who is our patron and what is our public policy for establishing relevance?" Cora B. Marrett, provost at the University of Massachusetts–Amherst and formerly the first assistant director of the Social, Behavioral, and Economic Sciences Directorate at the National Science Foundation, suggests that part of the reason funding for research in the social sciences has come under attack may lie in the fact that social scientists have not fully educated the public—

and Congress—about the impact their programs may have.[66] This suggestion applies to the natural science community as well. Natural scientists must take the initiative in educating the public about the value of their work. Given the current funding climate, they quite simply cannot afford to leave the scientific education of the public to anyone other than themselves.

CONCLUSIONS AND IMPLICATIONS FOR POLICY

Changes in the context in which science is practiced require changes in the scientific enterprise. The increase in the numbers of Ph.D. scientists and the subsequent increase in competition for jobs makes necessary a thoroughgoing reexamination of both notions of careers and career paths for science Ph.D.s. The argument that the problems of the new-generation scientist are due to a glut of science Ph.D.s is based on two important—but nevertheless implicit—assumptions: first, that young Ph.D.s should follow the same career path as their mentors (simply no longer possible given the decline in the numbers of tenure and tenure-track positions); and second, that "success" is implicitly defined as obtaining a full-time tenure-track position in a college or university. This definition is already inappropriate, because more than half of the new graduates with Ph.D.s in science fields—such as chemistry—already work outside academe.[67]

Perhaps the fundamental error has been examining the prospects for young Ph.D. scientists with a lens that focuses only on a single, narrow sector, namely, academe. If we take a wider view of the employment arena and define success for graduate students in science more broadly to encompass nonresearch, applied research, and development positions, we would see that there does appear to be a significant number of positions for science Ph.D.s. Moreover, these nontraditional career paths may be more appealing to underrepresented groups—such as non-Asian minorities and women in the science community. Indeed, the problem does not seem to be supply, but distribution. "Studies have shown that imbalances between supply and demand do not lead to crises; we do not have unfilled jobs, but jobs filled by people from other areas."[68] Broadening our conceptualization of successful careers for Ph.D. scientists entails reexamining how we train those scientists.

It seems that a narrow view has been taken of the purpose of graduate education in science. In addition to training researchers and teachers, graduate science programs provide the education, training, knowledge, and skills required to address a growing range of social and economic issues. Many science and engineering disciplines are experiencing rapid changes in their knowledge base. To be prepared for tomorrow's jobs, today's science students must be adaptable. Adaptability results as much from socialization as it does from education.[69] Therefore, it is necessary to inculcate in science Ph.D.s the skill to recognize opportunities to use their training, and the ability to take advantage of those opportunities. In addition to substantive knowledge, the research and analytical skills imparted through graduate programs in science are in demand for many jobs, such as those in aviation, finance, and industries in which technical skills are an advantage. Moreover, scientists could apply these skills to start their own businesses.

In the context of what some contend is a poor job market for science Ph.D.s, major scientific funding organizations—the National Science Foundation and the National Institutes of Health—continue to sponsor initiatives to increase the diversity of the scientific enterprise in the United States by increasing the representation of women and underrepresented racial/ethnic minority groups among the scientific community. Regardless of the job market, it is important to diversify the scientific labor force in order to broaden and deepen the science talent pool. Tomorrow's scientists are trained by today's scientists. Who does science determines who will do science insofar as scientists function as gatekeepers who recruit, train, socialize, and mentor other scientists.[70] As socialized human beings, scientists bring to their profession values, beliefs, and experiences that shape their approach to their work. Increasing the participation in science careers of people from underrepresented groups increases the probability that there will be scientists working on problems that are significant to the diverse groups comprising the US population. Who does science has significance for science in terms of which problems are selected for study and how they are framed; which populations are selected as subjects and which benefit from the research; how data are collected and analyzed; and how results are reported. In sum, diversifying the science talent pool enriches the entire S&E enterprise by expanding the perspectives reflected in the knowledge base.[71]

What appears in the narrow context of full-time tenure-track positions in colleges and universities to be a loss for science Ph.D.s obtaining "successful" positions can instead be considered a gain for the entire system as well as for individual science Ph.D.s. A scientist who earns a Ph.D. at a top-tier institution and whose first full-time position is at a third- or fourth-tier institution gives that institution the talent, training, and skills that it could not get in a different job market. This same principle applies to the science Ph.D. whose first full-time position is teaching science in elementary and secondary schools. What is the loss? Not salary, because Ph.D.s teaching science in some K–12 schools can start at approximately the same (or even higher) salary than that of a new assistant professor at some postsecondary institutions. Perhaps the only loss is that of perceived status based on an outdated set of expectations that people with science doctorates should only teach in a research institution. The education and training of science Ph.D.s who would be in another part of the employment arena under other conditions benefit the entire system. This is the polar opposite of a "dumbing-down" effect; it enhances the entire science employment arena, as well as society as a whole.

Certainly, however, employing Ph.D. scientists as teachers in elementary and secondary schools would require changing how they are trained. For example, they would have to take courses in education. This might create the demand for new courses to be taught by teacher's colleges or education departments. The example could be replayed for any number of heretofore "nontraditional" career paths for science Ph.D.s. Indeed, the notion that teaching science to K–12 students might become a viable career option for Ph.D. scientists seems less likely than other scenarios. Perhaps a more likely and viable option would be having them teach science to teachers who teach at the elementary and secondary levels. Some surveys indicate that these teachers report being uncomfortable with their knowledge of science. This discomfort is communicated to their students, who are then more likely to be uncomfortable with science as well. Perhaps Ph.D. scientists could break this cycle by teaching these teachers science.

Changes in the working conditions of the scientist as academic necessitate concomitant changes in how we conceptualize science. As the number of jobs in academe declines and competition for funding and jobs increases, we must think of the uses of scientific training in ways different than we did when grants and jobs were plentiful. This requires creativity and flexibility—creativity to identify new opportunities to which to apply the knowledge and skills of Ph.D. scientists, and flexibility to take advantage of these new opportunities and adapt to changed work conditions. Moreover, as more women and non-Asian minorities increase their participation in science, we must think of science in ways different than we did when the talent pool for the scientist as academic was predominantly white and male. This will affect not only how science is done but also who will do science in the future—and what science they will do.

It appears highly unlikely that we will ever return to the golden age of science. Rather than looking back and lamenting the differences between yesterday and today, we would do better to find ways to increase and enhance the opportunities available to the scientist as academic now and in the future.

ACKNOWLEDGMENTS

I am grateful to Willie Pearson, Jr., Jesse Ausubel, Stephen Graubard, and Burton Clark for helpful comments and insights.

ENDNOTES

[1] Richard H. Hall, *The Sociology of Work* (Thousand Oaks, Calif.: Pine Forge Press, 1994).

[2] Ibid.

[3] David F. Noble, "The Selling of the University," *The Nation,* 6 February 1982.

[4] David Dickson, *The New Politics of Science* (Chicago, Ill.: University of Chicago Press, 1988), 29.

[5] Ibid.

[6] Daniel Lee Kleinman, "Scientists Need to Change the Way They Respond to Their Critics," *Chronicle of Higher Education,* 29 September 1995, B1–2.

[7] Ibid.

[8]L. Seachrist, "Multidisciplinary Research Blurs Lines Between 'Hard' and 'Soft' Sciences," *The Scientist* 10 (22) (11 November 1996): A7.

[9]Jesse H. Ausubel and John H. Steele, "Flat Organiations for Earth Science," *Bulletin of the American Meteorological Society* 74 (5) (1993): 809–814.

[10]Daniel J. Kevles, "The National Science Foundation and the Debate over Postwar Research Policy, 1942–1945," in Ronald L. Numbers and Charles E. Rosenberg, eds., *The Scientific Enterprise in America: Readings from ISIS* (Chicago, Ill.: University of Chicago Press, 1996): 297–319.

[11]Ibid., 297.

[12]Cited in Dickson, *The New Politics of Science*, 260.

[13]Ibid.

[14]Ibid., 15.

[15]National Research Council, *The Path to the Ph.D.* (Washington, D.C.: National Academy Press, 1996).

[16]Dickson, *The New Politics of Science,* 104.

[17]Ibid.

[18]Robert K. Merton, "The Normative Structure of Science," in *The Sociology of Science* (Chicago, Ill.: University of Chicago Press, 1973).

[19]Dickson, *The New Politics of Science.*

[20]Myrna E. Watanabe, "Pressures Wearing Down Researchers," *The Scientist,* 18 September 1995, 1, 6, 7.

[21]This study was sponsored by the Department of Education's National Center for Education Statistics. Denise K. Magner, "The New Generation," *Chronicle of Higher Education,* 2 February 1996, A17–18.

[22]National Science Foundation, Directorate for Social, Behavioral, and Economic Sciences, *Data Brief* (1) (19 February 1997).

[23]Magner, "The New Generation."

[24]Robin Wilson, "At Harvard, Yale, and Stanford, Women Lose Tenure Bids Despite Backing from Departments," *Chronicle of Higher Education,* 6 June 1997, A10–11.

[25]Martha W. Tack and Carol L. Patitu, *Faculty Job Satisfaction: Women and Minorities in Peril* (Washington, D.C.: Association for the Study of Higher Education and ERIC, 1992).

[26]Alison Schneider, "Proportion of Minority Professors Inches Up to About 10%," *Chronicle of Higher Education,* 20 June 1997, A12–13.

[27]Unfortunately, in many instances data on "minority groups" are not further disaggregated by race, ethnicity, and gender, thereby resulting in the effects for some race/sex categories being masked.

[28]Tack and Patitu, *Faculty Job Satisfaction.*

[29]As reported in Magner, "The New Generation."

30P. H. Henderson, J. E. Clarke, and M. A. Reynolds, *Summary Report 1995: Doctorate Recipients from United States Universities* (Washington, D.C.: National Academy Press, 1996).

31National Research Council, *Summary Report 1995: Doctorate Recipients from United States Universities* (Washington, D.C.: National Academy Press, 1996).

32Magner, "The New Generation," A18.

33Franklin Hoke, "Growth in Untenured Academic Science Jobs Seen Hurting Careers," *The Scientist,* 18 September 1995, 1, 4.

34"Race and Ethnicity in the American Professoriate, 1995–96," Higher Education Research Institute, Graduate School of Education and Information Studies, University of California, Los Angeles.

35Kim A. McDonald, "Frustrated Young Scientists Find Solace on an Electronic Network," *Chronicle of Higher Education,* 6 January 1993, A9–10.

36Henderson, Clarke, and Reynolds, *Summary Report 1995: Doctorate Recipients from United States Universities.*

37Ibid.

38Committee on Science, Engineering, and Public Policy (COSEPUP), National Research Council, *Reshaping the Graduate Education of Scientists and Engineers* (Washington, D.C.: National Academy Press, 1995).

39See *Chronicle of Higher Education,* 15 March 1996, A19.

40Richard C. Wiggins, "Scientists Must Clarify the Societal Relevance of Research," *The Scientist,* 3 February 1997, 10.

41H. F .L. Mark, "The Plight of Women in Science Continues," commentary in *The Scientist,* 18 September 1995, 13.

42Colleen Cordes and Paulette V. Walker, "Ability to Win Grants Increasingly Dictates Clout of Departments within Universities," *Chronicle of Higher Education,* 14 June 1996, A14.

43In chemistry, about two-thirds of Ph.D.s take jobs outside of academe.

44These figures include Ph.D.s in postdoctoral appointments. National Academy of Sciences, "Reshaping the Graduate Education of Scientists and Engineers."

45COSEPUP, *Reshaping the Graduate Education of Scientists and Engineers.*

46McDonald, "Frustrated Young Scientists Find Solace on an Electronic Network."

47Robert Finn, "Study Finds Gender Disparity Even Among High Achievers in Science," *The Scientist,* 13 November 1995, 3, 9.

48Watanabe, "Pressures Wearing Down Researchers."

49Hoke, "Growth in Untenured Academic Science Job Seen Hurting Careers."

50Ibid.

51Ausubel and Steele, "Flat Organizations for Earth Science."

[52]David L. Wilson, "Internet Users Face Lines at Computers," *Chronicle of Higher Education,* 1 December 1995, A51.

[53]Jeffrey R. Young, "Classes on the Web," *Chronicle of Higher Education,* 3 November 1995, A27–28.

[54]Scott Huler, "Reinvigorating the Mathematics Culture: The Problems are Not Only Quantitative," *The Scientist,* 13 April 1992.

[55]Ibid., 9, 24.

[56]COSEPUP, *Reshaping the Graduate Education of Scientists and Engineers.*

[57]Magner, "The New Generation."

[58]COSEPUP, *Reshaping the Graduate Education of Scientists and Engineers.*

[59]M. C. Cage, "Some Graduate Programs Offer Training for Careers Outside Academe," *Chronicle of Higher Education,* 15 March 1996, A20.

[60]Ibid.

[61]COSEPUP, *Reshaping the Graduate Education of Scientists and Engineers.*

[62]Personal communication.

[63]Wiggins, "Scientists Must Clarify the Societal Relevance of Research."

[64]Comments on public policy at the 1996 meeting of the American Association for the Advancement of Science, Baltimore, Md.

[65]Wiggins, "Scientists Must Clarify the Societal Relevance of Research."

[66]Ibid.

[67]COSEPUP, *Reshaping the Graduate Education of Scientists and Engineers.*

[68]Cheryl B. Leggon, "National Needs and Technological Change: A Background Paper," in Committee on Skill Transferability in Engineering Labor Markets, National Research Council, *Fostering Flexibility in the Engineering Work Force* (Washington, D.C.: National Academy Press, 1990).

[69]Committee on Skill Transferability in Engineering Labor Markets, National Research Council, 1990.

[70]Cheryl B. Leggon, "The Impact of Science and Technology on African Americans," *Humboldt Journal of Social Relations* 21 (2) (1995): 35–53. See also Cheryl B. Leggon and W. Pearson, Jr., "Who Will Do Science in the United States? Implications for Indigenous Minorities," in R. Varela and L. Mayer, eds., *Los Grandes Problemas de la Ciencia y La Tecnologia* (Mexico City, Mexico: Universidad Autonoma Metropolitana, 1994), 77–88.

[71]Cheryl B. Leggon and Shirley M. Malcom, "Human Resources in Science and Engineering: Policy Implications," in Willie Pearson, Jr. and Alan Fechter, eds., *Who Will Do Science? Educating the Next Generation* (Baltimore, Md.: The Johns Hopkins University Press, 1994).

Sheldon Rothblatt

The "Place" of Knowledge in the American Academic Profession

TODAY'S ACADEMIC WORLD contains many communities and, in some instances, radically different kinds of institutions with distinct missions and clientele. There is overlap, without which certain other cardinal features of American higher education would not be possible, such as student transfer. Yet to focus the discussion, and to keep the paths of argument fairly clear, I will concentrate on the one segment of academe that historically regards research, in the sense of discovery or original scholarship, as one of its prime endeavors, and perhaps its most singular feature.

The question of the institutional structure for organizing knowledge is critically important. Presumably, whoever controls that structure determines the rules and means for acquiring knowledge, for legitimizing and passing it on to new generations of researchers, and for establishing career-advancement norms. I speak now of what has traditionally been defined as "basic" or primary research, the "research" part of the R&D equation. It has long been observed that one of the features of knowledge production in the United States has been the concentration of high-level research efforts in particular educational institutions. The universities of the nation undertake a larger share of basic research than the federal government (with laboratories like the National Institutes of Health), private industry, nonprofit institutes, or endowed foundations. The university's share has been estimated at half of all the basic research conducted in the United States, with a heavy concentra-

Sheldon Rothblatt is Professor of History at the University of California, Berkeley, and STINT Professor of History at the Royal Institute of Technology in Sweden.

245

tion of such efforts in less than fifty, or even ten, institutions. The federal government has been the principal sponsor, providing two-thirds of the funding for fundamental research, followed by industry.[1] The states of the Union provide small supplementary amounts.

By and large, sponsors have accepted the university's explanation for its dominant research presence, praising the research professoriate for providing opportunities for personal initiative, creativity, flexibility, and a willingness to take intellectual risks. Furthermore, universities have subsidized the national research effort through their faculty, although support staff and other researchers are usually paid for by outside funds. The comparatively low cost of research undertaken in the university has obviously been a selling point. However, it is entirely possible that as we enter another century this classic picture of the American research university as the dominant provider of basic knowledge and new technologies will alter. Universities have become heavily dependent on a statutory distinction between "basic" and "applied" research. What if that dichotomy should prove to be dubious—the two activities conflated or inseparably conjoined—simply because the characteristics of basic knowledge acquisition have changed? Surely that has already transpired in some fields.

Nevertheless, the research university is not likely to disappear. Universities have historically had enormous staying power. But if we take current developments into account, we have to consider at least the possibility that some fields of intellectual endeavor with a home in the university will be much more strongly represented outside the university in the years to come. Incentives and initiative may also shift to those institutions with a capacity to simulate university inquiry. The almost complete reliance on external funding for science and technology, or for certain areas of applied social science, certainly raises questions about the viability of the university in the absence of such support. If the research ethic continues to be the mainstay of university culture, a third possibility is that universities will lose much of their autonomy in determining which kinds of research should receive priority and how academic research is to be evaluated in relation to tenure and professional careers. The following observations are therefore aimed at exploring such questions, identifying some of the consequences for the culture or cultures of the research professoriate, while also identifying the organizational or institutional "place" of research in the contemporary university.

HOMES FOR KNOWLEDGE

A commonplace of historical thinking is that universities embody both continuities and discontinuities. The former—the supremacy of the lecture system, professional studies, the status hierarchies and symbolism of the university's inner circuitry, the machinery of examinations, the corporate/guild identity—often disguise the latter, which consist of changes in the governing structure as well as in knowledge production and delivery systems, a consumer orientation in conflict with supply-side conceptions of education, and a critical role in national defense and wealth generation. Where historical continuities were strong enough to resist innovation, there arose new internal structures or divisions (new degree programs and curricular tracks) as well as wholly new types of institutions where undervalued research could find working space, however unsatisfactory: royal academies, lighthouses, botanical gardens, astronomical observatories, specialized schools, polytechnics, various kinds of colleges, and, later, corporate classrooms and distance learning or open universities.

This is not the place to discuss the interesting and relevant question in the sociology of knowledge as to whether advanced forms of education create institutional homes for themselves or whether the homes in some sense precede disciplinary specialisms and anticipate them. Examples of both can be found in the historical record, depending upon the country and period. In origin some structural innovations have few direct connections to the production or dissemination of knowledge. The colleges of medieval universities were initially a means for providing professorial and other positions; the endowments of their canonries were frequently channeled into the universities. But one change that became vitally important for the history of the research university was the creation of the academic department, the main location of a discipline. This movement has not yet been studied in close historical detail, but its timing strongly suggests that it follows from changes in the methods of inquiry, in conceptualization, and from a sense of the significance of discovery for higher education. The movement was often resisted; it was seen as being inimical to existing forms of general or liberal education, including the "cohort system" of instruction wherein the undergraduates of a particular entering class advanced to their degrees simultaneously through a set curriculum with few or no electives. Departments pursuing the interests of their specialisms also threatened to produce a more expensive educational system, primarily because of the experimental and engineering sciences. And the appearance of the department meant the end of the European-style chairholder system in this country, the decline of a "faculty" dominated by deans and senior professors as a major factor in internal governance, and the proliferation of junior professors ascending a well-defined academic career ladder. Such features allowed American universities to take advantage of the migration of European talent following the fascist takeover of Germany and Italy.[2]

Disciplinary specialization, as represented in the academic departments, was not a nineteenth-century discovery. It was a natural tendency, an essential step in knowing (as Alfred North Whitehead once remarked), with a respected history in the works of the great philosophers and their taxonomies of knowledge. What was new, however, was the emergence of the department as a "place" for the many categories of knowledge-seeking, a location for learning as defined by the subgroups comprising the research professoriate. It was the institutional expression of the collective interests of like-minded researchers.

The department was in fact a structure waiting to be born. That it developed more slowly in other national contexts is attributable to the absence of the transforming features of America's society and economy. More rigorous secondary schooling in Europe allowed for the preservation of elite functions. Students moving from postcompulsory schools to universities were socialized early and prepared to undertake advanced instruction under the guidance of individual professors. Elite education was supported by policies favoring the traditional class structures or by civil service and ministerial control of the market for higher education. The competition between institutions for students, resources, and colleagues was effectively restrained, with the state almost always being the sole buyer of educational services. Since these conditions were absent from the United States—with its looser class structures, populist and democratic values, and constant search for status and identity—innovation was easier to effect. The department emerged as the location for new ambitions, where disciplines could advance their collective interests and norms.

In describing these leaps, it is easy to overlook such rigidities and complexities as undeniably existed, yet the general outcome was not in doubt. For the teaching and research professoriate, and for undergraduate and graduate students, the first object of loyalty has most often been the department, even within liberal-arts colleges. Choosing a major, and the anxiety that accompanies that decision, is never far from the minds of entering undergraduates. Normally encompassing two years, the major reaches downwards into the lower-division curriculum (where it competes with the need for "remediation") to impose some "prerequisites." Honors programs require even more specialized time and reduce the opportunities to explore additional electives. Yet, from another perspective, this is a gain since disciplines have a capacity for breadth, connecting certain forms of knowing and their methods with others, reaching outward into adjacent disciplines and fields of interest, and encouraging exploration by means of connected and systematic systems of evidence gathering and evaluation. Disciplines are not inherently narrow, as some critics imagine. All, even the most vocational, can effectively stretch the mind—although unfortunately some professors are assuredly narrow.

In Europe the seminar room and the laboratory were the institutional expressions of chairholder authority, with "assistants" in the early stages of their academic careers providing ancillary teaching services as specified by the professor. The graduate school as a separate structure, with its own admission requirements, curriculum, and degree programs, did not exist (although a different version, in an embryonic form, can be found today in Belgium, Germany, the Netherlands, and France). The *ordinarien* admitted their advanced students directly, and largely still do. The graduate school in the United States, creeping into research universities from the last decades of the nineteenth century onwards, was in league with departmental efforts to free itself from the burdens of an underprepared and underspecialized student population by providing an older and, in most institutions, a more carefully selected body of potential recruits to the academic or other professions.

The American university laboratory, though more of an extension of the departmental organization of knowledge than of the chairholder's authority, nevertheless similarly provided a capacity for independence, especially after the introduction of extramural grants applied for by and awarded directly to professors in charge of the laboratories. While for the most part the image of the lonely or heroic researcher dominated the humanities and most of the social sciences, a more cooperative conception of knowledge pursuit emerged from the developing structure of the academic laboratory, with teams composed of the senior professor, postdoctoral students, and graduate students.[3] The presence of undergraduates is a feature of recent decades, partially in response to external criticisms alleging the neglect of undergraduate teaching. During competitive recruitment today, the outfitting of a laboratory to suit the specific needs of the researcher requires very large sums of money—a serious worry for campus officials charged with the responsibility for raising the necessary financial support.

The American university is a composite or hybrid, responding in its structural differentiation to the external demands placed upon it. While the French *polytechnique* has a foothold in the United States, notably in places like MIT and Caltech, the specialized research institution tends towards the comprehensive model, and even the great technical foundations show an inclination to broaden their curricula and create departments outside engineering and the sciences that have some relevance for these predominant interests. In the comprehensive research university model, knowledge production competes for professorial time. Consequently, the research academy is divided in its opinion of the relevance of advanced specialization for undergraduate education.

Departments of dance, theater, and music, which extend their reach through performance, have alternative cultures that are closer in spirit to laboratories—cooperation between students or faculty is an absolute necessity and the usefulness of competition is often questioned. But the issue of whether knowledge generation should be a primary purpose of such departments remains problematical. Experiments with collegiate university structures on the model of Oxford and Cambridge are not characteristic of American universities, both because of expense and because of the strength and importance of the separate liberal-arts college as an indispensable part of the system of higher education. The federated collegiate university, in any case, has not been the locus for research; but where such institutions have existed, as seen in the much beleaguered and fascinating history of the University of California at Santa Cruz, or at Oxford and Cambridge, the fault lines between departments and colleges are very much in evidence. Departments and colleges compete for the authority to determine the curriculum, the teaching delivery system, and the recruitment and promotion of suitable talent for each structure.[4]

Even outside the hard sciences within the American research university, departments have had rivals. Research institutes and centers, especially for the social sciences (including history) have been attractive sources for multidisciplinary mixing since at least the 1950s, because they attract and distribute research funds, are less hierarchical or bureaucratic in character, are more flexible and swifter in decision-making, and make a good home for visiting scholars whose specializations fit better in institutes and centers than in departments. They are also largely "voluntary" communities and therefore have an advantage over "compulsory" affiliations. Institutes and centers are not based so much on disciplines—with their special internal history, ethos, pantheon of heroes, and methods of inquiry—as they are on more mixed fields of inquiry, often of an applied character. They have continual turnover, making them open to many influences. Research institutes may or may not have teaching functions; if they do, departmental cooperation is required, particularly to release regular faculty from teaching commitments. They can affiliate students from a great number of different specialties, providing jobs or research support through funded projects, and consequently serve as valuable training centers. Many have funds to employ both administrative and research staff. With some exceptions, however, the research institute does not exercise the same degree of career control over professors, which is both an advantage and a sign of comparative weakness. Nevertheless, it is within the multidisciplinary research center, or rather in what it ideally represents, that we begin to trace the integuments of yet another development in the history of university "places" for knowledge production—one that may well be having an impact on all disciplines but perhaps most radically on the humanities and social sciences.

THE NEW PRODUCTION OF KNOWLEDGE

The new development promises (or threatens) to affect the twentieth-century supremacy of the department, but we can speculate that the department has already been weakened by the kinds of partial defections already described, most notably those of the laboratory and the research institute. And just as the department historically was an organizational response to the knowledge revolution of the nineteenth century, an American invention to break the historical hold of collegiate styles of education and teaching on the research university, so is the new development a response to external changes in the production of knowledge and its use.

For some understanding of the transformations under way, we can turn to a composite work written by an international group of social scientists and first published in 1994.[5] This analysis of how knowledge pressures are creating new forms of research associations describes a situation quite unlike the classical model of the lonely or heroic researcher in competition with other researchers for income, reputation, and influence in a given area of intellectual inquiry. In fact, "intellectual inquiry" may not be a suitable description, implying as it does the kind of open-ended or "pure" investigations linked to an ethic of value-free knowledge, as understood at the end of the last century. As defined by the contributors, who call the new production of knowledge "Mode 2" (the old one is "Mode 1"), research has an imposed time limit for results (denominated "strategic or targeted research" in other accounts). Under funding pressures, commercialization, market and global competition, and the current preoccupation of nation-states (or large free-trading areas) with wealth production, the single researcher, or the single researcher in charge of a laboratory of acolytes, is replaced or augmented by a project group assembled for specific investigations. The group is disbanded when the project is completed and regrouped in a different configuration when the next assignment is received (note: not developed from within the group, but accepted from outside). The time required to move from a research idea to a design plan, and from there to prototypes, manufacturing contracts, and actual production—the process that had historically delayed the flow of discovery from universities into practical use—is vastly telescoped. Product turn-around time is more rapid than we have ever known under rust age manufacturing conditions. Furthermore, the actual producer or sponsor is directly involved from the start, and marketing considerations are written into the research design. All the separate historical steps of conception, research, development, and commercial application are conflated into one connected process.

That science projects should have an applied goal is hardly new; neither is the use of teams to accomplish laboratory-based tasks. Yet in the heyday of high-energy physics in the aftermath of World War II, critics of the university's involvement in defense-related research and secrecy impositions were particularly troubled by utilitarian requirements. It was an unwritten assumption that in an environment of plentiful resources no sunset clause was likely to be strictly invoked, and under the protective mantle of the project there would exist ample scope for investigations that for all intents and purposes were as "pure" as any traditional academic work could be without a practical outcome. In disciplines other than physics, or later bioengineering, the research team on a science model might be involved in city and transport planning, clinical psychology, or demography, often in connection with campus-based research institutes.

But Mode 2 knowledge production is not necessarily associated with existing campus units nor connected to departments in any significant way in the spirit of the established research institutes. The "new production of knowledge" represents an intensification of the tendency for any discipline-based activity to cross domain boundaries. While the department has protected the career interests of academics, creating subguilds of masters, journeymen, and apprentices, it has rarely prevented individual researchers from borrowing freely from adjacent and even distant fields, nor has it prevented the results of such intellectual adventures from reaching undergraduate audiences through lectures and seminar teaching. Some disciplines may take more readily to transdisciplinary activity than others; but all in academe have watched how language-based departments have for several decades embraced a wide variety of social scientific and philosophical approaches to literary criticism or linguistics, combining anthropology, psychology, sociology, and some forms of history. Professional schools are heavily multidisciplinary, even when subdivided into departments.

For science, the major impetus behind Mode 2 is the changing marketplace for knowledge, the growth of high-tech industries, and global competitiveness. A loss of faith in the interventionist state has shifted political attention away from the distribution of wealth to its production, heightening economic expectations throughout national populations and stimulating irresistible political pressures and tensions, especially but not exclusively in the former Soviet system. Yet at the same time there are strong consumer pressures aimed at improving opportunities and the quality of life. Societies around the world are demanding safer environments, accessible medical services, better transportation facilities, and other social amenities. We are currently experiencing tendencies that tie higher education research more closely to problem-solving.

But what about the humanities and "soft" social sciences that historically have been associated with general or liberal education, that is to say, individual self-realization or citizenship, to name two of the leading (and contradictory) justifications? For these disciplines, Mode 2 characteristics are less in evidence—or, rather, they are present but operate indirectly in cultural areas of society (including mass culture), or operate directly in the sense that, as universities create or sustain professions, the humanities and social sciences play an important role in generating the knowledge used by professions in the arts, journalism, or businesses allied to the arts.[6] Whether agreeable or not, the so-called impractical university subjects have become part of the nation's enormous entertainment industry.[7]

Have Mode 2 values and organization ended the notion of the heroic scholar toiling on his own, at least in certain fields of investigation? No, not universally or uniformly. Have career values changed so that the values of Mode 2 discovery affect the career chances of all academics? The answer is somewhat confusing, since Mode 2 values are themselves part of a system of external pressures long in evidence in the United States. The demands for some vague standard of immediate relevance or for projects that can attract money have been in existence for decades, but they are now intensified. Higher education costs, critics have complained, have risen faster than inflation. Research costs are notoriously difficult to contain. Resources are needed to support graduate students in all fields and to generate more resources, and occasionally one hears the accusation (and the lament) that the liberal arts do not do enough on their own to warrant the subsidies or overhead monies that they receive from others. The research academy has not only been pluralistic in its values for many decades (and possibly for centuries); it has long been divided into wealthy and less wealthy communities, favored and less favored subguilds, and not only between disciplines but within them and within departments. Multiple reward systems operate within single universities. Questions of individual equity, which arise continually, become subservient to market discipline. But even market factors are not applied uniformly. In professional schools, for example, the very fact of belonging to the school may automatically bring higher levels of compensation than in letters and science departments with similar specialties. In Europe, where historically the state placed a lid on salaries and where academic trade unions attempted to create more equitable conditions of income distribution, privatizing features have now appeared to upset historical understandings. So new and disturbing (or riveting) is this transformation that the *Times Higher Education Supplement* has taken to publishing the salaries of all vice chancellors of universities and directors of polytechnics, to the consternation of the lowly British lecturer struggling to make ends meet on small salary increases painfully negotiated by the unions. The new orthodoxy in Europe (but well established in the United States) is that high-priced leaders and researchers will bring payoffs to their institutions in the form of prestige, industrial and research council grants, and an abundance of fee-paying students.

We have in the making a knowledge production whose location within universities is uncertain and whose researchers are unclear as to their primary allegiances. In some cases—let us say, where Mode 2 circumstances are not present—the discipline and its extensions (the department, the learned society with its officers, committees, annual meetings, prizes, and distinctions) are central concerns. The individual researcher works in relative isolation. In others, where Mode 2 prevails, the team is more important than the individual, and the research organization, permanent or temporary, is as important to career-making as is the department. In the first example, the reward system is reasonably well defined— at least the elements of recognition are apparent. Tenure, promotions, and distinctions are decided either through markets or merit or a combination of the two, troubling as the contradictions may be to promotion committees. But how is the success of an academic career adjudicated in the second case? Confusion exists over who gets "credit" for innovation and discovery in the sciences—the old difficulty of "simultaneous discovery" in a new guise. Most of the great prizes (e.g., the Nobel) go to single researchers or a few collaborators. But what if there are many? For a decade or more this has been recognized as an acute problem, and several years ago the National Science Foundation was forced to consider ethical problems arising from multi-authored reporting. How, therefore, in a given Mode 2 project are we to distinguish among the contributions made by members of a team drawn from radically different fields of intellectual endeavor, with "hard" and "soft" hopelessly intertwined? It is conceivable that some members of the team may not be in academic careers at all but rather seconded from firms sponsoring the product, and thus they are informed by different intellectual rules. Furthermore, for several participants the project may be their only means of support, if they do not hold regular appointments in a university, company, government, or think tank. They have an obvious interest in supporting the project irrespective of its ramifications. Would the correct analogy be a dance company, an opera, or a movie production where the director, musicians, performers, set designers and builders, lighting experts, costume designers, publicity agents, and producers all share in the acclaim, if not exactly in all the wealth, and disband after the production?

Questions about how the members of a project team are educated, trained, or assembled will surely arise, as they already have. But an even more pressing question is how the importance of the project affects the operations of traditional disciplines centered in departments, i.e., their undergraduate programs of study and doctoral tracks. Even without Mode 2 systems of research, these questions would still be relevant. Will departments continue to have major responsibility for the training of research specialists, or will the transdisciplinary dimensions of research in time produce something like a separate training program (depending upon a project's life span)? Who is to undertake the task of undergraduate instruction? It is theoretically possible to associate honors students or other select undergraduates with projects but quite inconceivable that mass instruction can function under such conditions. And if teaching responsibilities fall only on those Mode 2 participants who hold teaching appointments, how can we distinguish their contributions from those who have no other assignments?

An even larger unanswered question is whether, or in what ways, Mode 2 concerns will contribute to the creation of a learning environment in which the highest and most visible rewards accompany problem-solving, so that whatever difference between pure and applied education that may still exist disappears. The implications for the university's funding base are as significant as the compensation of researchers. Who profits from Mode 2 contracts? What happens to overhead? How are patents and licensing affected? How much authority does the university retain over the composition of the research team? And who judges the quality of the project's output? The classic peer-review system may prove to be inadequate where so many diverse interests are represented on one team and where profit margins involve a different set of evaluation criteria.

KNOWLEDGE PRODUCTION AND THE NEW CLASSES

As if in response to the expansion of academic duties in the last forty years—the combination of professional obligations, consulting (where it exists), teaching in different degree programs, research, travel, campus administration, student consumer demands, and accountability work loads—research universities are filled with new classes of employees—professionals, semi-professionals, and the would-be professionals who comprise an enormous body of academics (and have grown faster and larger than the traditional faculty at certain institutions), who in some instances are unionized. In discussing how changes in the places where knowledge is pursued are leading to changes in academic rules and career values, it is advisable to mention the presence of sizeable support staffs, which in a sense also include part-time academics without the customary faculty privileges and standing. Heavy use has been made of such talent in the teaching of basic courses in, for example, foreign languages or mathematics, and in some cases security of employment has been granted as an acknowledgment of essential services that otherwise would have to be performed by the research faculty.

But another category of support personnel that may or may not perform teaching functions has been fashioned from hirees associated with a research university's investment in new technologies. Some of them are in the familiar category of soft-money appointments. Research grants bring with them a structure of grant administrators, accountants, project managers, and assistants. In general, every new or expanded undertaking by the university inevitably produces a staff or small bureaucracy: housing and food services, purchasing agents, conventions and outreach programs, curriculum advisers, coordinators and facilitators of every kind, and development and public-relations activities, not to mention fleets of lawyers to contend with the plentiful lawsuits of America's singularly litigious society. Now, in the age of computers, there are also hot-line attendants, software designers, and lab experts, who often find themselves supplementing actual instruction in the use of the new technologies. Their careers at the university provide various levels of satisfaction, ranging from disappointment at not achieving a better-paid position in industry to the pleasure of working with young people in a flexible educational environment. One change has been the equating of the academic with the technician. Another is a decline in the belief that knowledge brings wisdom or that a university education provides an understanding of experience and personal relationships.

We cannot as yet be sure as to where the dominant "place" of knowledge acquisition is likely to be as the new century opens. It is tempting to speculate that it will not be so wholly associated with universities as in the past, or even with specific universities. Just as Mode 2 production may include outsiders on the team or researchers drawn from industry, government laboratories, or nonprofit research foundations (which are heavily invested in social-science research at the moment), it may also include academics from more than one research university. Funding problems, the cost of certain kinds of equipment (as in the golden age of atomic physics), and the shortage of talent have long fostered inter-university cooperation along many lines, especially in jointly run hospitals (with mixed results), the sharing of library collections, or inner-city renewal undertakings. Research consortia, university/

industry partnerships, and science parks here and in Europe are forms of collaboration that we have known of for several decades. Some universities are in the business of providing start-up assistance to businesses in the high-tech field. Academic engineers, as well as other professional-school academics or professors in applied subjects, may have their own consulting or architectural firms. Professors of medicine in most countries have a proprietary interest in the running of university clinics. But there are also some new and serious rivalries. A race for domination in the market for interactive teaching software has opened up between universities, nonprofits, and for-profit institutions. Within single campuses, or federations, the several divisions are in competition or potential competition with one another, with university extension programs and distance learning centers pursuing mass audiences and demanding the right to give degrees (where it has not yet been obtained).

Major historical changes often have twofold and contradictory ramifications, and we can notice similar developments at present. A greater division of labor is occurring within and between institutions, including the noneducational institutions. At the same time there is a sharing of some functions hitherto assigned mainly to universities, driven partly by global economic developments but assisted by other factors.[8] The "overproduction" of doctorates in teaching specialties, for example, has had the positive effect of taking new talent into other areas of achievement, building the infrastructure for a nonuniversity world of education providers, transforming publishing, and turning some academics into "consultants" or "facilitators" rather than role models for young students, who in any case may not be as young as they were in the past.

THE DISAPPEARANCE OF "PLACE"

The fact that the research university is critically dependent upon outside support brings us to a final point about the contemporary university as—to use John Henry Newman's famous word—a place (happily rendered in a French translation as *milieu* when referring to dissemination but *not* production) of knowledge. Unlike most continental universities, and with several important exceptions, the Anglo-American university generally occupies an exclusive or boundaried physical space. Placemaking has been an outstanding feature of American college and university history, giving rise to the occupation of campus planning. Virtually all the great gardening traditions of the last two centuries have been employed in arranging and designating spaces, in giving campuses unique topographical qualities, accentuated through naming schemes—the Yard, the Oval, the Lawn, the Faculty Glade, and so on. The American campus was developed as and designed to be a place for growing up, an immense and sophisticated kindergarten, commingling personal retreats with public zones. For the most part, it has not been an urban institution, sharing space with cities for the purpose of educating the young. For historical reasons the American university has very often been anti-urban in nature— collegiate, in that sense, jealous of its perimeters and prerogatives, eager to extend its influence over the private time of undergraduates by providing amenities that in some countries are often associated with cities. The irony is that its very pluralism and comprehensiveness has turned it into a city with its own internal suburbs and neighborhoods, but that is another tale. The point to be made is that the new production of knowledge (whether it be Mode 2 or some other form of applied career role), aided but not caused by computer technologies, is driving research academics away from their institutions, although their emotional loyalty or affection is a more significant variable. Administrators complain that faculty absences are frequent (although I wonder if they are as frequent as in Europe), which for them also suggests that alumni support for their institutions may in some ways be compromised.[9]

Administrative insistence on income-generating activities, however, and faculty compliance in their own career interests have led to a situation of great internal ambivalence and mixed messages. Ideological conflicts and the culture wars of the last thirty years have made many department members uneasy with one another, stimulating a flow of initiative to crossdisciplinary projects and less conflict-ridden situations. Following the argument wherever it goes—the civilized educational ideal for Victorian thinkers like John Stuart Mill—is possibly less important today for some scholars than knowing where the argument is supposed to be going in the first place. University public relations officers, so set in promoting favorable images of their institutions, are naturally reluctant to discuss such matters, if they are even aware of them.

It is furthermore apparent that Mode 2 teams, or other similarly organized teams, do not really need to be campus-based anymore. No single institution can provide the resources of a CERN or a Fermilab. Electronic connections have strengthened the operations of invisible colleges that, through ordinary forms of correspondence, have existed from time immemorial. But there is an unusual intensification of the importance of such networks at present. Tony Becher's interviews reveal that the closest intellectual and friendship ties of many professors lie outside their departments and institutions, perhaps even outside their own countries.[10] And correspondents do not have to be professors. They can be full-time researchers in other competing institutions. In this scenario, already so real, the research university is not a place or a milieu but a pied-à-terre. Some academic researchers are even reporting in the academic press that they find life outside the university more stimulating; this conclusion depends heavily upon their fields, the institutions at which they once served, and the level of reward and satisfaction in the industries they have now joined.

It was once said that the great advantage of the research university over industry was that knowledge could be pursued according to the interests of the researcher. To insulate themselves from market discipline, which dictated that science be used as a source of entertainment for fee-paying audiences, experimental scientists of the Enlightenment were eager to hold positions within universities. In time an ethic of discovery took hold, but it was not really until our own century that research universities became tied to the aims of the nation-state.[11] Until then, secret research was not a major problem (although it did exist here and there as academics competed for prestige or, in some cases, gained from industry connections), patent agreements were a relatively simple matter, and tenure questions were decided largely on institutional criteria. The levels of control that each separate institution once possessed should not be exaggerated. Political interference and public opinion have always played a part in the functioning of America's research establishments. Yet in our present, chaotic, and alternately lively and frustrating academic university, we may well speculate about who really is in charge of the production of new knowledge, who gains from it and in what ways. Or is it the case that all university authority and all research decisions are in some fashion shared and that no one is truly in charge of intellectual products?

THE RESPONSIBILITY FOR KNOWLEDGE PRODUCTION

In the complicated internal university world of many jurisdictions, many actors, and many constituencies—which include managers, technocrats, pure and applied knowledge seekers, liberal-arts champions, and advocates of the service university—there is a quiet struggle for mastery that is currently in operation. It falls under the heading of "shared governance" and is a contest between trustees, system and campus administrations, faculties, and nonacademic staff, with probings and sightings taken frequently by legislators and governors. Such struggles are not absolutely new in a university system governed by lay boards with public-sector representation. Still, it is difficult to imagine a more differentiated universe than the present research university, with its seemingly infinite number of interest groups and opposing policies. In the absence of consensus-defining mechanisms, governance is confused. Increased outside political interest and media reporting on such issues as affirmative action, the use of federal overhead and charges to grants, and the culture wars have weakened internal management, once again bringing to life the vexed question of how effective campus leaders can possibly be selected. If we are not yet in Kafka's world, we are approaching Max Weber's bureaucratic environment. The paths of decision-making are unclear and the lines of responsibility uncertain. Personality is subordinated to management decision-making, which is slowly dragged out in the fashion of the Austrian civil service *juristen*. Initiative is shifting to the outside, where giant electronic firms and global pharmaceutical interests are clearer about their objectives.[12]

It is not certain that we are in a period of transition from Mode 1 to Mode 2 knowledge production. The two in fact occur together, dividing the campus yet again into distinct research communities. Yet for important bodies of knowledge to lose their "place" within the university, or to lose the initiative long associated with university-based research, would be an ironic outcome indeed. Guild development over the centuries—*gemeinschaft*—was based on the supposition that it was the guild and not the marketplace that determined the value of an enterprise. The historical truth of that flattering self-conception is questionable but less important than the academic code of self-regulation once derived from it.

ENDNOTES

[1] Patricia J. Gumport, "Graduate Education and Organized Research in the United States," in Burton R. Clark, ed., *The Research Foundations of Graduate Education* (Berkeley, Calif.: University of California Press, 1993), 243–244.

[2] Roger L. Geiger, *To Advance Knowledge: The Growth of American Research Universities 1900–1940* (New York: Oxford University Press, 1986), 239.

[3] Histories of laboratories show how distinct styles and cultures develop within them, e.g., the history of the Cavendish laboratory at Cambridge in the late nineteenth century under the Noble laureate J. J. Thomson.

[4] It appears that even the Oxbridge colleges may be losing their battles against university departments and schools, which in applied research have been signally resourceful in raising money under government privatizing policies.

[5] *The New Production of Knowledge: The Dynamics of Science and Research in Contemporary Societies* (London and Thousand Oaks, Calif.: SAGE Publications, 1994). The contributors are Michael Gibbons, Martin Trow, Helga Nowotony, Simon Schwartzman, Peter Scott, and Camille Limoges. Roger Svensson, Director of the Swedish Foundation for International Cooperation in Research and Higher Education, provided indispensable moral and administrative support. A capsule version of the argument appears as Michael Gibbons, "The University as an Instrument for the Development of Science and Basic Research," in *Emerging Patterns of Social Demand and University Reform: Through a Glass Darkly,* ed. David D. Dill and Barbara Sporn (Oxford and New York: Pergamon, 1995), 90–104.

[6] Caution is required lest we make the simple mistake of associating particular disciplines with ideal sets of values as virtually a matter of right. Given the transformation of the humanities in the last two decades under the influence of postmodern theories of epistemology and proof, we should not consider words like "humanities" to be anything more than taxonomic. As long ago as 1704 Jonathan Swift, in *The Battles of the Books,* pointed out that the fight between ancients (classics) and moderns (experimental science) was not necessarily a fight between disciplines but between mentalities. An ancient could be modern and vice versa.

[7] But how many disciplines remain "impractical"? Nearly thirty years ago Martin Trow and A. H. Halsey, in their study of British academics, empirically demonstrated that even then most of them were in some kind of ap-

plied field. A. H. Halsey and Martin Trow, *The British Academic* (London: Faber, 1971).

[8]Harold Perkin, in *The Rise of Professional Society: England Since 1880* (London and New York: Routledge, 1989), has written about the absence of significant value distinctions between professionals in private and public sectors. They appear to be one class, differing only in whom they temporarily serve.

[9]I have heard that many of the biggest Berkeley donors are not in fact alumni of the university, which raises some interesting questions about their motives and expectations.

[10]Tony Becher, *Academic Tribes and Territories* (Philadelphia, Pa. and Milton Keynes: Society for Research into Higher Education and Open University Press, 1989).

[11]Discussed in Sheldon Rothblatt, *The Modern University and Its Discontents: The Fate of Newman's Legacies in Britain and America* (Cambridge: Cambridge University Press, 1997), chap. 9.

[12]This may provide a windfall for America's liberal-arts colleges. While research can be simulated by other institutions (and today's high-tech industrial environment is said to possess far superior equipment), elite undergraduate education cannot be simulated, providing the historic colleges with a delicious monopoly. It is customary to think of expensive liberal-arts colleges pricing themselves out of the market. That will certainly remain a concern, but we can now wonder whether the research university will be able to retain its unique qualities in the years to come.

Theodore R. Mitchell

Border Crossings:
Organizational Boundaries and
Challenges to the American Professoriate

*For good or ill, civilized men have come to hold
that. . .the knowledge of things is the only end in life
that justifies itself. So that nothing more
irretrievably shameful could overtake modern
civilization than the miscarriage of this modern
learning, which is the most valued spiritual asset of
civilized mankind.*

—*Thorstein Veblen*
The Higher Learning in America[1]

THE STRUGGLE FOR THE IDENTITY OF THE UNIVERSITY has been waged for as long as there have been universities, and it shows no signs of abating.[2] If anything, a snapshot of higher education at the century's end shows an industry under great stress. Universities are challenged internally by declining resources, by new populations of students and faculty with new interests, and by unsettled and divisive disputes over the legitimacy of alternate knowledge claims. Simultaneously, universities are challenged externally by the rise of competing providers of educational services, by increasing demands for short-term relevance in both teaching and research, and by the spread of new technologies that seem, at one level, to threaten the meaning of the university as a place.[3] But snapshots are often misleading. Snapshots of higher

---

Theodore R. Mitchell is Vice Chancellor at the University of California, Los Angeles.

265

education at almost any period would show similar challenges, yet universities have survived and prospered. Indeed, one of the great strengths of the university as an organization has been its resilience in the face of significant and changing internal and external demands. It is this resilience and the resulting diversity of university forms over time and across different settings that has been the source of the university's great staying power as an institution.[4] In evolutionary terms, the university has adapted well to changes in its environment over time, exhibiting local variation as well as general shifts in structure and behavior.

From time to time there have been serious discontinuities in the historical evolution of American universities. The creation of land-grant universities is perhaps the most significant of these, altering the relationship between the state and higher education and institutionalizing a utilitarian focus for academic work that had been present to a far lesser degree in predecessor institutions. But for the most part, university adaptation has been a series of slow changes at the margins that have nudged rather than shocked the system. The introduction of modern languages into American universities at the turn of the eighteenth century, for example, was accomplished by setting up an alternate track for nonclassical studies without changing the classical course at all.[5] In organizational terms, the resilience of the American university, its ability to adapt and occasionally to change given alterations in its environment, might best be characterized as a function of the careful management of institutional boundaries.[6]

This is an essay about boundaries and their management. The analysis has three aims. First, it is an attempt to think critically about the ways in which universities historically have managed along the borders that set them apart from other organizations in society and from society itself. Second, it is an attempt to look critically at current efforts to manage boundaries within the context of the challenges facing universities. Finally, it is an attempt to assess the implications of current boundary pressures on the professoriate and upon academic leadership.

The essay's argument can be summed up in the following four propositions: 1) During much of the twentieth century, American universities have employed strategies to buffer their inner processes (research design, curriculum, faculty work in the traditional disciplines) from external forces by creating distinct organizational units (institutes, professional schools, external affairs offices) to accommodate or at least address external demands. 2) These "boundary-spanning" units have not merely buffered what James Thompson called the "technical core"; they have altered relationships and structures inside the university, actually reversing their original purpose by becoming conduits for external demands.[7] 3) Individual faculty find themselves in a family of organizations whose boundaries are less clear than ever, characterized by increasing penetration of environmental demands into the fundamental work processes of the university and into the daily lives of individual faculty. 4) A major leadership challenge in American higher education over the next decades will be the articulation of a unique organizational identity and the effective management of organizational boundaries.

OPEN SYSTEMS AND THE BOUNDARIES OF THE UNIVERSITY

The literature on organizational boundaries is an outgrowth of the more general inquiries into the relationship between organizations and the environments in which they exist. These "open systems" inquiries, initiated in the 1950s, hypothesize that organizations are parts of integrated and interdependent systems, shaped not only by internal logic but by a constant generative friction with organized and unorganized elements of the environment with which they interact. At its simplest level, this approach suggests that organizations change as their environments change.

Environmental pressures to change travel along several pathways. Organization researchers have identified several analytically distinct pathways—policy, resources, and information—that often converge or overlap in application. It is easiest to see the effect of environmental influences on the internal organization of universities in the area of policy. There, environmental pressures play out in terms of demands for new outputs or processes and are given coercive force. At a trivial level, regulatory demands that require public universities to report faculty work load on an annual basis, for example, require campuses to create internal units for collecting data and filing reports. This, in turn, deflects resources from other purposes. At a deeper level, Title IX and its recent interpretations in the courts have required many universities to restructure their intercollegiate athletics programs, against what many institutions see to be their self-interest and the interests of female athletes.

The interaction between institutions and their environment often involves the flow of resources. Changes in the flow of resources can create implicit or explicit demand for changes within the organization. In the university context, we can all think of the simplest variation on this theme, the donor who is willing to grant the university significant resources in return for its willingness to build this building or create that professorship. In small ways, these examples illustrate the larger point that resource dependency creates a kind of boundary breach wherein external demands exert pressure on internal processes and structures. One might, in this context, think of every agency's "Request for Proposals" (particularly their cost-sharing provisions) as an invitation to universities to change their internal priorities in response to external interest.

In a university, resources mean much more than dollars. Changes in the kinds of people who attend as students and work as faculty alter the nature of the enterprise in fundamental ways. The GI Bill (an interaction between policy and resources) is an example— some say the critical example—of an environmental change that altered both the financial incentives for universities and the human resource mix within the student body. That change, in turn, called for new curricula, new pedagogies, and the end of the collegiate system of paternal control over student life. Current proposals in California and elsewhere to eliminate the consideration of race, ethnicity, and gender in university admissions will offer obverse challenges to the organization, as universities seek to retain access to a diverse student body with no direct means of doing so.

Information is the third pathway by which external trends and phenomena travel into the organization in an "open systems" framework. Here, one might think of universities themselves as parts of each other's external environment and information about the activities of other universities as a source of external influence. Upon hearing in 1902 that Yale had begun to advertise its graduate school, Chicago's President Harper urged that his institution follow suit.[8] In the current era, the willy-nilly adoption of technology often smacks of imitation rather than careful planning.[9] In less formal ways, the movement of faculty from one institution to another hastens the exchange of ideas and fosters the process of imitation. The university model was carried across the nation by the nearly one thousand Ph.D. graduates of Johns Hopkins who held faculty appointments in American institutions of higher education by 1926.[10] Today, conferences, associations, informal networks, and publications like the *Chronicle of Higher Education* become settings for information transfer inside the higher education industry. Imitation—one response to this kind of information transfer—has been an important source of organizational change across even the diversity of American universities.

Information flows and information influences extend beyond the fraternity of universities. In many ways, this has always been so. Broad social trends toward professionalism, specialization, and credentialing have placed emphasis on the more utilitarian elements of university work. Similarly, broad changes in society, including the wider acknowledgment of civil rights, have informed the nature of access. These pathways remain open today. Increasingly, business processes designed to transform large industries (TQM, reengineering, etc.) have gained advocates within the institution and with important constituencies outside. Governors, boards of regents, and trustees, most of whom are businesspeople, increasingly demand that universities acknowledge this body of information and make appropriate changes in their organizations in response.[11]

Open systems depend upon these linkages to their environment for resource flows and for legitimacy, indeed for their very existence.[12] But at the same time, if universities are to retain the independence that is critical to their core purposes, to the "knowledge of things" that Veblen described as the "only end in life that justifies itself," openness to the environment cannot mean surrender to it.[13] It is precisely this tension that has dominated the evolution of universities in the twentieth century and that promises to dominate our entry into the twenty-first. Management of this tension will be a critical element of university leadership now as it was then.

Open systems without boundaries soon cease to be definable, differentiable organizations. Put another way, boundaries and limits define the uniqueness of any organization. A liberal-arts college, for example, that creates a law school at the behest of a donor might soon cease to maintain the internal focus on undergraduates required of its identity as a liberal-arts college. It is no wonder, as W. Richard Scott observes, that open systems "expend great energy in boundary maintenance."[14] Research into the boundary issues of open systems suggests that boundary maintenance has two characteristic forms: buffering and bridging.

In the first, organizations seek to absorb or deflect the demands of the external environment without altering its fundamental structure or processes. In Thompson's words, "Organizations seek to seal off their core technologies from environmental influences."[15] Much about universities is about buffering. The creation of segregated physical environments, the rich internal rituals, the scholarly ethic of distance from immediate problems, and the isolation of students all aim to the creation of what Erving Goffman aptly called a "total institution."[16] Like others of that ilk, including prisons, mental hospitals, and boarding schools, university culture relies on the substitution of its own norms for those of the broader society. In a university context, this buffering from the external world is essential if scholars and scientists are to pursue the "knowledge of things" unfettered by pedestrian demands that might short-circuit the process of discovery. Within the university, buffering aims at protecting the core processes of teaching and research from external demands. Often this buffering takes the form of careful processes that filter out unwanted influence. The academic personnel process is an example of this kind of buffering. In other instances, buffering is achieved through a lack of process, as when faculty choose readings and construct assignments for classes or when faculty individually or in groups write grant proposals or research articles. In both instances the result is to insulate individual faculty and the faculty as a whole from unwanted outside interference.

Researchers also suggest that buffering attempts to protect the technical core from fluctuations in the quality or quantity of needed inputs. By carefully "coding" or "screening" inputs, business organizations assure uniform quality. By "stockpiling" necessary inputs, business organizations protect themselves against a shortage. By "forecasting" demand and supply, business organizations seek to anticipate fluctuations and make adjustments before the changes occur. We can easily see analogues in the university setting as faculty hiring and student admissions processes carefully sort applicants in order to secure the highest attainable quality.

Endowments are stockpiled financial resources. And while it is difficult for individual institutions to stockpile human resources, one might argue that the overproduction of Ph.D.s in recent years has had the effect of creating a stockpile of available teaching resources. Moreover, the employment of these highly trained scholars as lecturers rather than as tenured faculty allows individual institutions to respond to unforeseen fluctuations in student demand, minimizing the need for accurate forecasting. In these ways, universities initiate buffering strategies in a manner consistent with other large organizations in an effort to protect core activities from undue intentional or unintentional environmental pressures.

The second major category of boundary maintenance mechanisms falls under the category of bridging strategies. Rather than insulate core processes from external influence, bridging strategies attempt to absorb the effect of external demand by creating delimited accommodations that do not compromise the core processes and values. Research contracts specifying that a certain set of activities be performed for specific amounts of money are examples of one kind of bridging strategy. More subtle forms of bridging take the form of co-optation, in which external actors are brought into the internal processes of the institution in order to be socialized into its set of values. In universities, nonfiduciary boards of visitors and many alumni associations seek just this outcome.

Structurally, two forms of bridging have been important to universities. The first are segregated joint ventures, in which boundary-spanning organizations are created that borrow resources from the core and put them to work in activities that respond to environmental demands, often funded by external resources. Many institutes and centers reflect this kind of segregated joint venture. Some respond to external demand for study of a particular problem, whether arms control or pollution. Others, including ethnic studies centers and institutes for multimedia or technology, respond to the demands of internal and external constituencies for concentrated representation and focused inquiry. Like most joint ventures, these centers and institutes are semipermanent features of the university organization, postulated to grow, shrink, or disappear entirely depending on external demand and relevance. What makes these joint ventures segregated are the boundaries that are set up and managed between them and the technical core, often buffered by the mechanisms described above. Take the example of most centers and institutes, funded by outside money and populated by a mixture of university faculty and nonacademic subject specialists. Few of these institutes possess the right to appoint faculty; virtually all must submit to the regular faculty appointment process, and faculty must be appointed to a mainline academic department. Thus, institutes and centers respond to external demands but do not allow those demands to alter a fundamental input to the core processes of teaching and research.

The second form of structural accommodation is the creation or absorption of subsidiaries, some close to the core and some farther away, that are constructed specifically to meet external demands. Unlike joint ventures, these subsidiaries tend to have long lives and often become permanent parts of the university apparatus. In the past, professional schools, extension departments, and women's divisions of (usually elite) institutions were first created to address external demands of this kind. What marks these subsidiaries is their durability. In the history of American universities, they have been critical elements. The most salient example of this kind of influence is Columbia University, created at the turn of this century through the amalgamation of fourteen separate colleges and institutes. Several, including Teachers College, retain independent endowments, an independent president, and their own board of trustees. As these examples suggest, over time the original nature of the relationship between core and subsidiary becomes clouded, with important institutional consequences.

Together, these buffering and bridging strategies typify the means by which the American university has remained resilient to successive waves of demand from its environment. No period is more illustrative of this resilience than the progressive era, the time, in Frederick Rudolph's phrase, of the "flowering of the university movement."[17]

PROGRESSIVE ERA CHALLENGES TO THE AMERICAN UNIVERSITY

The American university did not emerge full-grown from a well-developed template. Instead, it developed over time from a number of starting points.[18] As a result, the identification of the "core" processes of the university was itself an evolutionary process.

Understanding some of that process is integral to understanding the ways in which universities have, from their beginnings, confronted boundary issues and how they have managed those boundaries in accommodating external demands.

The most fundamental influence on the development of the core processes of the university was the growth of scientific and scholarly inquiry as independent endeavors and the subsequent emergence of scholarly activity as being central to institutional identity.[19] Some of this growth occurred through accretion and imitation, as at Harvard and Yale where experimental science gradually made inroads during the early decades of the nineteenth century. In other instances, new institutions took up science directly, as in the flurry of institution-building at the end of the nineteenth century. At the new Johns Hopkins University, conscious imitation of the German model of research and scholarship was a part of the founding charter. As Rudolph describes it, "For the revealed truth [of the denominational college] the new university in Baltimore substituted a search for scientific truth."[20] Clark University became the nation's first completely graduate institution. At the newly risen state universities, too, science became the key with which to unlock new knowledge in every field of human endeavor. By the early years of the twentieth century the reign of science and scholarship along the German model had created the general framework for the American model of the university and the general shape of core activities dominated by research and scholarship in basic disciplines. In institutions across the country, university life came to be defined by the image of doctorate-holding professors teaching undergraduates and working with groups of graduate students on their way to the Ph.D. to fold back the mysteries of the natural, social, and cultural worlds.[21]

But what made the American university different from all that had come before it, and many that would come after it, was the range of inquiry that would be placed under the rubric of science, a range that seemed without limit or boundary.[22] It was Daniel Coit Gilman, president of the University of California, who gave voice to this array in his inaugural address of 1872. In anticipation of the flowering of the university movement a quarter-century later, Gilman described the university as "the most comprehensive term that can be employed to indicate a foundation for the promotion and diffusion of knowledge." He described his own institution as "a group of agencies organized to advance the arts and sciences of every sort, and train young men as scholars for all the intellectual callings of life."[23] In usage, it was the very comprehensiveness of the term "university" that invited the boundary debates that so dominated the first decades of the twentieth century inside and outside the academy.

The "pattern of the new university," in Veysey's formulation, was a pattern that accepted a broad mission in exchange for broad support from a variety of internal and external constituencies. Undergraduate teaching, accommodating to a wide variety of specializations and elective courses after 1900, combined with research departments, graduate schools, professional schools, and training institutes. Each of these aimed to provide a bridge to important constituencies in the external environment. Over the first two decades of the century, internal faculty demands, propelled by an increasing number of Ph.D.s, quickly made research the high-status activity. By 1910, universities were competing for the most prolific researchers, advertising their most prolific scholars, and even, at Stanford, publicizing in the annual report the number of research papers written by each faculty member. As Veysey summed up the period, "As far as official demands upon the faculty were concerned, by 1910 research had almost fully gained the position of dominance which it was to keep thereafter."[24]

But while research may have become the high-status activity within American universities of the early twentieth century, it was not enough, alone, to support them. Clark University, the first institution to attempt survival on research and graduate teaching alone, nearly failed. Johns Hopkins, more successful than Clark, nonetheless struggled in its early years. The more typical pattern "was for researchers to form an enclave within a larger university devoted to other ends." These other ends, in our terms, were those aspects of university life—undergraduate education, professional training, and, increasingly, athletics—that satisfied environmental demands for assisting in adolescent development, in providing useful skills, and in entertainment, respectively. The symbiotic relationship that emerged between research activities and the more externally focused aspects of the university's work is one that prevails today. Professional schools, athletics, and undergraduate education support research by providing access to resources that would not otherwise come the university's way, and research supports these boundary-oriented activities by adding both the substance and the form of academic legitimacy.[25] What emerged from this formative period was a kind of institutional division of labor, in which boundary activities were assigned to professional and technical schools, the university administration, and extension departments that offered instruction to a broad and diverse constituency. Within this periphery, the core and now-dominant research activities of faculty in traditional disciplines were protected and buffered. But even at its origin, there were those who warned that this apparent equilibrium was not stable.

In 1916, pressed by both the lengthening shadow of World War I and the tumultuous energy of American Progressivism, Thorstein Veblen wrote his classic manifesto, *The Higher Learning in America*. It was at once a scathing critique of the university at the beginning of the century and a ringing endorsement of its importance to a rapidly changing society. Veblen understood the university's role in purely intellectual terms, its role to "conserve and extend the domain of knowledge." It followed that the work of a professor should be "the single-minded. . .pursuit of knowledge, together with whatever advisory surveillance and guidance he may consistently afford. . .students." In Veblen's ideal role, the institutionalized university protected this single-mindedness among its faculty by creating a gravity-free zone in which scholars would be protected from the weight of everyday demands. Isolation was of critical importance, as "the affairs of life, except the affairs of learning, do not touch the interest of the university. . .scholar or scientist." To those of us used to the competing demands of Kerr's modern "multiversity," the purity of Veblen's conception seems hopelessly idealistic and naive. But then this was Veblen's point, that without a clear vision and moral compass, determinedly idealistic universities had become whatever anyone wanted them to be, the product of "aimless survival" rather than of purposeful self-definition.[26]

Veblen's university, unlike Gilman's, was a domain of pure scholarship, "more closely identified with the quest of knowledge than any other" institution. The university "is the only accepted institution of the modern culture on which the quest of knowledge unquestionably devolves." Veblen regarded any retreat from this single focus as a dilution of the university's essential mission. Although an extremist on the issue, he was not alone. Palmer Ricketts, a faculty member at RPI at the turn of the century, reflected upon a particular set of environmental demands when he recalled that "the youngest among us here remembers how many of the academic schools were unwillingly forced to add scientific departments in compliance with public demand."[27] Veblen acknowledged these environmental demands by dismissing them, with a vigor that bespoke their currency in popular discourse. "It is true," he acknowledged, that "many other lines of work, and of endeavor that may not fairly be called work, are undertaken by schools of university grade." He observed also, "many other schools that call themselves 'universities' will have substantially nothing to do with the higher learning." The list of work of dubious legitimacy was a long one and included "professional training, undergraduate instruction, supervision and guidance of the secondary school system, edification of the unlearned by 'university extension' and similar excursions into the field of public amusement, [and the] training of secondary school teachers."[28] The evenhanded Veysey, writing fifty years later, could have been referring to Veblen and Ricketts when he remarked that "wedged among the other demands of the fully developed university, research had gained its power at the cost of the single-mindedness with which its more zealous partisans had sought to pursue it."[29]

What is significant about Veblen's list is not so much the identity of the suspect categories, but rather the manner in which American institutions of higher education dealt with the demands for these activities on their way to becoming universities. In each instance, universities in the making protected a core research faculty in the arts and sciences with an array of bridge institutions—professional schools, scientific institutes, extension divisions, and departments—that were technically part of the university but were held at an organizational distance from the "core" faculties and activities.

OF BRIDGES AND BUFFERS

A classic contradiction inherent in boundary-spanning or bridging strategies arises from their tendency to create or sustain external support for peripheral activities. This is, of course, their aim. The rationale for engaging in these kinds of activities is twofold. Either boundary spanning will yield support that will be translated inside the organization into support for the core, or core activities will find their support elsewhere and the effect of support for peripheral activities will be benign. An example of the first is an endowment for a chair in business that allows some funds to be diverted to Renaissance studies. An example of the second is a gift to renovate the campus quad. However, in a world of scarcity and, hence, resource competition, it is likely that resources and support that attach to peripheral activities will not be available at the core. Indeed, it is plausible to propose that in certain environments, the more successful an institution is at creating boundary-spanning organizations linked to the external environment, the less able it will be to generate resources directly for support of core activities.[30] This is a problem that has become particularly pressing today, and it has three aspects.

The first-order problem is a simple one. In environments in which resources are constant or declining and in which demand is high for activities and services that are different from those currently supported at the core, it follows mathematically that efforts to produce these activities and services will draw resources away from the core. This has been the fate of many arts and sciences faculties (where much of the core work takes place) across the nation in the last two decades, when resource growth has slowed and marginal new resources are directed towards the very services and activities (professional training, applied research, etc.) that Veblen criticized as having no place in the university.

One could well counter that marginal resources are earmarked in such a way that they never could be used for other, even core, purposes. This is the point. Take a simple schematic example: In the University of California, UCLA and UC Berkeley raise about the same amount of private money each year (UCLA slightly more, naturally). UCLA has a medical center and hospital on campus that raises about half of these dollars for applied medical research. Berkeley has no medical school but raises several times what UCLA does for basic research in the biological and natural sciences. One might wonder whether, if Berkeley suddenly grew a medical school or UCLA closed a hospital, there would be a shift in the way these new resources were raised. This is to say, simply, that the array of choices available determines, to some extent, resource acquisition. It has only been a three-decade rise in revenues that has kept this from being a more pressing issue. To the proposition that bridging strategies have failed to manage demands upon the core, we might therefore add the claim that this is typical of periods of declining resources, when every allocation decision becomes a trade-off of one kind of activity for another.

The second aspect of this problem is also linked to resource acquisition, but more indirectly. As universities have developed bridging institutions, like professional schools or athletic departments, to link with specific aspects of their environments (businesspeople, lawyers, those who enjoy athletics), they also create both internal and external constituencies for that work. Internal constituencies consist of those faculty and professionals who operate these units. External constituencies include alumni, boosters, and those who derive benefit from, for example, the applied research of a medical school or engineering school or the entertainment and prestige value of tickets on the fifty-yard line. With some unintended irony, the bridge organizations become the primary reference point for these constituencies, and they come to see the interests of these units as identical to or even proxies for the interest of the whole. This is a kind of ocular dysfunction that keeps the NCAA on the front pages of newspapers. Like the blindfolded men feeling the elephant, each constituency defines the university by its experience with a part of it. To many within these external constituencies, the bridge structures *become* the defining features of the university.

It follows that the more successful an institution is in developing bridging organizations and structures, the more entrenched and focused external constituencies will become in their support for these particular expressions of the university's identity. In turn, these entrenched constituencies become conduits for environmental demands and place demands not only on a particular professional school or administrative program but on the university as a whole. This is particularly so in circumstances, all too common, in which the clearly defined constituencies of professional schools, for example, compete against the diffuse constituency of the arts and sciences for resources and, ultimately, for the ability to define the identity of the institution.

The third means by which bridging organizations actually increase the penetration of external demands arises inside the organizational boundary of the university, as a result of the breakdown of the internal boundaries between disciplines and subunits. Perhaps the most obvious examples of these boundaries, and the most pertinent in terms of the future, are those that separate the faculties of arts and sciences from those of the professional schools. While these boundary conditions vary from institution to institution, the general point remains that the multiple external constituencies of professional schools, their definitional role in attending to the professions to which they are attached, separates much of the work of the professional school from the traditional arts and sciences disciplines. Here, once again, Veblen is anticipatory. He contrasts the "practical" work of professional schools with the work of "scientists and scholars," which is "not 'practical' in the slightest degree." Yet he understood, as we do, the important reciprocal relationship between these two activities. Professional schools (Veblen could not bring himself to call those who worked in them "faculty") "depend in large measure on the results worked out by the scientist," while "the scientists similarly depend on the work of technical men for information, and for correction and verification of their theoretical work."[31] While simplistic, Veblen's distinction is a useful starting point and reflective of the historical origins of both technical and professional schools, on the one hand, and research faculties, on the other.

As we have seen, there has been much gain for American universities in the coupling of professional schools and traditional disciplines. But, for Veblen, whose concern was the effect on individual scholars and not on the institution as a whole, the relationship produced neutral effects, at best. "There is," he argued, "nothing to gain by associating any given technical school with any given university establishment." While he understood that the best professional training drew from basic research and that research, in turn, drew questions and data from technical experience, he saw this exchange working best at a distance. As he saw it, technical and professional faculty draw upon "the general literature of [a] subject," not "the work of any particular men attached to particular schools." In fact, proximity was dangerous to the core research and inquiry functions in two ways.

First, by attaching professional and technical schools to a university, the faculty of these institutions "are necessarily included among the academic staff," and once inside the gates, these nonscholars "come to take their part in the direction of academic affairs at large." It is obvious that Veblen's construction of the dichotomy leads him to fear that the professional and technical faculty, "in what they do toward shaping the academic policy," will "not only count for all they are worth" but because of their training in the "world of affairs. . .are likely to count for something more than their due share in this respect."[32]

Leaving aside the last bit, Veblen's complaint can be rephrased in the terms of this argument. The creation of bridging organizations (professional and technical schools) creates internal boundary disputes between the disparate elements within the university, each claiming some due legitimacy as parts of the university whole. These boundary disputes are resolved institutionally in a variety of ways. In some institutions, thick buffers seek to prevent the kind of contamination against which Veblen warns. Academic personnel processes that are segregated by school or type of school sometimes attempt to keep the values of one kind of faculty from impinging on another. The creation of adjunct and other nontenure-track lines within schools, the restriction of voting rights for these lines, and the establishment of separate personnel processes for these faculty marks another type of segregation aimed at buffering the core values and processes of the research faculty. But far more common is an egalitarian spirit, perhaps first brought to full expression at Andrew White's Cornell, in which each discipline and each faculty, regardless of its focus, is treated in formally equal terms—sitting in judgment of each other's personnel actions, evaluating each other's research proposals, and working with each other's students. Within these institutions the maturation of successful professional and technical programs indeed serves the function Veblen feared, creating a conduit for the assertion of "practical" values into the core processes of the university.

If Veblen's first concern was structural and political—that the inclusion of technical and professional faculty in universities would contaminate academic decision-making—his second was more psychological, perhaps even epistemological. Research faculty should shun "intimate association with these 'utilitarians,'" since such contact "unavoidably has its corrupting effect on the scholars and scientists and induces in them also something of the same bias toward 'practical' results in their work." Individual faculty, attracted by the ease of practical work and by its rewards of fame and gain, "no longer pursue the higher learning with undivided interest, but with more or less of an eye to the utilitarian main chance."[33]

Veblen also understood that this flow works in both ways. If weak buffers between the research faculty and the professional faculty lead to the transmission of professional values to the research faculty, it is true that the values of the research faculty flow with at least equal force to the professional side. The attractions of scholarship, particularly the university status system that accords higher *internal* respect to scholars, leads faculties in professional schools "to court a specious appearance of scholarship." Although sympathetic to the effect on professional schools, Veblen's main concern was with the long-term effect of this "specious appearance" on the definition and broad understanding of scholarship itself. In the long run, he argued, people inside and outside the university might actually take this "make-believe scholarship" to be real research, thus cutting off the "knowing of things" at its very source.[34] Here, then, in this final and most elemental way, the bridging function of professional and technical schools alters how core processes are defined and how research and inquiry are conceptualized, thus amplifying rather than suppressing environmental demands.

CONTEMPORARY ISSUES

One need not subscribe to Veblen's absolutism to appreciate his basic concern that the cohabitation of professional schools and graduate faculties in the traditional disciplines has resulted in a blurring of distinctions between them. Neither must one reach his negative conclusions in order to acknowledge that the mechanisms universities have used to manage their boundaries and protect the core research functions in the basic disciplines have come to play just the opposite role, providing pathways for influence over core processes and decisions. Distilled in this way, these two observations inform much of the current state of unease among American universities.

Veblen's commentary reflected a particular historical moment and set of environmental demands. In 1916, when he wrote *The Higher Learning*, American universities were under extraordinary pressure, torn as Veblen saw it "between patriotism in the service of the captains of war, and commerce in the service of the captains of finance." Both pressures demanded a retreat from dispassionate scholarship and basic inquiry and an acceptance of utilitarian ends. Today, this same call for utilitarianism is strident and growing. Basic research, as an activity, is under assault for its lack of immediate connection to pressing problems. Undergraduate curricula are under attack for lack of reference to the job market. Even some professional schools, designed precisely to address these utilitarian demands, are under fire for being too academic. One need only review the current debates in Congress over research funding to understand that while it may still be true that "civilized men have come to hold that. . .the knowledge of things is the only end in life that justifies itself," support for that work can no longer be taken for granted.

Thus, today's turn of the century environmental demands on the university differ from their earlier counterparts in degree rather than in kind. But the organizational history of the intervening eight decades has changed the field on which these demands, and their accommodation, are played out. The long coexistence of professional schools with graduate and undergraduate faculties in arts and science has had some of the blurring effects Veblen anticipated. Professional schools have developed their own brands of scholarship and, in conjunction with their counterparts in traditional fields, have nurtured and matured new fields of basic inquiry, including neuroscience, organizational science, materials science, and information science. Belying Veblen's fears, much of this has been first-rate scholarship.

Over the same period, graduate and undergraduate faculties have responded to demands to engage in more focused and utilitarian inquiry. It is here that the playing field has changed to the greatest degree. Some of this change is an outgrowth of basic changes in the American economy, changes that have themselves been driven by applications of new scientific discoveries in the form of new technologies. The rise of biotechnology and of information and media technology, in particular, has created a family of industries and firms that facilitate the direct translation of basic research into a commercial product. These "boundary-piercing organizations" can and do reach directly into the faculty, providing inducements to the best scientists to sell certain discoveries and to pursue specific lines of research. Every physical sciences dean has a story to tell about the senior chemist recruited away by one firm or another. Venture capitalists troll professional and scientific meetings the way sports agents comb the practice fields, looking for new talent. Many within the traditionally buffered ranks of research faculty are now engaged on the boundary between universities and commerce in ways they could not have foreseen three decades ago.

Under these circumstances, buffering and bridging have come to take on new meaning and new forms. In the current generation, two of the major threats to basic research within the university are a decline in traditional sources of support and the existence of more opportunities for faculty, especially scientists, to find more lucrative employment in the for-profit world. In the terms we have been discussing, they appear at first glance to call for opposite boundary-management strategies. In the first case, declining support for basic inquiry suggests the creation of boundary units that can attract support for some aspect of the research enterprise that can in some way be channeled back into basic inquiry (or for simple retrenchment).[35] In the second case, the voracious appetite among businesses for academic talent seems to demand a raising of the boundaries for buffering strategies designed to keep faculty at work on issues of basic inquiry.

In fact, what has happened over the last fifteen years or so is that universities have used all of these strategies, and some have or are attempting to develop strategies that buffer and bridge at once. Boundary-bridging organizations, such as the Stanford Center for Integrated Systems, have succeeded in providing an intellectual site where basic inquiry, applied analysis, and experimental design are more or less integrated. Critically, support for the Center comes from industry, which is willing to pay a premium on their contributions to fund basic research in return for close contact with the applied side of the house. Similar kinds of centers and institutes have emerged across the nation as a way of meeting not just the growing demand of private industry but the application and dissemination requirements of many federal research grants. Buffering mechanisms, meanwhile, have focused on faculty incentives and sanctions. On the sanctions side, most universities attempt to regulate the amount and kind of time faculty spend working on for-profit concerns while they are also university employees.[36] This has two intended effects. One is to focus the majority of faculty time on core activities. The other is to force faculty who are tempted to leave the academy to make that decision with little direct experience of the "outside," thus increasing their uncertainty about leaving. In this, universities bet on basic risk aversion. Sometimes this strategy backfires, as initial and partial experiences show the alternative in the best possible light. Other sanctions include the deeply embedded cultural ones against individual faculty whose outside work diminishes their scholarly productivity. Faculty promotion committees do not look kindly upon colleagues whose work in the for-profit sector takes them away from research or even from teaching or committee meetings.

Far more interesting than these sanctions are the incentives universities are creating to retain faculty and to keep them productive in basic research. Most of these incentives seek to help investigators reap private-sector benefits while still remaining productive members of the research faculty. For example, university patent offices seek to make it as easy or easier inside the institution for faculty to convert their discoveries into commercial applications than it would be outside. Moreover, these offices often market patented discoveries to potential licensees, acting as agents and eliminating the need for faculty to devote time and energy to these directly commercial ends. This family of strategies has the second-order purpose of getting faculty "back to work" by handing off the commercialization of research to others inside the university. As the external demand for academic talent increases, so do the terms by which faculty share in the returns for this kind of integrated action. This year, for example, the University of California adopted a policy that gives a third of all patent income to investigators, with a third each going to the university and the sponsoring department.

Some universities have become even more aggressive in these areas, seeking to bridge and buffer at once by creating internal units whose mission it is to build businesses on the foundation of faculty research work and then to seek investment partners among the very same firms that under other circumstances would have been competitors for faculty time and brainpower. Like other buffering strategies, these "incubators" seek to limit the amount of time and energy faculty spend building a business and to keep faculty working inside the university. At the same time, like other bridging strategies, they make connections between the university and external demands (in this case, the demand that discoveries be brought to market) on the university's own terms.

What makes these boundary pressures and their management different from those that concerned Veblen at the turn of the twentieth century is their point of impact. As Veblen's commentary reflects, the impact point for environmental pressure was the institution. Pressures to add or sustain professional and technical schools, demands to add parallel degree tracks for "utilitarian" subjects—these affected the way the university's programmatic building blocks were assembled and maintained. Once assembled, as Veblen predicted and as we have seen, the internal boundaries separating these differentiated units began to break down, and the mechanisms meant to absorb or deflect environmental pressure began to attract and transmit that pressure deep into the organization. As a result, today's boundary pressures impact universities not only at an organizational level but, increasingly, at the level of individual faculty work.

Whether it is the faculty member who consults one day per week or the researcher who engages in a joint partnership to create a new biotech firm within a university incubator, individual faculty increasingly find themselves in the role of boundary spanners. The net result is that the division of labor between basic and applied work occurs less and less at the organizational level and more and more at the individual level. Perhaps the clearest examples come from the health sciences, where research faculty also maintain clinical practices under the control of the university and provide teaching to both future researchers and clinicians. In this way, faculty respond to the demands of society for more direct impact on health care, to students' demands for training, and to the internal demand of the university for basic research. This triple identity as researcher, clinician, and teacher has profoundly positive effects in terms of bridging basic inquiry and practice, yet it is also a drain on the energies of any one endeavor. Moreover, it creates a complicated set of trade-offs that must be managed by both the individual and the university if any kind of balance is to be maintained.

The breakdown of the institutional division of labor that in Veblen's era assigned border-crossing activities to a limited number of units, professional schools, extension departments, and the like has also affected those who have been well protected and buffered. For them, the increasing penetration of environmental concerns comes as a shock, if not an insult. For these faculty members, the ability to stand apart from environmental demands is testimony to the persistent success of buffering mechanisms in some disciplines, in some generations, and in some institutions. What has created shock in recent years is the combination of the slow changes that have made bridging organizations conduits of external demand with the rapid effects of declining resources; this has made the question of resource acquisition and resource use paramount. Resource questions have, in turn, brought virtually every faculty member to a greater realization of the importance of environmental demands, even if that importance is seen, as it often is, as a threat to the internal integrity of the institution.[37]

At the institutional level, managing boundaries has become increasingly about managing the way individual faculty spend their time, never the easiest of propositions. Again we return to Veblen's insights. As professional schools have adopted many of the norms of scholarship of their brethren in the arts and sciences, they have become less effective as a bridge to the environmental demands for direct intervention into social issues. Education schools have become particular points of vulnerability in this regard, as their increasing sophistication as research entities and the increasing sophistication of their faculty as researchers has made the faculty and their work less directly relevant to practice. Over time, this trend has led to broad dissatisfaction with education schools in the world of professional education and in society at large.[38] The perceived inadequacy of education schools to meet the nation's educational crisis has caused environmental demand to spill over into other domains of the university. To the frustration of many university administrators, education schools have not buffered the rest of the institution from these demands, nor have they bridged to the environment in such a way as to satisfy the need for university engagement on its own terms. As a result, demand is rampant and uncontained. In January of 1997, for example, the governor of California, fed up with precisely this issue, proposed language in his budget that would require the University of California campuses to establish charter schools providing direct educational services to children in kindergarten through grade twelve.

This kind of demand is nothing new for management schools. They are typically called upon to intervene directly in providing educational services to the world's businesses. Executive education programs have become pervasive and highly lucrative, for institutions and for individual faculty. It is not surprising that while some institutions are seeking to expand their executive education programs to meet environmental (and market) demand, others are examining ways to balance the potentially explosive growth in demand for these programs with the stagnant and declining demand (and support) for research. This means a recalibration of incentives for individual faculty, making it either less profitable for them to participate in executive programs or more profitable for them to pursue research and other types of teaching.

Neither of these examples speaks of good boundary management. Balance, and the ability to address multiple environmental demands, becomes increasingly problematic when the locus of the balancing shifts from organizational units to individuals. At the individual level, the multiple and competing demands on faculty time produce a situation in which faculty feel increasingly schizophrenic.[39] Especially in professional schools, faculty are torn between responsibilities to their research, responsibilities to their students, and responsibilities to their professional colleagues. As in the case of the health sciences cited earlier, the general case of the professional schools is one in which the interaction of teaching, research, and service produce positive results in the abstract. Yet in reality, this need for a personal division of labor produces stress and a lack of clarity about any of the three types of work.[40]

LIVES ON THE BOUNDARY

In answer to his own observations and concerns, Veblen recommended that "to the substantial gain of both parties, through with some lesion to the vanity of both, the separation between the university and the professional and technical schools should be carried through and made absolute."[41] To a degree that he would have found abhorrent, but to achieve purposes that we easily understand, universities have moved in the opposite direction. Looking back, we see the development of professional and technical schools as a part of a history of organizational initiatives that have sought to manage the boundaries between core research functions of the university and demands from the external environment. Looking forward, one sees increasing demands for some kind of boundary definition and boundary management. In all likelihood, this boundary management will take on two aspects of the problem.

First, university leaders will need to grapple with the increasing penetration of external demands and lures into the work lives of individual faculty. This will necessarily take place at a political level, where public universities, in particular, face pressures to increase undergraduate teaching and decrease research activities and graduate training. It will also need to take place organizationally, helping faculty achieve a reasonable balance between activities oriented toward inquiry and those oriented toward application or dissemination. In so doing, leaders will need to think seriously about new structures that tackle the hard questions of buffering and bridging. Second, and perhaps more significantly, university leaders will have to address a new wave of nonuniversity organizations that seek to provide teaching and training services to the public. In a twist Veblen could not have foreseen, new technologies and the market may create his desired separation between universities and technical schools.

Last year the governors of the western states launched an initiative to create a "virtual university." This year California's governor created a similar initiative within the state. Enrollments at Mind Extension University, the University of Phoenix, and other like concerns continue to climb. A major securities firm has proclaimed to its investors that education is "the largest market opportunity for private (for-profit) sector involvement since health care in the 1970s."[42] All of this suggests a social demand for teaching and training that is currently unmet by traditional universities. What makes these examples interesting to our discussion of boundaries is the sense that the mechanisms to meet this demand will emerge outside the traditional university sphere, even though many of these emerging organizations call themselves universities. In this environment, in which universities are losing their de facto monopoly over postsecondary teaching and training, leaders will need to make one of two choices. On the one hand, universities can enter this market and become players in a new kind of instruction that is both more focused in terms of subject and more distributed in terms of delivery. In this, one might expect universities to adopt traditional boundary management strategies, creating distance learning and lifelong learning units specifically designed to capture this burgeoning demand and to build links of political support to those demanding such services. On the other hand, universities can take Veblen's advice and take advantage of this moment to restrict their efforts to a set of core competencies around basic research and the training of scholars. Each strategy has its risks.

In the former case, the creation of new boundary organizations is likely, in the long run, to follow the same evolutionary pattern we have traced for professional schools, eventually contributing to the muddying of the university's identity and mission as it tries to build maximum political and financial support. In the latter case, the abandonment of the new markets for training and teaching isolates the university and forces university leaders to build financial and political support for one or two narrow sets of objectives. The question of whether the university can survive as a niche player, focusing on basic inquiry, is a question we have never answered affirmatively, and it is unlikely that we will do so in this generation. Instead, university leaders and faculty will be faced, as they have for a century, with living lives on the boundary and with seeking institutional means of managing the tensions and temptations that arise at the border crossings between the internal life of the university and the demands of society.

ENDNOTES

[1]Thorstein Veblen, *The Higher Learning in America* (New York: Hill and Wang, 1957), 8.

[2]For an interesting take on the earliest European version of the university form, see Stephen C. Ferruolo, *The Origins of the University: The Schools of Paris and Their Critics, 1100–1215* (Stanford, Calif.: Stanford University Press, 1985). The history of the American university is ably told by Laurence R. Veysey, *The Emergence of the American University* (Chicago, Ill.: University of Chicago Press, 1965).

[3]An exhaustive survey of this literature is a study in itself. For an overview, see Sheldon Rothblatt, *The Modern University and its Discontents* (Cambridge: Cambridge University Press, 1997); Derek Bok, *Universities and the Future of America* (Durham, N.C.: Duke University Press, 1990); Jonathan R. Cole, Elinor G. Barber, and Stephen R. Graubard, eds., *The Research University in a Time of Discontent* (Baltimore, Md.: The Johns Hopkins University Press, 1994); and C. Kumar Patel, ed., *Reinventing the Research University* (Berkeley, Calif.: University of California Press, 1993).

[4]See Burton Clark, ed., *The Academic Profession: National, Disciplinary, and Institutional Settings* (Berkeley and Los Angeles, Calif.: University of California Press, 1987) and Clark's essay in this issue of *Dædalus*.

[5]Frederick Rudolph, *The American College and University: A History* (New York: Vintage Books, 1962), chap. 6. This process of change by accretion is, of course, still the preferred mode. Yet as we will see, it becomes dysfunctional over time.

[6]W. Richard Scott, *Organizations: Rational, Natural, and Open Systems*, 2d ed. (Englewood Cliffs, N.J.: Prentice Hall, 1987), chap. 8; James Thompson, *Organizations in Action* (New York: McGraw-Hill, 1967), chap. 1; Jeffrey Pfeffer and Gerald R. Salancik, *The External Control of Organizations* (New York: Harper and Row, 1978) chaps. 2, 3, 5. More recent elaborations of the issue of boundaries, and more generally on the relationship between environmental demands and organizational response, can be seen in Walter W. Powell and Paul DiMaggio, eds., *The New Institutionalism in Organizational Analysis* (Chicago, Ill.: University of Chicago Press, 1991).

[7]Thompson, *Organizations in Action*, 19.

[8]Veysey, *The Emergence of the American University*, 331.

[9]See Martin Trow's essay in this issue of *Dædalus*.

[10]Rudolph, *The American College and University: A History*, 336.

[11]See Edward Whalen, *Responsibility Center Budgeting* (San Francisco, Calif.: Jossey-Bass, 1991) for an example of these ideas translated into a university context.

[12]John Meyer and Brian Rowan, "Institutionalized Organizations: Formal Structure as Myth and Ceremony," *American Journal of Sociology* 83 (2) (1977): 340–363.

[13]Several recent monographs have responded to what might be described as the "boundary crisis" in higher education. A. Bartlett Giamatti, *A Free and Ordered Space* (New York: Norton, 1976); Derek Bok, *Higher Learning* (Cambridge,

Mass.: Harvard University Press, 1986); Derek Bok, *Beyond the Ivory Tower* (Cambridge, Mass.: Harvard University Press, 1982); Henry Rosovsky, *The University: An Owner's Manual* (New York: Norton, 1990); and James O. Freedman, *Idealism and Liberal Education* (Ann Arbor, Mich.: University of Michigan Press, 1996) are fine sets of essays by university leaders who grapple with boundary issues. Jaroslav Pelikan, *The Idea of the University: A Re-Examination* (New Haven, Conn.: Yale University Press, 1992) and David Damrosch, *We Scholars: Changing the Culture of the University* (Cambridge, Mass.: Harvard University Press, 1995) are thoughtful analyses by faculty who find themselves in the midst of challenges to their own cultural understandings. Even Dinesh D'Souza's *Illiberal Education* (New York: Vintage, 1992) can be seen as a criticism of universities' openness to the demands of their environments.

[14]Scott, *Organizations: Rational, Natural, and Open Systems,* 82.

[15]Thompson, *Organizations in Action,* 19. This analysis follows Scott, *Organizations: Rational, Natural, and Open Systems,* chap. 8.

[16]Erving Goffman, *Asylums* (New York: Doubleday, 1961).

[17]Rudolph, *The American College and University,* 356–357.

[18]Here Veysey's treatment is superb; see especially Veysey, *The Emergence of the American University,* chaps. 3 and 5.

[19]See ibid., chap. 3.

[20]Rudolph, *The American College and University,* 274.

[21]Veysey, *The Emergence of the American University,* 165–177.

[22]There were, of course, holdouts. Rudolph tells the story of Ira Remsen, who upon asking for a small laboratory near his office at Williams College was told stiffly to "keep in mind that this is a college and not a technical school." Rudolph, *The American College and University: A History,* 271. See also Veysey, *The Emergence of the American University,* chaps. 1–4 for a discussion of alternative models for higher education that ultimately resolved themselves into the recognizable form we experience today.

[23]Daniel Coit Gilman, *The Building of the University: An Inaugural Address Delivered at Oakland, November 7, 1862* (San Francisco, Calif.: J. H. Carmany & Co., 1872), 6.

[24]Veysey, *The Emergence of the American University,* 321–325, 177.

[25]Ibid., 165–171. Recently there was a spirited discussion about whether UCLA's scarce basketball tickets should be allocated by the central development office or by the athletic department. The winners, the central development office, argued that the campus needed to use Pauley Pavilion as a fund-raising tool for the College of Letters and Sciences, for one, thus achieving a resource shift between the peripheral bridge of athletics to the core functions of the College.

[26]Veblen, *The Higher Learning in America,* 6, 8, 21.

[27]Ricketts, quoted in David Noble, *America By Design* (New York: Alfred A. Knopf, 1979), 22.

[28]Veblen, *The Higher Learning in America*, 11, 12.

[29]Veysey, *The Emergence of the American University*, 178.

[30]It is this tendency that has given rise to a number of regulations internal to universities to "tax" peripheral organizations for the sake of the core. Central taxes on gifts and tuition that are then redistributed to organizations and departments less likely to secure "outside" revenue are examples of these redistributive techniques.

[31]Veblen, *The Higher Learning in America*, 19–20.

[32]Ibid., 21–22. Presumably these "men of affairs" who populate the professional and technical schools will use their worldly wiles to trick the naive and guileless research faculty.

[33]Veblen, *The Higher Learning in America*, 22.

[34]Ibid., 23.

[35]See Patricia Gumport's essay in this issue of *Dædalus*.

[36]For example, the one day per week standard in the University of California is designed to accommodate simple consulting. Other restrictions limit engagements that include management responsibilities. This past year, the University's regulations were changed to make the one-day restriction applicable to a base week of seven days rather than five, effectively seeking to prevent faculty from engaging outside the university even on their "own time."

[37]Wellford Wilms, Cheryl Teruya, and Mary Beth Walpole, "Capturing Change: A Case Study," *Change* (forthcoming).

[38]See Geraldine Joncich-Clifford and James W. Guthrie, *Ed School: A Brief for Professional Education* (Chicago, Ill.: University of Chicago Press, 1988); also Rita Kramer, *Ed School Follies: The Miseducation of America's Teachers* (New York: Free Press, 1991).

[39]Burton R. Clark, "Listening to the Professoriate," *Change* XVII (September-October 1985): 36–43. See also Clark's essay in this issue of *Dædalus* and Alexander W. Astin, WIlliam S. Korn, and Eric L. Dey, *The American College Teacher: National Norms for 1989–90 HERI Faculty Survey* (Los Angeles, Calif.: Higher Education Research Institute, University of California, Los Angeles, 1991), 9–22.

[40]See Theodore R. Mitchell and Mike Rose, "Inquiry in Education," UCLA Graduate School of Education and Information Studies, Working Paper Series, April 1997.

[41]Veblen, *The Higher Learning in America*, 23.

[42]Michael T. Moe, R. Keith Gay, and Jodi C. Nelson, "The Emerging Investment Opportunity in Education," (San Francisco, Calif.: Montgomery Securities, 1996, 4–12.

Martin Trow

The Development of Information Technology in American Higher Education

I NFORMATION TECHNOLOGY IS A PROTEAN SUBJECT; it has many different aspects and is discussed from many different perspectives.[1] One important perspective centers on its use specifically in teaching and learning and on the development and use of courseware and other teaching and learning materials. Other questions are raised about its impact on the ownership of intellectual property and the problems it poses for quality assessment and control.

Diane Harley and I are trying to locate information technology (IT) in the broad framework of American higher education, asking how IT is likely to adapt itself and be adapted to the enormously diverse forms and conditions of American higher education. To do this, we must disaggregate the concept of American higher education, recognizing that the character and function of IT will vary from the large public research university to the small private liberal-arts college. Our point of departure is a close look at the University of California and other California institutions, believing that this will give us clues about what is happening across the country. Our concern is less with "What should be done?" than with "What is going on?"

HISTORICAL AND INSTITUTIONAL CONTEXT FOR IT

Discussions of IT are normally very narrowly framed in time— anything older than three months is pre-history, anything further

Martin Trow is Professor in the Graduate School at the Goldman School of Public Policy, University of California, Berkeley.

293

ahead than ten years is science fiction. This reflects the fact that discussions of IT are dominated by what the technology can do or is predicted to do and by efforts to explore and expand its educational capacities. But we face a paradox: the rapid rate of change for the technology and software makes it highly desirable to anticipate future development, but it is almost impossible for us to do so beyond a few years or even months. During the computer's brief history, very little has been accurately predicted about its future development, either technological or social. With IT the crystal ball is very cloudy indeed.

What we do know is that IT is embedded in and used by institutions that have a history. The historically shaped characteristics of colleges and universities are highly relevant to the ways IT will be used by (and over time transform) the existing structures of higher education. It is also likely that IT will cut its own channels, leading to the creation of institutions that differ from those of today, institutions where the weight of history does not condition and constrain IT's use. This possibility, and the question of what relation those new institutions might have to current ones, should be kept in mind.

Much discussion of IT is presently undifferentiated; the focus is on new technologies, new courseware, and issues of pedagogy that arise in connection with the new forms of instruction. In order to address policy and practice in American higher education, we need to divide this enormous sphere of contemporary life into segments that share similar aims, functions, and characteristics. The distinctions between elite, mass, and universal access to higher education point to different forms of teaching and learning, to differences in their contexts and uses.[2] Elite forms of higher education aim at a kind of adult socialization, the shaping of mind, character, and sensibility. Requiring a relatively prolonged association between students and teachers, it is marked by a high ratio of teachers to students; studies tend to be intensive and difficult, pursued without the distractions of family responsibilities, outside work, or other competitive involvements. In this country, its purest form is in our leading private liberal-arts colleges and in the undergraduate colleges of the leading private research universities. Of course, elite higher education is not just a matter of shaping the mind and character, for it offers marked status and career advantages as a result of its reputation and networks as well as higher rates of admission to leading professional schools and graduate departments. This partly accounts for its survival, despite its high costs.

Mass higher education centers on the transmission of knowledge rather than the shaping of character. Studies tend to be less intense and are compatible with, and often enriched by, simultaneous part-time employment during the school year. Work is oriented toward the earning of certificates of accomplishment, i.e., degrees, which can serve as a proxy for employers as an indication of the student's possession of useful skills and knowledge and, more often, as an indication of the recipient's capacity to learn at certain levels of difficulty.

Postsecondary education marked by universal access is more difficult to describe. Its chief characteristic is that it is not oriented primarily toward gaining certificates or credit toward degrees. The number of people involved in this kind of learning is growing very rapidly; they study all sorts of things for all sorts of reasons that escape categorization. But since they are not earning credits toward degrees, they fall outside the authority of existing colleges and universities; their studies need not meet traditional academic standards nor be accredited unless they claim public institutional or individual support. Even then, the external criteria are closer to those of consumer protection against fraud than to the more familiar standards for academic accreditation. The UC Extension school has a wealth of experience in maintaining the quality of its offerings, including those that do not provide credits toward degrees. But not all of its competitors do or will, and a serious question regarding issues of quality control will be raised by the expansion of noncredit distance learning through IT.

It is sometimes convenient to give whole institutions one of these labels, for example, to call the University of California an elite university; the California State University system, with its strong commitment to vocational and semi-professional studies, to mature and part-time students, California's instrument for mass higher education; and the community, open-door colleges our instrument for universal access. But that obscures the fact that all three of these public segments are internally highly diverse and that all three kinds of education can be found in all three segments, though in quite different distributions. I will not be discussing the various forms of education to be found in the other two segments, except to say that both mass and universal higher education can be found in both institutions, as can even elite forms in nooks and crannies here and there. The University of California is a home to all three forms, in different departments and even in different courses. The different forms and functions of education are adapting different forms of IT to their purposes.

I need hardly say that elite, mass, and universal access types of higher education are not sharply bounded but rather shade off into one another. Moreover, the very same educational provisions are used in different ways by different students; I have spoken of undergraduate education at UC as predominantly forms of mass higher education. However, undergraduates at UC who are knowledgeable and motivated—and motivation is crucial here—can create for themselves forms of education that are comparable to those one would find in the best small liberal-arts colleges. But the numbers who do so are relatively few. Most take the structure of education as it is presented to them, which is what I have described as mass higher education.

This elementary differentiation within the world of higher education allows us to draw some implications and raise some questions. For example, there seem to be three main motives for colleges and universities to add more IT to their curricula. One is enrichment and improved efficiencies in learning; a second is wider access; and a third is cost containment, and perhaps per-capita cost reduction. For UC, access and cost control seem to be closely related: IT is seen as one way to accommodate the Second Tidal Wave[3] of qualified students within the close constraints of future state support for the university, which will surely not be growing as rapidly as our enrollments. I make the conceptual distinction because broad access through electronic media may well be an aim of a university (and society at large) independent of the issue of savings—that is to say, even if it were at current per capita costs. Similarly, some may hope to save money through IT even at current enrollment levels, though I suspect that is unrealistic. Access and cost control are analytically distinguishable.

Elite forms of higher education, and those responsible for it, are motivated chiefly by the possibilities of educational enrichment and improved learning, whether that means bringing a live interactive video course by the leading historian of Armenia to Santa Barbara and Berkeley by using specially prepared rooms or the creation of hand-tailored software for advanced science courses that allow complex experiments to be run outside of labs. Broader access and cost control in such institutions are distinctly secondary to enrichment and may not be present as motivations at all. Our graduate programs are mostly elite forms of education: though they teach at high levels of complexity and difficulty, they are also in the business of professional and scholarly socialization, and that is best accomplished through direct personal relationships. So long as the academics have anything to say about it, the introduction of IT into our elite forms of education will be in addition to, but not at the expense of, direct and personal relations between teachers and students. If the slogan of universal-access education is "anywhere, anytime," the slogan of elite higher education is "here and now," propinquity and synchronicity.

By contrast, the noncredit learning of universal-access education is made to order for "anywhere, anytime;" this is what the correspondence wings of the university's extension school have been doing for a very long time and what its administrative arrangements and independent funding are suited to develop. Extension does not deal internally with a powerful academic senate; the administrators own the curriculum as well as the budget, and that makes innovation a good deal easier than in the rest of the university. UC Extension, with some four hundred thousand students, pays for itself and more; it knows how to market and charge for education. Extension already knows what much of the rest of the university has to learn, or it knows how to find out. It comes as no surprise that the extension school, very quietly, is UC's pioneer in the adaptation and use of IT, in ways that the rest of the university may find it useful to learn from. Naturally, there is a status hurdle for any research university to overcome in order to be able to do that.

Mass higher education is "here and now" education but without close teacher-student relationships and with an emphasis on skills, credits, and certificates. This is the bulk of what we provide in our lower division now and a good bit of our upper-division studies as well—mass higher education of a pretty high quality, taught or supervised by a distinguished faculty. For the average UC student, the experience is one of anonymity—marked by the difficulty of finding any teacher who knows her well enough to write a letter of recommendation to a graduate or professional school. Here, enrichment of the undergraduate experience through IT should not be difficult; what is at issue is who will do it, where the initiatives will come from, who will pay for it, how costs will be controlled, and what the prospects are for wider access at levels of quality that we can accept and assimilate to our current conceptions. Mass higher education in this university seems to be emerging as some combination of traditional forms of lectures and seminars, enriched by IT both here and now and at the student's convenience in time and place. Work is now being done along these lines to draw more and more of the faculty into the new world and to explore the full potential of new technologies for enriching and even transforming the traditional forms of mass higher education in the university. This is perhaps where the most interesting work is being done and where the immediate problems of organization and finance arise most sharply.

SOFTWARE AS INDUSTRIAL PRODUCT AND AS HANDICRAFT

Many statements about IT prematurely generalize about the whole of American higher education. For example, one observer suggests:

> Development costs [of digital courseware] are such that they can be justified only if the resulting materials are used by very large numbers of students—numbers far larger than are found in any single institution and often are larger than the numbers of students in a single state. Different institutional providers, with help from foundations and other third-party funders, or through consortia that allow them to pool funds, will undoubtedly continue their course and curriculum development activities. But the need remains to "create a market" for such materials and ensure that those materials are distributed to (and accepted by) an audience large enough to justify the initial investment costs.[4]

If this statement were true, it would pose a serious threat to many colleges and universities. If courseware has to be designed for "very large numbers of people," then, besides costing a great deal, it also undermines the ownership of a course by the faculty member teaching it—a long-standing element of American higher education, and particularly of elite higher education. College and university teachers are rewarded with higher status and salaries than their counterparts in K–12, largely due to their responsibility for the courses they teach and the knowledge, insight, and imagination they put into those courses. Academics claim to be experts in their subject, with a wide and deep knowledge augmented by their own research or scholarship. To give up ownership of their courses to specialists developing digital courseware is to surrender their claim to intellectual autonomy and the status of professionals—that is to say, to become indistinguishable from most secondary school teachers, whose curricula and syllabi are largely determined by others.

However, professors are beginning to take the initiative to develop their own courseware. Recently I saw a demonstration, by a young assistant professor of Spanish at UC Santa Barbara, of a first-year course on the culture and politics of Latin America in the 1960s. The course was largely carried by a web page developed by the teacher with the help of technical-support people at her university. The page not only had annotated reading lists but included links to video clips of Latin American musicians of the day, singing and playing politically charged songs. The lyrics of those songs appeared alongside, with translations elsewhere, and there were clips of text discussing the artists as well as the events or struggles the songs celebrated or mourned. Members of the class had interviewed some of the artists still alive, and their interviews were now on the website. The instructor found wide resources on the Internet, in libraries, and in museums worldwide to link to her course web site; she is now able to maintain the web site herself and add material as it surfaces. The first course had involved about fifty hours of technical support time—not inexpensive, but not prohibitive either, unless everyone at her university were clamoring to do the same thing in the same semester. It seems likely that these development costs will come down as the technical staff begins to rationalize the procedures of support and user education, or if the work is outsourced.[5] So the development of courseware is already being demystified; it will increasingly be part of the bread and butter of college and university teaching, not the monopoly of experts and the equally expensive development and marketing firms that insist thousands of students need to be supported.

I mention this case not because it is the most dramatic or impressive use of IT resources in courseware that I have seen (it is not) but because it was produced by an initially technologically naive teacher in a rather esoteric nontechnical subject without any thought to its commercial potential. What is not clear is how the new IT resources actually affect the design of the course and its contribution to the education of its students. The way the material draws students in deserves praise, but do the resources of the course encourage a subtle simplification of the issues? The musicians and their revolutionary songs, so dramatically incorporated into the courseware, were certainly part of the scene in Latin America during the sixties; seeing and hearing them may well shed light on popular moods and movements that the standard histories of the period slight or cannot convey as powerfully. But does the format itself make reasoned discussion of the complexity of those events more difficult? Social and political variations, class and ethnic relations, historical traditions, the very flow of events— these issues depend on the scholarship and professional judgment of the instructor. The material was good entertainment; I enjoyed it too much, making me a bit uneasy about what I was learning. This is not a reaction I have had watching courseware in, say, mathematics, which is also very effectively designed to draw unwilling students into active engagement with the material.

Commercial courseware, designed for use by others, can take several forms. Some is designed as modules, used like textbooks to supplement the instructors' own teaching and resources—and chosen by the teacher for those purposes. Such modules may resemble in their function the hand-crafted courseware discussed above, and they may be integrated with the instructor's own IT courseware. Over time, modules that are technically superior, and easier and cheaper to use, may begin to replace the teacher's IT courseware, just as commercial radios replaced the crystal sets built by hobbyists in radio's infancy. My own guess is that for some time handcrafted courseware in colleges and universities will be a mix of courseware created by the teacher and adapted commercial modules. But in these cases the teacher is still designing the course, choosing or creating IT materials to enrich what is offered.

In sharp contrast to this is commercial courseware that is designed for widespread use by many institutions and that largely replaces, rather than supplements, the teacher. Such commercial courseware may embody a high level of internal complexity, be useful to different kinds of students, and have great value if there is no competent teaching in place for a subject. The same courseware may also be used for continuing education through distance learning. Through feedback, such courses can be constantly modified to improve the parts of the course that are not effective. But the improvement is in the hands of the designers, not the teachers or support staff who may supplement the courseware.

As mentioned, the voluntary creation of courseware by instructors or their adoption of commercial modules requires time, motivation, incentives, and technical support. The adoption of commercially produced whole courses requires none of these, and perhaps is facilitated by their absence. Teachers who have no strong motivation to create their own unique course, do not have the authority to design their course, have no spare time, or cannot count on technical support for the creation of their own courseware are more likely to adopt or passively accept the introduction of packaged IT courses. These conditions are most likely to be found in situations that resemble secondary schools or in continuing education.

Whole-course commercial courseware is usually targeted at courses that do not lend themselves to the special talents or unique interests of academics—or are not perceived by many academics to do so. Typically, they are skill-transfer courses, rather than those that aim to shape minds and perspectives, or broaden and refine sensibilities.[6] It is not surprising that the most common packaged whole courses are in beginning language instruction and basic college mathematics (college algebra, calculus, and introduction to statistics). Since so many students take, or are required to take, these courses, the market is there. In addition, these basic courses give narrower scope to the professional skills and knowledge of regular academics and are most easily abandoned by them to teaching specialists or teaching assistants—or to developer-controlled courseware.

In most academic institutions other than the elite research universities and leading private liberal-arts colleges, promotion and salary are tied closely to seniority rather than achievement. In those places, there may be little incentive to create IT-based or IT-enriched courses and a lot of encouragement for adapting commercial packages into the curriculum, thereby expanding the student base (and income) at relatively low cost. Also, the time and support needed to design IT-based courses is simply not available to teachers in nonresearch institutions, where teaching loads are 12 to 20 contact hours a week and the number of courses are twice what the teacher in the research university carries.

While the conditions best suited to widely distributed, packaged IT courses are approximated most closely in high schools, they also are approached in many community colleges and in nonresearch universities. The extension branches of research universities, however, are different. While their teaching staffs are professionally weak, their full-time administrative staffs are relatively strong, and the users—often mature, well-educated professionals or semiprofessionals—provide an excellent market for distance learning. The extension branches of elite universities have the resources to provide support for teachers who want to develop or test IT-based courses for their large and varied clientele.

In its character, function, and consequences for existing institutions the courseware produced for a mass market is markedly different from what I have called hand-crafted courseware, developed by teachers for their own courses. To the technicians of IT the two kinds of courseware are not so different: they require a similar infrastructure, especially very wide bandwidths and carrying capacity; similar hardware and software; similar skills on the part of the users. But the differences to an educator are larger than the similarities and rest on who controls the software, its development, and use.

ARGUMENTS FROM ACCESS

The arguments for developer-maintained commercial courseware are commonly linked to arguments for broader access. Wide-market commercial courseware, it is said, will help meet growing demands in three areas: for constraining costs associated with wider access (arising from the anticipated rapid growth in enrollments in the next decade) to existing institutions of higher education as they confront constrained public budgets; for access to continuing education, in a society where skills are increasingly important for employment and where the skills are constantly changing, as are jobs and careers; for access by students in K–12 to better teaching and coursework than they now find there, in order to meet the demands of global competition and the new information age.

Like most public research universities providing both mass and elite forms of education, UC concentrates its efforts in this area on various forms of curricular enrichment, providing first the expensive infrastructure for making IT-linked courseware available to teachers and then the equally expensive technical support and training for new users. At the same time, it is in the university's interest to expand access through broad-spectrum or commercial software. UC is very concerned about the looming prospect of the Second Tidal Wave of students who will be eligible for and applying to the university over the next decade. Under the terms of the California Master Plan, the agreement UC made with the state to accept the top one-eighth of the graduates from California high schools, entry to one of the university's eight undergraduate campuses is an entitlement of these eligible students; the university is strongly committed to honoring that agreement, out of political necessity if nothing else. But to do so with the university's current structure would cost enormous sums, both for the initial capital investment and for continuing instructional costs that the state and university cannot meet. The idea of commercial courseware for teaching students off-campus has more appeal for the Office of the President, which has to deal with state government, than for the campuses, which are concerned chiefly with their national standing and reputation as research universities.

Commercial courseware seems to offer substantial savings as institutions meet the growing demand for places in colleges and universities. IT promises to do that by putting some parts of postsecondary education directly into people's homes or offices and by reducing both capital and instructional costs for students enrolling in existing institutions. As William Massy and Robert Zemsky put it:

> Using IT for more-with-less productivity enhancement requires that technology replace some activities now being performed by faculty, teaching assistants, and support personnel. With labor accounting for 70 percent or more of current operation cost, there is simply no

other way. Faculty will have to re-engineer teaching and learning processes to substitute capital for labor....Failure to substitute intelligently will undermine educational quality and thus negate productivity gains.[7]

But the subject is a sensitive one. No research university president or chancellor is about to tell his faculty to "re-engineer teaching and learning processes to substitute capital for labor." The authorities say there is no other way, but it remains for university administrators and academics to find alternatives. The idea of giving any teaching over to self-contained courseware with only minimal supervision by regular faculty is at odds with the university's traditions; it threatens its jealously defended reputation for a degree reflecting high academic standards. The first tentative moves in this direction are toward providing what we now call "remedial" education—in English and college-level algebra—through commercial courseware, but even that runs into resistance, not least from the interest groups already providing that instruction. Moreover, for many who do not teach at that level, the proposals appear to herald the advent of technology as a substitute for, rather than the servant of, the instructor.

The coming tidal wave of students poses problems of a magnitude that cannot be solved by off-loading remedial courses. The university is just beginning to think about how to mix remote, self-contained courses for undergraduates with the traditional coursework on campus. What part of an undergraduate education can be provided to students off-campus and still count as regular credits toward a UC degree? And how can that be monitored and supervised by the academic senate, as would surely be required? What in the experience of UC Extension might be useful to the university here? On the whole, the university would not want to get into this universal access aspect of IT, except that it might provide an answer to the financial problems posed by the next tidal wave.

The university is also interested in commercial courseware as a way to raise the quality of education in K–12 and thus the preparedness of students entering UC. There are the familiar complaints about the literacy and numeracy of entering freshmen, even the selective entry to UC.[8] But some of what is now taught in the first year at UC—and not just what is done in the remedial courses—might be done in the last year or two of high school. If more students were to enter UC with advanced standing, having taken college-level courses in high school, that could shorten their time-to-degree and increase the university's ability to meet its obligations without major new outlays for buildings and professors. In addition, the university is under moral and political pressure to maintain its cultural diversity after preferential admissions policies for minorities was outlawed. Sophisticated courseware, particularly in mathematics and English, promises to increase the proportion of graduates of these ethnic groups who qualify on their own for entry to the university.[9]

The university also envisions commercial courseware as a way to compete with other institutions in the growing area of continuing education—some traditional, like Stanford and the California State University campuses, and some, like the University of Phoenix, devoted chiefly to distance and part-time education for people with jobs. While much of this responsibility is shouldered by UC Extension, a growing segment of continuing education serves groups that already have high levels of formal education and are interested in remaining highly qualified in technically demanding fields, in ways that involve the university's core departments.

UC sees itself as active in every area of postsecondary education, and as innovative and preeminent in as many as possible. UC is exploring its potential role in distance learning ("anywhere, anytime") because other leading institutions are doing it and because the challenge is there. Some may ask whether that is properly part of UC's mission, whether it might not be a distraction from what the university already does. But for both practical and symbolic reasons, UC is likely to forge ahead as much for institutional survival as for its reputation as the leading public research university in the country.

GROPING FOR SOLUTIONS

The crucial difference between "hand-crafted" and "commercial" courseware is whether it is under the control of the teacher or the developer. The former is increasingly created in elite colleges and universities by academics fascinated by the educational possibilities of IT; the latter is driven by the concerns and motives discussed above, as well as by those who hope to profit from the commercial potentialities of these new substitutes for mass sales of textbooks.[10] At an institution like UC Berkeley, the senior administrative officers resemble the academics in their primary concern for the elite forms of education: research, graduate education, and the traditional faculty-owned and -created course. And that is where hand-crafted courseware is being developed at both the graduate and undergraduate levels—to enrich those courses, to increase the efficiency of learning, and to make them available at different levels of difficulty and complexity to students with disparate levels of talent and motivation.

Stanley Chodorow makes the point that multimedia courseware "will blur the distinction between elementary and advanced instruction."[11] This is important for courses presented to widely diverse students, in differing institutional contexts. Chodorow summarizes well the advantages of multimedia education through the web. As provost of a leading private research university, the University of Pennsylvania, he speaks chiefly of "hand-crafted" courses at very high levels of development:

> The multimedia packages are likely to evolve through use and by the actions of the users. Faculty and students will add materials and adjust relationships among the elements of the packages to suit their particular needs. Although the basic package may be on a CD-ROM, users will soon learn how to integrate files from their own disks with them. Every major package—such as on biochemistry or on the diseases of the liver—will need a user's group with an electronic bulletin board to keep people up-to-date on the enhancements to or the clever ways to use the package. In this environment, teaching the subject embodied by the package will become a collective enterprise, and the research community will also become a teaching community. This expansion of the subject of our communications will enhance our intellectual community, while it greatly increases the speed at which research results are introduced to our teaching materials.[12]

But the actual development of courseware does not reflect the sharp distinction between "hand-crafted" and commercial courseware, though the nature of institutions, the variable weight of tradition, and the authority of academics in different institutions gives the distinction a continuing usefulness. Between the two extremes we begin to see at least the potentialities for hand-crafted courseware, further developed and enriched, moving beyond a single course to serve a larger market, including students not technically enrolled in the originating course and not even in contact with the originating teacher. Along the same continuum, the commercial "boutique" course could be designed and controlled by one professor or a group of academics for a large though limited special market, for example, courses designed for the continuing education in some technical specialty of a population of electronic engineers in Silicon Valley. These two examples, breaking out of the confines of the single university course, are attractive to both faculty and administrators in elite research universities, although they do not deal with the problems of mass access and cost control.

Currently there is considerable confusion about what universities want to do and how they want to use these new opportunities. The difficulty is not with the courseware itself; that is being developed at every level of cost and complexity and will presumably find its own market. What is problematic for the research university is how to develop and exploit commercial courseware in ways that are consistent with faculty ownership of the curriculum in elite universities, and how to venture outside the boundaries of the institution—either to make money (for the institution or its innovative faculty), expand access, or control costs. How can these mostly elite universities get into the mass market for courseware within the constraints of their own values and structures?

The answer may lie in three directions: the creation of new structures—schools, institutes, and the like—whose mission is to project the elite university's educational resources beyond its boundaries for a price; the use of the university's own extension service to perform the same functions; or the development of partnerships with other institutions—such as community colleges or independent open-access institutions, such as the National Technological University—that can exploit the intellectual resources of the university without compromising its integrity or standards. The links between research universities and these open-access institutions are made possible by the blurring of the distinction between elementary and advanced instruction with IT-based instruction. The same courseware can be used by students of very different talent, motivation, and preparation, allowing the coursework to be part of the extension school as well as the university, with students assessed differently and credited differently. Even this early in the development of educational IT, we can say that IT can enrich our courses, and it can bring challenging forms of instruction to people who would not otherwise have access to those courses. What we do not know is whether it will also contain costs or save money. The savings promised by IT seem always to be in the future.

TEACHERS AND TEACHING

The use of IT for instruction is gradually expanding through the teaching faculty of the elite research universities and liberal-arts colleges, as it did for research and e-mail. The technology continues to improve in quality and fall in price. The use of IT for instruction becomes less discriminatory as more students acquire computers and get access to the Internet from home and dormitory. A small number of teachers will create their own courses on a home page; more will use various commercial products to supplement assigned books and lectures. More library resources will be available on-line, though at a cost to the availability of printed material, especially journals. The focus of IT in elite institutions is enrichment of the curriculum.

The impact of IT on academics in mass and universal-access higher education is less clear. In those institutions much more will depend on the character of leadership and how presidents, chancellors, and provosts view the new opportunities—whether they seize the opportunity to improve their teaching resources internally or try to cope with financial and political pressures by moving into distance learning and continuing education. Much will also depend on the creation of new courseware by both commercial and nonprofit agencies, its costs, and the adaptability of the institution. In these nonelite institutions leaders may be tempted to counter the resistance of the existing academic community by hiring younger teachers on short contracts. Insofar as IT shifts professional status and scholarly expertise to the developers outside the institution, it must weaken the standing of teachers in these institutions and ultimately the quality of recruitment to academic life. At the same time it will create new academic professions: a small elite designing courseware for wider use—something like the writers of textbooks—and another, larger population of technicians on each campus to stay abreast of continuing developments in IT and work closely with the teaching faculty to incorporate and adapt new resources into the curriculum. Some of these may hold or gain academic credentials, offering institutions the attractive package of disciplinary competence along with IT skills. This group will be augmented by academics gaining special technical skills, which over time may become a necessary qualification for teaching both the local and distant student served by the same institution. These trends will also be visible in the mass-education sections of elite universities, which will also be serving distant learners in advanced subjects.

All this may just accelerate the diversification of the academic community already well under way with the expansion of institutions, the specialization of academic subjects and subdisciplines, and the focus on outside sources of funds and support from both government and private industry. The atomization of the academic community increases the power of institutional administration and especially the administrators of technical services to coordinate and manage, if not initiate, the variety of activities taking place on campus. The transformations implicit in the introduction of IT to the curriculum are beyond the powers of academic senates—committees of amateurs—to govern or steer. An academic senate assumes that most issues in academic life can be sensibly addressed by ordinary academics, drawn from every department, applying the largely unspoken norms and values of academic life and the lessons of their own experience. These are less and less adequate for the problems and opportunities created by IT.

In theory, improved infrastructure (i.e., new hardware or support services with more nonacademic staff) should ease faculty efforts to experiment with the new instructional technologies. But relatively few faculty without access to additional resources, such as federal and foundation grants, and without institutional rewards in the form of released time are able to devote the time and energy necessary to build IT applications into their courses. So while the attempts of some faculty to exploit the enormous resources of IT in their own courses are impressive and illustrative of what can be done, the costs to ordinary faculty members—in time, money, and the loss of other teaching and research opportunities—prevent more academics from creating courseware. Most faculty still have to cobble together resources from a variety of funders, including their own departments and private industry and foundations; that in itself is time-consuming and often impossible for those outside the sciences and engineering. The result has been a piecemeal and uncoordinated effort to bring IT more widely and deeply into the instructional programs of the university.

Currently, the problems for student users are equally great. While three-quarters of the students at Berkeley own computers, those who must use the computer laboratories scattered around the campus are still at something of a disadvantage in a course built around the Internet. Similarly, the one-third of Berkeley students who have off-campus access to the Internet claim another big advantage, which troubles faculty designing courses for the Internet. In addition, the university's servers are overloaded, and students often have long waits before getting through. A university technician observed that "we are driving Model Ts on muddy roads," with the implication that all those problems will be solved by technology over time.

Chodorow also mentions a more subtle problem that arises from IT's disruption of traditional methods of time management. His respondents reported that while they loved the total-immersion intellectual experience of an on-line course, "it drove out other courses, and when they had by necessity to turn their attention to other courses, they felt the stress of falling behind in the electronically magnified course. If they could not check in on the discussion on the listserv an hour or so before real class began, they felt lost for a while in the class discussion."[13] We are just beginning to learn about these unanticipated and unintended consequences of IT in higher education.

Perhaps the most difficult effect of IT is its influence on instruction itself. We should anticipate differences among teachers in their adaptation to the new forms of instruction. But in addition to considering differences in temperament and talent among teachers as well as the developing possibilities of the technology, which include both video and written communication on-line, we need to anticipate students' reactions to the various forms of teaching. Will students come to lectures of a hundred students and engage in the kind of direct question and answer that is still possible in classes of that size if there are alternative ways to learn through IT? My guess is that the best students will want to engage teachers directly; less highly motivated students may prefer the anonymity of learning at a distance, even if the distance is only to a hall of residence.

LEADERSHIP AND ORGANIZATION

What insights can be gained about the patterns of leadership, organization, initiative, and funding of IT within the university from these perspectives? Moving from universal to mass to elite education, the role of central administration becomes weaker as that of the academics becomes stronger and initiatives by faculty themselves become more important. At Berkeley, there is much energy and activity in the area of IT, with discretionary money from varied sources available for experiments and trials from below, relatively little coordination from above, and a fair amount of communication among actors. At this early stage of the development of IT in higher education, leadership seems to involve not directing but facilitating: providing infrastructure, which is constantly changing and expanding, and services and education to users; communicating and circulating new ideas within the university; and making discretionary money available to innovators, especially seed money for trials and experiments.

At this stage of development, some forms of central planning may be counterproductive for several reasons. The university cannot be sensitive to the extraordinary diversity of education within it, which calls for equally diverse forms of IT. Also, public universities are accountable to public authority and therefore averse to risk, and IT is an area where risk and success are closely linked. In addition, a large public university is too big, and its authority too widely dispersed, to make rapid decisions. Individuals and units need to be able to make many small, rapid, risky, and relatively inexpensive decisions from below and have the opportunities and resources to experiment. Also needed are rich support services from the IT-expert community for the teachers and learners. There is certainly a place for more centralized resources and activities, but a key question involves the right balance between central and local sources of initiative for all the contexts in which IT will be employed in the university. Other questions involve ownership of intellectual property, the right balance of IT with traditional forms of instruction, and the allocation of university funds for upgrading the infrastructure as opposed to paying for student and faculty user support.

In the great research universities, there is tension between the deeply conservative norms and structures of academic communities, senates, and decision-making processes on the one hand, and the readiness of individual members of those communities to initiate and experiment boldly in research and teaching and in responding to market opportunities on the other. There also exists the tension between what Burton Clark has called the "bottom-heaviness" of American research universities, the weight of the individual scholar and scientist and their departments, and the apparent need for leadership to provide direction and establish priorities for the development of IT for the institution as a whole. The driving forces are rapidly changing technology and equally rapidly moving market forces that can develop, apply, and exploit this technology in a variety of ways, some of which will penetrate the university immediately. Commercial markets have already moved into the university's research laboratories, where academic scientists and engineers are perpetually alert to ideas and potential products that might be profitable, blurring the distinction between pure and applied research and between research and development.[14] I believe we are seeing a similar movement of market forces into the instructional life of the university, where ideas and people can be found to create, develop, and continually improve courseware, not only for use in the home university, but also potentially for wider audiences outside the university.

CONCLUSION

The expansion of the university's functions to provide broader access to high-level continuing education through IT poses problems for accreditation, for quality control, for the integrity of the university and its relation to its own academic staff, and for the ownership of the intellectual property represented in courseware. Some of these problems will resemble those emerging from the commercialization of university research, but some will be different.[15] The solutions will leave a recognizable structure to address all the functions of universities that technology and distance learning cannot fulfill. But it will change the university as well, perhaps by blurring the distinctions among elite-, mass-, and universal-access forms of higher education.

ENDNOTES

[1]This essay reports some of the early findings of a study I am conducting in collaboration with Diane Harley of the Center for Studies in Higher Education at Berkeley, and it reflects her very considerable contributions to it. My thanks to Elliot Brownlee and Gary Matkin for their help with earlier drafts.

[2]See M. A. Trow, "Problems in the Transition from Elite to Mass Higher Education," in *Policies for Higher Education,* the general report of the Conference on Future Structures of Post-Secondary Education (Paris: OECD, 1974), 55–101; and "Elite Higher Education: An Endangered Species?" *Minerva* 14 (3) (Autumn 1976): 355–376.

[3]This is Clark Kerr's term for the big growth in enrollments that demographics promise for California higher education over the next decade. One informed estimate points to an increase in enrollments in California colleges and universities of some 400,000 students by the year 2005. "Strategies to Enhance Quality and Opportunity in California Higher Education," a report of the California Higher Education Policy Center, June 1996. This compares with current enrollments of 150,000 in the University of California and roughly 300,000 in the California State University. At current per-capita costs, this expansion would run into billions of dollars. Unlike the federal government, state governments cannot incur recurrent deficits.

[4]Dennis P. Jones, "Higher Education and High Technology: A Case for Joint Action," briefing paper for the Western Governors' Association, 14 November 1995.

[5]Commercial firms are already offering to help instructors set up courses on web sites.

[6]Participants at a meeting at Stanford in April of 1995 believed that "technology's greatest impact on instruction would fall in the area of so-called codified knowledge—the transmission of facts, theories, and the development of cognitive skills." "Leveraged Learning: Technology's Role in Restructuring Higher Education," *Stanford Forum for Higher Education Futures* (1995): 7.

[7]William F. Massy and Robert Zemsky, "Using Information Technology to Enhance Academic Productivity," EDUCOM National Learning Infrastructure Initiative.

[8]As Derek Bok has recently reminded us, "We cannot expect our schools to raise student proficiency in algebra or biology when the American Academy for the Advancement of Science can declare that 'few elementary school teachers have even rudimentary education in science and mathematics and

many junior and senior high school teachers of science and mathematics do not meet reasonable standards of preparation.' Whatever the defects of standardized tests, only blind optimists would expect our teachers to succeed in conveying higher-order skills if their average College Board scores continue to fall close to the bottom third of all takers." Derek Bok, *The Cost of Talent* (New York: The Free Press, 1993), 179. This pattern is a long-standing one that is not likely to change soon. See M. Trow, "The Second Transformation of American Secondary Education," *International Journal of Comparative Sociology* II (2) (September 1961): 157, n. 2. This fact, little discussed in the literature, has been a major motivation in the search for technological alternatives to the teacher in the classroom. The failure of earlier enthusiasms is the source of much of the skepticism about the impact of IT. See Neil Postman, "Making a Living, Making a Life: Technology Reconsidered," *The College Board Review* (1995).

[9]UC Berkeley already has such programs in place to raise the quality of instruction in K–12, and especially in its main feeder high schools, through an "Interactive University Project." Thirty campus departments are involved with school districts around the Bay Area, public libraries, and community-based organizations. The project was recently awarded a grant of $650,000 by the Department of Commerce to develop a national model for how the university can best use the Internet for educational outreach to K–12 schools.

[10]Of course, any particular individual may well embody more than one of these concerns and motives. A developer of commercial IT products might hope to provide wider access to an effective piece of courseware while making money from it. "Commercial" refers to the courseware's dependence on and sensitivity to its market rather than its orientation to profits, which may be absent or low.

[11]"Educators Must Take the Electronic Revolution Seriously," the Alan Gregg Memorial Lecture, Annual Meeting of the Association of American Medical Colleges, October/November 1995. But Chodorow does not address here the questions of cost, access, and accreditation that arise when the "multimedia package" moves outside the walls of the campus where it was created.

[12]Ibid.

[13]Ibid, 5.

[14]See Michael Gibbons et al., *The New Production of Knowledge: The Dynamics of Science and Research in Contemporary Societies* (London: Sage Publications, 1994).

[15]This essay does not address the peculiarly knotty problems of ownership of intellectual property that are raised by the presence of IT in intellectual life. Indeed, some observers see those issues as so weighty that the future of IT in higher education will depend on how they are solved or resolved. But these intertwined issues of technology, law, and market forces do not seem to allow easy resolution, nor do I believe it is necessary to wait for their resolution before trying to understand current developments. The issue does carry the warning that such external forces can heavily affect all the matters discussed in this essay. For a view of the international implications of the problem, see Jukka Liedes, "Copyright: Evolution, Not Revolution," *Science* 276 (11 April 1997): 223–225.

Philip G. Altbach

An International Academic Crisis? The American Professoriate in Comparative Perspective

HE ACADEMIC PROFESSION FACES significant challenges. Financial pressures have contributed to ever-increasing demands for accountability. The privatization of public higher education and the expansion of private academic institutions in many countries have changed the configuration of academe. Questions about the relevance of much of academic research have been linked to demands that professors teach more. The traditional high status of the professoriate has been diminished by unrelenting criticism in the media and elsewhere. This essay provides a discussion of the problems facing the contemporary university and their effects on the academic profession; it is presented in a comparative and international context because similar issues affect higher education worldwide and an international perspective can shed light on American realities.

The academic profession, in the United States and abroad, continues to function without basic change or even much consciousness of the external forces that buffet the universities. Yet change is inevitable, and it is quite likely that the working conditions of the professoriate will deteriorate. The profession's "golden age," characterized by institutional expansion, increased autonomy, availability of research funds, and growing prestige and salaries, at least in the industrialized countries, has come to an end.

Philip G. Altbach is Monan Professor of Higher Education and Director of the Center for International Higher Education at Boston College.

315

The modern American university is an international institution. It traces its origins to the medieval University of Paris, was deeply influenced by academic models from England, Scotland, and nineteenth-century Germany, and today educates students from all over the world.[1] The American university stands at the center of a world system of science and scholarship and is the largest producer of research and scholarly publications. The English language dominates world science and is, in a sense, the Latin of the twenty-first century. The American professoriate operates in an international system at the same time that it is embedded in a national environment.

The American academic profession is today the largest in the world, with a half-million full-time scholars and scientists. It is very difficult to generalize about the professoriate—divisions by discipline, institution, rank, gender, race, and ethnicity characterize the profession. There are some common elements—the experience of having undergone that most arcane of rituals, studying for the doctorate; the practice of teaching; and perhaps the most elusive thing of all, a commitment to the "life of the mind." There is a vague but nonetheless real understanding that an academic career is a "calling" as well as a job.[2]

INSULARITY AND INTERNATIONALISM

The contemporary professoriate is poised between the national and the international. In terms of numbers, American universities are more international than ever, educating 450,000 students from other countries and employing staff members from around the world. Professors, mainly from the research universities, are involved in research and teaching in many countries. At the same time, the most recent survey sponsored by the Carnegie Foundation for the Advancement of Teaching notes that among scholars from fourteen countries the American professoriate is the least committed to internationalism.[3] Only half of American faculty feel that connections with scholars in other countries are very important, and while more than 90 percent of faculty in thirteen countries believe that a scholar must read books and journals published abroad to keep up with scholarly developments, only 62 percent of Americans are of this opinion. American faculty are similarly unenthusiastic about internationalizing the curriculum; fewer than half agree that the curriculum should be more international.[4] Americans travel abroad for research and study less frequently than do their counterparts in other countries. The Carnegie data show that 65 percent of American academics did not go abroad for study or research in the past three years, compared with 25 percent of Swedes, 47 percent of Britons, and 7 percent of Israelis. At the same time, American professors have much more contact with international students than do faculty in other countries—96 percent indicate that foreign students are enrolled at their institutions. There are, of course, significant variations among the American professoriate, with faculty teaching at the prestigious research universities reporting higher levels of international involvement. Academics who are more cosmopolitan in their approach, focusing on their disciplines and on research, seem to be more international than those who are more local in their orientation, stressing the campus and teaching.[5]

These attitudes indicate a complex relationship with internationalism. American faculty feel that US higher education is at the center of an international academic system; the world comes to the United States, and therefore international initiatives are superfluous. Of course, there is a grain of truth to this perception, and it is reinforced by the relative ignorance of foreign languages on the part of American faculty. Besides being the language of science and scholarship internationally, English is the dominant language of the new communication technologies (such as the Internet). International conferences often use English as the primary language. And, increasingly, journals edited and published in such countries as Sweden, Japan, Taiwan, the Netherlands, and Germany are in English so that they can achieve an international readership and join the ranks of the top international journals. Even the large multinational academic publishers, such as Dutch-owned Elsevier or Germany's Bertelsmann or Springer, publish increasingly in English.

American academics do not often cite work by scholars in other countries in their research. The American research system is remarkably insular, especially when compared to scientific communities in other countries. Singapore and Hong Kong, for example, make it a priority to hire scholars from abroad, frequently from the United States, precisely to ensure an international perspective.

The American system accepts scholars and scientists from abroad, but only if they conform to American academic and scientific norms. To be sure, generations of foreign-born and foreign-trained scholars have been welcomed in the American academic system and have contributed much to science and scholarship. Their role in the New School for Social Research, in influencing the social sciences after World War II, and their involvement in the research that contributed to the Manhattan Project come immediately to mind. Ultimately, however, they have been assimilated into the American system. Their research and scholarly accomplishments may have had an impact, but their ideas about higher education have had little salience.[6]

Other countries look to the United States as the academic center. In most disciplines, Americans are among the leaders, and scholars from abroad find the United States an attractive place to work. In 1995, more than 59,000 visiting scholars studied in the United States.[7] Americans still win a preponderance of Nobel prizes. And although its preeminence is decreasing, the United States remains by far the largest producer of basic research. American academics have an ambivalent relationship with the rest of the world. They welcome scholars from abroad as visitors or as permanent colleagues and eagerly accept foreign students in their classes and seminars. But they pay little attention to the knowledge that the rest of the world produces, are unlikely to travel outside the United States for study or research, and are unenthusiastic about internationalizing the curriculum.

CENTERS, PERIPHERIES, AND KNOWLEDGE NETWORKS

Being at the center of the world academic system places American professors in a powerful position and also imposes special responsibilities on them. The advent of new technologies for knowledge distribution complicates matters, but it may also strengthen the position of the United States. A small segment of the American professoriate—the top 10 to 20 percent or so, who are located at the major research universities and can be characterized as the "research cadre"—is the arbiter of many of the scientific disciplines for much of the world. This group includes full-time faculty who are more interested in research than in teaching and whose positions require them to be regularly engaged in research. This research cadre is composed of fewer than 20 percent of all academics and 37 percent of those in research universities,[8] but it produces much of the research published in the mainstream academic journals, obtains a large proportion of research grants, and edits the major journals.

The American research cadre consists of fewer than one hundred thousand scientists and scholars. They are largely tenured (88 percent), male, and in the sciences. These academics teach mainly in the research universities—the 236 universities that fit into the doctoral and research categories of the Carnegie classification. These institutions constitute 6.1 percent of all institutions but claim 31.4 percent of all enrollment.[9] This group dominates knowledge production and its distribution; they are the primary producers and gatekeepers of science and scholarship. The research cadre, not surprisingly, publishes more than other faculty. For example, faculty at research universities published well over twice as many journal articles in a three-year period as faculty at nonresearch colleges and universities.[10] The leaders of this group occupy the commanding heights of a complex knowledge system and hold tremendous power to determine what becomes legitimate science. There are, of course, some fields in which US domination does not hold sway, such as literary theory, which is dominated by European thinkers. And there are many prominent scholars and scientists working in other countries.

The United States is the largest market for new academic "products" of all kinds. The library market alone, although it has suffered significant cutbacks in recent years, remains the world's largest purchaser of scientific materials. The sheer size of the academic community and the number of institutions—more than three thousand colleges and universities—gives the United States advantages in both size and scope. Technological innovations such as the use of the Internet for scholarly communications, on-line journals, bibliographical services, and document delivery through computer-based means have all been developed and are most widespread in the United States. Americans are by far the most active users of computers, e-mail, and other data-base services. The American professoriate remains far ahead of other academic communities in the use of these and other new technologies. The bulk of e-mail communication worldwide is in English, and many of the new data services operate primarily in English, giving further advantages to academic communities that use English. It is perhaps significant that only American e-mail addresses do not have to list a country identifier—an artifact, no doubt, of the American origins of the Internet and symbolic of US domination of this key communications tool. The agencies that have developed data-base services, bibliographical resources, and document delivery arrangements are for the most part American, and their origins and ownership make a difference. For example, the ERIC (Educational Resources Information Center) system, the most important source of research and bibliographical assistance in the field of education, is based in the United States and funded by the US Department of Education. It is not surprising that the orientation of the material available through ERIC is American, and very little research or documentation from other countries is available.

The American professoriate, and especially those academics active in research, are at the center of the international knowledge network. Their paradigms tend to be most influential simply because they are the key decision makers—as well as the major users—of the new systems. Most American scholars do not consider the international dimensions of their decisions simply because, as noted earlier, they do not have a high degree of international consciousness. In this respect, their insularity works to the detriment of academic communities in other countries, which are to some extent excluded from the mainstream.[11] Academics in other countries depend on the major international journals, publishers, and increasingly the new technologies. In some ways, they reinforce their peripherality by emphasizing the mainstream international journals, sometimes requiring publication in them to qualify for academic promotion.

Academics even in such highly developed countries as Denmark have become in part peripheral to the American scientific center. So too are scholars and scientists in the United States, particularly those at small liberal-arts colleges, who are not part of the mainstream research system and are to some extent marginalized.[12] Those who wish to publish in the major internationally circulated publications often must adhere to the trends of the dominant elites in the discipline. Researchers who do not teach at research universities often find themselves at a disadvantage in terms of access to publication outlets and research funds from major foundations and governmental agencies—it is estimated that 80 percent of federal research funds go to scholars and scientists at the top one hundred universities.

Academe has always been stratified and hierarchical. These characteristics, which can be observed internationally as well as within a large university system such as that of the United States, differentiate the profession and are salient factors for academic careers. Hierarchies in the disciplines combine with a pecking order of institutions to forge a powerful system of centers and peripheries. Although access to knowledge has been made easier by the new technologies, the ability to participate in the system remains controlled by scientific elites in the various disciplines.

THE DECLINE OF THE TRADITIONAL PROFESSORIATE

The traditional concept of the professoriate is being supplemented by new hiring and promotion arrangements across the United States, and in other countries as well. The proportion of the professoriate in tenured and tenure-track positions is steadily declining in many countries. In the United States, approximately 35 percent of all faculty are part-timers, and over one-third of the full-time faculty hold term appointments.[13] Criticism of the concept of tenure itself is heard in policy circles, and the recent unsuccessful efforts by the regents of the University of Minnesota to modify the tenure system are but the first voices in what is bound to be a continuing debate. These changes come at a time of significant financial pressure on higher education—universities and colleges are trying to squeeze more productivity from the one segment of the academic enterprise heretofore thought to be immune, namely, the professoriate.

The full-time tenured and tenure-track professoriate will very likely continue to decline as a proportion of the academic work force, although it will remain the "gold standard" to which all aspire. Academic institutions gain flexibility and incur lower costs by hiring nontenure-track teachers, but significant nonmonetary costs enter into this shift. The traditional faculty are those who perform the complex governance functions of the institution. They serve on committees, design new curricula, become department chairs, and later fill some senior administrative positions of the university; they also produce most of the research. Perhaps most importantly, they have loyalty both to the institution and to the academic profession. They are, in short, the traditional core of the university. Indeed, the statutes of most colleges and universities reserve full participation in governance, including voting on important academic decisions, for the full-time faculty, and usually only those with "regular" appointments.

The American university is becoming a kind of caste system, with the tenured Brahmins at the top and the lower castes occupying subservient positions. The part-timers are equivalent to the Untouchables, relegated to do the work that others do not wish to do and denied the possibility of joining the privileged. In this hierarchical order, the traditional faculty ranks may constitute half (or even less) of the profession. The new and growing middle category of full-time but nontenure-track faculty is increasing rapidly. Hired mainly to teach, these new ranks have more contact hours, are not expected to engage in research, and have only a limited role in institutional governance. They receive the standard benefits from the institution, but their terms of appointment are limited by contract to five years or some other finite period. Paid somewhat less than tenure-track faculty, these staff members are part of the academic community but are not fully involved in the affairs of the university. They provide a reliable teaching force. They also permit the institution flexibility in staffing, since the considerable turnover in positions can be used to meet the demands of enrollment changes or institutional priorities. This institutional category is new at most institutions, but we can expect it to grow rapidly.

Part-time faculty have been part of the academic landscape for a long time, and they are a rapidly growing segment of the academic labor force. Hired to teach a specific course or two, provided no benefits, often given no office space, and expected simply to show up to teach a class, part-timers are the *ronin* of traditional Japan—the masterless samurai who traveled the countryside offering their services and hoping to be chosen as apprentices. These *ronin* have all the qualifications of samurai; they lack only a sponsor (permanent employer). Part-timers are exploited in the sense that they are paid very modestly on a per-course basis. Not surprisingly, part-time faculty feel little loyalty to the institution.

The implications of this emerging caste system for American higher education are significant. The structure of the academic profession will be altered. One of the traditional strengths of the American pattern of academic organization has been its relative lack of hierarchy, especially when compared to Europe or Japan. The American academic department is a community of equals, with participation dispersed among all faculty. This is in sharp contrast to the Japanese "chair" system, where basic academic power resides with a small group of full professors and emanates from them.[14] This pattern, borrowed from Europe but modified there by the reforms of the 1960s, remains a powerful influence.

The changing structure of the profession also has implications for the future of research in the universities. Only the full-time faculty have the time, commitment, support, and professional obligation to engage in research and publication. Indeed, many universities permit only full-time faculty to serve as principal investigators on grants. In the research-oriented universities, academic work is arranged so that research is an integral part of the career of most academics. If one believes that teaching and research are related, and that teaching benefits from the engagement of a faculty member in active research, the new hierarchy places fewer researching faculty in the classroom; the quality of teaching, at least in the top-tier schools, may suffer as a result.

The new structure of the professoriate will affect the various sectors of the American higher education system differently. The top-tier research universities and selective liberal-arts colleges will be least affected, in terms of traditional academic work. The new category of full-time nontenure-track faculty will likely expand significantly at these institutions, while part-time staff may be cut back. The greatest alterations will likely take place at the less-selective colleges and comprehensive universities, where reliance on part-time and nontenure-track faculty will grow in order to meet student demand in a context of diminishing fiscal resources and the need for institutional flexibility. These differential changes will exacerbate the already considerable variations in academic prestige and quality. The quest of many of these institutions and individual professors to join the top ranks of academe may be ended as a result of tighter controls on professorial time and greater institutional accountability.

Examples from other countries can help us understand some of the changes taking place in the United States. In Germany and a number of other European countries, full-time nontenure-track academic employees have long been responsible for teaching or research.[15] These appointees have no possibility of obtaining a regular (permanent) position, and in general their contracts cannot be extended. They often circulate to different universities on term appointments and compete for regular positions away from their home institutions. In recent years, this "underclass" of academics has again become a growing feature of the German university system. Since full professors are seldom promoted from within the institution, the term-appointment *Mittelbau* staff do not seriously alter the academic balance in the German academic system.[16]

The Latin American academic profession, where a majority of those teaching in the universities are part-timers, is also a useful point of comparison for the United States. There is a long tradition of the "taxicab" professor who rushes from his or her professional job to teach a class at the university.[17] The large proportion of part-time staff has helped to shape the ethos of the Latin American university and has hindered the emergence of a modern academic culture. Contemporary reformers have argued that a full-time professoriate is a prerequisite for a competitive and effective academic system. Indeed, countries such as Brazil, Mexico, Chile, and Argentina have expanded full-time staff. Reliance on part-timers has meant that university governance is in the hands of a very few senior faculty, little research takes place, and teaching is limited to lectures given by busy professionals who have little interaction either with students or colleagues.

While it is generally agreed that research and innovative teaching and curriculum development cannot be built on the basis of part-time staff, reliance on part-time faculty has given the universities much-needed flexibility and has permitted higher education to be offered at a low cost. Tuition levels are very low in the public institutions, and government allocations to postsecondary education are modest when compared to international norms. The public universities in Latin America have thus been able to expand their enrollments in order to meet increasing demand.

The growth of private universities in Latin America and elsewhere has significant implications for the academic profession. Although the prestigious older private universities in Latin America, largely sponsored by the Catholic Church, maintain high standards and have many full-time professors, most of the newer institutions rely almost exclusively on part-time faculty. In Latin America as well as in the former communist countries of Central and Eastern Europe, private institutions are educating an increasing segment of the student body. The quality of many of these new universities has yet to be measured—and the implications of their employment patterns for an emerging professoriate are similarly unmeasured.

TENURE

The tenure system is again under attack. As a result of difficult economic circumstances, a perceived need by academic institutions to increase staffing flexibility, and the perennial complaint that professors who hold tenure are not accountable to anyone, the tenure system has come under widespread criticism.[18] This has ranged from attacks on putative faculty "deadwood" or professorial laziness to issues relating to institutional priorities.[19] The Minnesota case, mentioned earlier, is indicative of the strong feelings on this volatile issue. The faculty ultimately won that struggle, although tenure rules were slightly modified. Professorial job security is an increasingly volatile issue in other countries, too.

The central issues in the current debate relate to accountability, post-tenure review of faculty, and institutional concerns about financial and programmatic flexibility. The interplay between the imperatives of the tenure system and its linkage to academic freedom, on the one hand, and pressures for change, on the other, will result in some alterations in traditional arrangements. However, in most institutions, tenure will probably be retained with only modest modifications.[20] The important point is that there will very likely be, for the first time in close to a century, a number of changes in the tenure system.

Post-tenure review is one likely reform. Pressure for institutional accountability is being extended to individual faculty members. Moves are afoot to hold tenured faculty accountable for their teaching and to measure both teaching and research productivity more closely. Clearly, the era of unfettered professorial autonomy following the award of tenure is coming to a close. Another possible change is that fewer faculty members will receive tenure. A cadre of full-time nontenure-track faculty is emerging, who will not have the protection of the tenure system. Some will have the possibility of a periodic renewal of contracts, while others will be appointed for a limited period without any prospect of renewal.

It should be kept in mind, of course, that for most colleges and universities tenure in American higher education has never been ironclad. Tenured faculty members can be dismissed in times of financial exigency or for reasons of programmatic restructuring (such as the closing down of departments). While relatively few institutions have resorted to such measures, some have, and their actions have been upheld in the courts. During a financial crisis in the 1970s, the State University of New York dismissed several faculty members when specific academic programs were being eliminated; although the American Association of University Professors censured the administration for this action, the courts upheld it. Top-tier institutions have been less likely to resort to firing tenured staff at times of restructuring or fiscal crisis.

International trends regarding academic employment and tenure present a mixed picture. There is variance, but permanent employment after a probationary period is the norm worldwide, although some policy changes are under way. American professors undergo perhaps the longest probationary period and one of the most rigorous evaluations of performance prior to awarding tenure found anywhere in the world. In Europe, young scholars are appointed to university posts, "confirmed" after a relatively short probationary period of approximately three years, and are given permanent appointments if performance in teaching and research is satisfactory. The evaluation conducted is not nearly as rigorous or elaborate as that which is standard practice in the United States. Salary increases are typically based on longevity and are not performance based. Once a scholar is appointed to a "permanent" post, tenure is often protected not only by university statutes but by civil service regulations and, as in the case of Germany, by the constitution itself.

Promotion to a higher rank, however, is not automatic and often involves a rigorous evaluation. In some countries, promotion to the rank of full professor requires open advertisement and competition, and the promotion of a person already in the university is not assured. In countries with the tradition of the "chair system," a relatively small number of academics are promoted to this high rank, and it is by no means certain that most academics will end their careers as full professors. As European academic systems experience financial problems, fewer senior professorships are authorized, and as a result a growing proportion of the academic profession either cannot be promoted to a senior academic rank or must be content with temporary appointments.[21]

There are even some countries where formal tenure does not exist. In Taiwan and South Korea, for example, there is no formalized tenure system, and it is possible for professors to lose their positions. Yet virtually all academics hold "de facto" tenure, and few, if any, are actually fired. England is undergoing a dramatic experiment with the modification of permanent appointments. Traditional tenure was abolished by the government for new incumbents in the academic profession during Margaret Thatcher's prime ministership, and the country is currently witnessing considerable change in the nature of academic careers.[22] The government's policy was universally condemned by the academic profession at the time it was implemented.

Patterns of academic appointment, security of tenure, and provisions for the guarantee of academic freedom vary considerably. Legal as well as administrative arrangements differ. In India, for example, most full-time academics have permanent appointments, but weak legal and administrative protection means that institutions can violate tenure with relative impunity.[23] Even in the United States policies vary. Protection for faculty at the University of Minnesota has been immutable, while in New York tenure regulations, even in a unionized environment, are much weaker.

It is perhaps surprising that one-fifth of the American professoriate feels that academic freedom is not well protected and that almost half worry about ideological restrictions on publication.[24] This may reflect concern about "political correctness" or other debates in recent years over the ideological basis of the curriculum (although 71 percent of American academics feel that this is an especially creative and productive time in their fields—among the most favorable ratings in the fourteen-country Carnegie study).[25] Or it may relate to unease about the tenure system, a difficult job market, or other uncertainties.

SCHOLARSHIP RECONSIDERED AND ASSESSED

Among the most important implications of the fiscal and institutional pressures discussed here is a significant reconfiguration of academic work. The debate that began with the publication of Ernest Boyer's *Scholarship Reconsidered* continues today and may be starting to have an impact on the profession.[26] Boyer's argument—that the professoriate should pay more attention to teaching and learning and that the definition of scholarship should be broadened so that it goes beyond traditional publication of research findings and analysis—came at a time when academic institutions were seeking more productivity and accountability from the faculty. A sense that the emphasis on research that has characterized the top tier of American higher education may have gone too far has increasingly entered the debates about higher education in the 1990s.

Financial reality, institutional necessity, and the ideology of reform have come together in the movement to reemphasize teaching as the central responsibility of the academic profession. The American professoriate itself is committed to teaching as its central role. When asked if their interests were primarily in teaching or research, 63 percent of American academics respond that their commitments primarily lean toward teaching. This compares with 44 percent in England, 28 percent in Japan, and 33 percent in Sweden. In these nations, and others in the Carnegie survey, faculty are more focused on research.[27] Not surprisingly, because of their publication records, American faculty members in the research cadre are more focused on research, yet even these individuals indicate a strong commitment to teaching.

However, American academics are dissatisfied with many of the conditions under which they teach and conduct research. For example, 42 percent feel that the pressure to publish reduces the quality of teaching at their institutions, 71 percent believe that research funding is now more difficult to obtain, and 75 percent believe that it is difficult to achieve tenure if they do not publish.[28] Half or more are critical of library, computer, and classroom facilities for their teaching. They also judge many of their students to be insufficiently prepared for their studies. But their views are by no means inimical to the teaching role in higher education.

While there is a perception that things are modestly deteriorating in academe, there is certainly no ground swell from the professoriate for a greater emphasis on teaching, new procedures for assessment, or a reorientation of American higher education. Yet it is unlikely that most faculty would be opposed to a renewed emphasis on teaching and a diminished focus on research. Most academics produce relatively little published scholarship or research, and most express strong loyalty to teaching. Many, as the Carnegie survey indicates, feel that they are under too much pressure to do research. Assessment, mainly in the form of student evaluations of teaching, is nearly universal in the United States. Additional assessment, if not too time-consuming or intrusive, is unlikely to be strongly opposed.

Critics often overemphasize the innate conservatism of the professoriate. While it is unlikely that the academic profession will press for drastic change, a commitment to teaching and to the goals of higher education will make the professoriate receptive to proposals for change. The American professoriate, more focused on teaching than their colleagues in Europe or Japan, is likely to be more amenable to reform. Even in England, where the professoriate was united against the Thatcher changes and expressed traditional views on a range of issues, the academic profession adjusted to a new academic environment and has been willing to implement changes that have introduced assessment of teaching and research and a greater emphasis on accountability at all levels of the academic system.

In the United States, a Carnegie report entitled *Scholarship Assessed* represents the next step in the effort to place more emphasis on teaching and to expand the concept of intellectual work as well as to assess the totality of academic work.[29] The report's focus is on better means of assessing teaching so that it can be evaluated, along with research, as an element of academic work. Guidelines are provided for covering service as well as teaching. This initiative is part of an ongoing effort in higher education to assess, measure, and evaluate all academic work. The outcome of these efforts remains uncertain—the techniques for effective measurement of teaching and learning are still debated. The widespread acceptance of modified norms of professorial performance will also require something of a cultural shift in the profession.

The research cadre, and indeed most faculty at the top-tier research-oriented institutions, will see relatively little change in their working lives. Those at less-selective colleges and universities will probably be most affected, coming under increasing pressure to emphasize teaching and to downplay a commitment to research. Most colleges already emphasize the teaching role, although they may benefit from greater sophistication in the measurement of teaching effectiveness. Assessment and accountability are at the top of the institutional agenda. So far, the financial and governmental pressures on American higher education have been felt largely at the institutional level and have not yet touched on life in the classroom, but this is about to change.

In a few countries, mainly in the English-speaking academic community, there has also been an emphasis on assessment and evaluation. Britain has been most active in this field, with policies implemented to measure academic performance in both research and teaching, and there are plans to ensure that those who enter postsecondary teaching have some preparation in pedagogy specifically relevant for university teaching.[30] The British approach is to provide training for postsecondary teaching and then to assess the quality of academic performance. Australia and Canada have also paid attention to issues of assessment.

MORALE

In general, there is little sense of crisis among academics; most seem unaware of the magnitude of the problems facing American higher education.[31] Overall, most faculty are remarkably content with their careers but are less pleased with their institutional surroundings, increasingly critical of their students, and especially alienated from the administration of their institutions. Nevertheless, more than 75 percent are happy with their job situation as a whole and express satisfaction with the opportunities they have to pursue their own ideas. A majority feel that this is a good time to become an academic, and only 11 percent say that if they had to choose careers again, they would not choose academe. Faculty report that they are generally content with their colleagues, and 79 percent are satisfied with their job security, although only 61 percent report that they are tenured. Faculty are even relatively happy with their salaries—46 percent describe their salaries as excellent or good. This is a surprisingly high proportion in view of the reality of relatively stagnant academic salaries during much of the 1990s.[32] Ninety-six percent are satisfied with the courses that they teach, although they are somewhat critical of their students. A quarter of the faculty reported that their students are less qualified now than they were five years ago. Overall, they feel that academic freedom is protected. In short, in their departments and in the classroom, the professoriate expresses general satisfaction. Faculty feel content with their overall professional autonomy. The Carnegie data suggest that if an academic feels professionally autonomous, secure in his or her job, and respected by campus colleagues, he or she is likely to give a positive rating to the job situation as a whole, even if some other, less central aspects of the job are seen as unsatisfactory.[33]

It is interesting that there is little worry over what some have called the crisis of "political correctness" on campus. The Carnegie survey shows that most faculty are comfortable with the level of academic freedom and feel few constraints in their teaching and research. However, 34 percent are of the opinion that there are some restrictions on what a scholar can publish, perhaps reflecting a concern about "PC." There is, however, scant evidence to support the claims of conservative analysts that the campus is seething with conflict over the nature of scholarship, the "canon," multiculturalism, and other issues.[34]

Faculty report dissatisfaction in a number of key areas, most notably, as indicated, with the administration, with a number of institutional arrangements, and to some extent with students. Unhappiness with the academic administration is a near-universal phenomenon; in all of the fourteen countries in the Carnegie survey, it was a strong theme among the faculty.[35] This alienation from administrative authority tells us a good deal about attitudes within the academic profession. While faculty express satisfaction with their colleagues at the department level, they are deeply unhappy with institutional governance and policy. Similar dissatisfaction is expressed with governmental involvement in higher education. Only 10 percent of American faculty agree that the government should have responsibility for defining overall purpose and policy for higher education. Thirty-four percent feel that there is far too much governmental interference in important academic policies. Faculty are alienated from the people who run their colleges and universities and from the governmental authorities who provide the funding as well as shape broad approaches toward research, student aid, and affirmative action. There is a large gap between the satisfaction felt about the "local" aspects of academe and the discontent with the broader policy direction of higher education.

The faculty would like to be permitted to pursue teaching and research unfettered by governmental interference or administrative restrictions. Most academics enjoy what they do, believe that they do their work well, and consider themselves reasonably well prepared for their jobs. There is a vague sense of unease with the institutional climate and with trends in higher education, and this seems to be reflected in negative feelings toward institutional leaders and their policies.

FUTURE REALITIES AND PROFESSORIAL PERCEPTIONS

The average full-time American professor remains largely insulated from the broad changes taking place in higher education. Not only that, the professoriate seems to have little understanding of these trends. The majority of tenured faculty has been unaffected by the deteriorating academic labor market, although job mobility has become more limited. In some respects, academic work has changed. Classes have become larger, research funding is more difficult to obtain, and enrollments in many schools have increased while full-time faculty numbers remain steady or have even declined. Part of the slack has been taken up by part-time staff, graduate student instructors, and an increase in class size. The full-time professoriate has become somewhat more "productive" in terms of numbers of students taught. Although there is little hard evidence, most academics are of the opinion that obtaining tenure has become more difficult, especially at the research universities. New doctorates cannot find full-time positions and must content themselves with insecure part-time teaching and repeated postdoctoral assignments.

Most academics do not see these trends as very alarming and do not recognize them as part of a permanent change in the landscape of American higher education. They have not yet experienced the new realities for themselves. Presidents and other leaders have not communicated the idea that the faculty shares responsibility for institutional adjustment and survival in the current period, and they have not involved the professoriate in responding to the new financial pressures and other realities. Faculty members do not yet realize that if institutions are going to survive and the traditional prerogatives of the professoriate maintained, the profession will need to take an active role in ensuring institutional well-being.

The professoriate is faced with difficulties and diminished circumstances almost everywhere. The Carnegie survey portrays an academic profession that has a vague sense of unease but little sense of crisis. It is instructive and relevant to examine some of the trends evident abroad. Britain has seen the most far-reaching reform, with the abolition of the tenure system, the amalgamation of the polytechnics with the universities that more than doubled the size of the university system, and, most recently, the imposition of performance measures for teaching and research and the allocation of funds to universities based on these measures. These policies have had considerable impact on the professoriate, as indicated by the low morale of the British respondents to the Carnegie survey.[36] The British academic profession has been significantly affected by these structural changes, as well as by forced retirements and deteriorating conditions of teaching.

There has also been a less marked deterioration in the conditions of the professoriate in most Western European countries, where little structural change has taken place. Most pronounced in Germany but also evident in France, Italy, and to some extent the Netherlands, increases in student numbers have not been accompanied by growth in the professoriate, and the conditions for teaching and learning are declining. Few jobs are available for younger scholars, and research funding has been cut or at least has not kept up with costs. There have been few, if any, initiatives to reform the universities or the basic terms and conditions of the academic profession.

Eastern Europe and the former Soviet Union, on the other hand, present a dramatic picture of decline and deterioration. In all of these countries, higher education has come under severe financial pressure, with cutbacks in government funding for the universities. Support for research has been especially hard hit. The Russian universities have suffered severe enough financial declines that the conditions necessary for research and advanced scholarship no longer exist. The establishment of new private universities has also changed the equation since few, if any, of these new institutions offer tenured appointments. The professoriate has had to adjust to a changed environment. Many have left the universities, pursuing careers in other fields or finding positions abroad. Others find that they cannot survive financially and take extra part-time academic jobs. The universities and the academic system remain in a period of transition, with the future unclear.

In a trend most evident in China but also seen in other countries (including the United States, to some extent), universities are increasingly asked to generate their own revenues. Chinese universities are now charging many of their students tuition and other fees. The universities have also established consulting departments, profit-making laboratories, and even businesses. Beijing University, China's most prestigious academic institution, runs a successful software company and other enterprises. Many professors are involved in these enterprises, and in private consulting as well. As a result, they naturally pay less attention to campus life and to their students. The professoriate is increasingly seen as a source of direct income for academic institutions. In the United States, university-industry collaboration has an element of Chinese-style academic entrepreneurship.

In very few countries is the academic profession secure in its traditional role. Even in Hong Kong, which may have the highest academic salaries in the world, new performance evaluation and accountability standards are being implemented. Many faculty are also worried about the impact of the transition to Chinese sovereignty on academic freedom and on higher education as a whole. In Australia, the new conservative government's promises of significant cuts in higher education funding have the professoriate profoundly worried. In Japan, current reform efforts aimed at improving undergraduate education may affect the traditional autonomy and insularity of the Japanese professoriate. Heavy reliance on part-time faculty has been part of the Latin American academic system for a century or more; this will be of interest to the United States as the balance steadily shifts.

CONCLUSION

The American professoriate is part of an international academic community that now faces diminished circumstances, decreased autonomy, and threats to the perquisites and even the traditional roles of the professoriate. While each academic system is embedded in its own national issues and circumstances, there are some common realities, especially in the realm of fiscal problems and demands for accountability, that make it possible to learn from the experiences of other countries.

The largest and arguably the most powerful in the world, the American academic profession is faced with unprecedented challenges. Its world scientific and research leadership is reasonably secure because of the size and complexity of the academic system. At the same time, it must function in an increasingly multipolar world in which international skills and connections are important, and it is ill prepared for this role. American scholars and scientists remain remarkably insular in their attitudes and their activities. Domestic challenges also abound, and again the professoriate seems poorly prepared for the future. There is little understanding of the complex realities facing American colleges and universities; prevalent attitudes reflect little sense of crisis. Indeed, the distrust felt by many academics toward the leadership of American higher education makes innovation more difficult.

At the same time, the academic profession has weathered difficulties in the past. The wave of creative energy that resulted in the establishment of the American research universities at the end of the nineteenth century and the professionalization of the academic profession shortly thereafter prove that reform and change is possible. Academics met the challenges of the economic depression of the 1930s and the expansion of the postwar period creatively.[37] With leadership and energy, there is no reason why the early twenty-first century cannot rival the early twentieth century as a creative period for higher education.

ENDNOTES

[1]Joseph Ben-David and Awraham Zloczower, "Universities and Academic Systems in Modern Societies," *European Journal of Sociology* 3 (1) (1962): 45–84.

[2]Edward Shils, *The Academic Ethic* (Chicago, Ill.: University of Chicago Press, 1983). See also Edward Shils, *The Order of Learning and the Crisis of the University,* ed. and with an introduction by Philip G. Altbach (New Brunswick, N.J.: Transaction, 1997).

[3]Material in this essay is cited mainly from two volumes related to the Carnegie Foundation's international survey of the academic profession. These are Philip G. Altbach, ed., *The International Academic Profession: Portraits of Fourteen Countries* (Princeton, N.J.: Carnegie Foundation for the Advancement of Teaching, 1996) and Ernest L. Boyer, Philip G. Altbach, and Mary Jean Whitelaw, *The Academic Profession: An International Perspective* (Princeton, N.J.: Carnegie Foundation for the Advancement of Teaching, 1994). Additional material is cited from tables prepared by the Carnegie Foundation from the survey. The countries included are the United States, England, Germany, the Netherlands, Russia, Sweden, Hong Kong, Japan, Korea, Brazil, Chile, Mexico, Israel, and Australia. A common questionnaire of more than two hundred items was developed, and a common methodology for the selection of institutions and individuals was used. For a discussion of the research design of this study, see Mary Jean Whitelaw, "The International Survey of the Academic Profession, 1991–1993: Methodological Notes," in Altbach, ed., *The International Academic Profession,* 669–678.

[4]Results taken from Boyer, Altbach, and Whitelaw, *The Academic Profession,* tables 63 and 66.

[5]Alvin Gouldner, "Cosmopolitans and Locals: Toward an Analysis of Latent Social Roles," *Administrative Science Quarterly* 2 (December 1957): 281–303.

[6]Hyaeweol Choi, *An International Scientific Community: Asian Scholars in the United States* (Westport, Conn.: Praeger, 1995).

[7]Todd M. Davis, ed., *Open Doors, 1995/96: Report on International Educational Exchange* (New York: Institute of International Education, 1996).

[8]J. Eugene Haas, "The American Academic Profession," in Altbach, ed., *The International Academic Profession,* 355–356.

[9]*A Classification of Institutions of Higher Education, 1994 Edition* (Princeton, N.J.: Carnegie Foundation for the Advancement of Teaching, 1994).

[10]Haas, "The American Academic Profession," 363.

[11]See, for example, Philip G. Altbach, "Gigantic Peripheries: India and China in the World Knowledge System," *Economic and Political Weekly* 28 (12 June 1993): 1220–1225.

[12]See Harriet Zuckerman, *Scientific Elite: Nobel Laureates in the United States* (New Brunswick, N.J.: Transaction, 1996) for a discussion of how the elite scientific system works.

[13]Judith M. Gappa and David W. Leslie, *The Invisible Faculty: Improving the Status of Part-Timers in Higher Education* (San Francisco, Calif.: Jossey-Bass, 1993).

[14]William K. Cummings, *The Changing Academic Marketplace and University Reform in Japan* (New York: Garland Publishing, 1990).

[15]Jürgen Enders, *Die wissenschaftlichen Mitarbeiter: Ausbildung, Beschäftigung, und Karriere der Nachwuchswissenschaftler und Mittelbau-angehörigen an den Universitäten* (Frankfurt am Main: Campus Verlag, 1996).

[16]Jürgen Enders and Ulrich Teichler, "The Academic Profession in Germany," in Altbach, ed., *The International Academic Profession*, 437–490.

[17]Philip G. Altbach, "The Pros and Cons of Hiring 'Taxicab' Professors," *Chronicle of Higher Education,* 6 January 1995, B3.

[18]See Richard P. Chait, "The Future of Academic Tenure," *Priorities* 3 (Spring 1995): 1–12. *Priorities* is a publication of the Association of Governing Boards. See also Cathy A. Trower, "Tenure Snapshot," New Pathways: Faculty Careers and Employment for the Twenty-First Century, a project of the American Association for Higher Education, working paper, Washington, D.C., 1996.

[19]See Charles J. Sykes, *ProfScam: Professors and the Demise of Higher Education* (Washington, D.C.: Regnery, 1988) and Martin Anderson, *Impostors in the Temple* (New York: Simon and Schuster, 1992).

[20]Matthew W. Finken, ed., *The Case for Tenure* (Ithaca, N.Y.: Cornell University Press, 1996). See also Richard P. Chait, "The Future of Academic Tenure," in William F. Massy and Joel W. Meyerson, eds., *Revitalizing Higher Education* (Princeton, N.J.: Peterson's, 1995), 19–36.

[21]See Maurice Kogan, Ingrid Moses, and Elaine El-Khawas, *Staffing Higher Education: Meeting New Challenges* (London: Jessica Kingsley, 1994).

[22]Rob Cuthbert, ed., *Working in Higher Education* (Buckingham, England: Open University Press, 1996).

[23]Suma Chitnis and Philip G. Altbach, eds., *The Indian Academic Profession* (Delhi: Macmillan, 1979).

[24]Boyer, Altbach, and Whitelaw, *The Academic Profession*, tables 54 and 57.

[25]Ibid., table 37.

[26]Ernest L. Boyer, *Scholarship Reconsidered: Priorities of the Professoriate* (Princeton, N.J.: Carnegie Foundation for the Advancement of Teaching, 1990).

[27]Boyer, Altbach, and Whitelaw, *The Academic Profession*, table 17.

[28]Ibid., tables 18, 21, and 23.

[29]Charles E. Glassick, Mary Taylor Huber, and Gene I. Maeroff, *Scholarship Assessed* (San Francisco, Calif.: Jossey-Bass, 1997).

[30]See Roger Ellis, ed., *Quality Assurance for University Teaching* (Buckingham, England: Open University Press, 1993) and Angela Brew, ed.,

Directions in Staff Development (Buckingham, England: Open University Press, 1995).

[31]The material in this section is based on the results of the Carnegie study of the international academic profession. See Boyer, Altbach, and Whitelaw, *The Academic Profession.* See also Haas, "The American Academic Profession."

[32]Denise K. Magner, "Increases in Faculty Salaries Fail to Keep Pace with Inflation," *Chronicle of Higher Education,* 3 July 1997, A8.

[33]Haas, "The American Academic Profession," 347–348.

[34]For opposite sides of this debate, see John K. Wilson, *The Myth of Political Correctness: The Conservative Attack on Higher Education* (Durham, N.C.: Duke University Press, 1995) and George Roche, *The Fall of the Ivory Tower: Government, Corruption and the Bankrupting of American Higher Education* (Washington, D.C.: Regnery, 1994).

[35]Lionel S. Lewis and Philip G. Altbach, "Faculty Versus Administration: A Universal Problem," *Higher Education Policy* 9 (3) (1996): 255–258.

[36]Oliver Fulton, "The Academic Profession in England on the Eve of Structural Change," in Altbach, ed., *The International Academic Profession,* 389–436.

[37]Clark Kerr, *The Uses of the University* (Cambridge, Mass.: Harvard University Press, 1995).

Index